P9-EDP-790

THE HISTORY
OF FRANCE

From the Earliest Times to 1848

BY M. GUIZOT AND
MADAM GUIZOT DE WITT
TRANSLATED BY ROBERT BLACK

Volume VII

THOMAS Y. CROWELL & COMPANY
PUBLISHERS : : NEW YORK

TABLE OF CONTENTS—VOL. VII.

THE HISTORY OF FRANCE.

CHAPTER VII.

THE CONSULATE (1799—1804).

FOR more than ten years, amid unheard of shocks and sufferings, France had been seeking for a free and regular government, that might assure to her the new rights which had only been gained through tribulation. She had overthrown the Monarchy and attempted a Republic; she had accepted and rejected three constitutions, all the while struggling singlehanded with Europe, leagued against her. She had undergone the violence of the Reign of Terror, the contradictory passions of the Assemblies, and the incoherent feebleness of the Directory. For the first time since the death of King Louis XIV., her history finds once more a centre, and henceforth revolves round a single man. For fifteen years, victorious or vanquished, at the summit of glory, or in the depths of abasement, France and Europe, overmastered by an indomitable will and unbridled passion for power, were compelled to squander their blood and their treasure upon that page of universal history which General Bonaparte claims for his own, and which he has succeeded in covering with glory and crime.

On the day following the 18th Brumaire, in the uncertainty of parties, in face of a constitution audaciously violated, and a government mainly provisional, the nation was more excited than apprehensive or disquieted. It had caught a glimpse of that natural power and that free ascendancy of genius to which men willingly abandon themselves, with a confidence which the most bitter deceptions have never been able to extinguish. Ardent and sincere republicans, less and less numerous, felt themselves conquered beforehand, by a sure instinct that was not misled by the protest of their adversaries. They bent

before a new power, to which their old hatreds did not attach,
which they believed to be in some sort created by their own
hands, and of which they had not yet measured the audacity.
The mass of the population, the true France, hailed with joy
the hope of order and of a regular and strong administration.
They were not prejudiced in favor of the philosophic constitution so long propounded by Sieyès. In the eyes of the nation,
the government was already concentrated in the hands of General Bonaparte; it was in him that all were trusting, for repose
at home and glory and peace abroad.

In fact, he was governing already, disregarding the prolonged
discussions of the two legislative commissions, and the profound developments of the projects of Sieyès, expounded by
M. Boulay. Before the Constitution of the year VIII. received
the sanction of his dominant will, he had repealed the Law of
Hostages, recalled the proscribed priests from the Isle of
Oléron, and from Sinnamari most of those transported on 18th
Fructidor. He had reformed the ministry, and distributed
according to his pleasure the chief commands in the army. As
Moreau had been of service to Bonaparte in his *coup d'état*, he
was placed at the head of the army of the Rhine joined to the
army of Helvetia, taken from Masséna on the morrow of his
most brilliant victories. Distrust and ill-will struggled with
his admiration of Bonaparte in the mind of the conqueror of
Zurich; he was sent to the army of Italy, always devoted to
Bonaparte. Berthier remained at Paris in the capacity of
minister of war. Fouché was placed at the police, and Talleyrand undertook foreign affairs. By a bent of theoretical fancy,
which was not borne out by experience in government, the
illustrious mathematician Laplace was called to the ministry
of the interior. Gaudin became minister of finances; he replaced immediately the forced loans with an increase of direct
taxes, and introduced into the collection of the public revenues
some important improvements, which paved the way for our
great financial organization.

At the same time, without provocation and without necessity, as if simply in compliance with the mournful traditions
of past violence, a list of proscriptions, published on the 23rd
Brumaire, exiled to Guiana or the Île de Ré nine persons—a
mixture of honest republicans opposed to the new state of
things, and of wretches still charged with the crimes of the
Reign of Terror. Only the name of General Jourdan excited
universal reprobation, and it was immediately struck out.

The measure itself was soon mitigated, and the decree was never executed.

Through the revolutionary storms and the murderous epochs which had successively seen all the great actors in the political struggles disappear from the scene, the Abbe Sieyès emerged as a veteran associated with the first free impulses of the nation. In 1789, his pamphlet, "What is the Third Estate?" had arrested the attention of all serious minds. He had several times, and in decisive circumstances, played an important part in the Constituent Assembly. Since his vote of the 20th January, and until the 9th Thermidor, he remained in voluntary obscurity; mingling since then in all great theoretical discussions, he had exercised a preponderating influence in recent events. From revolution to revolution. popular or military, he came out in the part of legislator, his spirit escaping from the influence of pure democracy. He had formerly proposed the banishment *en masse* of all the nobility, and he still nursed in the depths of his soul a horror for all traditional superiority. He had said, "Whoever is not of my species is not my fellow-creature; the nobles are not of my species; they are wolves, and I fire upon them." He had, however, been brought, by his reflections and the course of events, to construct eccentric theories, of a factitious aristocracy, the wielders of power to the exclusion of the nation, recruited from a limited circle—a disfigured survival of the Italian republics of the middle ages, without the free and salutary action of representative government.

"Confidence ought to proceed from below, and power to act from above," declared the appointed legislator of the 18th Brumaire. He himself compared his political system to a pyramid, resting on the entire mass of the nation, terminating at the top in a single man, whom he called the Great Elector. He had not the courage to pronounce the word king.

Five millions of electors, constituted into primary assemblies, were to prepare a *municipal* list of 500,000 elected who in their turn were entrusted with the formation of a *departmental* list of 50,000 names. To these twice sifted delegates was confided the care of electing 5000 as a *national* list, alone capable of becoming the agents of executive power in the whole of France. The municipal and departmental administrations were to be chosen by authority from their respective lists.

The *Conservative Senate*, composed of eighty members, self-elective, had the right of appointing the members of the Corps

Législatif, the Tribuneship, and the Court of Cassation.
It was besides destined to the honor of choosing the Great
Elector. The senators, richly endowed, might exercise no
other function. The Corps Législatif was dumb, and limited
to voting the laws prepared by the Council of State, and discussed by the Tribunate. The Great Elector, without actively
interfering in the government, furnished with a civil list of
six millions, and magnificently housed by the state, appointed
the two councils of peace and war, upon whom depended the
ministers and all the administrative *personnel* of prefects and
sub-prefects entrusted with the government of the departments. In case the magistrate, so highly placed in his sumptuous indolence, should seem to menace the safety of the State,
the Senate was authorized to *absorb* him by admitting him
into its ranks. The same action might be exercised with respect to any of the civil or military functionaries.

So many complicated wheels calculated to hinder rather than
to sustain each other, so much pomp in words and so little
efficacy in action, could never suit the intentions or the character of General Bonaparte. He claimed at once the position
of Great Elector, which Sieyès had perhaps secretly thought
to reserve for himself.

"What!" said he, "would you want to make me a pig in a
dunghill?" Then demolishing the edifice laboriously constructed by the legislator, "Your Great Elector is a slothful
king," said he to Sieyès; "the time for that sort of thing is
past. What! appoint people to act, and not act himself! It
won't do. If I were this Great Elector I should certainly do
everything which you would desire me not to do. I should
say to the two consuls of peace and war: 'If you don't choose
such and such a man, or take such and such a measure, I shall
send you about your business.' And I would compel them to
proceed according to my will. And these two consuls—How
do you think they could agree? Unity of action is indispensable in government. Do you think that serious men would be
able to lend themselves to such shams?"

Sieyès was not fond of discussion, for which indeed he was
not suited; with the prudent sagacity which always characterized his conduct, he recognized the inferiority of his will
and his influence in comparison with General Bonaparte.
Three consuls were substituted for the Great Elector and his
two chosen subordinates—equal in appearance, but already
classed according to the origin of their power. As first consul,

Bonaparte was not to be subjected to any election; he held himself as appointed by the people. "What colleagues will they give me?" said he bluntly to Rœderer and Talleyrand who served him constantly as his agents of communication. "Whom do you wish?" He named Cambacérès, then minister of justice, clever and clear-sighted, of an independent spirit joined to a docile character; and Lebrun, the former secretary of the Chancellor Maupeou, minister for foreign affairs under the Convention, and respected by moderate republicans. Some had spoken of M. Daunou, honestly courageous in the worst days of the Revolution; the clever author of the Constitution of the year III., and whom Bonaparte had taken a malicious pleasure in entrusting with the drawing up of the new Constitution. A certain number of voices in the two legislative commissions had supported his name. The resolution of M. Daunou was known; Bonaparte did not complete the counting of the votes. "We shall do better," said he, "to keep to those whom M. Sieyès has named." Cambacérès and Lebrun were appointed consuls. Sieyès received from the nation a rich grant and the estate of Crosne. In concert with Roger-Ducos and the new consuls, he formed the list of the Senate, who immediately completed its numbers, as well as the lists of the 300 members of the Corps Législatif, and the 100 members of the Tribunate. Moderation presided over the composition of the lists; Bonaparte attached no importance to them, and took no part in their preparation. He had formed with care the Council of State, many capable men finding a place in it. It was the instrument which the First Consul destined for the execution of his ideas. Once only, on the 19th Brumaire, he came for a moment into contact with the assemblies. Henceforth he left them in the shade; all power rested in his hands. Under the name of Republic, the accent of an absolute master resounded already in the proclamation everywhere circulated on the day following the formation of the new government:—

"Frenchmen,

"To render the Republic dear to citizens, respected by foreigners, formidable to our enemies, are the obligations which we have contracted in accepting the chief magistracy.

"It will be dear to citizens if the laws and the acts of authority bear the impress of the spirit of order, justice and moderation.

"The Republic will be imposing to foreigners if it knows how to respect in their independence the title of its own independence, if its engagements, prepared with wisdom and entered upon with sincerity, are faithfully kept.

"Lastly, it will be formidable to its enemies, if the army and navy are made strong, and if each of its defenders finds a home in the regiment to which he belongs, and in that home a heritage of virtue and glory; if the officer, trained by long study, obtains by regular promotion the recompense due to his talents and work.

"Upon these principles depend the stability of government, the success of commerce and agriculture, the greatness and prosperity of nations.

"We have pointed out the rule, Frenchmen, by which we ought to be judged, we have stated our duties. It will be for you to tell us whether we have fulfilled them."

"What would you have?" said the First Consul to La Fayette. "Sieyès has put nothing but shadows everywhere; the shadow of legislative power, the shadow of judicial power, the shadow of government; some part of the substance was necessary. Faith! I have put it there." The very preamble of the Constitution affirmed the radical change brought about in the direction of affairs. "The powers instituted to-day will be strong and lasting, such as they ought to be in order to guarantee the rights of citizens and the interests of the State. Citizens, the Revolution is fixed upon the same principles which began it. It is finished!"

It was not the apotheosis, but the end of the Revolution that the authors of the Constitution of the year VIII. arrogantly announced. In the first impulse of a great spirit brought face to face with a difficult task, Bonaparte conceived the thought of terminating the war like the Revolution, and of re-establishing, at least for some time, the peace he needed in order to govern France. Disdainful of the ordinary forms of diplomacy, he wrote directly to George III., as he had formerly written to the Archduke Charles (18th December, 1799).

"Called by the will of the French nation to be first magistrate, I deem it expedient on entering upon my charge to communicate directly with your Majesty.

"Must the war which for eight years has ravaged the four quarters of the globe, be eternal? Is there no other means of arriving at a mutual understanding?

"How can the most enlightened nations of Europe, powerful and strong beyond what their security and independence require, sacrifice the interest of commerce, the prosperity of their people, and the happiness of families, to ideas of vainglory?

"These sentiments cannot be foreign to the heart of your Majesty, who governs a free nation with the sole aim of rendering it happy.

"Your Majesty will see in these overtures only my sincere desire to contribute effectively, for the second time, to a general pacification by a prompt procedure, full of confidence and divested of those forms which, necessary perhaps, in order to disguise the dependence of feeble States, only reveal between strong States a mutual desire to deceive each other.

"France and England, by the abuse of their power, may for a long time yet retard its termination; but I dare to say that every civilized nation is interested in the close of a war which embraces the whole world."

At the same time, and in nearly the same terms, Bonaparte wrote to the Emperor Francis. He had treated formerly with this sovereign, and would not perhaps have found him inflexible; but Pitt did not believe the Revolution finished, and had no confidence in a man who had just seized with a victorious hand the direction of the destinies of France. A frigidly polite letter, addressed by Lord Granville to Talleyrand, the minister of foreign affairs, repelled the advances of the First Consul. The English then prepared a new armament intended to second the attempts which the royalists were at that time renewing in the west. In enumerating the causes of European mistrust with regard to France, Lord Granville added, "The best guarantee, the most natural guarantee, for the reality and the permanence of the pacific intentions of the French government, would be the restoration of that royal dynasty which has maintained for so many ages the internal prosperity of France, and which has made it regarded with respect and consideration abroad. Such an event would clear away all the obstacles which hinder negotiations for peace, it would ensure to France the tranquil possession of her ancient territory, and it would give to all the nations of Europe that security which they are compelled to seek at present by other means."

During the violent debate raised in Parliament by the pacific propositions of the First Consul, Pitt based all his arguments upon the instability and insecurity of a treaty of peace with the French Revolution, whatever might be the name of its chief rulers. "When was it discovered that the dangers of Jacobinism cease to exist?" he cried. "When was it discovered that the Jacobinism of Robespierre, of Barère, of the five directors, of the triumvirate, has all of a sudden disappeared because it is concentrated in a single man, raised and nurtured in its bosom, covered with glory under its auspices, and who has been at once the offspring and the champion of all its atrocities? . . . It is because I love peace sincerely that I cannot content myself with a vain word; it is because I love peace sincerely that I cannot sacrifice it by seizing the shadow when the reality is not within my reach. *Cur igitur pacem nolo? Quia infida est, quia periculosa, quia esse non potest!*"

More moderate in form, Austria had in reality replied like England. War was inevitable, and in the internal disorder in which the Directory had left affairs, in the financial embarrassment and in the deplorable state of the armies, the First Consul felt the weight of a government that had been so long disorganized and weak, pressing heavily on his shoulders. His first care was to achieve the pacification of the west, always agitated by royalist passions. For a moment the chiefs of the party thought it possible to engage General Bonaparte in the service of the monarchical restoration: they were speedily undeceived. But the First Consul knew how to make use in Vendée of the influence of the former curé of St. Laud, the Abbé Bernier; he made an appeal to the priests, who returned from all parts to their provinces, "The ministers of a God of Peace," said the proclamation of the 28th December, 1799, " will be the first promoters of reconciliation and concord; let them speak to all hearts the language which they learn in the temple of their Master! Let them enter temples which will be reopened to them, and offer for their fellow-citizens the sacrifice which shall expiate the crime of war and the blood which has been made to flow!" Always in intimate unison with the religious sentiment of the populace who fought under their orders, the Vendean chiefs responded to this appeal, laying down their arms. In Brittany and in Normandy, Georges Cadoudal and Frotté continued hostilities; severe instructions were sent, first to General Hédouville, and then to General Brune. "The Consuls think that the generals ought to shoot on the spot the principal rebels taken with arms in hand. However cunning the Chouans may be, they are not so much so as Arabs of the desert. The First Consul believes that a salutary example would be given by burning two or three large communes, chosen from among those who have behaved themselves most badly." Six weeks later the insurrection was everywhere subdued; Frotté, and his young aide-de-camp Toustain, had been shot; Bourmont had accepted the offers of the First Consul, and enrolled himself in his service; Georges Cadoudal resisted all the advances of him whom he was soon to pursue with his hatred even to attempting a crime. "What a mistake I have made in not stifling him in my arms!" repeated the hardy chief of the Chouans on quitting General Bonaparte. He retired into England. The civil war was terminated; the troops which had occupied the provinces of the west could now rejoin the armies which were preparing on the frontiers. Carnot, who had just re-entered France, replaced at the ministry of war General Berthier, called upon active service. It was the grand association connected with his name, rather than the hope of an active and effective co-operation, which decided the First Consul to entrust this post to Carnot; possibly he wished to remove it from the little group of obstinate liberals justly disquieted at the dangers with which they saw freedom menaced. Already the journals had been suppressed, with the exception of thirteen; the laws were voted without dispute; and, "in a veritable whirlwind of urgency," the government claimed to regulate the duration of the discussions of the Tribunate. Benjamin Constant, still young, and known for a short time previously as a publicist, raised his voice eloquently against the wrong done to freedom of discussion. "Without doubt," said he "harmony is desirable amongst the authorities of the Republic; but the independence of the Tribunate is no less necessary to that harmony than the constitutional authority of the government; without the independence of the Tribunate, there will be no longer either harmony or constitution, there will be no longer anything but servitude and silence, a silence that all Europe will understand."

The past violence of the assemblies, and their frequent inconsistencies, had wearied feeble minds, and blinded short-sighted spirits. The speech of Benjamin Constant secured for his friend Madame de Staël a forced retirement from Paris. The law was voted by a large majority, and the adulations of flatterers were heaped up around the feet of the First Consul. He himself took a wiser view of his position, which he still considered precarious. On taking up his residence at the Tuileries, in great state, on February 19, 1800, he said to his secretary, "Well, Bourrienne, we have reached the Tuileries: the thing is now to stop here."

Already, and by the sole effort of a sovereign will, which appeared to improve by exercise, the power formerly distributed among obscure hands was concentrated at Paris, under the direction of a central administration suddenly organized; exactions borne with difficulty resulted in abundant resources from the conquered or annexed countries, at Genoa, in Holland, at Hamburg. The young King of Prussia, sensible and prudent, had refused to transform his neutrality into alliance; but he had used his influence over the smaller states of the empire, to induce them to maintain the same attitude. The Emperor Paul I., tossed to and fro by the impetuous movements of his ardent and unhealthy spirit, was piqued by the defeats of Suwarrow, and offended by the insufficiency of the help of Austria; he was discontented with the English government, and ill-humoredly kept himself apart from the coalition. The resumption of hostilities was imminent, and the grand projects of the First Consul began to unroll themselves. Active preparations had been till then confined to the army of the Rhine under Moreau. The army of Liguria, placed under the command of Masséna, with Genoa as a centre of operations, had received neither reinforcements nor munitions; its duty was to protect the passage of the Appenines against Mélas, whilst Moreau attacked upon the Rhine the army of Suabia, commanded by Marshal Kray. The occupation of Switzerland by the French army impeded the movements of the allies, by compelling them to withdraw their two armies from each other; the First Consul meditated a movement which should give him all the advantages of this separation. Moreau in Germany, Masséna in Italy, were ordered at any cost to keep the enemy in check. Bonaparte silently formed a third army, the corps of which he cleverly dispersed, distracting the attention of Europe by the camp of the army of reserve at Dijon. Already he was preparing the grand campaign which should raise his glory to its pinnacle, and establish his power upon victory. In his idea everything was to be sacrificed to the personal glory of his successes. He conceived a project of attack by crossing the Rhine. Moreau, modest and disinterested, accepted the general plan of the war, and subordinated his operations to those of the First Consul; in his military capacity independent and resolute, he persisted in passing the Rhine at his pleasure. Bonaparte was enraged. "Moreau would not seek to understand me," cried he. He yielded, however, to the observations of General

Dessoles, and always clever in subjugating those of whom he
had need, he wrote to Moreau to restore him liberty of action.
" Dessoles will tell you that no one is more interested than
myself in your personal glory and your good fortune. The
English embark in force; what do they want? I am to-day a
sort of manikin, who has lost his liberty and his good fortune.
Greatness is fine but in prospective and in imagination. I
envy you your luck; you go with the heroes to do fine deeds.
I would willingly barter my consular purple against one of
your bridadier's epaulettes" (16th March, 1800).

The army of Italy had been suffering for a long time with
heroic courage; the well-known chief who took the command
was more than any other suited to obtain from it the last
efforts of devotion; it was the first to undergo the attack of
the allied forces. The troops of Masséna were still scattered
when he was assailed by Mélas. The fear of prematurely
exhausting the insufficient resources of Genoa had prevented
him from following the wise councils of Bonaparte, by mass-
ing his troops round that town. After a series of furious
combats upon the upper Bormida, the French line found itself
cut in two by the Austrians; General Suchet was obliged to
fall back upon Nice, Masséna re-entered Genoa. A new effort
forced back General Mélas beyond the Appenines. The attempt to rejoin the corps of General Suchet having failed,
Masséna saw himself constrained to shut himself up in Genoa,
in the midst of a population divided in opinion, but whose confidence he had already known how to win. Resolved to
occupy by resistance and by sorties all the forces of the allies,
the general made preparations for sustaining the siege to the
last extremity. All the provisions of the place were brought
into the military magazines; the most severe order reigned in
the distribution, but already scarcity was felt. The forces of
Masséna, exhausted by frequent fights, diminished every day;
bread failed; and the heroic obstinacy of the general alone
compelled the Austrians to keep a considerable corps d'armée
before a famished town (5th May, 1800). Mélas had in vain
attempted to force the lines of Var, behind which General
Suchet, too feeble to defend Nice, had cleverly entrenched
himself.

Moreau delayed to commence the campaign; his material
was insufficient; Alsace and Switzerland, exhausted of resources, could not furnish the means of transport required by
his movement. The First Consul urged him. " Obtain a success

as soon as possible, that you may be able by a diversion in some degree to expedite the operations in Italy," he wrote to him on April 24; "every day's delay is extremely disastrous to us." On April 26, Moreau passed the Rhine at Strasburg, at Brisach, and at Basle, thus deceiving General Kray, who defended the defiles of the Black Forest, whilst the different divisions of the French army reascended and repassed the Rhine, in order to cross it afresh without difficulty at Schaffhausen. The Austrians had not yet collected their forces, dispersed by the unlooked-for movement they found themselves obliged to execute; the French corps were themselves dispersed when the battle commenced, on May 3, at Engen. After a furious struggle at several points, General Moreau achieved a splendid victory; two days later the same fortune crowned the battle of Mœsskirch; the loss on both sides was great. The action was not well combined; Marshal Kray at first fell back behind the Danube; by the advice of his council of war he decided to defend the magazines at Biberach. He repassed the river, and offered battle to the corps of Gouvion St. Cyr, then hampered with Moreau, bearing his direction with difficulty. The positions occupied by the Austrians were everywhere attacked at once; their troops, already demoralized by several defeats, retired in disorder. Kray fell back on Ulm, where an entrenched camp was ready for him. General Moreau was compelled to weaken his army by detaching a corps of 1800 men, necessary for the operations of the First Consul. He attempted without success a movement intended to turn the flank of General Kray, and resolved to blockade him in his positions, and wait for the result of the manœuvres of Bonaparte. On the 27th May he wrote to Bonaparte, "We await with impatience the announcement of your success. M. de Kray and I are groping about here—he to keep his army round Ulm, I to make him quit the post. It would have been dangerous, especially for you, if I had carried the war to the left bank of the Danube. Our present position has forced the Prince of Reuss to remove himself to the passes of the Tyrol, to the sources of the Lech and the Iller; thus he is no longer dangerous for you. If M. de Kray comes towards me, I shall still retreat as far as Meiningen; there I shall join General Lecourbe, and we shall fight. If M. de Kray marches upon Augsburg, I shall do the same; he will quit his support at Ulm, and then we shall see what will have to be done to cover your movements. We should find more advantages in carrying on the war upon the left bank of the Danube, and making Wurtemberg and Franconia contribute to it; but that would not suit you, as the enemy would be able to send detachments down into Italy whilst leaving us to ravage the provinces of the Empire.

"Give me, I pray you, some news of yourself, and command me in every possible service I can render you."

All was thus prepared in Germany and Italy for the success of that camgaign of the First Consul of which the enemy were still ignorant. Always deceived by the fictitious concentrations carried on at Dijon, the Austrians saw without disquietude the departure of Bonaparte, who left Paris, as it was said, for a few days, in order to pass in review the army of reserve. The French public shared the same illusion; the preparations eagerly pushed forward by the First Consul, remained secret. He set out at the last moment, leaving with regret, and not without uneasiness, his government scarcely established, and new institutions not yet in working order. "Keep firmly together," said he to Cambacérès and Lebrun; "if an emergency occurs, don't be alarmed at it. I will return like a thunderbolt, to crush those who are audacious enough to raise a hand against the government." He had in advance, by the powerful conceptions of his genius arranged the whole plan of operations, and divined the movements of his enemies. Bending over his maps, and designating with his finger the positions of the different corps, he muttered in a low voice, "This poor M. de Mélas will pass by Turin, he will fall back upon Alessandria. I shall pass the Po, and come up with him again on the road of Placenza, in the plains of the Scrivia; and I shall beat him there, and then there." The Tribunate expressed their desire that the First Consul might return soon, "conqueror and pacificator." An article of the Constitution forbade him to take the command of the armies; Berthier received the title of general-in-chief. The First Consul passed in review the army of conscripts and invalids assembled at Dijon. On May 13, he combined the active forces at Geneva; the troops coming from Germany under the command of General Moncey had not yet arrived; they were to pass by the St. Gothard. General Marescot had been ordered to reconnoitre the Alps; the pass of the St. Bernard, more difficult than that of the Simplon or Mont Cenis, was much shorter, and the passage from it could be much more easily defended. "Difficult it may be," replied the First Consul to the report of Marescot, "but is it possible?" "I think so," said the general, "with

VII.—2

extraordinary efforts." "Ah, well! let us set out," said Bonaparte.

From Geneva to Villeneuve the journey was easy, and vessels carried provisions to that point. The First Consul had carefully arranged places for revictualling all along the road. At Montigny half the mules, requisitioned at great cost in the neighborhood, were loaded with victuals and munitions of war; the other half were attached to the gun carriages relieved of the cannon, which were to be again put in working order at San Remi, on the other side of the pass. The cannon themselves were enveloped in the hollowed trunks of trees; they could then be dragged over the ice and snow. The number of mules proving insufficient, and the peasants refusing to undertake this rough work, the soldiers yoked themselves to the cannon, and dragged them across the mountain without wishing to accept the rewards promised by the First Consul. He rode on a mule at the head of the rear-guard, wrapped in a gray greatcoat, chatting familiarly with his guide, and sustaining the courage of his soldiers by his unalterable coolness. After a few hours' rest at the hospice of St. Bernard commenced the descent, more difficult still than the ascent. From the 15th to the 20th of May the divisions followed each other. Lannes and Berthier, who commanded the vanguard, had already advanced to Aosta, when they found themselves stopped by the little fort of Bard, built upon a precipitous rock, and with artillery commanding the defile. It was now night; a layer of straw and refuse was spread over the frozen foot-path; the wheels of the gun-carriages were encased in tow; at the break of day the passage had been safely cleared. The French army, descending like a torrent into the valley, seized upon Ivry, and repulsed the Austrians at the Chiusella on May 26th. All the divisions of Bonaparte's army assembled by degrees; the corps of Moncey debouched by the St. Gothard, 4000 men under the orders of General Thureau crossed by Mont Cenis. General Mélas still refused to believe in the danger which menaced him, and already an imposing army was advancing against his scattered and divided forces. Already Lannes had beaten General Ott at Montebello, after a hotly disputed engagement. "I heard the bones crackle like a hailstorm on the roofs," said the conqueror.

Bonaparte threw himself upon Milan, neglecting Genoa, which he might have delivered without risk; thereby condemning Masséna and his army to the sufferings of a prolonged siege, terminated by a sad defeat. He had conceived vaster projects, and the design of annihilating the Austrian army by a single blow. Everything had to give way to the consideration of personal success and his egotistical thirst for glory. The Lombard populace received the First Consul with transport, happy to see themselves delivered from the Austrian yoke, and beguiled in advance with the hope of liberty. General Mélas was at Alessandria, summoning to his aid the forces that were attacking Suchet on the Var, and the troops of General Ott, detained by the siege of Genoa. He was assured of the impossibility of any succor being sent by Marshal Kray. It was necessary to conquer or die. In the prison in which the Austrian army detained him, Masséna had divined the situation of the enemy. He was still hoping for the assistance that had been promised him; already General Ott had sent him a flag of truce. "Give me only provisions for two days, or one day," said he to the Genoese, "and I will save you from the Austrian yoke, and spare my army the sorrow of surrender."

All resources were exhausted; the horrors of famine had worn out the courage of the inhabitants; even the soldiers were yielding to discouragement. "Before he will surrender," said they, "the general will make us eat his boots." For a long time the garrison had lived on unwholesome bread made with starch, upon linseed and cocoa, which scarcely sufficed to keep the soldiers alive; the population, reduced to live on soup made of herbs gathered on the ramparts, died by hundreds; the prisoners cantoned in the port in old dismasted vessels, uttered cries that reached the ears of their old generals. The latter had refused to send in provisions for the prisoners, in spite of the promise of Masséna to reserve it for them. The last food was used up; on the 3rd of June the general censented to receive the flag of truce. He asked for, and obtained, the honors of war; the army was authorized to depart from Genoa with arms and baggage, flags displayed, and free to direct its course towards the corps of General Suchet. "Without that I should issue arms in hand, and it should be seen what eight thousand famished men could do." War and famine had reduced to this number the soldiers in condition to carry arms. After their cure, the sick, who filled the hospitals, were to be sent to the quarters of General Suchet. Masséna defended the interests of the Genoese, and asked in their favor for a free government. The Austrian generals refused to make any engagement. "In less than a fortnight I shall be back again in

Genoa," declared the French general. "You will find there the men whom you have taught how to defend it," replied St. Julien, one of the plenipotentiaries. General Soult remained in the place, seriously wounded. Masséna brought his exhausted troops to the Var. In the depths of their souls, generals and soldiers cherished a bitter resentment for the manner in which they had been abandoned. When the Austrian troops, beaten by Suchet, had retired towards Alessandria, Masséna did not allow him to pursue them; he contented himself with guarding the gates of France.

Bonaparte had just quitted Stradella, which he had occupied after leaving Milan. He had been obliged to disperse his forces, in order to cut off all the passages open to the enemy. When he entered, on June 13th, the plain that extends between the Scrivia and the Bormida, near the little village of Marengo, he was badly instructed as regards the movements of the enemy, as well as the resources of the country. On the morning of the 14th, General Mélas, constrained by necessity, evacuated Alessandria, and, passing the Bormida upon three bridges, attacked General Victor before Marengo. Lannes was at the same time surrounded on every side, and obliged to retreat in spite of prodigies of courage. Marengo had been destroyed by the artillery of the enemy, when Bonaparte arrived upon the field of battle with his guard and his staff officers, at once drawing upon himself the brunt of the fight. Meanwhile the retreat continued; the army seemed about to be cut in two; the Austrian general, old and fatigued, believing himself assured of victory, re-entered Alessandria. It was now three o'clock, and Bonaparte still hoped and kept on fighting. He despatched an aide-de-camp to Desaix, returned from Egypt two days before, and whom he had detached in the direction of Novi; upon his return depended the fortune of the day. Desaix had divined this, and forestalled the message of Bonaparte; before he could be expected he was beside the general, who questioned him as to the aspect of affairs. "Well," said Desaix, after having rapidly examined the situation of the different corps, "it is a lost battle; but it is not late; we have time to gain another." His regiments were forming whilst he spoke, stopping the march of the Austrians. "My friends," said the First Consul to the reanimated soldiers, "remember that it is my custom to sleep upon the field of battle."

At the same moment Desaix advanced at the heads of his troops. "Go and tell the First Consul that I am about to charge," said he to his aide-de-camp, Savary; "I need to be supported by cavalry." He was crossing an undulation in the ground when a ball struck him in the breast; from daybreak he had been oppressed by gloomy presentiments. "I have been too long making war in Africa," said he; "the bullets of Europe know me no longer." On falling he said to General Boudet, "Conceal my death; it might unsettle the troops." The soldiers had perceived it and rushed forward to avenge him. Kellermann arrived at the same instant, urged forward by one of those sudden inspirations which mark great generals; hurling his dragoons upon the Austrian cavalry, which he broke through, he attacked the column of grenadiers which arduously sustained the assault of the division of Desaix. Their ranks fell into disorder; one entire corps threw down its arms. General Zach, entrusted with the command in the absence of Mélas, was forced to give up his sword. When the old general hurried up in agitation, the battle was lost. The Austrian troops, repulsed and routed, and crowded against the banks of the Bormida, blocked up all the bridges, or cast themselves into the river, everywhere pursued by the victorious French. The cannon, which stuck fast in the Bormida, fell into the hands of the conquerors. The staff was decimated.

The First Consul regretted the loss of Desaix, the only one among the companions of his youth who had seemed able to inspire in him any particular regard. He was, however, triumphant, and this great day made him in fact the master of Italy. He had the wisdom to perceive it. The needs of government recalled him to France; the conditions he proposed to Mélas, although hard, were such as could be accepted. The Austrian army was authorized to retire with the honors of war; but it was to surrender to the French troops all its positions in Liguria, Piedmont, Lombardy, and the Legations, whilst evacuating the Italian territory as far as the Mincio. To the protests of Mélas, Bonaparte replied by a formal refusal to listen. "Sir," said he, "my conditions are irrevocable. I did not begin to made war yesterday. Your position is as well known to me as to yourself. You are in Alessandria, encumbered with the dead, the wounded, and the sick, and destitute of provisions; you have lost the *élite* of your army; you are surrounded on all sides. I could exact everything, but I only demand of you that which the situation of affairs imperatively requires. Return to Alessandria; you will have no other conditions."

Mélas signed, pledging his word until he should receive a reply from Vienna. On the same evening, before quitting the field of battle, the First Consul wrote for the second time to the Emperor Francis Joseph. He was moved to the very depths of his impassable and haughty soul by the spectacle of the carnage and fury of the battle. In subsequent calmer moments he perhaps regretted his letter. "It is upon the battlefield of Marengo," said he, "in the midst of agonies, and ¡surrounded by 15,000 corpses, that I conjure your Majesty to listen to the cry of humanity, and not permit the children of two brave and powerful nations to massacre each other for interests which are foreign to them. It is for me to press this upon your Majesty, since I am the nearest to the theatre of war. Your heart cannot be so keenly alive to it as mine. The arms of your Majesty have achieved sufficient glory. You govern a large number of States. What then can those in the cabinet of your Majesty allege in favor of the continuation of hostilities? Is it the interests of religion and of the Church? Why do they not counsel your Majesty to make war on the English, the Muscovites, and the Prussians? They are further from the Church than we. Is it the form of the French Government, which is not hereditary but simply elective? But the government of the Empire is also elective; and besides, your Majesty is thoroughly convinced of the powerlessness of the entire world to change the desire which the French people have received from nature to govern themselves as they please. Is it the destruction of revolutionary principles? If your Majesty will take account of the effects of war you will see that it tends to revolutionize Europe, by increasing everywhere the public debt and the discontent of the people. In compelling the French people to make war, you compel them only to think of war, only to live in war; and the French legions are numerous and brave. If your Majesty wishes for peace it is done; let us give repose and tranquillity to the present generation. If future generations are foolish enough to fight— well, they will learn after a few years of war to become wise and live in peace. I might take captive the entire army of your Majesty. I am satisfied by a suspension of hostilities, having hopes that it may be the first step towards the repose of the world; an object for which I can plead all the more forcibly because, nurtured and schooled by war, I might be suspected of being more accustomed to the evils it drags after it. If your Majesty refuses these proposals, the hostilities will recommence; and let me be permitted to tell you frankly, in the eyes of the world you alone will be responsible for the war."

Peace was still to be delayed, but the Convention of Alessandria was concluded at once; and the success of General Moreau sustained in Germany the victorious arguments of the First Consul. The former passed the Danube near Hochstedt; after a very brilliant action, which lasted eighteen hours (June 19), he took 5000 prisoners, and captured twenty pieces of cannon and considerable magazines. Kray, menaced with the probability of having his line of retreat cut off, had abandoned his position at Ulm, forcing his march so precipitately that General Moreau had not been informed of it. Meanwhile he attacked the Grisons and the Tyrol, repulsed the Prince of Reuss, and established himself upon the Isar. On the 15th of July a suspension of arms was signed at Parsdorf, near Munich. Like the soldiers of the army of Italy, the soldiers of the army of the Rhine were about to take some repose.

Masséna had re-entered Genoa on the 24th of June, justifying to the letter his glorious bravado; his ill-humor was dissipated, and he remained entrusted with the chief command of the army of Italy. The First Consul had received at Milan the eager homage of the Lombards, but the Cisalpine Republic was not reconstituted; a Grand Council governed it under the Presidency of Pétiet, the French minister. At Turin, General Jourdan directed the provisional government; at Genoa, General Dejean filled the same functions; everywhere the paraded power of France was substituted for the semblance of liberty; the Roman States were still in the hands of the Neapolitans. The new Pope, Barnabus Chiaramonti, formerly Bishop of Imola, who had shown himself well disposed towards the French, had just arrived unexpectedly at Ancona, whence he negotiated his re-entry into the eternal city. The First Consul assured him of his good intentions as regards the Catholic Church, and the Holy See. The far-seeing *finesse* of the Court of Rome did not permit it to be deceived. The Secretary of the Sacred College, Monsignor Consalvi, had said during the conclave, "It is from France that we have received persecutions for ten years past; well, it is from France that will perhaps come in the future our succors and our consolations. A very extraordinary young man, and even more difficult to be judged, rules there to-day. There is no doubt he will soon have reconquered Italy. Remember that he protected the priests in 1797, and that he has recently rendered funeral honors to Pius VI. Let us not neglect the resources which offer themselves to us on this side." On the day after the battle of Marengo preliminary negotiations already commenced. The First Consul was officially present at the grand *Te Deum* chanted in the cathedral of Milan. "Our atheists at Paris may say of it what they will," wrote Bonaparte to Cambacérès.

During the night of the 2nd and 3rd July, 1800, Bonaparte re-entered Paris, overwhelmed on the way by evidences of public joy, which were most brilliantly manifested at Lyons. He had forbidden all preparations for his return: "My intention is to have neither arches of triumph nor any species of ceremony," he wrote to his brother Lucien, who had replaced Laplace at the ministry of the interior. "I have too good an opinion of myself to hold such baubles in much estimation. I know no other triumph than the public satisfaction."

The day would come when public satisfaction, of a truth much mitigated by long sufferings, would no longer suffice for the triumph of the absolute master who dragged exhausted France across fields of battle; the remembrance of his return to Paris after the victory of Marengo was to recur to his sorrowful mind when he dictated at St. Helena the memoirs explanatory of his life: "It was a great day," said he.

Already the adulations and mean worship of courtiers were encompassing him; already, also, was revealed the provisional character of that power which depended so completely upon the life of a single man. Sinister reports were circulated during the campaign in Italy; the names of Carnot, Moreau, and La Fayette had been put forward. The triumphant arrival of the First Consul promptly baffled the intrigues in which the principals interested had never taken part; nevertheless, he nursed against Carnot an unjust feeling, which soon betrayed itself in his dismissal. Lucien Bonaparte had forestalled, or badly comprehended, the wishes of his brother; he had got Fontanes to write a pamphlet entitled "Cæsar, Cromwell, and Bonaparte," which revealed projects and hopes in favor of the First Consul for which the public was not prepared. "Happy for the Republic," it was said, "if Bonaparte were immortal? But where are his successors? Who is the successor of Pericles? Frenchmen, you slumber over an abyss, and your sleep is madly tranquil."

It was too soon to allow these premature pretensions to be thus made public. The *finesse* of La Fayette enabled him to penetrate the secret hope of the First Consul, who was already occupied, and for most serious reasons, with the re-establishment of religion in France. He was able to say to him, with an irony that was a little scornful, "Come, general, confess that this has no other aim than to get the little phial broken on your head." Public opinion was not yet calling for the re-establishment of the monarchy; it did not connect the idea of hereditary power with a victorious general, still young, and who had scarcely seized the reins of the government of the interior. The pamphlet, and the insinuations it contained, had no success; Fouché was openly reprimanded for allowing the publication. Lucien Bonaparte was sent as ambassador to Madrid, bearing, he has declared, the manuscript of the pamphlet, with four corrections in the handwriting of the First Consul. The latter began to surround himself with a court. Madame Bonaparte had already her ladies and chevaliers of honor.

St. Julien had just arrived at Paris with the ratification of the treaty of Alessandria, and for the purpose of sounding the First Consul as to his intentions on the subject of a definitive peace. Major-general of the imperial armies, and little versed in diplomatic usages, he, in all simplicity, avowed his ignorance to Talleyrand. The latter profited by this to prevail upon the Austrian ambassador to sign the preliminary articles. "So be it," said St. Julien, "but they will have no authority until after their ratification by my sovereign." The major-general was not authorized to treat; and the conventions he had accepted being vague as to the most important point, the settlement of the frontiers of Italy, were disavowed at Vienna. Thugut proposed the opening of a congress, in which England was disposed to take part. General Duroc, aide-de-camp of the First Consul, who had accompanied St. Julien on his return to Vienna, was not admitted to negotiate, and found himself compelled to return to Paris.

Bonaparte's temper was quick; his irritation against England was old and inveterate. For more than two years that power had hindered the success of his favorite enterprises; and he struggled against her in her commercial interests, as well as in her military efforts, with a perseverance worthy of Pitt. He had already won over the United States to the doctrine of the greater part of European States as to the rights of neutrals, and concluded with their diplomatists the treaty of Morfontaine; he then worked to raise up against England a formidable coalition, at the head of which the Emperor Paul

I. had just placed himself. Strongly influenced in favor of
France by the offer the First Consul had made to cede to him
Malta, then besieged by the English, the Czar also received
with satisfaction the 6000 Russian prisoners whom Bonaparte
sent to him without ransom, after having vainly solicited ex-
changes with England and Russia. The maritime powers of
the north of Europe had to complain of vexatious interference
with merchant-vessels on the part of England. The law of the
seas, said they, authorized them to carry on commerce between one power and another, goods contraband of war alone
excepted; as the flag covered the merchandise, English vessels
could not legitimately stop and visit ships of neutral countries,
in order to seize French or Spanish commodities. The theory
of England was different, serving her own commercial and
military interests. In 1800 the Emperor Paul embraced the
cause of the maritime powers, and formed against England the
League of Neutrals, whilst he entered into amicable relations,
and a sort of alliance, with the First Consul. At the same time
Bonaparte negotiated with the King of Spain, offering him
Tuscany, with the title of King of Etruria, for his son-in-law
the Duke of Parmo, on condition that France should receive
back Louisiana, formerly ceded to Spain by Louis XV. for an
indemnity claim. Charles IV. also engaged himself to use his
influence to have the ports of Portugal closed against England.
Before admitting England to the congress, the First Consul
demanded that the continental armistice should be extended to
naval forces, as the suspension of maritime hostilities would
permit him to revictual Malta and Egypt; he accepted on
these terms the common negotiations.

England rejected, and could not but reject, these proposals.
She already held the conquest of Malta as certain; and since
Bonaparte himself had quitted Egypt, the English soldiers and
marines no longer doubted the ultimate success of their efforts
against us, everywhere united with those of the Porte. Egypt
was henceforth a point so important for England that she had
resolved never to yield to the passionate caprices which had led
General Bonaparte to establish the French dominion there.
In the month of August, 1800, she could not accept an arm-
istice which would of necessity have prolonged the war in the
East. In the month of November, 1799, letters of General
Kléber, sincere and discouraged, had fallen into the hands of
the English Government. Entrusted since the departure of
General Bonaparte with the chief command, Kléber displayed

to the Directory the sad state of his army and his finances. Five months had passed, and nothing new had taken place; no succor had arrived from France. Kléber had lent his ear to the proposals of the vizier and Sir Sidney Smith. Bonaparte himself had foreseen the circumstances under which the evacuation of Egypt would become necessary; he had left upon this subject peremptory and haughty instructions. Kléber forestalled the term marked out by the general who had let his mantle fall upon his shoulders, and he concluded the treaty of El Arish, a monument of his sorrow and desolation. The signature of Desaix, who negotiated it, was mournfully wrung from him, after he had required from the general-in-chief a formal order to put his name to it. Negotiated between military men, it was not countersigned with the signature of the plenipotentiary, who himself had not better authority to negotiate. The Government of Great Britain, informed of the distress of General Kléber, sent to Admiral Keith a formal injunction forbidding him to treat with the French army, unless they surrendered as prisoners of war. Sir Sidney Smith immediately made known to Kléber the orders he had received; the honorable conditions which the French general had previously accepted were already in process of execution; several places had been given up to the Turks; the vizier had advanced. Kléber, however, did not hesitate. He published to the army the letter of the English commodore, with these words: "Soldiers! such insolence as this is only answered by victories: prepare to give battle."

It is a noble spectacle, that of resolute men reduced to extremities without fleeing from danger. On March 20 the French army went out from Cairo; diminished by death and sickness it numbered no more than 12,000 men, who formed themselves into squares, according to the old tactics of the troops of Egypt, in front of the ancient ruins of Heliopolis. Kléber estimated at 70,000 or 80,000 men the Turkish army which was to assail him. "My friends," said he in passing along the ranks, "you possess in Egypt only the ground which you have beneath your feet! If you retreat a step, you are lost!" Having thus spoken, he gave the order to carry the entrenched village of El Matarieh. The little redoubts were already in our possession when the Janissaries made their first rush upon the Friant division. The squares remained immovable, keeping up a continuous fire, enveloped in smoke, and scarcely distinguishing the mass of the enemies who were falling at their feet. When the clouds began to disperse, a rampart of corpses surrounded all the French corps ; in the distance were seen the enemy in flight. Kléber order a pursuit, which was continued during three days. When the general-in-chief at length reached the camp of the vizier at Salahieh he only found a few detachments of the enemy. The chiefs had disappeared in the desert, with their best troops. The French soldiers pillaged the tents: they were loaded with rich spoils when they retook the road to Cairo.

The capital of Egypt, never in complete submission, and disturbed by frequent insurrections, had revolted at the announcement of the evacuation and the departure of the French army; crimes had been committed, and the Christians had been massacred in several quarters. Kléber laid siege to it; the resistance was long and furious, and it was as conquerors that the French re-entered the city which formerly cost them such slight efforts. All the rebel cities of Lower Egypt were again brought back into obedience to France. The war indemnities and the prizes taken from the enemy restored the finances. Kléber labored for the completion of the forts scattered over the hills; he enrolled Copts, Syrians, and some blacks from Darfour; he treated with Murad Bey, who had driven from Upper Egypt the Turkish corps of Dervish Pacha; Ibrahim Bey and Nassif Pacha, who had sustained the revolt of Cairo, obtained an authorization to retire. Egypt appeared to be once more submissive ; but the illusions which the Mohammedans had conceived were promptly dissipated: they recognized their traditional enemies, and the old fanaticism was reawakened. An assassin had already arrived in Cairo from Palestine, and shut up in the great mosque he had confided to the shieks his project of killing General Kléber. They sought to dissuade him from it, but without informing the French. On the 14th of June, as the general was walking in his garden with the architect of the army, Suleiman presented himself before him, pretending to ask alms, and struck him several times with his dagger. The architect was wounded in striving to defend Kléber. When the soldiers came hurrying up the general had already breathed his last. The assassin made no attempt to flee; he expired under torture. At Cairo, and on the battlefield of Marengo, Kléber and Desaix succumbed on the same day, and almost at the same hour, both young, and serving to their last day the designs of the chief to whom they were very unequally attached. The First Consul

KLÉBER.

wished to unite them in the same patriotic honors; he had never had much liking for Kléber, but he did not the less keenly feel the greatness of his loss. General Menou, who took by seniority the command of the army of Egypt was incapable, and of a chimerical spirit. Bonaparte comprehended the danger which threatened that one of his conquests to which he attached the most importance; he increased the reinforcements of men and munitions, but he was in want of generals, and the war was recommencing in Europe. The English had just succeeded at last in taking Malta.

The armistice had been prolonged for eighty-five days, and the Emperor of Austria had paid for this moment of peace by the surrender of the cities of Ulm, Philipsburg, and Ingoldstadt; the preliminaries, which Cobentzel had drawn out to great length, had brought about no result. Austria refused to negotiate without England, to whom she was allied by a treaty of subsidies. In contempt of the convention of Alessandria, the French troops occupied Tuscany; Masséna no longer commanded the army of Italy. Quarrels had arisen with the Italian administrations, who said they were victims of heavy exactions. Masséna was accused; in the depth of his soul he was discontented, and was always little favorable te the First Cousul. Brune had replaced him. At the expiration of the armistice, and in spite of the new attempts at negotiations, the troops entered on the campaign. General Bonaparte still remained at Paris, ready to proceed at need to the threatened points. All eyes were fixed on Germany; by a common instinct great military events upon this theatre were look forward to.

The Archduke John was young and daring; he conceived the hope of cutting off the army of General Moreau, and imprudently crossing the Inn, the difficult passage of which the French dreaded, he advanced immediately towards the Isar, intending to reascend the river in our rear. But already the difficulties of the enterprise became apparent; the young general resolved to give battle immediately. An advantage gained on the 1st of December, over the left wing of the French army, emboldened him to the point of pushing forward across the forest of Hohenlinden, in the vain hope of encountering no resistance. General Moreau waited for him in the plain between Hohenlinden and Harthofen; Generals Richepanse and Decaen had been directed to take the Austrians in the rear. Moreau had exactly calculated the time necessary for this operation.

The battle commenced at the exit from the forest; as fast as they debouched upon the plain the Austrian corps encountered the attack of our troops. Across the snow, which fell in great flakes, the general-in-chief discerned a little confusion in the ranks of the enemy. "The moment has come to charge," he cried; "Richepanse has taken them in the rear." General Ney rushed forward at the head of his division; he rejoined his companions at the centre of the defile mingled with the confused crowd of the enemy, which they drove before them. The centre of the Austrian army was completely hemmed in; the left wing had been thrown back upon the Inn by Decaen. The French divisions who were engaged on the right, repulsed for a moment, had in their turn forced the Austrians to redescend into the valley. The plain of Hohenlinden remained in the hands of the French army. The enemy lost 8000 men killed or wounded, 12,000 prisoners, and eighty-seven pieces of cannon. General Lecourbe passed the Inn close behind the Archduke John, the division of Decaen crossed the Salza and seconded the movement of Lecourbe; General Moreau crossed the Traun, and advanced towards the Ens. The Archduke Charles, drawn from his disgrace by the danger of his country, resumed the command of the Austrian troops. It was too late to snatch back victory; he accepted the sorrowful duty of arresting the conqueror's progress by negotiations. Moreau had arrived at Steyer, a few leagues from Vienna: the ardor of his lieutenants urged him to march forward. "It would, without doubt, be a fine thing to enter Vienna," he replied; "but it is a much finer thing to dictate peace." The armistice was signed on the 25th of December, 1800, delivering to the French all the valley of the Danube, with the Tyrol, various fortresses, and immense magazines. The army of Augereau, which had had adventure enough on the Rednitz, was included in the armistice; the generals commanding in Italy and in the Grisons, Macdonald and Brune, were to be engaged to accept a suspension of arms. The modest prudence and consummate cleverness of General Moreau had assured to our arms advantages which at length promised peace. Bonaparte perceived this, not without secret heart-burning; but for a time he felt himself compelled to dissemble. "I cannot tell you all the interest I have taken in your admirable and wise manœuvres," he wrote to Moreau; "in this campaign you have surpassed yourself."

The orders of the First Consul caused the war in Italy to be ardently pushed forward. "Wherever a couple of men can plant their feet, an army can find the means of passing," said General Bonaparte; and Macdonald had led his 15,000 men across the passes of the Splügen, among rocks and glaciers, obliged to open a path by the oxen, who trod down the snow in order to permit the soldiers to advance; he left behind him numerous victims of cold and fatigue. The army of the Grisons had arrived at Trent, the efforts of General Wukassovich having failed to arrest its progress. Brune had conducted his operations more gently; when he marched towards the Mincio, in order to cross it at two points, the imprudence of the attack and the division of the forces led to a great shedding of blood; it was only on the 31st December that the passage of the Adige was at last effected. The corps of General Moncey rejoined the forces of Macdonald at Trent; the Count of Laudon, close pressed, could only save his troops by a subterfuge, by forestalling the armistice, which did not yet extend to the armies of Italy. He had rejoined the Count of Bellegarde, when all military operations were suspended by a convention signed at Treviso.

Cobentzel and Joseph Bonaparte had remained at Lunéville during the resumption of hostilities, negotiating mutual concessions, of which the cannon every day altered the conditions. The success of his armies, and the attitude of the powers of the north, enlarged the pretensions of the First Consul; the Austrian plenipotentiary defended with persevering courage the frontier of the Adda, and the re-establishment of the Italian princes in their States, when the instructions of Bonaparte to his brother were all of a sudden altered. Order was given to retard the conclusion of peace; at the same time, as if for the purpose of calling upon Austria to bow to imperious necessity, the First Consul sent to the Corps Législatif a message, which was a bold evidence of the newest phase of his diplomacy.

"Legislators, the Republic triumphs, and its enemies once more implore its moderation.

"The news of the victory of Hohenlinden has resounded throughout Europe; that day will be reckoned in history as one of the grandest examples of French valor. But it has been thought little of by our defenders, who only think themselves victors when the country has no more enemies. The army of the Rhine has passed the Inn; every day has been a battle, and every battle a triumph. The Gallo-Batavian army has conquered at Bamberg; the army of the Grisons, through snow and ice, has crossed the Splügen, in order to turn the for-

midable lines of the Mincio and the Adige. The army of Italy
has carried by main force the passage of the Mincio, and has
blockaded Mantua. Lastly, Moreau is no more than five days'
march from Vienna, master of an immense tract of country,
and of all the magazines of the enemy.

" It is at this juncture that the Archduke Charles has asked,
and the general-in-chief of the army of the Rhine has accorded,
the armistice of which the conditions are about to be placed
before you.

" Cobentzel, plenipotentiary of the Emperor at Lunéville,
has declared himself ready to open negotiations for a separate
peace. Thus Austria is freed from the influence of the English
Government.

" The Government, faithful to its principles and to the prayer
of humanity, confides to you, and proclaims to France and
entire Europe, the intentions which animate it.

" The left bank of the Rhine shall be the limit of the French
Republic ; she claims nothing on the right bank. The interests
of Europe will not permit the emperor to pass the Adige. The
independence of the Helvetic and Batavian Republics shall be
assured and recognized. Our victories add nothing to the
claims of the French people. Austria ought not to expect from
its defeats that which it would not have obtained by victories.
Such are the unchangeable intentions of the Government. It
will be the happiness of France to restore calm to Germany and
Italy ; its glory to enfranchise the continent from the covetous
and malevolent influence of England.

" If our good faith is still deceived, we are at Prague, at
Vienna, at Venice."

So many rigorous conditions, thus arrogantly announced,
were, and could not fail to be, the object of discussions and
stubborn resistance. But even these did not satisfy the will of
the First Consul, and his resolution to snatch the last concessions from the conquered. The Emperor Paul, in his capacity
of Grand Master of the Order, demanded from England the
cession of the island of Malta. Upon the refusal of the British
Government, he placed an embargo on all English vessels found
in his ports, at the same time announcing the despatch of a
plenipotentiary to Paris. In accord with Prussia, he admitted
the principle of the granting of indemnities to the deposed
Italian princes by the secularization of the ecclesiastical territories in Germany. Cobentzel was constantly opposed to this
arrangement ; he equally refused to deliver Mantua to France

as a condition of the armistice in Italy. Abandoned by the neutral powers, isolated in Germany, and separated from England, who alone remained openly hostile to France, the Austrian envoy saw himself constrained to accept conditions harder than those the rigor of which he had formerly deplored. On the 9th February, 1801, the treaty of Lunéville was at last signed. A single concession had been accorded to Cobentzel; France had consented to surrender the places which she held on the right bank of the Rhine. She insisted, however, that the fortifications should be demolished. "Dismantle them yourselves," said the Austrian plenipotentiary, sorrowfully, "and we will engage that they shall remain in the condition in which they are surrendered." This was the last hope, and the last effort of diplomacy. Upon the very morning of the signature, and with reference to the obstinate persistence of Cobentzel, Joseph Bonaparte declared, in language which was not his own, "that if the termination of the war was favorable to France, the house of Austria ought to expect to find the valley of the Adige on the crest of the Julian Alps; and that there was no power in Europe which did not see with pleasure the Austrians expelled from Italy."

The bases of the treaty of Lunéville were identical with those of the treaty of Campo Formio. Austria lost in Germany the bishopric of Salzburg, assured as an indemnity to the Grand Duke of Tuscany, and in Italy the territories of this prince were granted to the Duke of Parma. The articles made no mention of Piedmont or Parma, or of the Pontifical States. The First Consul did not wish to commit himself on this point or encounter the sluggish proceedings of a congress. The Emperor of Austria had treated for the Empire as for himself. The Diet assembled at Ratisbon simply ratified the conditions of the treaty. Henceforth England found itself isolated in Europe, as France had been in 1793. The duel continued between Bonaparte and Pitt.

So much *éclat* abroad, so much glory and success terminating in an almost general peace, did not absorb all the thoughts of the First Consul, and had not yet succeeded in founding his power on a lasting basis. He felt it bitterly, and the irritation which he experienced habitually manifested itself against the remnants of the Jacobin party, the declared enemies of the order of things which he wished to establish, capable, he thought, of any crimes, and whose works he had had the opportunity of judging. This exclusive preoccupation sometimes turned

VII.—3

away his attention from more pressing perils and bolder
enemies. A conspiracy to which the police had lent themselves, and which had failed without any of the accomplices
daring to put their hands on their arms, roused public attention, in the month of October, 1800, to the dangers which
pursued the First Consul. Since then there had been seized,
at the house of a mechanician named Chevalier, an explosive
machine which had given rise to certain suspicions; but no
attempt had been made, and the conspirators, who plotted in
the dark, were as yet only known to Fouché, the minister of
police, clever and foreseeing, constantly hostile to the old
enemies of the Republic, and more disquieted than the First
Consul at the royalist manœuvres. It was to the Chouans
and men of that class that the police attributed the brigandage
which infested the roads in the departments of the west, the
centre, and the south; it was the descents of their former
chiefs upon the Norman coasts which preoccupied Fouché. At
one period the royalists had thought General Bonaparte
capable of playing the *rôle* of Monk, and accepting that modest
ambition.   On the 20th of February, 1800, Louis XVIII. wrote
to him with his own hand, " Whatever may be their apparent
conduct, men like yourself, monsieur, never inspire uneasiness. You have accepted an eminent place, and I am thankful for it.   Better than any one you know how much force and
power are needed to make the happiness of a great nation.
Save France from its own madness, and you will have accomplished the first desire of my heart; restore to it its king, and
future generations will bless your memory. You will always
be too much a necessity of the State for me ever to discharge by
the highest appointments the debt of my forefathers and my
own."

This letter remained unanswered. Louis XVIII. thought he
ought to write again. " For a long time, general," said he
yon ought to know that you have won my esteem. If you
have any doubt as to my being susceptible of gratitude, appoint your place, and decide as to the position of your friends.
As to my principles, I am French; merciful by character, I
should be still more so by reason.

" No, the conqueror of Lodi, of Castiglione, of Arcola, the
conqueror of Italy and Egypt, cannot prefer a vain notoriety
to glory. But you are losing precious time. We can assure
the peace of France; I say *we*, because I need Bonaparte for
that, and he cannot do it without me.

"General, Europe observes you, glory waits for you, and I am impatient to restore peace to my people."

Sad illusions of exiles, who in a remote country know not how to judge either men or circumstances! Louis XVIII. and his friends were blind as to the state of men's minds in France, which they believed ripe for a monarchical restoration; they comprehended neither the character nor the still veiled designs of the man who had conquered, by the audacity of his genius, military glory and the civil authority. In the depth of his soul, and in spite of his firm design to mount the throne by means of absolute power, Bonaparte was, and remained, revolutionary—hostile to the remains of the past by conviction as well as by personal ambition. He wrote to Louis XVIII. on the 7th September, 1800. "I have received, monsieur, your letter; I thank you for the fair words you have spoken. You ought not to desire your return to France; it would be necessary for you to march over 500,000 corpses. Sacrifice your interests for the repose and happiness of France; history will take account of you for it.

"I am not insensible to the misfortune of your family. I shall contribute with pleasure to the comfort and tranquillity of your retreat."

Five hundred thousand corpses of French soldiers were yet to strew the soil of Europe to serve the ambition of Bonaparte, without hindering that return of the House of Bourbon which he declared to be so disastrous. In 1800 the First Consul deigned to promise his benevolence to the descendants of Henry IV., and felt no fear as to royalist intrigues in France. Since the troubles had ceased in the west, only Georges Cadoudal had continued sometimes to attract his attention. A letter in the month of July had ordered Bernadotte to pursue him: "Have this miserable Georges arrested, and shot within twenty-four hours," he wrote. Georges had returned to England.

He was back again in France on the 24th December, 1800, when the coach of the First Consul was stopped in the Rue St. Nicaise by a small cart which barred the way; the coachman urged forward the horses, and passed it. At the same instant an explosion was heard; the dead and the wounded fell round the carriage of Bonaparte, shaken by the violence of the shock, all the windows being broken. Bonaparte stopped his carriage, and comprehended at once the cause of the accident. "Drive to the opera!" said he. Madame Bonaparte was waiting for him there. When the public was reassured by his presence, he returned to the Tuileries. A barrel of powder, loaded with grape-shot, had been placed upon the road; the victims were numerous, and the assassins escaped.

The general fright was of use to the anger and emotion of the First Consul. The enemies of Fouché denounced a police everywhere favorable to the old Jacobins. The suspicions of Bonaparte were all directed against these known and furious enemies of his person and his policy. He was enraged in his irritation, and disdained, according to his custom, the legal forms and the justice of the tribunals. "We must make the number of the convicted equal to the number of their victims," he said, "and transport all their adherents. I will not have all quarters of Paris successively undermined. There are always Septembrisers, miscreants covered with crimes, in square battalion against every successive government. It is necessary to make an end of them." Fouché, silent but imperturbable, for a long time on the traces of the conspiracy, persisted in seeing in the infernal machine the work of the agents of Chouannerie. The Council of State proposed to institute a military commission and authorize the First Consul to remove the men who appeared dangerous. Bonaparte was irritated by this slowness of justice. "The action of a special tribunal will be slow," said he; "it will not get hold of the truly guilty. It is not a question of judicial metaphysics. There are in France 10,000 miscreants who have persecuted all honest men, and who are steeped in blood. They are not all culpable in the same degree, far from it. Strike the chiefs boldly and the soldiers will disperse. There is no middle course here; it is necessary to pardon all, like Augustus, or else there must be a prompt and terrible vengeance proportionate to the crime. It is necessary to shoot fifteen or twenty of these miscreants, and transport 200 of them. I am so convinced of the necessity of purging France from these sanguinary dregs that I am ready to constitute myself sole tribunal—to bring forward the guilty, examine them, judge them, and have their condemnation carried into effect. It is not myself that I seek to avenge here. I am as ready to die as First Consul for the preservation of the Republic and the Constitution as to fall upon the field of battle; but it is necessary to reassure France, who will approve my policy."

The members of the council listened, struck with consternation at such absolutist and revolutionary violence, but already too much dismayed to defend the cause of the most elementary

justice. Admiral Truguet alone suggested doubts as to the
true authors of the crime. "It is desired," said he, "to defeat the miscreants who trouble the Republic, so be it; but the
miscreants are of more than one kind. The returned emigrants menace those who have acquired national property,
the Chouans infest the highways, the priests inflame the passions of the people, the public spirit is corrupted by pamphlets."
The First Consul blushed violently at this allusion; the re-
minder of the unfortunate attempt of Lucien Bonaparte increased his anger. Advancing towards the admiral, "Of what
pamphlets do you speak?" cried he. "You know as well as I
do," without giving way, answered the brave sailor.

The First Consul paced the hall; the councillors of State
watched him, vaguely recognizing in the outbursts of the anger of the master the powerful instinct of government, which
discerned the permanent hostility of the revolutionaries without being able to divest itself of their principles or of their
modes of action. "Do people take us for children?" he cried.
"Do they expect to draw us aside with these declamations
against the emigrants, the Chouans, and the priests? Because
there are still a few partial attempts in Vendée, must we be
called upon to declare the country in danger? If the Chouans
commit crimes, I will have them shot. But must I commence
proscribing for a quality? Must I strike these because they
are priests, those because they are old nobles? Must I send
away into exile 10,000 old men, who only ask to be allowed to
live peaceably in obedience to the established laws? Do you
not know, gentlemen, members of the council, that excepting
two or three you all pass for royalists? You, Citizen Defer-
mon, don't they take you for a partisan of the Bourbons?
Must I send Citizen Portalis to Sinnamari, and Citizen De-
vaisne to Madagascar, and then must I make for myself a Ba-
beuf council? No, no, Citizen Truguet, you won't get me to
make any change; there are none to fear except the Septembrisers. They would not spare even you yourself, and it would
be in vain for you to tell them that you defended them at the
Council of State. They would cut your throat, just the same
as mine or the throats of your colleagues."

He went out without giving time for any one to answer him.
Cambacérès, moderate and prudent, equally clever in giving
counsel and at yielding when counsels were useless, deemed
the anger of the First Consul too passionate to admit of contradiction. The Council of State, several times consulted, was

brought over with repugnance to the idea of an extraordinary measure. The First Consul wished a law; it was decided to involve the great bodies of the State in the arbitrary act which he was about to commit. "The consuls do not know what may happen," said he. "So long as I am alive I am not afraid of any one daring to ask me an account of my actions; but I may be killed, and then I cannot answer for my two colleagues. You are not very firmly placed in your stirrups," he added, turning to Cambacérès, with a smile. "Better to have a law now as well as for the future." The Council of State hesitated from a repugnance to form a proscription list, assuring him that it would be rejected by the Tribunate and the Legislative Body. "You are always afraid of the Tribunate," said Bonaparte, "because it rejected one or two of your laws; but there are only a few Jacobins in the Legislative Body, ten or twelve at most. The others know well that but for me they would all have been massacred. The law will be passed."

At last, Talleyrand, who had previously remained silent, said that since there was a Senate, some use should be made of it. The proscription list was sent to the Senate. It had been written by Fouché, who knew the real criminals; and the statement of reasons were drawn up by the two sections of the Council of State who were at first unanimously opposed to the measure: the Senate voted, the First Consul having signed the act. "All these men have not taken the dagger in their hands," said the preamble, "but they are all universally known to be capable of sharpening it and taking it." Two days afterwards 133 Jacobins sailed from Nantes for Guiana—formerly members of the Convention and the Commune, proved or supposed to have had a part in the massacres of September, all certainly loaded with crime, and worthy of the punishment which they underwent, strangers to the attempt to assassinate the First Consul, and condemned without regard to moral or legal justice. At the same time, and as if to clear off all old accounts with the conspirators, the four men accused in October, Aréna, formerly a representative, and recently employed by the Committee of Public Safety, and the artists Ceracchi and Topino-Lebrun, were at last tried, and condemned to perish on the scaffold. Chauveau-Lagarde defended them, as he had formerly defended Charlotte Corday and the men of Nantes denounced by Carrier. His efforts were not crowned with success; whether acknowledged or only suspected, the Jacobin conspiracy was everywhere repressed with the same rigor.

Nevertheless, Fouché had at last recovered the temporarily lost traces of the real criminals. Two assistants of Georges Cadoudal, Limoëlan and St. Réjant, who had formerly taken part in the civil wars, entered into partnership with a man of the lower orders named Carbon, who bought them the cart, the horse, and powder. He was found concealed in Paris; Limoëlan had fled abroad. St. Réjant, who had let off the infernal machine, had not yet recovered from the injuries caused by it; and Carbon having betrayed his place of concealment, and all the details of the plot, they were both executed. Fouché's penetration on this occasion gained him still greater confidence with the First Consul. "He was right," repeated Bonaparte; "his opinion was better than that of the others. The returned emigrants, the royalist plotters, and people of that sort, ought to be closely watched. I am pleased, however, to be rid of the Jacobin staff."

Neither the banishment of the old revolutionists, nor the condemnation of those who had contrived the infernal machine, had disturbed the repose of public opinion, then in close alliance with the steady and firm power which ruled France. The abstract principles of justice were no longer thought of by men in general: the desire for permanent freedom had given place to the longing for rest and quiet, and all were pleased with the energy which the government had shown against disturbers of the peace; and the oppressive laws being modified, prosperity was reappearing. The state of the finances became more satisfactory: a part of the public funds had been paid, and that which still remained had just been registered in the "Great Ledger;" the fundholders accepted without too much difficulty the delay in paying the first dividend. The national property not yet sold was set apart for the liquidation, excepting what was assigned for public instruction and the support of the Invalides. Everywhere roads were being made or repaired, canals dug, and three bridges were built over the Seine. In spite of the formation of extraordinary tribunals, the great Code of Civil Law was being slowly made—destined to rule France and extend her useful action. An agent, almost unknown at Rome and only recently arrived in Paris, was already discussing with Abbé Berniér those great questions of order and organization which were afterwards to introduce the concordat. Peace, even when partial and precarious, was everywhere bearing its fruits; at home, France displayed that wonderful recuperative power so frequently and painfully put to the proof by the severe shocks of our modern history; abroad, her importance in Europe was daily increasing, and caused more disquiet to all her enemies. The government of England, however, was soon to pass from Pitt's hands: the whole English nation called loudly to stop a war of which they had financially borne the burden, even though their armies had generally had little share in it.

In the south of Europe the First Consul, while negotiating with the Pope, and occupying Piedmont without diplomacy, had no longer any enemy to subdue worthy of his power. Murat had invaded the kingdom of Naples, causing so great terror that the queen herself was on the point of accepting an armistice by which the ports of the Two Sicilies were closed to the English. The treaty of definitive peace was signed at Florence on the 18th of March, 1801, the conditions being the same as those of the armistice, with the important addition that the territory of Elba, a dependency of the kingdom of Naples, was to be ceded. By a secret article, the sovereign of the Two Sicilies was obliged to receive and maintain a body of fifteen thousand men, which the First Consul intended to transport to Egypt, important armaments being prepared in our ports in order to be sent to the same place, their real destination being yet concealed. A Franco-Spanish expedition, nominally commanded by Prince de la Paix but really directed by General Gouvion St. Cyr, was to attempt in April the conquest of Portugal. In spite of repeated promises, the government of that small State remained obstinately faithful to England.

England was suffering from a scarcity of food which threatened to become a famine, constantly made worse by the hindrances put in the way of her commerce. The difficulties of the home government increased those of the diplomatic and military isolation which she underwent in Europe. At the moment of the conclusion of the Treaty of Union, Pitt had entered upon engagements with the Irish Catholics which he felt himself bound to fulfil. The conscientious but short-sighted and narrow-minded George III. opposed every act of toleration with respect to his Catholic subjects: he refused to give his assent, and Pitt by resigning his post sacrificed, at a perilous crisis for his country, foreign policy to the duties and obligations of parliamentary tactics. The reason of King George, already tottering, was unable to undergo so much agitation; he remained faithful to his convictions, but was for a short time out of his mind. When he regained his faculties,

Pitt, who was moved to the heart by the trouble which he had caused to his aged king, and disturbed by the evils which threatened England under the regency of the Prince of Wales, undertook never to raise the question of the emancipation of the Catholics during the life of George III. He had no seat, however, in the new cabinet, which was obviously incapable, and unequal to the difficult task which it had undertaken, and in their earlier proceedings still influenced by Pitt's action, and following the line of policy which he had traced. Scarcely had Addington become prime minister, when an attempt which had long been projected against Denmark was put in execution. Nelson had charge of it under the superior command of Sir Hyde Parker, who was above him in the order of seniority. "This is no time to feel nervous," said Nelson to his superior as they were setting sail. "Dark nights and mountains of ice matter little; we must take courage to meet the enemy."

Having passed the Sound, the English squadron blockaded the fleet which covered Copenhagen. The Danes made an heroic defence, and the old Admiral Parker, somewhat alarmed, gave the signal for the action to cease. "I'll be d——d first!" cried Nelson in a passion: "I have the right of seeing badly"—putting his telescope to the eye which he had lost at Aboukir. "I don't see the signal. Nail mine to the mast. Let them press closer on the enemy. That's my reply to such signalling." It was Nelson, moreover, who, when the battle was gained, arranged with the Prince Royal of Denmark the terms of the armistice which separated his country from the number of the neutral states.

Almost at the same moment the coalition of maritime powers underwent a more fatal check. For several months the strange workings of the mind of the Emperor Paul I. had become more obvious. Everybody trembled before him, and even the empress, as well as her sons, had been threatened with banishment to Siberia. A caricature was published representing the Czar holding in one hand a paper on which was written the word "order;" in the other, the word "counter-order;" on his forehead was read the word "disorder." A conspiracy was formed, including the principal nobles and the most intimate members of his household. "They are conspiring against me, Pahlen," said the emperor to the Governor of St. Petersburg. "Let your Majesty's mind be easy," replied the Russian, coolly; "I am up to them." He really was so, and on the night of the 23rd March, 1801, he entered the Michael palace with the conspirators. The next in importance to him, General Benningsen, had afterwards the honor of fighting bravely against the Emperor Napoleon when subduing Poland; he was already distinguished, and had been decorated with all the orders of the empire. On making his way to the bedroom of the Czar, who was asleep, the two Hungarians who formed the only guard ran away after striking one or two blows; the palace-guard were already on an understanding with the conspirators. The unfortunate Czar, pursued by the assassins, took refuge behind a screen. Benningsen observing him held out a paper: "There is your act of abdication," said he; "sign it and I answer for your life." The emperor resisted; the conspirators crowded into the room; the lamp fell and was extinguished, and in that moment of darkness a scarf was tightened round the neck of Paul I., and he was struck on the head with the pummel of a sword. When a light was brought in he was dead.

Count Pahlen had not entered the room, being engaged in guarding the doors with a troop of soldiers: he went to call on the new emperor. Alexander was not ignorant of the plot formed to force from his father an abdication which had become necessary; but he had not considered, and did not anticipate, the fatal consequences of that enterprise. Pahlen's silence was the only reply to his questions about the Czar: the young man burst into tears, hiding his face in his hands and heaping reproaches upon the Governor of St. Petersburg, who still remained motionless before him. But by this time the empress, out of her mind from sorrow, and suddenly seized with an ill-regulated ambition, sent to announce to her son that she was resolved to take possession of the power. Count Pahlen at once threw off his apathy. "Enough of childish tears," said he to the young emperor; "now, come and reign!" He then presented him to the troops, by whom he was well received.

A few days afterwards the Emperor Alexander was crowned. "Before him marched his grandfather's murderers," wrote Madame de Bonneuil, "beside him those of his father, and behind him his own." Count Pahlen's ambition was to govern the young monarch, but he was not to reap the fruits of his crime. The empress-mother insisted upon the banishment of the murderers of Paul I. In the retirement of his country estate, where he lived a long time, the count on the 23rd of March made himself drunk from daybreak, in order to pass in oblivion the dreaded anniversary which awoke in his mind a remorse which was only slumbering. "That's the regular mode of deposition in Russia," said Talleyrand, cynically, on hearing of the emperor's assassination. The First Consul's anger overcame his judgment. "The wretches!" he exclaimed; "they failed here on the 3rd Nivôse, but they have not failed in St. Petersburg." And bent on showing his spite towards his enemies, he had the following note inserted in the *Moniteur:* "Paul I. died on the night of the 23rd March, and the English squadron passed the Sound on the 31st. History will inform us the relation that possibly exists between these two events."

History has done justice to those false insinuations, unworthy even of him who pronounced them. Admiral Nelson felt no joy at the death of the Emperor Paul, which finally broke the league of the neutrals, and deprived him of the easy triumph which he made sure of gaining over the Russian fleet. It was of service, however, to England, and contributed to assist the wish for peace which was beginning to be awakened in the mind of the First Consul. Scarcely was the Emperor of Russia dead, when Piedmont, long protected by his favor, was reduced to the condition of a French department: but it was in vain that Bonaparte pretended to reckon on the alliance of the young Czar, in vain that Duroc was despatched to St. Petersburg with a mission of confidence; he was not deceived as to the Emperor Alexander's leaning to ally himself with England. In fact, M. Otto, who had been sent to London to arrange the exchange of prisoners, had already several weeks previously been authorized to meet favorably the advances made by Lord Hawkesbury, then the foreign minister. On both sides they tried to gain time. The great question which then separated France and England, the possession of Egypt, remained undecided, and both sides determined that it should be settled. On the 7th of March, 1801, the English squadron of the Mediterranean, which was long stationed at Mahon, and had recently been directed towards Malta, suddenly disembarked a body of 18,000 soldiers under the orders of Sir Ralph Abercromby. Thus, with a Turkish contingent and the regiments of sepoys brought from India, there were 60,000 men united against the army of occupation, which was reduced to 15,000 or 18,000 soldiers, commanded by dissatisfied officers, and generals who could not act together. Unfortunate in his relations to his colleagues, and showing little tact in his application of

European methods of organization to the native population, General Menou was unable to take the necessary precautions against the English invasion of Egypt; and in spite of his bravery, General Friant, who was in charge of 15,000 men defending Alexandria, could make only a feeble resistance to the landing of the English. Assisted by General Lanusse, he again joined battle, 13th March, on the road to Ramanièh; while General Menou—"Abdallah Menou," as his soldiers called him after he became a Mussulman—was on march with all his troops to assist Alexandria. After committing the fault of allowing the English army to land, it was necessary to make haste to fight it before it should have received the expected re-inforcements. The battle of Canopa was fought on the 21st March under disadvantageous circumstances; and General Lanusse being killed in the action, General Reynier's disposi-tion prevented his supplying his chief's incapacity. The battle, though remaining indecisive, left the English masters of the coast, and constantly revictualled by the fleet.

For more than two months, the French army hoped and waited for the assistance which had been promised them. Ad-miral Ganteaume, provided with the best vessels of our navy, a body of picked soldiers, and supplies and resources of every kind, had in fact set sail on the 23rd January, leaving Brest in the midst of a frightful tempest in the hopes of escaping the English cruisers. After being beaten about and somewhat damaged by the sea, the French vessels made for the Straits of Gibraltar, without any accident except a short engagement be-tween the frigate "Bravoure" and an English one. The ad-miral hesitated; in spite of his personal courage, he felt loaded with too great a responsibility. Bringing back his squadron almost within view of Toulon, he thought he saw Mahon's English fleet making straight for him, and as the struggle threatened to be unequal he returned into the harbor of Toulon. Leaving it on the 19th of March, after his vessels were repaired and urgent orders were received from the First Consul, he again delayed, on account of an accident which had happened to one of his ships, and it was only on the 22nd that he finally put to sea. On the 26th he was delayed by the collision of two vessels at Cape Carbonara in Sardinia, and becoming dis-couraged and uneasy, the admiral again entered Toulon on the 5th of April, at the moment when the English fleet were pass-ing Rosetta. The town was badly defended and fell into the hands of the enemies, who thus became masters of the mouth of the Nile; and sending some gun-boats up as far as Fouèh, they soon took it. Generals Lagrange and Morand held Ramanièh; and Menou delaying to lend the assistance which he promised, Lagrange fell back upon Cairo, and communication with Alexandria was interrupted. General Billiard, who commanded in the capital of Egypt, made a sally to repulse the vizier's troops; but in spite of several skirmishes he could not reach the main body of the army, and returning to the town, he offered to capitulate. The English were anxious to finish, being afraid of one of those strokes of good fortune to which the French arms had so often owed their success. The most honorable conditions were granted to the army, the troops evacuating Egypt being carried back to France at the expense of England, and in their vessels (27th June, 1801). Almost at the same moment (24th June), Admiral Ganteaume, with his squadron reduced by sickness, at last anchored before Derne, several marches from Alexandria; but as the people on the coast opposed his landing, and the undertaking was hazardous and the land route difficult, he again put to sea, thinking himself fortunate in finding in the Straits at Candia an English ship, which he captured and brought triumphantly to Toulon. General Menou, now alone, and shut up in Alexandria, obstinately and heroically resisted in vain. When at last he surrendered, he had been long forgotten in his isolation. Thus though Bonaparte's thoughts often went back to that famous and chimerical conquest of his youth, Egypt was definitively lost to France.

The negotiations with England had undergone the fluctuations inseparable from the vicissitudes of a distant war, the events of which remained still doubtful in Europe several weeks after their occurrence. The successes gained by Admiral Linois against the English before Algesiras and Cadiz, and the danger of Portugal threatened by the Spanish army, had their influence no doubt upon the English cabinet, but it was still haughty and exacting. The First Consul himself drew up a minute for the minister of foreign affairs, giving an abstract of the concessions which he was disposed to accept. "The French Government wishes to overlook nothing which may lead to a general peace, that being for the interests both of humanity and of the allies. It is for the King of England to consider if it is also for the interests of his policy, his commerce, and his nation: and if so, a distant island more or less can be no sufficient reason for prolonging the unhappiness of the world.

"The question consists of three points: the Mediterranean—the Indies—America.

"Egypt will be restored to the Porte.

"The Republic of the Seven Islands will be recognized.

"All the ports of the Adriatic and Mediterranean occupied by French troops will be restored to the King of Naples and to the Pope.

"Mahon will be restored to Spain.

"Malta will be restored to the Order; and if the King of England should consider it conformable to his interests as a preponderating naval power to destroy the fortifications, that clause will be admitted.

"In India, England will keep Ceylon, and so become unassailable mistress of those immense and wealthy countries.

"The other establishments will be restored to the allies, including the Cape of Good Hope.

"In America, all will be restored to the former possessors. The King of England is already so powerful in that part of the world that to wish for more is, being absolute master of India, to wish to be so of America also.

"Portugal will be preserved in all its integrity.

"Such are the conditions which the French Government is ready to sign.

"The advantages which the British Government thus derive are immense: to claim greater ones is not to wish a peace which is just and reciprocally honorable.

"Martinico not having been conquered by the English arms, but placed by the inhabitants in the hands of the English till France should have a government, cannot be considered an English possession.   France will never give it up.

"All that now remains is for the British Government to make known the course they wish to adopt; and if these conditions do not satisfy them, it will be at least proved before the eyes of the world that the First Consul has left nothing undone, and has shown himself disposed to make any sacrifice, in order that peace may be restored and humanity spared the tears and bloodshed which must inevitably result from a new campaign."

The concessions were in fact great, the First Consul abandoning points which had long been disputed,—Egypt, Malta, and Ceylon; and he showed extreme annoyance when Lord Hawkesbury refused to admit the principle of complete restitution in America.   Several threatening articles were inserted in the *Moniteur*, and Bonaparte urgently hurried the preparation of a fleet of gun-boats at Boulogne, which were supposed to be intended for the invasion of England. It had long been an idea of the First Consul's thus to intimidate the English Government, but it was only the people on the coast who were really alarmed. Nelson wrote immediately to the Admiralty, that "even on leaving the French harbors the landing is impossible were it only for the difficulties caused by the tides: and as to the notion of rowing over, it is impracticable humanly speaking." An attempt to land a large army on the English coast was soon to become a fixed idea in Bonaparte's mind; but then he used his armaments to disquiet the British Government. Twice Nelson attempted to destroy our fleet, and twice he failed completely: in the second attack, which was begun at night, and vigorously carried on to boarding, Admiral Latouche-Tréville compelled the English ships to withdraw, after inflicting severe losses upon them. Nevertheless, England still insisted on obtaining possession of the island of Trinidad, which belonged to Spain. The First Consul refused for a long time, but the Prince de la Paix had betrayed the hopes of his imperious ally. Bonaparte had guaranteed the throne of "Etruria" to the young Duke of Parma, and recently received in Paris the new sovereign, and his wife, the daughter of the King of Spain, and showed the nation that the prince was a simple lad, to be easily bent to his purposes. In return for so many favors, the Spanish troops had with difficulty conquered a few provinces, and King Charles IV., already reconciled to his son-in-law, the King of Portugal, concluded the treaty of Badajoz, which closed the harbors to the English, and granted an indemnity of twenty millions to France. The First Consul was extremely indignant, having counted on the threat of a war in Portugal to exercise a preponderating influence in the negotiations in London. At first he insisted that the treaty must be broken. "At the very time," said he, "when the First Consul places a prince of the house of Spain on a throne which is the fruit of the victories of the French nation, the French Republic is treated as the Republic of San Marino might with impunity be treated. Let the Prince de la Paix know that if he has been bought by England, and has drawn the king and queen into measures contrary to the honor and interest of the Republic, the last hour of the Spanish monarchy has struck."

The Prince de la Paix made ample excuses, but refused to

break the treaty of Badajoz. The real intention of the First Consul was to have peace: he had three vessels granted him by Portugal, and abandoned the island of Trinidad to the demands of the English Government. At one time England also claimed Tobago, but the very terms of the treaty were displeasing to Bonaparte's pride, and he assumed the insulting tone which he had been accustomed to use with foreign diplomatists. "The following is what I am directed to tell you," wrote Talleyrand: "excepting Trinidad, the First Consul will not yield, not only Tobago, but even a single rock, if there is one, with only a village of a hundred people; and the ground of the First Consul's conduct is, that in the treaty he has yielded to England to the last limit of honor, and that further there would be for the French nation dishonor. He will grant nothing more, even if the English fleets were anchored before Chaillot."

Lord Hawkesbury withdrew his demands as to Tobago, and the First Consul modified his threats, both nations being eagerly desirous of peace. The preliminaries were at last signed in London, on the 1st October, 1801; and when, two days afterwards, the ratifications were brought from Paris by Colonel Lauriston, the welcome news caused an irresistible outburst of joy amongst the populace. The horses of the French envoy's carriage were unharnessed, that he might be drawn in triumph to Lord Hawkesbury's house; and everywhere in the streets there were shouts of "Long live Bonaparte!" At the banquets the First Consul's health was drunk, and cheered as loudly as the speeches in favor of the friendship of the two nations. The same excessive delight was shown in Paris, which was soon crowded with the foreigners whom war had long kept away; and Fox was received by the First Consul with such flattering attentions as made a deep impression on his mind. Party feeling had so influenced the mind of the illustrious orator as to partially efface his patriotic sentiments. A few days after the preliminaries were signed, he wrote to his friend Lord Grey, "I confess to you that I go farther than you in my hatred of the English Government: the triumph gained by France excites in me a joy I can scarcely conceal."

The public joy and hopes, both in France and England, were founded on motives superior to those which inspired Fox's satisfaction, but they were not more permanent, or better founded. On the day after signing the preliminaries of London, and as if to increase the renown of his successes, the First Consul took pleasure in concluding successively treaties with Portugal, the

Sublime Porte, the Deys of Algiers and Tunis, Bavaria, and finally Russia. One clause of the last treaty stipulated that both sovereigns should prevent criminal conduct on the part of emigrants from either country. The House of Bourbon and the Poles were thus equally deprived of important protection. The situation of the King of Sardinia was to be regulated in every way according to actual circumstances. Each of the conventions, and especially the treaty of peace with England contained reticences and obscurities, which were fertile in pretexts for war and in unfriendly interpretations. The First Consul wished to secure an interval of rest and leisure, to consolidate his conquests at home and abroad. He had not renounced the glorious and ill-defined project of the imperial government which he affected to exercise over Europe. "If England made a new coalition," he wrote to M. Otto, "the only result would be a renewal of the history of the greatness of Rome."

It was to the honor of the First Consul, in the midst of this brilliant political and military renown, and in spite of his impulsive and ungovernable disposition, that he understood that the restoration of peace, the joy of victory, and the hope of a regular government, were unable to satisfy all the wants or regulate all the movements of the human soul. Personally without experience of religious prejudices or feelings, free from any connection with philosophical coteries, Bonaparte did not limit himself to a sense of the support which religion could lend in France to the new order which he wished to establish: he understood the higher wants of minds and consciences, and the supreme law which assigns to Heaven the regulation of human life. The doctrines of Christianity, as well as the divisions of the Christian Church, were indifferent to him; he did not understand their importance, and would have thought little of them; but he knew that, in spite of the efforts of the eighteenth century philosophy—in spite of the ravages caused by the French Revolution, the attachment and respect of many for the Catholic religion had still great power. He knew also that Catholicism could not be re-established in France, under his auspices, without the assistance and good will of the Court of Rome. No impression was made on his mind by the attempts made to persuade him to found in France an independent church freed from all connection with the Papacy, or by the arguments used in favor of Protestantism. His traditional respect, as well as the religious sentiment of the mass of the

VII.—4

French nation, were in favor of Catholicism. His good sense, as well as his profound instinct of the means of action in government, had long urged him towards religious toleration. During his last campaign in Italy, a circular to the curés of Milan had revived the hopes of the Roman Court; and after Pope Pius VII. returned to his capital, on its evacuation by the Neapolitan troops, M. Spina, at first envoy at Turin, had followed the First Consul to Paris. He treated with Abbé Bernier who had skilfully negotiated to bring about the pacification of Vendée—a man of great ambition, determined to serve the government which could raise him to the episcopal purple. The *pourparlers* were prolonged; the situation was difficult; the new powers founded in France by the Revolution and by victory raised pretensions which were contrary to the Roman tradition. They were, moreover, embarrassed by the unequal position of the ecclesiastics who were performing in France their sacred functions, some having submitted to the republican demands rather than leave their country and their flocks, others believing it was their duty to sacrifice everything to their former oaths. Proscribed and outlawed, they had for a long time preached, said mass, and given the sacraments in spite of an unrelenting persecution. A large number had decided to take to flight, but having now returned, the faithful were divided between them and the priests who had remained in France. Almost alone in Paris, and among those men whose opinion he was accustomed to consult, the First Consul persevered in his idea of again joining the French Church to the general Catholic body. His patience, however, was exhausted by the delay of the Holy College, and he resolved to have recourse to means which were more efficacious, and more in accordance with his character. On the 13th May, 1801, he wrote to M. Cacault, French minister at Rome, that he had determined to accept no longer the irresolution and dilatory procedure of the Court of Rome; if in five days the scheme sent from Paris, and long discussed by the Sacred College, was not accepted, Cacault must leave Rome to join, in Florence, General Murat, the commander-in-chief of the army of Italy.

The emotion at the Vatican was great. Shortly before, when giving Cacault his final instructions, the First Consul said, "Forget not to treat the Pope as if he had 200,000 men at his orders." The French minister had faithfully observed this injunction, which agreed with his personal opinions: he knew the obstacles which still separated the new master of France

from the Roman Court. The scheme of ecclesiastical organization proposed by Bonaparte was simple: sixty bishops
named by the civil power and confirmed by the Pope, the
clergy salaried by the State, the ecclesiastical jurisdiction
transferred to the Council of State, and the official management of religious bodies to the temporal authority. Pius VII.
agreed to accept this new condition of the Church exclusively
restored to her spiritual functions. The situation in the
Church of the priests who had taken the oath to the civil constitution of 1789, their reconciliation to the papacy, the tacit
admission of the appropriation by the State of the ecclesiastical
property, the nomination of new bishops and consequent
resignation or deprivation of those already holding the titles,
—such were the various questions which occupied Pope Pius
VII. and his skilful minister Cardinal Consalvi. Cacault tried
to persuade them that the cardinal himself must go to Paris.
" Most Holy Father," said the French minister, "it is necessary that Consalvi himself carry your reply to Paris. What
alarms me most is the character of the First Consul; that man
is never open to persuasion. Believe me, something stronger
than cold reason advises me in this matter: a mere animal instinct some would call it, but it never deceives. What inconvenience if somehow or other you appear yourself? You
are blamed. What did they say? They wish for a 'Concordat' of religion; we anticipate them and bring it, there it
is!"

Pope Pius VII. had long felt for General Bonaparte an at-
traction caused by a mixed feeling of alarm and confidence.
Alarm reigned in the mind of his minister, who made up his
mind to set out for Paris as if he were going to martyrdom.
" Since a victim is necessary," said he, " I devote myself, and
go to see the First Consul: let the will of God be done!" He
rode in Cacault's carriage from Rome to Florence, whence the
French minister wrote to Talleyrand,—

" Citizen Minister, here I am, arrived in Florence. The
cardinal secretary of state set out with me from Rome, and
we have travelled together in the same carriage. We were
looked upon everywhere with great astonishment. The cardinal was much afraid people should think I had withdrawn on
account of a rupture, and kept saying to everybody, ' This is the
French minister.' This country, crushed under the recent evils
of war, shudders at the least thought of military disturbance.
The Roman Government has still greater fear of its own dis-

satisfied subjects, especially those who have been allured to authority and pillage by the sort of revolution just gone through. . . . The cardinal set out this morning for Paris, and will arrive shortly before my despatch, as he goes extremely quickly. The wretched man feels that if he fails he will be irretrievably lost, and that all will be lost for Rome. He is eager to know his lot. I tried at Rome to bring the Pope to sign the Concordat only; and if he had granted me that point, I should not have left Rome; but that idea was unsuccessful.

"You understand that the cardinal is not sent to Paris to sign that which the Pope has refused to sign at Rome; but being the prime minister of his Holiness, and his favorite, it is with the Pope's mind that you will be in communication. I hope the result will be an agreement as to the modifications. It is a matter of phrases and words, which can be turned in so many meanings that at last the good meaning is got hold of."

The First Consul had resolved to make from the very first an impression on the mind of the pontifical envoy by the display of his power. Scarcely had the cardinal stepped out of his carriage when he received a visit from Abbé Bernier, whom he at once employed to ask an audience for him. The same day, at the Tuileries, before the crowd of courtiers who were thronging to one of the grand receptions, Cardinal Consalvi was presented to the First Consul. "My astonishment," says he in his correspondence, "was like that felt in the theatre by the sudden scene-shifting, when a cottage, prison, or wood is unexpectedly changed to the dazzling spectacle of the most magnificent court. You can easily imagine that a person arriving at Paris on the night preceding, without being told beforehand, without knowing anything of the habits, customs, and dispositions of those before whom he appeared, and who was in a measure considered responsible for the bad success of the negotiations so far as they had been carried, must, at the sight of such grandeur, as imposing as it was unexpected, have felt not only profound emotion, but even a too evident embarrassment." As the cardinal approached the three consuls, alone in the midst of a magnificent drawing-room filled with a brilliant throng, Bonaparte left him no time to speak. "I know the object of your journey to France," said he. "I wish the conferences to be immediately opened. I leave you five days' time; and I tell you beforehand that if at the expiration of the fifth day the negotiations are not finished, you must return to Rome; whilst as for me, I have decided what to do in that case."

Consalvi came to Paris ardently wishing to bring to a successful completion the difficult negotiations which had been entrusted to him. His Italian cunning was not deceived as to the motive of the display of magnificence, and the rough reception of himself which signalized his first audience. He was conscientious and resolute without narrowness of mind, and he understood the immense importance to religion and politics of the restoration of agreement between France and the Court of Rome. He appeared neither astonished nor disturbed with reference to the First Consul. When they came to the discussion of the questions which had brought him to Paris, the Pope's envoy showed himself easily influenced on most of the points. Bonaparte himself summarized the whole of the Concordat in a few words: " Fifty emigrant bishops, paid by England, manage all the French clergy, and their influence must be destroyed. The authority of the Pope is necessary for that. He deprives them of their charge, or obliges them to resign. As it is said that the Catholic religion is that of the majority of the French, the exercise of it should be organized. The First Consul nominates the fifty bishops; the Pope institutes them; they name the curés, and the State pays their salaries. They take the oath: the priests who refuse to submit are removed, and those who preach against the government are referred to their superiors. After all, enlightened men will not rise against Catholicism; they are indifferent."

A rather keen opposition, however, was raised among the courtiers and in the army against the Concordat, which assisted in hampering the progress of the negotiations. Most of the military men were still imbued with the spirit of the Revolution, and suspicious of the influence of the priests. The constitutional clergy, who had no serious objection to the Concordat, the only means of securing them a regular ecclesiastical standing, feared lest they should be sacrificed in favor of the priests who had refused to take the oath. Several of them were married, and had thus increased the difficulties of their position by new ties. So many personal interests and different motives kept the First Consul's advisers in a state of hostility to the claims of the Holy See. Even the preamble of the Concordat gave room to long discussions. On the refusal to apply the title "State religion" to the Catholic religion, Cardinal Consalvi agreed to the simple statement of the fact that the Catholic Apostolic and Roman religion was the religion of the great majority of the French people. On the other hand, the Pope admitted the great advantage that religion should derive from the re-establishment of Catholic worship in France, and from the personal profession of it made by the consuls of the republic. He at the same time agreed to ask the old titular bishops to resign. The resignation of the constitutional bishops had been already secured. The First Consul wrote to Pius VII.: "Most holy Father, Cardinal Consalvi has showed me your Holiness' letter, and I recognize the evangelical sentiments which distinguish it. The cardinal will inform your Holiness of my intention to do all that may contribute to your happiness. It will depend only on you to find again in the French Government the support which it has always granted to your predecessors, when they have classed with their principal duties the preaching of maxims which help to confirm peace, morality, and obedience to the civil power.

"It only depends on me that the tears of Europe cease to flow, that the revolutions and wars be followed by general peace and order.

"On all occasions, I beg your Holiness to reckon upon the assistance of your devoted son."

Cardinal Consalvi had made several concessions; the French negotiators had more than once extended as they chose the exact sense of his concessions; but he refused absolutely to entrust the regulation of the public worship to the civil authority. In view of the cardinal's conscientious obstinacy, the First Consul at last agreed to important modifications of this point. When the day for signing arrived, Joseph Bonaparte, who had always a share in diplomatic negotiations, being one of the appointed signatories, the cardinal went to his house with the Abbé Bernier, both bringing a copy of the act. At the moment when the papal envoy was taking the pen, he cast his eyes over the text of the convention, and saw that the article referring to the exercise of worship had been restored to the form which he had objected to. Reading further, and finding other changes and additions, the cardinal protested against it. Joseph Bonaparte declared that he knew nothing of it. "The First Consul wished it to be so," said Bernier with some confusion, "declaring that anything may be changed so long as it is not signed. Besides, the draft agreed upon did not please him: and he insists upon the articles being so modified

The time was short, the First Consul having announced his intention of announcing publicly the signature of the Concordat at a great banquet the same evening. The outbursts of his anger even reached the cardinal's ears. He had torn the Concordat, and threatened to declare the rupture of the negotiations if Consalvi did not consent to give way. "I underwent the agonies of death," said the cardinal. But he was convinced of his duty, and went to the Tuileries as unbending in his resolution as the First Consul in his imperious will. Bonaparte came to him as he entered the drawing-room, and called loudly, "Well, cardinal, you wish then to break! I have no need of Rome! Let it be so! I have no need of the Pope! If Henry VIII., who had not the twentieth part of my power, was able to change the religion of his country, I am much more able to do so! By that change of religion I shall change the religion through nearly the whole of Europe, wherever the influence of my power extends. Rome will be sensible of the losses she brings on herself. She will lament them, but there will be no remedy. You wished to break. . . . Very well! let it be so, since you wished it. When do you set out?" "After dinner, general," replied the cardinal with calmness.

Consalvi did not set out. Next day, in spite of the reiterated attempt made to influence him, in spite of the weakness of the majority of his legation, the Pope's secretary of state held firm. The First Consul gave way, cr pretended it, in order afterwards to withdraw the concessions granted, but sufficiently to satisfy the conscience of the cardinal, and persuade him to put his signature to the Concordat. The ratification at Rome quickly succeeded, and a legate was sent to Paris, chosen at the First Consul's express desire. After Cardinal Caprara's arrival, the publication of the Concordat was still delayed by the choosing of the new bishops. Thirteen of the former prelates, who had taken refuge in England, alone refused to resign at the command of the Holy See; and thirty-three bishops, still abroad or already returned to France, obeyed generously and without reluctance. The constitutional bishops had just dissolved their council, which Bonaparte had authorized in order to influence the Court of Rome; but he ordered its cessation as soon as the Concordat was signed. His resolution to place several constitutional priests among the new bishops annoyed and disturbed the Pope. The First Consul became angry, making charges of systematic delay which prevented him from publishing the Concordat, and introducing

into their dioceses the prelates nominated during Lent. The
legate quietly claimed the submission which the constitutional
priests had promised. "There is haughtiness in asking it,"
exclaimed Bonaparte; "there would be cowardice in submitting." The conduct of the constitutional prelates remained
doubtful: ten, however, were nominated. Cardinal Caprara
was both less resolute and less clear-sighted than Consalvi: at
one time frightened, at another easily persuaded. In spite of
his resistance, "his cries and tears," he at last yielded to the
pressing demands of the First Consul. On the 18th April, 1802,
Easter Sunday, the Concordat was proclaimed in the streets of
Paris. At eleven o'clock an immense crowd thronged Notre
Dame, curious to see the legate officiating, and gaze again on
the pompous ritual of the Catholic service; but still more eager
to look at the First Consul in the brilliancy of his triumph and
power, surrounded by his companions in arms, all compelled
by his will to assist at a ceremony at variance with the opinions of several of them. The concessions of the Court of Rome
and the obedience of the generals could not conceal the vast
gulf that separated Revolutionary France from the religious
tradition of the past. Bonaparte felt this. He wished for the
Concordat, understanding its lofty aim and practical utility;
he had conceded more in appearance than he intended to
grant in reality. The *Te Deum* was chanted: the bishops were
confirmed, and had now set out for their dioceses. In every
district, along with the Concordat, and as if invested with the
same sanction, the First Consul published a series of "organic
articles," regulating in detail the relations of the civil power
with the religious authority. Already, when discussing the
Concordat the representative of the Holy See had rejected
most of Bonaparte's pretensions on that subject; but he now
reproduced them, transformed, by the power of his will alone,
into administrative measures, voted like the Concordat by the
Corps Législatif, and having equal force for the Catholic
Church, the Protestant Church, and the Jewish form of worship. The anger and sorrow of the Court of Rome had no
effect in modifying the resolution of the First Consul. Cardinal Caprara was constantly passing from submission to despair.
"He who is fated to treat with the First Consul," he wrote to
Cardinal Consalvi, "must bear always in mind that he is
treating with a man who is arbiter of the affairs of the world—
a man who has paralyzed, one might say, all the other powers
of Europe, who has conceived projects the execution of which

seemed impossible, and who has conducted them with a success which astonishes the whole world. Nor should it be forgotten that I am appointed here in a nation where the Catholic religion has not a ruling power, even in peace. Here all the powerful personages are against her, and they strive as much as possible against the First Consul. He is the only man who watches over her. Unfortunately, her future depends on his intention, but at least that intention is sure of completion. When the First Consul is against us, things proceed with a frightful rapidity." The Pope felt obliged to protest against the organic articles in an allocution to the Consistory, and to address his claims to the First Consul, who took no notice of them. In his communications with the religious authority in France, he proved imperious and insolent. "If the morality of the gospel is insufficient to direct a bishop," he wrote Portalis, "he must act by policy, and by fear of the prosecution which government might institute against him as a disturber of the public peace. I could not be otherwise than full of sorrow at the conduct of certain bishops. Why have you not informed the *préfets?*"

The ecclesiastical organization in France would have been incomplete, had Bonaparte not extended his care to the Protestant churches. In a kindly report addressed to him on the subject, it was stated that "the government, in declaring that Catholicism was in a majority in France, had no wish to authorize in its favor any political or civil pre-eminence. Protestanism is a Christian communion, bringing together, in the same faith and to the same rites, a very large number of Frenchmen. In recent times the Protestants were in the foremost ranks under the standards of liberty, and have never abandoned them. All that is secured to the various Christian communions by the articles of agreement between his Holiness and the Government of the Republic is equally guaranteed to the Protestants, *with the exception of the pecuniary subvention.*"

The original idea of Bonaparte had, in fact, been to leave to the Protestants the full liberty of their internal government, as well as the charge of their worship. The principle, admitted by the Constituent Assembly, of compensating the Catholic clergy for the confiscation of their property, was not applicable to the Protestant Church. On a consideration of the administrative advantages of a church paid by the state, Bonaparte decided that the law of the 18th Germinal, year X., should be drawn up, regulating the nomination of pastors and

consistories after the manner of the interior government of
the Protestant Church. The principle which, in this respect,
equalized the Protestant and Catholic modes of worship was
hailed with satisfaction by the reformers. The Jews established
in France were admitted to enjoy the same privileges.

At the same time that an alliance between religion and the
state was being re-established in France, Chateaubriand, still a
very young man, published his " Genius of Christianity." The
sense of the poetic beauty of Christianity then reawakening in
men's minds, the success of the book was deservedly great. It
marked in recent history the epoch of literary admiration for
the greatness and beauty of the gospel. We have since sadly
learnt that it was only a shallow and barren admiration.

Peace seemed again established in the world and the church.
In spite of several difficulties and suspicions, the definitive
treaty with England was at last to be signed at Amiens. But
rest seemed already to weigh heavily on the new master of
France, and the increasing ambition of his power could not deceive men of foresight as to the causes of disturbance in Europe
which were perpetually reappearing. Scarcely were the preliminaries of peace signed in London, when the Batavian Republic—recently composed, after the example of the French Republic, of a Directory and two Legislative Chambers—found
itself again undergoing a revolution, the necessary reaction of
what was being done in France. On a new constitution being
proposed to the Chambers they rejected it. The Dutch Directory, with the assistance of General Augereau, effected at the
Hague, in September, 1800, the *coup d'état* which took place in
Paris on the 18th Brumaire; the representatives were dismissed,
and the people were assembled to pronounce upon the new
constitution. Only 50,000 voters out of 400,000 electors presented themselves in the Assemblies. A president was chosen
for three months. The absolute authority of the First Consul
was secured in the Batavian Republic.

In Switzerland, an agitation diligently kept up throughout
all the cantons, rendered a government there impossible. The
French minister at Berne, "a powerless conciliator of the divided parties," as Bonaparte called him, received secret instructions from him. " Citizen Verninac must, under all the circumstances, say publicly that the present government can only
be considered provisional, and give them to understand that,
not only does the French Government not rely upon it, but it
is even dissatisfied with its composition and procedure. It is a

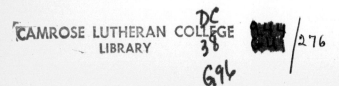

mockery of nations to believe that France will acknowledge as the intention of the Helvetic people the will of the sixteen persons who compose the Legislative Body." The French troops had evacuated Switzerland. The First Consul was scheming to annex the canton of Valais to the two departments of Mont Terrible and Léman, which he had already taken from the Helvetian territory. After several months passed, the seeds of discord began to bear fruit; and Aloys of Reding, formerly Landamman, being overthrown, Dolder, the leader of the radicals, was raised in his place. As a concession to the patriotic wishes of the Swiss, the French troops were suddenly recalled from their territory. When freed from that constant menace, interior dissensions burst forth; the Landamman Dolder, replaced at Berne by Mulinen, took refuge in Lausanne, where he founded a new government. The cantons were already taking sides, when the First Consul launched a proclamation as the natural arbiter of the destinies of Switzerland:—

" People of Helvetia, you have been disputing for three years without understanding each other. If you are left longer to yourselves, you will kill yourselves in three years without understanding each other any better. Your history, moreover, proves that your civil wars have never been finished unless by the efficacious intervention of France. I shall therefore be mediator in your quarrels, but my mediation will be an active one, such as becomes the great nation in whose name I speak. All the powers will be dissolved. The Senate alone, assembled at Berne, will send deputies to Paris; each canton can also send some; and all the former magistrates can come to Paris, to make known the means of restoring union and tranquillity and conciliating all parties. Inhabitants of Helvetia! revive your hopes!" At the same time Bonaparte said to Mulinen, who had already escaped to Paris, " I am now thoroughly persuaded of the necessity of some definitive measure. If in a few days the conditions of my proclamation are not fulfilled, 30,000 men will enter Switzerland under General Ney's orders; and if they thus compel me to use force it is all over with Switzerland. It is time to put an end to that; and I see no middle course between a Swiss government strongly organized, and friendly to France, or no Switzerland at all."

On the 15th October, 1802, General Ney received orders to enter Switzerland, and publish " a short proclamation in simple terms, announcing that the small cantons and the Senate had asked for the mediation of the First Consul, who had granted it; but a handful of men, friends of disorder, and indifferent to the evils of their country, having deceived and led astray a portion of the people, the First Consul was obliged to take measures to disperse these senseless persons, and punish them if they persisted in their rebellion." At the same time, after an imperious summons, the chiefs of the Swiss aristocracy, Mulinen, Affry, and Watteville, joined the radical deputies in Paris. There could be no long discussion, as the plan of the Helvetic Constitution was decided upon in the mind of the First Consul. He had recognized the inconveniences arising from the "unitary government:" he next abolished the old independent institutions of the cantons, and systematically weakened the central power, as the Diet, composed of twenty-five deputies, was to sit by rotation in the six principal cantons; he at the same time nominated Affry as President of the Helvetian Confederation, after carefully securing his services. Henceforward the Swiss cantons, free in their internal government, fell as a state under the rule of France. "I shall never permit in Switzerland any other influence than my own, though it should cost me 100,000 men," Bonaparte had said to the assembled deputies. "It is acknowledged by Europe that Italy, Holland, and Switzerland are at the disposition of France." At the same time (11th September, 1802), and as if to justify this haughty declaration, the territory of Piedmont was divided into six French departments, the Isle of Elba was united to France, and the Duchy of Parma was definitively occupied by our troops.

For a long time the north of Italy was subjected to the laws of its conqueror, and he arrogantly made it bear the whole burden. When the Congress of Vienna had begun its sittings, Talleyrand absolutely forbade Joseph Bonaparte to allow the usurpations of France in Europe to be discussed. "You will consider it a fixed point that the French Government can listen to nothing regarding the King of Sardinia, the Stadtholder, or the internal affairs of Batavia, Germany, Helvetia, or the Italian republics. All these subjects are absolutely unknown to our discussions with England."

England admitted the truce of which she stood in need. She tacitly accepted the reticences of the negotiators; and without any protest on her part the First Consul set out for Lyons, where he had summoned the 500 members of the Italian Consulte. Overwhelmed with the gifts of her conqueror, the Cisalpine Republic was now to receive from his hands a definitive

THE CONGRESS OF VIENNA

After a crayon drawing by Jean Baptist Isabey.

constitution. Lombardy as far as the Adige, the Legations, the Duchy of Modena, had sent their deputies to France, prepared to vote by acclamation for the constitution, which had been carefully prepared by several leading Italians under the eyes of the First Consul. The Consulte of Milan had accepted it. Bonaparte reserved to himself the direction of the choice of functionaries, and the important nomination of the President of the Republic. Lyons was in grand holiday, crowded by the Italians and numerous bodies of troops. The old army of Italy, on arriving from Egypt, had been ordered to Lyons; and the populace hailed with delight the arrival of the First Consul, who was always popular personally. The Consulte opened its sittings with distinction; and soon the Italian deputies understood who was the president designed for them by the solicitude of General Bonaparte. They accepted without repugnance his proclamation:—" The Consulte has appointed a committee of thirty persons," wrote the First Consul to his colleagues; "they have reported that, considering the internal and external circumstances of the Cisalpine, it was indispensable to allow me to conduct the first magistracy, till such time as the situation may permit, and I may judge it suitable, to name a successor." To the request of the Consulte, in humble terms, the general replied, "I find no one among you who has sufficient claims upon public opinion—who would be sufficiently independent of local influences—who, in short, has rendered to his country sufficiently great services, for me to trust him with the first magistracy." The Count Melzi accepted the vice-presidentship of the Republic. On the 28th January, after reviewing the army of Egypt, the First Consul, president of the Italian Republic, started again for Paris.

He was now waiting for news of the expedition which he had recently sent to St. Domingo. The horrors which signalized the violent emancipation of our negroes and their possession of the territory, was succeeded by a state somewhat regular, largely due to the unexpected authority of a black, recently a slave, who displayed faculties which are very unusual in his race. In his difficult government, Toussaint Louverture had given proofs of a generalship, foresight, courage, and gentleness which gave him the right to address Bonaparte, the object of his passionate admiration, in the following terms: "The first of the blacks to the first of the whites." Toussaint Louverture loved France, and rendered homage to it by driving from the island the Spanish and Eng-

lish troops. He claimed the ratification of his Constitution,
and sent his sons to France to be properly educated.

The instructions given by the First Consul to his brother-in-
law, General Leclerc, are still secret. He had placed under
his command 20,000 men, excellent troops, borrowed from the
old army of the Rhine, the generals and officers of which
were unwilling to resign during the peace. The squadron, in
charge of Admiral Villaret-Joyeuse, was a large one. The
English had been informed of the expedition, by a note signed
by Talleyrand but drawn up by Bonaparte himself. "Let
England know," said he, "that in undertaking to destroy the
government of the negroes at St. Domingo, I have been less
guided by commercial and financial considerations than by the
necessity of smothering in all parts of the world every kind
of inquietude and disturbance—that one of the chief benefits
of peace for England at the present moment was that it was
concluded at a time when the French Government had not
yet recognized the organization of St. Domingo, and afterwards the power of the negroes. The liberty of the blacks
acknowledged at St. Domingo, and legitimized by the French
Government, would be for all time a fulcrum for the Republic
in the New World. In that case the sceptre of the New
World must sooner or later have fallen into the hands of the
negroes; the shock resulting for England is incalculable,
whereas the shock of the empire of the negroes would, with
reference to France, reckon as part of the Revolution."

At the same time, and in contradiction to the intentions
which he announced to England, Bonaparte wrote to Toussaint
Louverture: "We have conceived esteem for you, and we
are pleased to recognize and proclaim the services which you
have rendered to the French people. If their flag still floats
over St. Domingo, it is to you and the brave blacks it is due.
Called by your talents and the force of circumstances to the
first command, you have overthrown the civil war, curbed
the persecution of several fierce men, restored honor to
religion and the worship to God, to whom everything is due.
The Constitution which you have made contains many good
things: the circumstances in which you are placed, surrounded on every side by enemies, without the power of being
assisted or provisioned by the capital (mother country), have
rendered legitimate the articles of the Constitution which
otherwise are not so. We have informed your children and
their tutor of our sentiments towards you. We shall send

them back to you. Assist the general by your advice, your influence, and your talents. What can you desire? The liberty of the negroes? You know that in every country in which we have been, we have given it to the peoples who had it not. Hence consideration, honors, fortune! After the services which you have rendered, which you can render in this matter, with the personal feelings which we entertain for you, you ought not to be doubtful as to the position before you. Consider, general, that if you are the first of your color who has arrived at so great power, and is distinguished by his valor and military talents, you are also before God and before us the most responsible for their conduct. Count without reserve upon our esteem, and let your behavior be that which becomes one of the principal citizens of the greatest nation of the world."

One of the incurable evils of a long state of slavery is the distrust begot in those who have undergone it, though it is also the defence and instinctive protection of weakness. Along with his admiration for the First Consul and his traditional attachment to France, Toussaint Louverture remained uneasy and suspicious as a slave. Already, under the orders of General Richepanse, the expedition was being prepared which was to re-establish slavery in Guadeloupe, in spite of the decrees of the Constituent Assembly and the formal declaration of the First Consul in a statement of the State of the Republic (November 30th, 1801). When the French squadron was signalled at St. Domingo, and the negro dictator ascertained the crushing force brought to impose upon him the will of the mother country, he made preparations for defence, entrusted his lieutenant, Christophe, with the guard of the shore and the town of Le Cap, ordering him to oppose the landing by threatening the white population with fire and sword should they offer to assist the French troops. Toussaint, counting upon the effect of threats, had not estimated the savage horror of slavery which animated his companions, nor the ferocity which could be displayed by men of his race when let loose upon their former masters. On entering the roads the French squadron began to fire; the negroes set the town on fire, put chains on some of the principal white men, and withdrew to the mountains or hills. Toussaint having preceded them, the army of negroes was again formed round him. The coast, however, being already taken by General Leclerc, the white population joined them; and a large number of the negroes, becoming alarmed, accepted the conditions offered by the general. Then, after offering some defence, several of Touissaint's lieutenants, one after another, surrendered. The most ferocious of them, Dessalines, had just been driven from St. Marc, where he committed great atrocities. Toussaint was pursued to his retreat, and after his entrenchments were forced he accepted a capitulation, and withdrew to his plantation at Ennery. The climate of St. Domingo caused frightful ravages to the French army, and the consequent weakness of his troops greatly increased General Leclerc's alarm. He had, moreover received peremptory orders, the severity of which he frequently modified. "Follow exactly my instructions," General Bonaparte wrote to him on the 16th of March, 1802, "and as soon as ever you have got rid of Toussaint, Christophe, Dessalines, and the leading brigands, and the masses of the blacks are disarmed, send away all the blacks and men of color who shall have played any part in the civil troubles." A certain agitation continued to reign among the blacks, and Leclerc seized upon this pretext to summon Toussaint to a conference. The vanity of the former dictator was flattered, and triumphed over his mistrust. "These white gentlemen who know everything still have need of the old negro," said he, and he set out for the French camp (June 10, 1802). Immediately arrested and cast into a frigate, he was taken to the town of Le Cap; his family had been captured as well as himself, and he found them on board the vessel that carried him to France. He was alone when he was imprisoned in the Temple, and afterwards transferred to the fortress of Joux, in the icy casemates under the canopy of the mountains. The only question asked him was where he had hidden his treasures. The dictator of the blacks gave no answer; he had fallen into a deep lethargy. On the 27th April, 1803, he at last expired, the victim of cold, imprisonment, and solitude. A few months later (November, 1803) the mournful remains of our army evacuated St. Domingo, for ever lost to the power of France. General Leclerc was dead of fever, as well as the greater part of his officers, like Richepanse at Guadeloupe. The climate of his country had avenged Toussaint Louverture; the instruments of Bonaparte had perished, the enterprise had failed. The sister of General Bonaparte returned to France, ready for higher destinies; the wife and children of the dictator of St. Domingo pined away slowly in exile.

This check was insignificant in the midst of so much success for his armies, and so many easy triumphs over the subdued nations; but the jealous susceptibility of the First Consul kept increasing. He had punished Toussaint Louverture for the resistance he had encountered in St. Domingo; he was irritated against the remnants of isolated opposition which he encountered at times among a few members of the Tribunate. The treaties of peace, so brilliantly concluded after the signature of the preliminaries of London, had been ratified without difficulty by the Corps Législatif. A single article of the treaty with Russia raised strong objections; it was obscure, and assured the Czar of the repression of Polish plots in France. The republican pride was irritated at the word *subjects* which was found in the clause. "Our armies have fought for ten years because we were citizens," cried Chenier, "and we have become subjects! Thus has been accomplished the desire of the double coalition!" The treaty was, nevertheless, ratified by an immense majority. But the anger of the master had been roused; "The tribunes are *dogs* that I encounter everywhere," he often exclaimed. The Tribunate and the Corps Législatif soon incurred his displeasure afresh—the one by discussing, the other by rejecting, a few preliminary articles of the new civil code. The First Consul was present at the discussions of the Council of State, often taking part in them with singular spirit and penetration, sometimes warped by personal or political prejudices. He had adopted as his own the work of the learned lawyers who had drawn up and compiled for the honor and utility of France the wisest and the simplest doctrines of civil and commercial law. "We can still risk two battles," said Bonaparte, after the rejection of the first head of the code. "If we gain them we will continue the march we have commenced. If we lose them we will enter into our winter quarters, and will advise as to the course to be taken."

The second head of the code was voted; the third, relative to the deprivation of civil rights, was excessive in its rigor; it was rejected. At the same time, and as if to give proof of its independence, the Corps Législatif, which had just chosen as its president Dupuis, author of a philosophical work, then famous, upon the "Origin of all Religions," sent up as candidates for the Senate the Abbé Grégoire and Daunou. The former had been dismissed from his charge as constitutional bishop at the time of the Concordat, the second was honored of all men, moderate in a very firm opposition. The

VII.—5

Abbé Grégoire was elected. The First Consul had presented Generals Jourdan, Lamartillière, and Berruyer, accompanying their candidature with a message. He broke out violently during a sitting of the Senate. "I declare to you," he said, "that if you appoint Daunou senator, I shall take it as a personal injury, and you know that I never suffer that!" General Lamartillière was appointed, but the slight notion of independence in the constitutent bodies had troubled and displeased Bonaparte; he recoiled before the risks that awaited the Concordat and the great project of public instruction presented for the acceptance of the Corps Législatif. On the 8th of January, 1802, a message was brought in during the sitting. "Legislators," said the First Consul, "the government has resolved to withdraw the projects of law of the civil code. It is with pain that it finds itself obliged to defer to another period laws in which the interests of the nation are so much involved, but it is convinced that the time has not yet come when these great discussions can be carried on with that calm and unity of intention which they require."

This was not enough to assure the repose of General Bonaparte and the docile acceptance of his wishes; Consul Cambacérès, clever at veiling absolute power with an appearance of legality, proposed to confide to the Senate the task of eliminating from the Tribunate and the Corps Législatif the fifth who ought regularly to be designated by lot. The legislative labors were suspended; the First Consul had set out for Lyons, in order to guide the destinies of the Italian Republic. He wrote thence to his colleagues: "I think that I shall be in Paris at the end of the decade, and that I shall myself be able to make the Senate understand the situation in which we find ourselves. I do not think it will be possible to continue to march forward when the constituted authorities are composed of enemies; the system has none greater than Daunou; and since, in fine, all these affairs of the Corps Législatif and the Tribunate have resulted in scandal, the least thing that the Senate can do is to remove the twenty and the sixty bad members, and replace them by well-disposed persons. The will of the nation is that the government may not be hindered from doing well, and that the head of Medusa may no longer be displayed in our Tribunes and in our Assemblies. The conduct of Sieyès in this circumstance proves perfectly that, after having concurred in the destruction of all the constitutions since 1791, he still wishes to try his hand against this one. It is very extraordinary that he does not see the folly of it. He ought to go and burn a wax taper at Notre Dame for having been delivered so happily and in a manner so unhoped for. But the older I grow the more I perceive that every one has to fulfil his destiny."

When the First Consul returned to Paris, the opposition, more brilliant than effective, of a few eloquent members, had ceased in the Tribunate; the Corps Législatif had undergone the same purification. Faithful servants had been carefully chosen by the Senate—some capable of ill-temper and anger, like Lucien Bonaparte and Carnot; others distinguished by their administrative merit, like Daru—all fit to vote the great projects which the First Consul meditated. He did not, however, condescend to submit to them the general amnesty in favor of all the emigrants whose names had not yet been erased from the fatal list. Perhaps he still dreaded some remains of revolutionary passion. This act of justice and clemency was the object of a Senatus Consultum. The First Consul kept in his own hands the unsold confiscated property of emigrants—a powerful means of action, which he often exercised in order to attach to himself men and families of consideration by direct or personal restitution.

He created at the same time a new instrument of government the fruit of a powerful mind and profound acquaintance with human nature. Formerly the honorary orders successively founded by kings of France had been reserved for a small number of privileged persons; in this limited circle they had been the object of great ambition and of long intrigues. By the institution of the Legion of Honor, Bonaparte resolved to extend to the entire nation, in the camp and in civil life, that rivalry of hopes and that ardent thirst for honors which formerly animated the courtiers. He had proved the importance which the military attached to arms of honor, and he was impatient of the objections which the Council of State brought before him on this subject. " People call this kind of thing a bauble," said he. " Well ! it is with baubles that men are managed. I would not say it to a Tribune, but I do not believe that Frenchmen love liberty and equality ; they have not been changed by ten years of Revolution ; like the Gauls, they must have distinctions. It is one means more of managing men." The experience of the rulers who have succeeded him has justified the far-seeing and cynical conception of Bonaparte. It has proved once more what abuses can be brought about, and what weaknesses can be created, by an institution originally intended to appeal to noble sentiments. The passion for equality was much stronger than the First Consul thought; the institution of the Legion of Honor encountered great opposition in the purified Tribunate and Corps Législatif, and was only voted by a small majority.

A great law on public instruction prepared the way for the foundation of the University, from that time one of the favorite ideas of the First Consul. Primary instruction remained neglected, as it had been practically by the Convention. The communes were entrusted with the direction and construction of schools; no salary was assured to the instructor beyond the school fees. The central schools were suppressed; their method of mixed instruction had succeeded badly. The project of the First Consul instituted thirty-two Lycées, intended for instruction in the classical languages and in the sciences. He had little taste for the free exercise of reflection and human thought; instruction in history and philosophy found no place in his programme. "We have ceased to make of history a particular study," said M. Rœderer, "because history properly so called only needs to be read to be understood." The great revival of historic studies in France was soon to protest eloquently against a theory which separated the present from the past, and which left in consequence a most grievous blank in education. Military exercises were everywhere carefully organized. Six thousand four hundred scholarships, created by the State, were to draw the young into the new establishments, or into the schools already founded to which the State extended its grants and its patronage. Without being officially abolished, the freedom of secondary instruction was thus subjected to a destructive rivalry, and the action of the government penetrated into the bosom of all families. "What more sweet," said M. Rœderer, "than to see one's children in a manner adopted by the State, at the moment when it becomes a question of providing for their establishment?" "This is only a commencement," said the First Consul to Fourcroy, the principal author of the project, and its clever defender before the Corps Législatif; by and by we shall do better."

The Treaty of Amiens had already been signed several months (25th March, 1802), but it had not yet been presented for the ratification of the Corps Législatif; this was the supreme satisfaction reserved for it, and the brilliant consummation of its labors. It was at the same time the price paid in advance for a manifestation long prepared for, but which, however, still remained obscure even among those most trusted by the all-powerful master of France. The destinies of the nation rested in his hands, but the power had been confided to him for ten years only; it was necessary to insure the prolongation of this dictatorship, which all judged useful at the present moment, and of which few people had foreseen the danger. Bonaparte persisted in hiding his thought; he waited for the spontaneous homage of the constituent bodies in the name of the grateful nation. Cambacérès was acquainted with this desire, and he exerted himself to prepare the votes in the Senate. A certain mistrust reigned in some minds. The Tribunate, alone permitted to speak, at length took the initiative. Its President, Chabot de l'Allier, the friend of Cambacérès made this proposal:—"The Senate is invited to give the consuls a testimony of the national gratitude." This wish, transmitted to the Senate, was at the same time carried to the Tuileries; Siméon was entrusted with presenting it to the First Consul. "I desire no other glory than that of having entirely completed the task which was imposed on me," replied Bonaparte; "I am ambitious of no other recompense than the affection of my fellow-citizens; life is only dear to me for the services I can render to my country; death itself will have for me no bitterness, if I can only see the happiness of the Republic as well assured as its glory."

So many protestations of disinterestedness deceived nobody; the thirst for power betrayed itself even in the most modest words. Through ignorance, or uneasiness as to the future, the Senate made a mistake as to the measure of an ambition that knew no limit. It voted for General Bonaparte a prolongation of his powers during ten years; Lanjuinais alone protested against the dictatorship, as he had formerly protested against demagogy. The officials, badly informed, ran with eagerness to the Tuileries; they were received with evident ill temper. The first impulse of Bonaparte was to refuse the proposal of the Senate; prudent counsels opened to him another way.

It was from Malmaison, the pretty country-house dear to Madame Bonaparte, that the First Consul replied to the message of the Senate. "Senators," said he, "the honorable proof of esteem embodied in your deliberation of the 18th will be always graven upon my heart. In the three years that have just passed away, fortune has smiled upon the Republic;

but fortune is inconstant, and how many men whom she has loaded with her favors have lived more than a few years!

"The interest of my glory and that of my happiness would seem to assign as the term of my public life the moment when the peace of the world is proclaimed.

"But you judge that I ought to make a new sacrifice for the people; I will do it if the wish of the people commands what your suffrage authorizes."

In all times, and under all forms of arbitrary government, the appeal to the people has offered to power an easy resource; Cambacérès had cleverly suggested it to the First Consul. In explaining to the Council of State the reasons which rendered the vote of the Senate unacceptable, he formulated immediately the proposal which ought to be put before the nation: "Napoleon Bonaparte, shall he be consul for life?" To this first question Rœderer proposed to add a second, immediately rejected by the explicit wish of the First Consul himself: "Shall he have the right of appointing his successor?" For three weeks, in all the cities and in all the villages, the registries of votes remained open. The Tribunate and the Corps Législatif presented themselves in a body at the Tuileries, in order to vote into the hands of the First Consul. The Senate had the honor of casting up the votes. It remained mute and powerless in consequence of its awkward proposal. "Come to the help of people who have made a mistake in trying to divine your purposes too deeply," said Cambacérès to the First Consul. 3,577,259 "Yeas" had agreed to the Consulate for life. Rather more than 800 "Noes" alone represented the opposition. La Fayette refused his assent; he wrote upon the registry of votes, "I should not know how to vote for such a magistracy, inasmuch as political liberty will not be guaranteed."

The feeble and insufficient guarantees of political liberty were about to undergo fresh restrictions. In receiving from the Senate the return of the votes, the First Consul said, "The life of a citizen is for his country. The French people wish mine to be entirely consecrated to it; I obey its will. In giving me a new pledge—a permanent pledge of its confidence, it imposes upon me the duty of basing the legal system on far-seeing institutions." A Senatus Consultum, reforming the Constitution of the year VIII., substituted for the lists of notables, the formation of Cantonal Colleges, Colleges of Arrondisements, and Colleges of Departments, the members of which, few in number, and appointed for life by the cantonal assemblies, were to nominate candidates for selection by the executive authority. The Tribunate was limited to fifty members; the Council of State saw its importance diminished by the formation of a Privy Council. The number of senators was fixed at eighty, but the First Consul was left at liberty to add forty members at his pleasure. This assurance of the docility of the Assembly was not sufficient. The Senate was invested with the right of interpreting the constitution, of suspending it when necessary, or of dissolving the Tribunate and the Corps Législatif; but it might not adopt any measure without the initiative of the government. The First Consul reserved for himself the right of pardon and the duty of naming his successor. This last clause was forced on him by reasons of State policy, but he deferred it for a long time. His mind could only be satisfied with the principle of hereditary succession, and he had no children. Madame Bonaparte feared a divorce, the principle of which had been maintained by the First Consul in the Council of State with remarkable earnestness. The choice of a successor remained an open question, which encouraged many hopes. The brothers of the First Consul were loaded with honors; the family of the master took rank by themselves from the moment when the name they bore in common appeared with a freshness which was in part to eclipse its glory. In imitation of the Italian Consulate, the Senate proclaimed Napoleon Bonaparte Consul for life.

A few prudent friends of liberty in France began to feel uneasy at this unheard-of aggrandizement of power without a curb. To the fear which France in anarchy had caused in Europe already succeeded the disquietude inspired by an absolute master, little careful of rights or engagements, led by the arbitrary instincts of his own mind, susceptible by nature or by policy, and always disposed to use his advantages imperiously. Peace was already beginning to be irksome to him; he cherished hopes of new conquests; his temper became every day more exacting, and the feebleness of the English minister furnished him with occasions of quarrel. A stranger to the liberal spirit of the English constitution, a systematic enemy to the freedom of the press, Bonaparte required from Addington and Lord Hawkesbury that they should expel from England the revolutionary libellers, whose daily insults in the journals irritated him, and the emigrant Chouans, whose criminal enterprises he dreaded. To the demands of the French minister at London was added the official violence of the *Moniteur*, edited and in-spired by Barère.   "What result," said the journal of the First Consul, "what result can the English Government expect by fomenting the troubles of the Church, by harboring, and re-vomiting on our territory, the scoundrels of the Côtes-du-Nord and Morbihan, covered with the blood of the most important and richest proprietors of those unfortunate departments? Does it not know that the French Government is now more firmly established than the English Government? Does it imagine that for the French Government reciprocity will be difficult?   What might be the effect of an exchange of such in-sults—of this protection and this encouragement accorded to assassins?"

The irritation was real, and its manifestations sincere; but they cloaked more serious incentives to anger, and pretensions fatal to the repose of Europe.   For a long time the First Consul had repelled with scorn any intervention of England in the affairs of the new States he had created, and which the English Government had constantly refused to recognize.   The com-plaints of Lord Hawkesbury on the subject of the French me-diation in Switzerland provoked an explosion of anger and threats.   "Whatever may be said or not said," wrote Talley-rand to Otto, "the resolution of the First Consul is irrevocable. He will not have Switzerland converted into a new Jersey. You will never speak of war, but you will not suffer any one to speak to you of it.   With what war could they threaten us? With a naval war?   But our commerce has only just started afresh, and the prey that we should afford the English would be scarcely worth while.   Our West Indies are supplied with acclimatized soldiers!   St. Domingo alone contains 25,000 of them.   They might blockade our ports, it is true; but at the very moment of the declaration of war England would find herself blockaded in turn.   The territory of Hanover, of Hol-land, of Portugal, of Italy, down to Tarento, would be occupied by our troops.   The countries we are accused of domineering over too openly—Liguria, Lombardy, Switzerland, Holland—instead of being left in this uncertain situation, from which we sustain a thousand embarrassments, would be converted into French provinces, from which we should draw immense re-sources; and we should be compelled to realize that empire of the Gauls which is ceaselessly held up as a terror to Europe. And what would happen if the First Consul, quitting Paris for Lille or St. Omer, collecting all the flat-bottomed vessels of

Flanders and Holland, and preparing the means of transport for 100,000 men, should plunge England into the agonies of an invasion—always possible, almost certain? Would England stir up a continental war? But where would she find her allies? In any case, if the war on the continent were to be renewed, it would be England who would compel us to conquer Europe. The First Consul is only thirty-three years old; he has as yet only destroyed States of the second rank. Who knows but that he might have time enough yet (if forced to attempt it) to change the face of Europe, and resuscitate the Empire of the West?"

The violence of these words went beyond the thought of the First Consul; he had not yet firmly made up his mind for the recommencement of hostilities. France submissive, Europe silent and resigned, accepting without a murmur the encroachments of his ambition—such were for him the conditions of peace; England could not accept them. With Piedmont and the island of Elba annexed to France, Holland and Switzerland subdued, and the Duchy of Parma occupied, England had eluded the agreements relative to the island of Malta. Profiting by the difficulties which opposed themselves to the reconstitution of the order of things guaranteed by the great powers, she had detained in her hands this pledge of empire in the Mediterranean. It was the object of continual complaints from the First Consul, and the pretext for his outburst of anger. "The whole Treaty of Amiens, and nothing but the Treaty of Amiens," Otto kept constantly repeating to Lord Hawkesbury. The minister of foreign affairs responded by a declaration equally peremptory: "The condition of the continent at the time of the Treaty of Amiens, and nothing but that condition." The mutual understandings and reticences which had enabled a truce to be arranged, little by little disappeared. The truth began to come to light. A mission of General Sébastiani to Egypt resulted in awakening general uneasiness.

The report of the First Consul's envoy was textually published in the *Moniteur;* it enumerated the forces at the disposal of England and Turkey in the East, and in conclusion expressed its opinion that "6000 Frenchmen would now be sufficient to reconquer Egypt."

This was, perhaps, saying more than Napoleon Bonaparte had resolved upon; and the ambassador's desire to please had responded to the remote and vague desires of the master. England was much disturbed at it, and yet more so at the haughty declarations of the First Consul in a statement of the condition of the republic. "In England," said he, "two parties contend for power. One has concluded peace and appears resolved on its maintenance; the other has sworn implacable hatred to France. Whilst this strife of parties lasts, there are measures which prudence dictates to the government. Five hundred thousand men ought to be, and shall be, ready to defend and to avenge her. Whatever be the success of her intrigues, England will not be able to draw other nations into new leagues, and the government declares with just pride that England alone could not now contend with France." The spirited indignation of the English people prevailed over the moderation and weakness of the government. George III., in a message to his Parliament, said, "In view of the military preparations which are being made in the ports of France and Holland, the king has believed it to be his duty to adopt new measures of precaution for the security of his States. These preparations are, it is true, officially intended for colonial expeditions; however, as there exists important differences of sentiment between his Majesty and the French Government, his Majesty has felt it necessary to address his Parliament, counting on its concurrence in order to assure all the measures which the honor and interests of the English people require." The public voice demanded the return to power of Pitt. "It is an astonishing and sorrowful fact," said his old adversary, Sir Philip Francis, "that in a moment like this all the eminent men of England are excluded from its government and its councils. For calm weather an ordinary amount of ability in the pilot might suffice; the storm which is now brewing calls for men of greater experience. If the vessel founders, we shall all perish with her."

The ambassador from England had just arrived at Paris. Lord Whitworth was a man of resolute and simple character, without either taste or ability for the complicated manœuvres of diplomacy; he was well received by the First Consul, and conversation soon began. "He reproaches us above all with not having evacuated Egypt and Malta," wrote the ambassador to Lord Hawkesbury. "'Nothing will make me accept that,' he said to me. 'Of the two, I would sooner see you master of the Faubourg St. Antoine than of Malta. My irritation against England is constantly increasing. Every wind that blows from England bears to me the evidence of its hatred and ill-will. If I wanted to take back Egypt by force, I could have had it a month ago, by sending 25,000 men to Aboukir; but I should lose there more than I should gain. Sooner or later Egypt must belong to France, either by the fall of the Ottoman Empire, or by some arrangement concluded with it. What advantage should I derive from making war? I can only attack you by means of a descent upon your coasts. I have resolved upon it, and shall be myself the leader. I know well that there are a hundred chances to one against me; but I shall attempt it if I am forced to it; and I assure you that such is the feeling of the troops, that army after army will be ready to rush forward to the danger. If France and England understand each other, the one, with its army of 480,000 men which is now being got in readiness, and the other with the fleet which has rendered it mistress of the seas, and which I should not be able to equal in less than ten years—they might govern the world; by their hostility they will ruin it. Nothing has been able to overcome the enmity of the English Government. Now we have arrived at this point: Do you want peace or war? It is upon Malta that the issue depends.'" Lord Whitworth attempted in vain a few protestations. "I suppose you want to speak about Piedmont and Switzerland? These are bagatelles! That ought to have been foreseen during the negotiations; you have no right to complain at this time of day."

The warlike ardour of the Parliament and the English nation was the answer to the hostile declaration of the First Consul. He had counted upon a more confirmed desire for peace, and upon the disquietude his threats would produce. He attempted once more the effect produced by one of those outbursts of violence to which he was subject, and of which he was accustomed to make use.

The message of George III. to Parliament was known to the First Consul when, on Sunday, March 13, 1803, the ambassador of England presented himself at the Tuileries. Bonaparte was still in the apartment of his wife; when Lord Whitworth was announced, he entered immediately into the salon. The crowd was large; the entire corps diplomatique was present. The First Consul, advancing towards Lord Whitworth, said, "You have news from London;" then, without leaving the ambassador time to answer: "So you wish for war!" "No," replied Lord Whitworth; "we know too well the advantages of peace." "We have already made war for ten years; you wish to make it for another fifteen years; you force it upon me." He strode with long steps before the amazed circle of diplomats. "The English wish for war," said he, drawing himself up before the ambassadors of Russia and Spain—Markoff and Azara; "but if they are the first to draw the sword, I will not be the last to put it back in the scabbard. They will not evacuate Malta. Since there is no respect for treaties, it is necessary to cover them over with a black pall!" The First Consul returned to Lord Whitworth, who remained motionless in his place. "How is it they have dared to say that France is arming? I have not a single vessel of the line in our ports! You want to fight; I will fight also. France may be killed, my lord; but intimidated, never!" "We desire neither the one nor the other," replied the ambassador; "we only aspire to live on a good understanding with her." "Then treaties must be respected," cried Bonaparte. "Woe to those who don't respect treaties."

He went away his eyes sparkling, his countenance full of wrath—when he stopped for a moment; the sentiment of decorum had again taken possession of his mind. "I hope," said he to Lord Whitworth, "that the Duchess of Dorset* is well, and that after having passed a bad season in Paris, she will be able to pass a good one there." Then suddenly, and as if his former anger again seized him: "That depends upon England. If things so fall out that we have to make war, the responsibility, in the eyes of God and man, will rest entirely upon those who deny their own signature, and refuse to execute treaties."

It was one of Bonaparte's habits to calm himself suddenly after an outburst of violence. A few days were passed by Talleyrand and Lord Whitworth in sincere efforts to plan pacific expedients; the ambassador had received from the English Cabinet its ultimatum: "1. The cession of the isle of Lampedusa. 2. The occupation of Malta for ten years. 3. The evacuation of the Batavian Republic and Switzerland. 4. An indemnity for the King of Sardinia. On these conditions England would recognize the Kingdom of Etruria and the Cisalpine Republic."

The warmth of public opinion in England had obliged the minister to take up a fixed attitude; the consequences could not be doubtful. In vain Lord Whitworth retarded to the utmost limits of his power the departure for which he had received orders. The advances of Talleyrand and the conces-

---

* Wife of Lord Whitworth.

sions of the First Consul did not seriously touch the essence of the questions in dispute. The decision of Napoleon remained the same: "I will not let them have two Gibraltars in the Mediterranean, one at the entrance and another in the middle." The ambassador quitted Paris on the 12th of May, journeying by short stages, as if still to avert the inevitable rupture between the two nations; at the same time General Andréossy, accredited at the court of George III., quitted London. The two ambassadors separated on the 17th of May at Dover, sorrowful and grave, as men who had striven to avert indescribable sorrows and struggles from their country and the world.

It was the harsh and barbarous custom of the English navy to fall upon the merchant vessels of an enemy's country immediately peace was broken. Two French ships of commerce were thus captured on the day following the departure of General Andréossy for Paris. The First Consul replied to this act of hostility by causing to be arrested, and soon afterwards interned at various places in his territory, all the English sojourning or travelling in France. Some had recently received from Talleyrand the most formal assurances of their safety. "Many English addressed themselves to me," said Napolean in his "Mémorial de Sainte-Hélène;" "I constantly referred them to their government. On it alone their lot depended." England did not claim its citizens, it resolutely persisted in leaving upon its author the full weight of this odious act, disapproved by his most faithful adherents. No Frenchmen were annoyed on English soil.

Europe was agitated and disquieted, still entrenched in its neutrality, more or less malevolent, and terrified at the consequences it foresaw from the renewal of the strife between France and England. "If General Bonaparte does not accomplish the miracle that he is preparing at this moment," said the Emperor of Germany, Francis II., "if he does not pass the straits, he will throw himself upon us, and will fight England in Germany." "You inspire too much fear in all the world, for it to dream now of fearing England," cried Philippe de Cobentzel, ambassador of Austria at Paris. It was upon this universal fear that the First Consul had counted. Already his troops had invaded Hanover, without England thinking it possible to defend the patrimonial domains of its sovereign. The Hanoverian army did not attempt to resist: Marshal de Walmoden concluded with General Mortier at Suhlingen a

convention which permitted the former to retire beyond the
Elbe with arms and baggage, on condition of not serving
against France in the present war. These resolutions not having been ratified by George III., the Hanoverian army was
disbanded after laying down its arms; 30,000 Frenchmen continued to occupy Hanover. The uneasiness of Germany continued to increase. The Emperor of Russia offered himself as
mediator; the King of Prussia offered to arrange for the neutrality of the north; but the First Consul remained deaf to
these advances. He sent Gouvion de Saint Cyr into the gulf of
Tarento, formerly evacuated after the peace of Amiens. The
forces intended for this expedition were to live at the expense
of the kingdom of Naples. "I will no more suffer the English
in Italy than in Spain or Portugal," he had said to Queen
Caroline. "At the first act of complicity with England, war
will give me redress for your enmity."

The attitude of Spain was doubtful, and its language little
satisfactory. By the threat of invasion by Augereau, whose
forces were already collected at Bayonne, the First Consul
acted on the disgraceful terrors of the Prince de la Paix; he
only exacted money from his powerless ally. As he now found
it impossible to occupy Louisiana, Bonaparte conceived the idea
of ceding it to the United States for a sum of 80,000,000 francs,
which the Americans hastened to pay. Holland was to furnish troops and vessels, Etruria and Switzerland soldiers.

It was upon a maritime enterprise that the efforts and
thoughts of the First Consul were at this moment entirely
concentrated. The attempt at an invasion of England which
the Directory had formerly wished to impose on him, and
which he had rejected with scorn on the eve of the campaign
in Egypt, had become the object of his most serious hopes.
To throw 150,000 men into England on a calm day by means
of a flotilla of flat-bottomed boats, which should be rowed
across whilst the great vessels of the English navy would be
immovable through the absence of wind—such was the primi-
tive conception of the enterprise. Bonaparte prepared for it
with that persevering activity, and that marvellous pre-
arrangement of details with a view to the entire plan, which
he knew how constantly to carry out in administration as in
war. To the original project of the Directory he had added
more masterly combinations, which still remained secret. A
squadron was preparing at Brest, under the orders of Admiral
Ganteaume; the Dutch vessels, commanded by Admiral

Verhuell, were collected at Texel; Admiral Latouche-Tréville, clever and daring, was to direct the squadron of Toulon destined for a decisive manœuvre. Admiral Brueix was entrusted with the conduct of the flotilla of the Channel; everywhere boats had been requisitioned, gun-boats and pinnaces were in course of construction; the departments, the cities, the corporate bodies, offered gifts of vessels or maritime provisions; the forests of the departments of the north fell under the axe. Camps had been formed at Boulogne, at Étaples, at St. Omer; fortifications rose along the coast; the First Consul undertook a journey through the Flemish and Belgian departments, accompanied by Madame Bonaparte and all the splendor of a royal household. The presence of the Legate in the *cortége* was to impress with respect and confidence the minds of the devout populations of the north. The first point at which Napoleon Bonaparte stayed his progress was at Boulogne; he pressed forward the works, commenced, and ordered new ones. On his return from the triumphal march to Brussels and back, he resumed himself the direction of his great enterprise. Established in the little chateau of Pont de Briques at the gate of Boulogne, he hastened over to St. Cloud, and returned, with a rapidity which knew no fatigue. Without cessation, on the shore, in the workshops, in the camps, he animated the sailors, the workmen, and the soldiers with the indomitable activity of his soul. The minister of marine, Decrès, clever, penetrating, with a nature gloomy and mournful, suggested all the difficulties of the expedition, and yielded to the imperial will that dominated all France. Admiral Brueix, already ill, and soon afterwards dying, was installed in a little house which overlooked the sea, witnessing the frequent experiments tried on the new vessels, sometimes even the little encounter that took place with the English ships. The First Consul braved all inclemencies of weather; he was eager "to play his great game." "I received your letter of the 18th Brumaire," wrote he to Cambacérès. "The sea continues to be very bad, and the rain to fall in torrents. Yesterday I was on horseback or in a boat all day. That is the same thing as telling you I was continually wet. At this season nothing can be accomplished without braving the water. Fortunately for my purpose, it suits me perfectly, and I was never better in health."

Already the night expeditions, intended to exercise the sailors and inure the soldiers, had commenced; the ardor of the chief spread to the army. On the 7th of January, 1804, the minister of marine wrote from Boulogne to the First Consul: "In the flotilla they are beginning to believe firmly that the departure will be more immediate than is generally supposed, and they have promised to prepare seriously for it. They shake off all thoughts of danger, and each man sees only Cæsar and his fortunes. The ideas of all the subalterns do not pass the limits of the roadstead and its currents. They argue about the wind, and the anchorage, and the line of bearing. As for the crossing, that is your affair. You know more about it than they do, and your eyes are worth more than their telescopes. They have implicit faith in everything that you do. The admiral himself is in just the same condition. He has never presented you any plan, because in fact he has none. Besides, you have not yet asked him for it; it will be the moment of execution which will decide him. Very possibly he will be obliged to sacrifice a hundred vessels to draw down the enemy upon them, whilst the rest, setting out at the moment of the defeat of the others, will go across without hindrance."

The First Consul, ceasingly watching the sea which protected his enemies, wrote to Cambacérès on November 16th: "I have passed these three days in the midst of the camp and the port. I have seen from the heights of Ambleteuse the coasts of England, as one sees the Calvaire from the Tuileries. You can distinguish the houses, and the movements going on. It is a ditch, which shall be crossed as soon as we shall have the audacity to attempt it."

So many preparations, pushed forward with such ardor, disquieted England. The most illustrious of her naval officers —Nelson, Lord Cornwallis, and Lord Keith—were ordered to blockade the French ports, and hinder the return of distant squadrons. Everywhere corps of volunteers were formed, and actively exercised on the coasts. Men of considerable note in the political or legal world—Pitt and Addington, as well as the great lords and the great judges—clothed themselves in uniform, and commanded regiments. Pitt proposed to fortify London. Insurrectionary movements were being fomented in Ireland; the French squadron at Brest was destined to aid them.

In the midst of this warlike and patriotic agitation, it was only natural that the excitement should gain a party, naturally restless and credulous. The French emigrants could not but feel a desire for action, in the hope of taking an active part in the general struggle waged against the enemy who kept them far from their country by the very fact of his existence and his power. The First Consul had offered an amnesty to all the emigrants, restored their property to some, and attracted a certain number of them round his own person; he had recalled the priests, and re-established the Catholic religion; but he had repelled the advances of the House of Bourbon. His hostility to the restoration of the monarchy had always been flagrant; the throne might be re-erected, but it should be for his own profit. He alone was the obstacle to the hopes cherished by the exiled princes and their friends, in presence of the re-establishment of order and the public prosperity. Delivered from his yoke, that pressed heavily upon her, France would salute with enthusiasm the return of her legitimate sovereign.

It was in England even, and amongst the circle that surrounded the Count d'Artois, that expression was given to these hopes and ignorant illusions as to the true state of men's minds in France. The Princes of the House of Condé, recently enrolled with their little army in the service of England, held themselves ready to fight, without conspiring. Louis XVIII. lived in Germany, withdrawn from the centre of warlike preparations; he was cold, sensible, and prudent; he thought little of plots, and had a healthier judgment than his brother as to the chances which might restore his fortune. The actual resources, the noisy agents of the emigration, were collected in England: there were found the chiefs of the Chouans, with Georges Cadoudal at their head; there dwelt the generals who had had the misfortune to abandon their country or betray their honor—Willot, Dumouriez, Pichegru; there were hatched chimerical projects, impressed from the first with the fatal errors and the terrible ignorance which doom to inevitable sterility the hopes and the efforts of exiles.

By his counsels, or his orders, Georges Cadoudal had taken part in the plot which had been discovered in 1801. After the failure of the infernal machine of St. Réjant he had felt regret, and some repugnance, for such proceedings. He proposed to go to Paris, with twenty or twenty-five resolute men, to attack the guard of the First Consul while he passed along the street, and strike him in the midst of his defenders. In order to profit by this bold stroke intrigues were to be carried on beforehand with discontented generals, who might be able to dispose the forces necessary for the sudden overthrow of the consular government. Bonaparte dead, the Count d'Artois and his son the Duc de Berry, secretly brought into France, would rally their friends round them, and proclaim the restoration of the House of Bourbon.

Two principal actors were indispensable to the execution of the project; Georges at Paris, unknown to the prying police of the First Consul; and General Moreau, favorable to the fall of Bonaparte, if not to his assassination. A nearly complete rupture had succeeded to the professed regard which for a long time covered the secret jealousy of the First Consul with respect to his glorious companion-in-arms. At the summit of his power and glory, Napoleon Bonaparte was never exempt from a recollection of rivalry with regard to the former chiefs of the republican army, his old rivals, and who had not bowed before the prestige of his recognized superiority. He liked neither Kléber, nor Masséna, nor Gouvion St. Cyr. As regards Moreau, he experienced a concealed uneasiness; it was the only military name that had been mentioned as that of a possible successor to himself. Wounded susceptibilities, and the quarrels of women, had aggravated a situation naturally delicate and strained. Moreau was spirited as well as modest; he felt himself injured; he dwelt in the country, living in grand style, sought after by the discontented, and speaking of Bonaparte without much reserve. The emigrant conspirators believed that circumstances were favorable for engaging him in their plans. General Pichegru had formerly been his friend. Moreau had long concealed the proofs of the former treason; perhaps he regretted having given them up at the moment of his comrade's just disgrace: he was known to be favorable to the return of Pichegru to France. It was in the name of Pichegru, and for his interests, that Moreau was to be approached. The first agent sent to Moreau was soon arrested; he has said in his "Mémoires," "Moreau would have nothing to do with conspiracy, and said, 'he must cease to waste men and things.'" Other emissaries had no better success. An active intriguer, General Lajolais, an old friend of Pichegru, meanwhile left Paris for London; he repeated the bitter words of Moreau respecting the First Consul—words which created illusions and hopes. On the 21st August, 1803, Georges landed at the cliff of Biville, crossing the rocks by the footpaths of smugglers. The police had for some time been on the traces of the conspiracy: they were, perhaps, actively con-cerned in it.   A few Chouans, obscure companions of Cadoudal, were arrested and put in prison, without their trial being pro-ceeded with; their chief succeeded in reaching Paris safely, where he hid himself.   Two successive arrivals completed the band of conspirators; on January 16th, 1804, General Pichegru, the Marquis de la Rivière, Jules and Armand de Polignac, landed in France.   On the same day, and by a coincidence which suggests the idea of a certain knowledge of the situation, the First Consul said in his statement as to the condition of the republic,—

" The British Government will attempt to cast, and has per-haps already cast upon our shores, a few of those monsters which it has nourished during the peace, in order to injure the land which gave them birth.   But they will no longer find the impious bands who were the instruments of their first crimes; terror has dissolved them, or justice has purged our country of their presence.   They will no longer find that credulity they abused, or that hatred which once sharpened their daggers.   Surrounded everywhere by the public power, every-where within the grasp of the tribunals, these horrible wretches will be able henceforth neither to make rebels, nor to resume with impunity their profession as brigands and assassins."

The conspirators succeeded in assuring themselves that, con-trary to the hopes of some English diplomatists, an insurrec-tion was no longer possible in Vendée or Brittany.   Already a certain amount of discouragement was influencing their minds as to the success of their perilous enterprise.   At their first interview, by night, on the Boulevard of La Madeleine, Moreau showed himself cold towards Pichegru.   Georges, who had accompanied the latter, was dissatisfied and gloomy.   "This looks bad," said he, at once.   The two generals conferred. Moreau displayed no repugnance towards the overthrow of the First Consul; he would form no project of conspiracy, but he believed himself sure of becoming the master of power if Bonaparte happened to disappear; he was, and he remained, a republican.   He reproached Pichegru with being mixed up with men unworthy of him.   The general had more than once bitterly felt this.   "You are with us *(avec nous)*," the Chouans used to say to him.   "No gentlemen," cried Pichegru, one day; "I am in your company *(chez vous)*."

"Poor man!" said the conqueror of Holland, on quitting the conqueror of Hohenlinden, "he also has his ambition, and wishes to have a turn at governing France: he would not be its master for twenty-four hours." Georges Cadoudal laughed scornfully; "Usurper for usurper! I love better the one who is ruling now than this Moreau, who has neither heart nor head!" The conspirators felt their danger. Their preliminary interviews had led to no result; the murmurs of discontent had not developed into serious promises, still less into effective actions. La Rivière lost hope every day; the First Consul every day became better informed as to what was going on.

He had recently suppressed the ministry of police; Fouché continued, without authority, the profession which he had always practised with enthusiasm; he informed Napoleon as to the result of his researches. The latter had ardently cherished a hope of pursuing, and striking down at one blow, enemies of diverse origin, dangerous on different accounts. Amongst the Chouans arrested in the month of August, two had remained obstinately silent, and had been shot; a third was less courageous. "I have secret information which makes me believe that they only came here to assassinate me," wrote Bonaparte to Cambacérès. Querelle revealed all he knew of the plot; he named the place of disembarkation; General Savory was sent there in disguise, ordered to wait for that arrival of a prince, as had been promised to the conspirators. Already his doom was determined on in the mind of the First Consul.

Fresh arrests had taken place in Paris, for a servant of Georges had given information. One of his principal officers, Bouvet de Lozier, vainly attempted to kill himself; rescued from death, he asked to see the chief judge. Régnier sent in his place Réal, the counsellor of state, more penetrating and more clever than himself. It is supposed that the latter was no stranger to the drawing up of the deposition of Bouvet, who implicated General Moreau in the gravest manner. "Here is a man who comes back from the gates of the tomb, still surrounded by the shadows of death, who demands vengeance upon those who by their perfidy have thrown him and his party into the abyss where they now find themselves. Sent to sustain the cause of the Bourbons, he finds himself compelled either to fight for Moreau, or to renounce an enterprise which was the sole object of his mission. Monsieur was to pass into France, to put himself at the head of the royalist party. Moreau promised to unite himself to the cause of the Bourbons; the royalists arrived in France, and Moreau retracts. He proposes to them to work for him, and to get him named Dictator.

Hence the hesitation, the dissension, and the almost total loss of the royalist party. I know not what weight you will attach to the assertions of a man snatched an hour ago from the death to which he had devoted himself, and who sees before him the fate which an offended government has in reserve for him. But I cannot withhold the cry of despair, or refrain from attacking the man who has reduced me to this."

Réal hastened to the Tuileries. The First Consul was less astonished than himself: he was acquainted with the interviews of Moreau and Pichegru. He was well aware that the opinions of Moreau were quite opposed to any thought of monarchical restoration. The general returned to Paris, after a visit to Grosbois, on the morning of the 15th of February; he was arrested on the bridge of Charenton, and taken to the Temple. Lajolais was arrested at the same time. The trial was directed to take place before the civil tribunal of the Seine. Cambacérès had proposed a military commission. "No," said the First Consul; "it would be said that I desire to disembarrass myself of Moreau, and to get him judicially assassinated by own creatures." The jury was chosen in the department of the Seine; a report upon the causes of the arrest of Moreau was sent to the Senate, the Corps Législatif, and the Tribunate.

The commotion in Paris was great, and the public instinct was favorable to General Moreau. The presumed accomplices of his crime had not yet fallen into the hands of the government. People refused to believe him guilty, a traitor to the opinions of a lifetime, and mixed up in a royalist conspiracy. The attitude of the general was firm and calm. For a moment, the First Consul conceived the idea of seeing him. "I pardon Moreau," said he; "let him own everything to me, and I will forget the errors of a foolish jealousy." General Lajolais had recounted the details of the interviews of Moreau with Pichegru; the accused persisted in denying everything. "Ah, well!" replied Napoleon, "since he will not open with me, it will be necessary for him to yield to justice." Anger broke forth, in spite of the efforts of the First Consul to preserve the appearance of a sorrowful justice. The brother of Moreau, was a member of the Tribunate; he had loudly pleaded in favor of the accused. "I declare," cried he, "to the assembly, to the entire nation, that my brother is innocent of the atrocious crimes that are imputed to him. Let him be given the means of justifying himself, and he will do so. I demand that he may be judged by his natural judges." The president of the Tribunate dared to style the accusation against Moreau **a** *denunciation;* the First Consul warmly criticised this expression. "The greatness of the services rendered by Moreau is not a sufficient motive for screening him from the rigor of the laws," cried he. "There is no government in existence where a man by reason of his past services may screen himself from the law, which ought to have the same grasp on him as on the meanest individual. What! Moreau is already guilty in the eyes of the highest powers of the State, and you will not even consider him as accused!" "Paris and France have only one sentiment, only one opinion," wrote he to Comte Melzi, vice-president of the Italian Republic.

The pursuit had become rigorous. It was known that Pichergru and Georges were hidden in Paris; the gates of the city were closed, egress by the river watched by armed vessels. The Corps Législatif voted a measure condemning to death whoever should conceal the conspirators, to the number of sixty. Whoever should be cognizant of them without denouncing them, was liable to six years in irons. One night General Pichegru went to ask asylum of Barbé-Marbois, formerly intendant of St. Domingo, transported, like himself, to Sinnamari, and now become a minister of the First Consul. Barbé-Marbois did not hesitate to receive him. When he avowed it afterwards to Napoleon, the latter warmly congratulated him upon it.

A few days passed by; General Pichegru, shamefully betrayed by one of his former officers, was arrested on the 28th of February, bravely resisting the agents of the police. Georges, seized in the street on the 9th of March, blew out the brains of the first gendarme who seized the bridle of his horse. La Rivière and Polignac were also in prison. Moreau had given up his system of absolute denials; at the prayer of his wife and his friends he wrote to the First Consul, simply recounting his relations with Pichegru, without asking pardon, and without denying the past transactions, seeking to disengage his cause from the Royalist conspiracy—less haughty, however, than he had till then appeared. Bonaparte had the letter affixed to the process of the trial. He appeared moved at the situation of Pichegru. "A fine end!" said he to Réal: "A fine end for the conqueror of Holland. It will not do for the men of the Revolution to devour each other. I have long had a **dream** about Cayenne; it is the finest country in the world for

PICHEGRU.

founding a colony. Pichegru has been proscribed, as he knows; ask him how many men and how much money he wants to create a great establishment; I will give them to him, and he will retrieve his glory by rendering a service to France." The general did not reject the proposition, but he persisted in his silence. "I will speak before the tribunal," said he. Before the supreme day when the trial was about to take place before human justice, Pichegru had appeared before a more august tribunal; on the morning of the 6th of April he was found dead in his bed, strangled, it was said, by his own hands.

The royalist conspirators at first proudly avowed the aim of their enterprise. "What did you come to do in Paris?" asked the prefect of the police of Georges Cadoudal. "I came to attack the First Consul." "What were your means?" "I had as yet little enough; I counted on collecting them." "Of what nature were your means of attack?" "By means of living force." "Where did you count on finding this force?" "In all France." "And what was your project?" "To put a Bourbon in the place of the First Consul." "Had you many people with you?" "No, because I was not to attack the First Consul until there was a French prince in Paris, and he has not yet arrived."

This was the prince for whom General Savary had been waiting in vain for nearly a month on the cliff of Biville. The anger of the First Consul continued to increase. "The Bourbons think they can get me killed like a dog," said he. "My blood is worth more than theirs; I shall make no more of their case than of Moreau or Pichegru; the first Bourbon prince who falls into my hands, I will have shot remorselessly." The Comte d'Artois and the Duc de Berry were announced, and did not arrive. Napoleon stretched forth his arm to seize an innocent prince, whose misfortune it was to be within his reach. On the 10th of March, 1804, he wrote to General Berthier: "You will do well, citizen minister, to give orders to General Ordener, whom I place at your disposal, to repair at night, by post, to Strasburg. He will travel under another name than his own, and see the general of division. The aim of his mission is to throw himself upon Ettenheim, invest the city, and carry away from it the Duc d' Enghien, Dumouriez, an English colonel, and any other individual who may be in their suite. The general of division, the marshal of the barracks of gendarmes, who has been to reconnoitre Ettenheim, as well as the commissary of police, will give him all necessary information."

The young Duc d'Enghien, son of the Duc de Bourbon, and grandson of the Prince of Condé, resided in fact at Ettenheim, in the grand duchy of Baden. Drawn at times to Strasburg, by his taste for the theatre, he was held fast in this little city by a passionate attachment for the Princess Charlotte of Rohan, who lived there. He was young and brave, and was waiting for the call from England to take part in the war. He was not implicated in the plot hatched round the Comte d'Artois, and was absolutely ignorant of it. A few emigrants—very few in numbers, and without political importance—resided near him; one of them was the Marquis de Thumery, whose name, mis-pronounced with a German accent, gave rise to the error which supposed the presence of Dumouriez at Ettenheim. This supposition might for a moment deceive the First Consul as to the complicity of the Duc d'Enghien; it was cleared up when, after having violated the territory of the Grand Duke of Baden (for which Talleyrand was careful to apologize), he learnt the arrival of the unfortunate prince at Strasburg; all the papers seized at Ettenheim were in his hands.

The first movement of the Duc d'Enghien had been to defend himself. "Are you compromised?" asked a German officer who was at his house. "No!" replied the young man with astonishment. Resistance was useless; he surrendered. There was one single ground of accusation against him: like all the princes of his house, and thousands of emigrants, he had borne arms against France. Nearly all the nobility had been per-mitted again to tread the soil of their country; he alone was about to expiate the fault of all. The minister of France at Baden, Massias, felt compelled to bear witness that "the con-duct of the Prince had always been innocent and guarded." A few days later the *Moniteur* had to announce the assembling of emigrants, with a staff of officers and bureaux of officials round a prince of the House of Bourbon. Massias had before-hand given the lie to this rumor. The Duc d'Enghien was brought to Paris; detained for a few hours at the barriers, he was then conducted to the chateau of Vincennes. On the same morning the First Consul had sent this order to his brother-in-law, General Murat, whom he had just named governor of Paris: "General, in accordance with the orders of the First Consul, the Duc d'Enghien is to be conducted to the castle of Vincennes, where arrangements are made to re-

ceive him. He will probably arrive at his destination to-night.
I pray you to make such arrangements as shall provide for the
safety of this prisoner at Vincennes, as well as on the road
from Meaux by which he comes. The First Consul has ordered
that the name of this prisoner, and everything relative to him,
shall be kept a profound secret. In consequence, the officer
entrusted with his guard ought not to be made acquainted
with the name and rank of his prisoner; he travels under the
name of Plessis."

Bonaparte was at Malmaison, gloomy and agitated; since the
day when the order had been given to arrest the Duc d'Enghien, the intimate companions of the First Consul had no doubt
as to his fatal resolution. Cambacérès had warmly insisted
upon the deplorable consequences of such an act; Madame
Bonaparte had cast herself at his feet, but he raised her up ill-
temperedly. "You have grown very saving over the blood of
the Bourbons," said he bitterly to Cambacérès. "I shall not
allow myself to be killed without being able to defend myself."
The fatal moment approached. Madame de Remusat, playing
at chess with Napoleon, heard him repeating in a low voice the
noble words of Augustus pardoning Cinna, and she believed the
prince saved: he had just entered the castle of Vincennes, and
already the judges were awaiting him.

Murat had loudly declared his repugnance for the functions
imposed on him by his brother-in-law. "He wants to stain
my uniform with blood," said he with anger. He was not
called to Vincennes. General Savary, devoted without reserve
to the First Consul, had set out with a corps of gendarmes.
Already the Duc d'Enghien, weighed down by fatigue, was
asleep; he was roused up at midnight. A captain, as judge
advocate, was entrusted with a first examination. He being
asked his names, Christian names, age, and place of birth, in
reply said " he was named Louis-Antoine-Henri de Bourbon,
Duc d'Enghien, born at Chantilly, the 2nd of August, 1772."
Being asked at what time he quitted France, in reply he said,
"I cannot say precisely, but I think it was on the 16th July,
1789, that I set out with the Prince de Condé my grandfather,
my father the Comte d'Artois, and the children of the Comte
d'Artois." Being asked where he had resided since leaving
France, in reply he said, "On leaving France I passed with
my parents, whom I always accompanied, by Mons and Brussels; thence we returned to Turin, to the palace of the king,
where we remained nearly sixteen months. Thence, always

with my parents, I went to Worms and the neighborhood, upon the banks of the Rhine. Lastly the Condé corps was formed, and I was with it throughout the war. I had before that made the campaign of 1792, in Brabant, with the Bourbon corps, in the army of Duke Albert. We terminated the last campaign in the environs of Grätz, and I asked permission of the Cardinal de Rohan to go into his country, to Ettenheim, in Brisgau, the former bishopric of Strasburg. For two years and a half I remained in this country, with the permission of the Elector of Baden." Being asked if he had ever passed into England, and if that power had always accorded him a grant of money, in reply he said he had never been there; that England always accorded him a grant of money, and that he had only that to live upon. Being asked if he kept up correspondence with the French princes in London, and if he had seen them for some time, he said that naturally he kept up a correspondence with his grandfather, and that equally naturally he corresponded with his father, whom he had not seen, so far as he could recollect, since 1794 or 1795. Being asked if he knew General Pichegru, and if he had any relations with him, he said, "I believe I have never seen him; I have had no relations with him. I know that he has desired to see me. I am thankful not to have known him, after the vile means of which it is said he has desired to make use, if it is true." Being asked if he knew the ex-general Dumouriez, and if he had had relations with him, he said, "On the contrary, I have never seen him." Being asked if, since the peace, he had not kept up correspondence with the interior of the republic, he said, "I have written to a few friends who are still attached to me, who have been my companions in war, about their affairs and my own; these correspondences are not, I think, those to which it is intended to refer."

Upon the minute of the examination, beneath his signature the Duc d'Enghien wrote, "I earnestly entreat to have a private audience with the First Consul. My name, my rank, my way of thinking, and the horror of my situation, make me hope that he will not refuse me my request." The request was foreseen, and the answer, according to instructions given, that under no pretext would the First Consul be willing to receive the Duc d'Enghien.

At two o'clock in the morning the military commission was assembled presided over by General Hullin formerly life-guard of Louis XVI., and one of the insurgent leaders before the Bastille. The same questions were addressed to the prince, more briefly—less explicitly, as if the time was short, and the enemy threatening. Sometimes the president interfered with an appearance of rude benevolence. General Savary did not speak. When the examination was finished he rose up. "Now this is my concern," said he. The judges deliberated a moment. The sentence, signed in blank, was already in their hands. The Governor of Vincennes, Harel, appeared at the gate carrying a light. He had formerly delivered to Bonaparte the conspirators of the plot of Aréna and Topino-Lebrun; to-day he preceded in the sombre corridors the prisoner, escorted by a piquet of troops. The prince did not pale; he reiterated his request for an audience, which was harshly denied. Already the grave was dug in the ditch of the chateau; a detachment of gendarmes waited for the condemned.

The Duke stopped. "Comrades," said he loudly, "there is without doubt among you a man of honor who will charge himself with receiving and transmitting my last thoughts." And as a young officer stepped out of the ranks, "Has any one here a pair of scissors?" asked the Prince. He cut a lock of his hair, and joining it in the form of a ring, he pronounced in low tones the name of the person for whom he intended this souvenir; then pushing back with his hands the bandage with which they wished to cover his eyes, he made one step towards the soldiers: they fired, and he was dead. General Savary went to tell his master that he was obeyed.

Shakespeare has depicted remorse with that terrible truthfulness which carries home to our minds the horror of crime. Lady Macbeth passes before us haunted by a vision, and ceaselessly washing her blood-stained hands. During all his life, even in his exile, Napoleon vainly sought to wash off the innocent and illustrious blood which he caused to flow in the fosse of Vincennes on the 20th of March, 1804. The men whom he had employed as the instruments of his heinous crime struggled like himself under this terrible responsibility. In vain has Bonaparte reproached Talleyrand with having perfidiously urged him on in the fatal path; in vain has Réal affirmed that an order reached his house during the night assuring to the prisoner a new examination, unfortunately forestalled by his death. All explanations, and all accusations have failed before the severe justice of history and the infallible instinct of the public conscience. The odious burden of a cowardly assassination was constantly weighing upon him who had ordered it.

The blood of his victim created round him an abyss that all the efforts of supreme power could never succeed in filling up.

When the news spread in Paris, on March 21st, it was received with stupor; people wept, even at Malmaison. Caulaincourt, previously entrusted with the explanatory letter for the Elector of Baden, complained bitterly of the stain upon his honor. Fourcroy was sent to dissolve the Corps Législatif; Fontanes, who presided over the assembly, replied to the counsellor of state without making allusion to the catastrophe, the intelligence of which the latter had mixed up with matters of business. His speech was modified in the *Moniteur*. Fontanes had the courage to protest against the approbation which had been attributed to him. The same journal contained the judgment of the military commission which had condemned the Duc d'Enghien; like the speech of Fontanes, the wording had been altered.

Alone amongst the public functionaries of every rank or origin, young Chateaubriand, minister of France to the republic of Valais, felt himself constrained to give in his resignation. Louis XVIII. sent back the collar of the Golden Fleece to the King of Spain, who remained the ally of Napoleon. The courts of Russia and Sweden put on mourning for the Duc d'Enghien.

Thus was preparing in Europe, under the impulse of public opinion, the third coalition, which was to unite all the sovereigns against France. Alone till then, England had hatched against us the plots in which its diplomatic agents were found compromised; but the denunciations of the First Consul against Spencer and Drake vanish, and lose all importance in presence of the crime committed at Vincennes. Prussia, long and obstinately faithful to its policy of neutrality, and recently disposed to draw nearer to us, began to incline towards Russia, with whom she soon concluded an alliance. Austria evinced neither regret nor anger, but the action of the German powers was silently influencing her. The First Consul broke out against the Emperor Alexander, violently hurling a gross insult at him. "When England meditated the assassination of Paul I., if it had been known that the authors of the plot could be found at a place on the frontiers, would not you have been inclined to have them seized?" General Hédouville, ambassador of France at St. Petersburg, received the order to set out in forty-eight hours. "Know for your direction," said he to the chargé d'affaires, "that the First Consul does not wish for war, but he does not fear it with anybody."

In presence of this general perturbation of Europe, of the loud indignation of some and the dull uneasiness of others—in order to respond to the denunciations of the royalists, who understood the fatal consequences of the blow that Bonaparte had dealt to his own glory, the First Consul resolved to take at length the last step which separated him from supreme greatness. A year before he had been appointed Consul for life of the French Republic; the murderer of a prince of the house of Bourbon, he raised again on his own account the overturned throne. Still without children, he founded in his person an hereditary monarchy, assured of finding in the nation the assent of admiration as of lassitude and fear. Eight days had scarcely passed since the execution of the Duc d'Enghien; the brothers of the First Consul were absent and discontented. Cambacérès was opposed to the projects which he had divined in the mind of Napoleon Bonaparte. In his place, Fouché, always eager to serve the man whose favor he courted, cleverly prepared the minds of the Senate. No equivocation was possible as to the desires of Napoleon. On March 27th the first assembly of the state addressed to the supreme chief this humble request: "You found a new era," said the Senate, "but you ought to make it eternal. Splendor is nothing without duration. You are harassed by circumstances, by conspirators, by the ambitious. You are also in another sense harassed by the uneasiness which agitates all Frenchmen. You can conquer the times, master circumstances, put a curb on conspirators, disarm the ambitious, tranquillize all France, by giving it institutions which shall cement your edifice, and prolong for the children what you have done for the fathers. In town and country if you could interrogate all Frenchmen one after another, no one would speak otherwise than we. Great Man, complete your work by rendering it as immortal as your glory; you have drawn us forth from the chaos of the past, you make us blessed in the benefits of the present—make us sure of the future."

The clever manœuvre of Fouché gave Napoleon the opportunity of declaring himself; he wished to be invited to speak. His answer was not, and could not, be ready; he asked of the Senate time to reflect. Meanwhile he set himself to sound the courts of Europe. On the morrow of the insult he had offered to all the sovereigns by the murder of the Duc d'Enghien, their good-will was doubtful: the earnest adhesion of Prussia and Austria astonished and satisfied him; he was at war with

England, embroiled with Russia; the rest of Europe seemed to be at his feet. Clever at managing those of whom he had need, he wished to assure himself of the disposition of the army still agitated by the arrest of Moreau. He wrote to General Soult, who commanded the camp of Saint Omer: "Citizen General Soult, I have received your letter. The Councils-General of the departments, the Electoral Colleges, and all the great bodies of the State, ask that an end should be at last put to the hopes of the Bourbons, by placing the republic in safety from the shocks of elections and the uncertainty of the life of a single man. But up to this moment I have decided upon nothing; meanwhile I desire that you should instruct me in great detail as to the opinion of the army on a measure of this nature. You perceive that I would not be drawn into it except with the sole object of the nation's interest, for the French people have made me so great and so powerful that I can desire nothing more."

The malcontents in the army were silent; the ambitious, the courtiers, the faithful and devoted servants of the great general, brought him the protestation of their devotion; the addresses from the departments succeeded each other in great numbers. On April 25 the First Consul sent a message to the Senate: "Your address of the 6th Germinal has not ceased to be present to my thoughts," said he. "You have judged the hereditary succession of the chief magistrate to be necessary to shelter the French people from the plots of our enemies, and the agitation born of rival ambitions. Many of our institutions have at the same time appeared to you to require to be improved in order to assure without reversal the triumph of equality and public liberty, and to offer to the government and the nation the double guarantee of which they have need. In proportion as I have fixed my attention on these great objects, I have perceived more and more that, under circumstances as novel as they are important, the counsels of your wisdom and of your experience are necessary to me in order to fix all my ideas. I invite you then to let me become completely acquainted with all your thoughts. I desire that on the 14th July this year we shall be able to say to the French people: Fifteen years ago, by a spontaneous movement, you rushed to arms; you required liberty, equality, and glory. To-day, this best of all national wealth, assured to you without fear of reversal, is protected from all tempests. Institutions conceived and commenced in the midst of the storms of internal and external war, developed with constancy, have been brought to their climax amidst the noise of the efforts and plots of our mortal enemies, by the adoption of all that the experience of ages and of peoples has demonstrated as fit to guarantee the laws which the nation has judged necessary for its dignity, its liberty, and its honor."

On the day following the 14th of July, 1789, the Duc de Rochefoucauld said, with prophetic sadness, "It is very difficult to enter into true liberty by such a gate." General Bonaparte was destined to confirm this solemn truth, so often and so sorrowfully misunderstood by our country. France, exhausted and disgusted by the enthusiasms of demagogy and the bloody tyranny of the Terror, had been tossed by shock after shock into the arms of the conqueror who promised her order and energy in government; she had forgotten for a time those great and salutary conquests of the liberty which she unreservedly yielded up at his feet.

By a tardy return towards the convictions of the past, Carnot alone raised his voice in the Tribunate to recall the Republic, abandoned by all, in the name of that liberty which he wrongly attributed to it. "Was liberty then always to be shown to man without his being able to enjoy it? Was it ceaselessly offered for his desires, like a fruit to which he could not stretch forth his hand without being in danger of death? No! I cannot consent to regard this gift, so universally preferable to all others, without which the others are nothing, as a simple illusion. My heart tells me that liberty is possible, that its rule is easy and more stable than any arbitrary or oligarchic government. You say that Bonaparte has effected the salvation of his country, that he has restored public liberty; is it then a recompense to offer up to him this same liberty as a sacrifice?"

On the 3rd of May, on the proposal of Curée and the report of Jard-Panvillier, the Tribunate sent to the Senate a proposal to the effect: "Firstly, that Napoleon Bonaparte, at present Consul for life, be appointed Emperor, and in this capacity entrusted with the government of the French Republic. Secondly, that the title of Emperor and the imperial power be hereditary in his family, from male to male, in order of primogeniture. Thirdly and lastly, that in deciding as regards the organization of the constituted authorities upon the modifications required by the establishment of hereditary power—equality, liberty, and the rights of the people, be preserved in their integrity."

The Senate was resolved not to lose the fruits of its initiative; the project of the senatus-consultum was ready, and was immediately carried to the First Consul, accompanied by the views of all the great bodies of the State. When it returned to the Senate, amended and modified by the will of the supreme chief, the authority which the senators had sought to arrogate to themselves had been taken away. "The senators, if they were allowed to do it, would go on to absorb the Corps Législatif, and, who knows? perhaps even to restore the Bourbons," said the First Consul to the Council of State. "They wish at once to legislate, to judge, and to govern. Such a union of powers would be monstrous; I shall not suffer it!" The Tribunate ceased to exist as an assembly, and could no longer discuss except in sections; the Corps Législatif were permitted to debate in secret committees only. A High Court was to be constituted, to judge the crimes of personages too important for the jurisdictions of ordinary tribunals. In order to satisfy the vanity of Joseph and Louis Bonaparte, alone entitled to the succession of the empire, two officers were borrowed from the constitution devised by Sieyès, and from mediæval history; the one became Grand Elector, and the other Constable. Sagacious and docile counsellor of the First Consul in their apparent equality, Cambacérès was appointed arch-chancellor of the empire, and Lebrun became arch-treasurer. Four honorary marshals * and fourteen active marshals † were grouped around the restored throne. Alone and beforehand the Senate decided upon the destinies of France, arrogantly called upon to ratify decisions over which it exercised no authority; on May 19th, 1804, at the close of the sitting, all the senators went together to St. Cloud, and by the voice of Cambacérès prayed his *Imperial Majesty* that the organic arrangements might come into force immediately. "For the glory, as for the happiness of the country, we proclaim at this very moment Napoleon Bonaparte Emperor of the French."

Those present cried, "Long live the Emperor!" Only the sanction of the law of hereditary succession was submitted to the popular vote. By the force of his genius as much as by the splendor of his military glory, Napoleon had conquered France more completely than Italy or Egypt.

---

* Kellermann, Pérignon, Lefèvre, Sérurier.

† Murat, Berthier, Masséna, Lannes, Soult, Brune, Ney, Augereau, Moncey, Mortier, Davout, Jourdan, Bernadotte, Bessières.

CHAPTER VIII.

GLORY AND SUCCESS (1804—1805).

ON the eve of the declaration of the Senate in favor of the empire, Cambacérès had said to Lebrun, "All is over! the monarchy is re-established! But I have a presentiment that what they are now constructing will not be durable. We made war upon Europe to give it republics, which should be daughters of the French Republic; now we shall make it to give Europe monarchs, sons or brothers of ours; and France, exhausted, will finally succumb to such fatal attempts."

A year before that, when the consulship for life was proclaimed, the wise and virtuous Tronchet, when a sorrowful witness of the revolutionary crimes against which he had defended King Louis XVI., had shown the same inquietude and fatal presentiment. "This young man begins like Cæsar," he said of General Bonaparte; "I am afraid he may end as he did."

The daggers of the Roman conspirators had arrested Cæsar in his course. Napoleon had found neither a Brutus nor a Cassius: he reigned without contest, by a triumphal acclamation of 3,572,329 suffrages against 2569 "Noes." The country was eager to salute its new master, with a curiosity mixed with confidence in the unexpected resources of his genius. The courtiers alone around him who had found no place in the prodigal distribution of honors, muttered their murmurs. They served him nevertheless; and Talleyrand remained minister of foreign affairs, even when all the important posts of the empire had escaped his desires.

With more calmness and pride than the courtiers, Moreau and the royalist conspirators waited in prison for their verdict. Napoleon was as eager as they were, being in haste to rid himself of an embarrassment which could become a danger. In proportion as the trial proceeded, Moreau's case was more and more kept distinct from that of the other prisoners. The mode of defence adopted by the royalists tended entirely to prove his innocence. "We entered France," they said, "de-

VII.—7

ceived by false reports, and with the hope of securing our restoration: General Moreau refused us his assistance, and our
project failed." The general did not appear disturbed by the
irregular jurisdiction to which his case was to be referred.
"Strive," he wrote to his wife, "to make sure that those who
are to judge me are just men, incapable of betraying their
conscience. If I am judged by persons of honor, I cannot
complain, although they have apparently suppressed the
jury."

The public interest was lively, and openly shown, in spite of
the evident annoyance of the emperor. The friends of the
royalist prisoners were numerous and ardent; and, whether
from admiration or indifference, the public believed General
Moreau innocent of all conspiracy, and made excuse for the
dissatisfaction or ambition which he might have manifested.
The sharers of his renown—Dessoles, Gouvion St. Cyr, Macdonald, Lecourbe—were faithfully present at every sitting. I
borrow from the interesting recollections of Madame Récamier
the picture of the spectacle then seen in the hall of the Palace
of Justice, every approach to which was choked by the crowd.
"The prisoners, of whom there were forty-seven, were for the
most part unknown to each other, and filled the raised seats
facing those where the judges sat. Each prisoner was seated
between two gendarmes; those near Moreau were full of
respect. When I raised my veil the general recognized me,
and rose to salute me. I returned his salute with emotion and
respect. I was deeply touched at seeing them treat as a criminal that great general whose reputation was then so glorious
and unstained. It was no longer a question of republic and
republicans. Excepting Moreau, who I am certain was an entire stranger to the conspiracy, it was the royalist loyalty
that alone was on its defence against the new power. This
cause of the ancient monarchy had as its head a man of the
people, Georges Cadoudal.

"That fearless Georges! We looked at him with the thought
that that head, so freely and energetically devoted, must fall
on the scaffold; or that he alone, probably, would not escape
death, as he did nothing for that purpose. Disdaining to defend himself, he only defended his friends; and when they
tried to persuade him to ask for pardon, as the other prisoners
had done, he replied, 'Do you promise me a fairer opportunity
of dying?'

"In the ranks of the accused, Polignac and Rivière were

still noticeable, interesting from their youth and devotion. Pichegru, whose name will remain historically united with Moreau's, was missing at his side—or rather, one believed his shade was visible there, because it was known that he also was not in the prison.

"Another recollection, the death of the Duc d'Enghien, increased the sorrow and terror of many minds, even among the most devoted partisans of Bonaparte."

Taken as a whole, and in spite of the embarrassment caused by the persistence of two or three of the accusers, the public judicial examination was favorable to General Moreau. On being accused of having agreed to a reconciliation with the traitor Pichegru, he replied, "Since the beginning of the Revolution there have been many traitors. There were some who were traitors in 1789, without being so in 1793; there were others who were so in '93 but were not in '95, others who were so in '95 but have not been so since. Many were republicans who are not so now. General Pichegru may have had an understanding with Condé in the year IV.; I believe that he had; but he was included in the proscription of Fructidor, and must be considered as one of those who were then proscribed. When I saw other Fructidorians at the head of the authorities of state—when Condé's army filled the Parisian drawing-rooms and those of the First Consul, I might very well take a share in restoring to France the conqueror of Holland. I am credited with the absurd idea of making use of royalists in the hope of regaining power if they were successful. I have made war for ten years, and during those ten years I am not aware of having done absurd things." When they laid emphasis on his interview with Pichegru and Georges, he said, "A quarter of an hour is but little for the discussion of a plan of government. It is said that Pichegru was dissatisfied; probably we were not of the same mind." On the president regretting that he had not denounced Pichegru and the royalists, saying that he owed it to a government that loaded him with benefits, Moreau exclaimed, "The conqueror of Hohenlinden is not a denouncer, M. le Président. Do not put my services and my fortune in the same balance, for there is no possible comparison between the things. I should have fifty millions to-day, had I made the same use of victory which many others have done!"

Moreau wished to plead himself the cause of his life and renown. "It is only by my counsel," he said, "that I wish to address justice"—here the illustrious general looked round upon the attentive multitude—"but I feel that both on your account and mine I ought to speak myself. Unfortunate circumstances, produced by chance or caused by hatred, may for an instant obscure the life of the most honorable man; and a clever criminal may keep off suspicion and the proof of his crimes. The whole life of a prisoner is always the most certain testimony against him and for him. I therefore set my whole life to witness against my accusers and prosecutors; it has been public enough to be known: I shall only recall a few of its epochs: and the witnesses whom I shall summon will be the French people, and the people whom France has conquered. I was devoted to the study of law at the beginning of that revolution which was to establish the liberty of the French people; and the object of my life being thus changed, I devoted it to arms. I became a warrior because I was a citizen: I bore this character beneath our standards, and have always preserved it. I was promoted quickly, but always from step to step without passing any; always by serving my country, never by flattering the committees. On being appointed commander, when victory obliged us to march through the countries of our enemies, I was as anxious that our character should be respected as that our arms should be dreaded. War, under my orders, was a calamity only on the battlefield. I have the presumption to think that the country has not forgotten my services then, nor the ready devotion which I showed when fighting as a subordinate; nor how I was appointed to the command-in-chief by the reverses of our arms, and, in one sense, named general by our misfortunes. It is still remembered how I twice recomposed the army from the fragments of those which had been scattered, and how, after having twice restored it to a condition of being able to cope with the Russians and Austrians, I twice laid down the command to take another of greater responsibility. I was not during that period of my life more republican than during the others, though I seemed so. It is well known that there was a proposal to put me at the head of a movement similar to that of the 18th Brumaire. I refused, believing that I was made to command armies, and having no desire to command a Republic. I did more; on the 18th Brumaire I was in Paris. That revolution, instigated by others, could not disturb my peace of mind; but directed by a man surrounded by great renown, I might have hoped for happy results from it. I took part in it

MOREAU.

to assist it, whilst some other parties urged me to lead them in opposing it. I received in Paris General Bonaparte's orders, and, in seeing them executed, I assisted in raising him to that high degree of power which circumstances rendered necessary. When, shortly afterwards, he offered me the command of the army of the Rhine, I accepted it from him with as much devotion as from the hands of the Republic itself. Never had my successes been more rapid, more numerous, or more decisive, than during that period; and their renown was reflected upon the government which accuses me. What a moment for conspiring, if such a scheme had ever entered my mind! Would an ambitious man, or a conspirator, have let slip the opportunity when at the head of an army of 100,000 men so often victorious? I only thought of disbanding the army before returning to the repose of civil life.

"During that rest, which has not been without glory, I enjoyed my honors (such honors as no human power can deprive me of), the recollections of what I had done, the testimony of my conscience, the esteem of my country and of foreigners, and, to be candid, the flattering and pleasant presentiment of the esteem of posterity. My mind and disposition were so well known, and I kept myself so far aloof from any ambitious project, that from the victory of Hohenlinden till my arrest my enemies were never able to accuse me of any crime except freedom in speaking. Do conspirators openly find fault with that which they do not approve? So much candor is scarcely reconcilable with political secrets and plots. If I had wished to adopt and follow the plans of any conspirators, I should have concealed my sentiments, and solicited every appointment which might have restored me to power. As a guide on such a route, in default of the political talent which I have never had, there were examples known to all the world and rendered imposing by success. I might have known that Monk retained command of his armies when he wished to conspire, and that Cassius and Brutus came nearer Cæsar's heart in order to pierce it."

When the pleading was finished, the emperor and the public anxiously waited for the sentence. The fact of the royalist plot being proved, the condemnation of the prisoners was certain, and the inquietude and hopes of all were concentrated on Moreau. "Towards the close of the trial," said Madame Récamier, "all business was stopped, the entire population were out of doors, they talked of nothing but Moreau." The emperor had informed the judges that he would not demand that the general be condemned to death unless in the interest of justice, and as a salutary example, his fixed intention being to grant him pardon. One of the members of the tribunal, Clavier, a man of great virtue and learning, said, on hearing General Murat's proposition, "And who will pardon us ourselves, if we pass judgment and condemnation against our consciences?" At the first deliberation of the tribunal, seven judges out of twelve voted for acquittal pure and simple: being afraid of Napoleon's anger, they sentenced Moreau to two years' imprisonment. "Why, that's a punishment for a pickpocket!" exclaimed the emperor in a passion. By wise counsel he was induced to show a prudent clemency. Moreau, nearly ruined by the expense of the trial, and as annoyed by the sentence as Napoleon was, refused to ask any favor. "If it was certain that I took part in the conspiracy," he exclaimed, "I ought to have been condemned to death as a leader. I undergo the extremity of horror and disgrace. Nobody will believe that I played the part of a corporal."

His young and handsome wife, being near confinement, asked for and obtained permission to sail to America with her husband, and when delayed at Cadiz by child-birth, was urged to set out on the voyage through Fouché's influence in the Spanish court. "Four years ago about this time," wrote the general, "I gained the battle of Hohenlinden. That event, so glorious for my country, procured for my fellow-countrymen a repose which they had long wanted. I alone have been unable to obtain it. Will they refuse it me at the extremity of Europe, 500 leagues from my native land?"

Moreau carried with him into exile the cruel recollection of the name "brigand" (ruffian), which had been formerly abusively replied to him, and that keen desire for vengeance which was one day to prove so fatal to his renown.

Of the royalist prisoners, twenty were condemned to death. In spite of Murat's eager pleading, eleven perished on the scaffold with Georges Cadoudal, equal to him in the imperturbability of their political and religious faith. Rivière and Polignac, General Lajolais, and four others owed their lives to the supplications of their families, judiciously assisted by the kindness of the Empress Josephine. They were all sent to prison.

Napoleon felt with more justice than Moreau himself that the conscience of the judges had been opposed to his supreme will. In spite of the silence which he imposed upon the organs of the press, more and more roughly treated by him, public opinion remained equally stirred up against the murder of the Duc d'Enghien. A thought which had arisen in his mind from the day of his elevation to the empire, gained fresh forces from the feeling of silent disapprobation of all honorable men. He wished to place a religious stamp upon his greatness, and instructed Cardinal Caprara to ask the Pope to come to Paris to consecrate him. " It is most unlikely," said he, " that any power will make objection to it either in right or in fact. Therefore broach the subject, and when you have transmitted the reply, I shall make the suitable and necessary arrangements with the Pope."

As in the case of the Concordat, the emperor's confidential advisers were not favorable to the idea of consecration. The discussion in the Council of State was lively, characterized by all the philosophical and revolutionary suspicion as to the pretensions of a power being invited to bestow the crown and thus probably believing it had the power to withdraw it. Napoleon had formed a better judgment of the profound and permanent effect of the condescension which he asked from the Pope. "Gentlemen," said he to his council, "you are deliberating in Paris in the Tuileries; suppose that you were deliberating in London in the British cabinet, that in a word, you were ministers of the King of England, and that you were told that at this moment the Pope was crossing the Alps to consecrate the Emperor of the French, would you consider that as a triumph for England or for France?"

The council had not insisted, and the court of Rome felt their force of resistance becoming weaker every day. The death of the Duc d'Enghien had caused the Pope much sorrow: —" My tears flow," said Pius VII., " at the death of the one and the attempt upon the other." The French bishops who had not resigned had renewed their protestations against the Concordat. The Sacred College, when consulted as to the journey of the holy father, were divided in their opinion. Five cardinals declared that by so doing the Pope would ratify all the usurpations of which the new Emperor of the French had rendered himself culpable; fifteen showed less severity, but all insisted upon surrounding the solicited favor with numerous conditions. "The actual advantage to religion expressly professed in the invitation which his Holiness is about to accept, but actually injured in the result, can alone excuse

in the eyes of Catholics the temporary abandonment of
the holy seat," wrote Cardinal Consalvi to Cardinal Caprara:
"the dignity and honor of the head of religion both require
it." He also wrote, "The form of oath taken by the emperor
raises great difficulties. We cannot admit the oath *to respect
and caused to be respected the laws of the Concordat,* which is
the same thing as saying that one must respect the organic
articles and cause them to be respected. *To respect the
liberty of worship* supposes an engagement not to tolerate and
allow, but to sustain and protect, and extends not only to persons, but to the thing, that is to say to all forms of worship.
But a Catholic cannot defend the error of false forms of
worship."

Cardinal Caprara, as papal legate in Paris, and Cardinal
Fesch, as French ambassador in Rome, explained away or
avoided the difficulties. The legate, always timid and easily
persuaded, gave grounds for hopes which he was not always
able to realize; the cardinal, haughty and violent, divided
between devotion to his all-powerful nephew and his own
restoration to ecclesiastical practices and sentiments, was at
Rome lavish of presents and threats. He at the same time
advised the court of Rome to claim the Legations, whatever
were the scruples of the Pope to confound temporal questions
with spiritual concessions. Skilful in making use of the real
intentions or wishes which he was aware of, without compromising his government by any formal engagement, Cardinal
Fesch at last triumphed over the repugnances of the Pope by
avoiding most of the conditions of the Holy College, and on
the 30th September, 1804, he presented to Pius VII. General
Caffarelli, the emperor's deputy at Rome, instead of the two
bishops formerly insisted upon. Still less explicit than his
ambassador, Napoleon gave no hopes to the holy father of the
important concessions with which the latter was fondly flattering himself.

"Very Holy Father," said the emperor, "the happy result
evinced in the morality and character of my people by the re-
establishment of the Christian religion, leads me to pray your
Holiness to give me a new proof of the interest which your
Holiness takes in my destiny and that of this great nation, in
one of the most important periods shown in the annals of the
world. I beg your Holiness to come and give a religious
character of the highest degree to the ceremony of the consecration and coronation of the first Emperor of the French. That

ceremony will acquire a new lustre if done by your Holiness. It will bring upon us and our peoples the blessing of God, whose decrees govern according to His will the lot of empires and of families.

"Your Holiness knows the friendly feeling which I have long had towards you, and must therefore infer the pleasure which I shall have in giving you fresh proofs.

"Thereupon we pray God, most holy father, that He may keep you for many years in the rule and government of our mother the holy Church.

" Your devoted son,

" NAPOLEON."

The Pope had determined to set out, being convinced that resistance was impossible, and harassed by a serious inquietude the importance of which was afterwards confirmed, and by the vague fears of a sickly old man. He was offended by the contemptuous terms which the foreign ambassadors applied to the condescension of him whom they called the "French emperor's chaplain." His Italian subtilty was disturbed, and his natural kindness chafed by the dryness of the emperor's message. "This is poison which you have brought to me," said he to General Caffarelli, after reading Napoleon's letter. He set out nevertheless, obstinately refusing to take with him Cardinal Consalvi, in whose hands he had placed his abdication. "If they keep me here," said he one day in Paris, "they will find that they only have in their power a wretched monk called Barnabus Chiaramonti."

The Pope's departure had been much hastened by the repeated urgency of the emperor, and his journey was so also. The time for the ceremony was fixed without consulting him. As Cardinal Consalvi said in his Memoirs, "they made the holy father gallop from Rome to Paris like an almoner summoned by his master to say mass."

On the 25th November, 1804, about mid-day, the emperor was hunting in the forest of Fountainebleau, and went towards Croix St. Herem at the moment when the Pope's carriage just reached that spot. The carriage stopped, and "the holy father stepped out in his white dress; as the road was muddy he could not soil his silk stockings by stepping on the ground." He got out, however, whilst the emperor, leaping from his horse, advanced to him and embraced him. The meeting had been skilfully arranged in order that the new master of France might be spared the annoyance of a deference which he considered excessive. Both doors of the emperor's carriage were opened at once, and Napoleon entering by the right, Pius VII. naturally took the left. The empress and imperial family were waiting for the Pope at the great portico of the palace. The emperor seemed triumphant. The Pope was full of emotion, affected by the kind reception he had met with by the people during his journey. "I have passed through a population all on their knees," said he.

The Emperor Napoleon was not on his knees, and Pius VII. was even sensible of it. Several questions had remained un- decided before the holy father's departure for France: Napo- loon had resolutely disposed of them, and yielded only on one point. Still bandied about between his own uncertainty, the love which he still felt for the Empress Josephine, the intrigues of her family, who were opposed to him, and the passionate longing to have a son to inherit his crown, he had been on the point of demanding a divorce a few days previously, but on the empress making the Pope her confidant their union was confirmed, and on the eve of the coronation, with the greatest secrecy, the religious marriage of the emperor with Josephine was celebrated by Cardinal Fesch. Pius VII. declared that it was impossible for him to proceed with the ceremony of the double consecration so long as that act of reparation remained unaccomplished.

Those who had charge of the arrangements for the great spectacle, the Abbé Bernier, lately appointed Bishop of Or- leans, and the Arch-chancellor Cambacérès, had frequently discussed the ceremonial of the coronation properly so-called. In France the peers, in Italy the bishops, formerly held the crown above the head of the sovereign, who then received it from the hands of the pontiff. "All the French emperors, all those of Germany who have been consecrated by the popes were at the same crowned by them. The holy father, in order to decide as to the journey, must receive from Paris the as- surance that in this case there will be no innovation contrary to the honor and dignity of the sovereign pontiff." At Rome the replies had been vague; at Paris the emperor had calmed the zeal and inquietude of his servants. "I shall arrange that myself," said he. On the 2nd December, 1804, the ceremony of consecration took place according to the solemn ceremonial, and the emperor, after being anointed with the holy oil, held out his hand towards the crown which the Pope had just taken from the altar. Pius VII., completely taken by surprise, made no resistance, and Napoleon himself placing on his head the emblem of sovereign power, then crowned with his own hands the empress, who was in tears kneeling before him. Mounting his throne whilst his brothers held up his robe, being compelled to that act of humility by his imperious will, and their sisters bore the train of the empress, the Pope pronounced the solemn formula, " Vivat in æternum Augustus!" And under the very eyes of the holy pontiff, the Emperor Napoleon took the oath in the form which had been so much opposed in Rome. His victory was complete: he triumphed over the old revolutionary prejudices, whilst at the same time confirming in Notre Dame, in spite of the scruples of the court of Rome, the principles of liberty acquired by the French Revolution.

When the Pope, sad and discouraged, at last set out for Rome, 4th April, 1805, he had obtained none of the favors which he thought he had a right to expect. The emperor was inflexible on the question of the " organic articles," making no concession as to their application. The statement presented by the Pope and drawn up by Cardinal Antonelli, the most enthusiastic of his councillors, was on Napoleon's orders replied to by Portalis, who was skilful in concealing the refusal under the grave phraseology of legal and Christian language. Urged to extremity, Pius VII. applied to the emperor himself to ask the restoration of the Legations. Talleyrand wrote in reply, "France has very dearly bought the power which she enjoys. It is not in the emperor's power to take anything from an empire which is the fruit of ten years' war and bloodshed, continued with an admirable courage and accompanied with the most unhappy agitation and an unexampled constancy. It is still less in his power to diminish the territory of a foreign state which, by entrusting him with the care of governing, had laid upon him the duty of protecting it." A few sentences added by the emperor to the diplomatic document left room for vague hopes of certain consolations. The illusions of Pius VII. began to disappear; without compensation or recompense, he had worked to consolidate for a short time the throne of the conqueror; the conquests which he had won were not of this world; the complete submission of the constitutional bishops, and the genuine respect with which the French people constantly surrounded him were due to the personal veneration which he inspired. When at last he crossed the mountains the Emperor Napoleon had reached Italy before him, as if to indicate more emphatically the condescension which the sovereign pontiff had shown to him. It was at Turin that he finally took leave of Pius VII., letting him return to Rome while he took in the cathedral of Milan the iron crown of the Lombard kings, and placed it on his head before an immense crowd of on-lookers, using the traditional words of the ancient Lombard monarchy, "God has given it me, who dare touch it?"

The Cisalpine Republic no longer existed, and the Emperor of the French, King of Italy, boasted of the moderation he had evinced in keeping the two crowns apart. At one time he intended raising his brother Joseph to the new throne, but the latter was afraid of compromising his right to succeed to the imperial crown. Louis Bonaparte refused to govern in the name of the child which he had by Hortense de Beauharnais, daughter of the Empress Josephine by her first marriage, whom he had married with regret. Compelled to unite, on his own head, the two crowns of France and Italy, Napoleon entrusted the care of the government to his son-in-law, Eugene de Beauharnais. His protestations of respect for the independence of the allied peoples did not prevent his annexing to the kingdom of Italy the territory of Genoa, whilst forming the domains of Lucca and Piombino into a principality in favor of his eldest sister, Elisa Baciocchi. The storm was already threatening the feeble government of Naples: the queen, obsequious in her alarm, had sent to Milan an ambassador to congratulate the emperor and king. "Tell your queen," exclaimed Napoleon, "that her intrigues are known to me, and that her children will curse her memory, for I shall not leave in her kingdom enough of land to build her tomb upon."

So much brilliance and severity in the display of his sovereign power proved of service to the irreconcilable enemies who were stirring up Europe against the already uncontrollable ambition of the new emperor. Pitt had already returned to power (19th May, 1804), though with less support in Parliament, and very infirm in health. He felt himself sustained by the breath of public opinion, and by the firm confidence of the mass of the nation. In this great duel, of which he was not to see the end, it was the consolation, as well as the honor of the illustrious minister, that he had constantly defended the principles of true liberty, as well as European independence,

JOSÉPHINE.

EMPRESS OF FRANCE.

against the encroachments and contagion of the revolutionary powers, and those of anarchy or absolutism.

It was in the name of the same principles that the young Emperor of Russia then proposed to Europe a mediation which was soon to end in a coalition. Generously chimerical in his inexperience, Alexander dreamt of a general rearrangement of Europe, which was to secure forever the peace of every nation. Poland itself was to be reconstituted, Italy and Germany to recover their independence, and a new code of the rights of nations on sea and land was to regulate the relations of civilized states. Nowosiltzoff was entrusted to discuss this scheme with Pitt.

It was by the prudence and skilful tact of the English minister that the scaffolding of ambitious hopes was overthrown, and the Emperor Alexander brought to the practical consideration of a durable alliance. England and Russia engaged to carry out the formation of a great European league and the legitimate re-establishment of the states. Hanover and Northern Germany were to be evacuated, the independence of Holland and Switzerland guaranteed, the King of Piedmont re-established, the kingdom of Naples consolidated, Italy delivered. In order to bring Prussia into that alliance, Pitt proposed to grant him the Rhenish provinces. He refused formally to evacuate Malta, and pleaded the English prejudices against the Russian overtures with reference to the Turkish territory. The Emperor Alexander still hoped to obtain important concessions from Napoleon. Trusting in his sincere disinterestedness, the young monarch had got Prussia to ask passports for his envoy; Napoleon was in Italy, and said he could not receive Nowosiltzoff before July. "I expect nothing from this mediation," he wrote to the King of Prussia: "Alexander is too fickle and feeble; Russia is too far, too foreign to colonial and maritime interests; the Woronzovs too much influenced by English money, for one to have reasonable hopes of an advantageous general peace. Whenever propositions are passed at St. Petersburg to reach Paris, there is no wish to come to an understanding: in London they wish to gain time, dazzle the eyes of all the peoples, and perhaps form a coalition which should bring disgrace upon England. My brother, I wish for peace, but I do not wish to agree to my people being disinherited of the commerce of the world. I have no ambition: I have twice evacuated the third part of Europe without being compelled to do so. I owe Russia no more as to Italian affairs than she owes me with reference to Turkish and Persian affairs. Russia has not the right to take that tone with anybody, and with me still less than with anybody whatever."

The Emperor Napoleon had already given his reply to Europe. The annexation of the territory of Genoa, and the threat to the Neapolitan government sufficiently proved his intentions. The treaty provisionally signed on the 11th April between England and the Emperor Alexander was confirmed; and on the 9th August, Austria, which already had a secret engagement with Russia, adhered to the Anglo-Russian alliance. Sweden joining soon after, the third coalition was now complete. Prussia remained as a common object for the negotiations and advances of all. Napoleon gave her hopes of obtaining Hanover.

He had just set out for Boulogne, always the centre of his adventurous plans. Already in the previous year he believed that he had reached the accomplishment of the project so carefully matured and prepared with that mixture of foresight and boldness which so often secured the unexpected success of his attempts. His enormous preparations were at last completed, the Dutch squadron alone being waited for; and the emperor deceived the impatience of his troops and his own agitation by reviews and military ceremonies. On the 2nd July, he wrote to Admiral Latouche-Tréville, whom he had put in command of his Toulon squadron: "By the same messenger let me know on what day you will weigh anchor. Let me know also what the enemy is doing, and where Nelson is located. Reflect upon the great enterprise which you are about to execute, and before I sign your definite orders let me understand the manner in which you think they would be most advantageously carried into effect. I have appointed you Grand Officer of the Empire, Inspector of the Coasts of the Mediterranean; but I desire much that the operation you are about to undertake may enable me to elevate you to such a degree of consideration and honor, that you may have nothing more to desire. The squadron of Rochefort (commanded by Admiral Villeneuve), composed of five vessels, of which one is a three-decker, and of four frigates, is ready to weigh anchor; it has before it only five of the enemy's ships. The squadron of Brest (commanded by Admiral Ganteaume) is of twenty-one ships; these ships have just weighed anchor in order to harass the enemy and compel him to keep there a large number of vessels. The enemy have also six ships before the Texel, and there blockade the Dutch squadron, consisting of eight vessels, four frigates, and a convoy of thirty ships in which the corps of General Marmont is embarked. Between Etaples, Boulogne, Wimereux and Ambleteuse (two new ports which I have constructed) we have 1800 gun-boats of various kinds, and 120,000 men, and 10,000 horses; only let us be masters of the strait for six hours, and we shall be the masters of the world.

"The enemy have before Boulogne, before Ostend, and at the Downs, two ships of seventy-four guns, two of sixty-four guns, and two or three of fifty guns. Until now Admiral Cornwallis has had only fifteen vessels, but all the reserves from Plymouth and Portsmouth have come to reinforce him before Brest.

"The enemy keep also at Cork, in Ireland, four or five ships of war; I do not speak of frigates or small vessels, of which they have a large number. If you deceive Nelson, he will go to Sicily or to Egypt or to Ferrol. It would then appear to me best to make a considerable roundabout, and arrive before Rochefort; thus making your squadron one of sixteen ships and eleven frigates; and then, without dropping anchor or losing a single instant, arrive before Boulogne. Our squadron at Brest, twenty-three vessels strong, will have on board an army, and will be constantly under sail set, so that Cornwallis will be obliged to press close to the shore of Brittany in order to try and prevent the escape of our fleet. For the rest, in order to fix my ideas upon this operation, which has its risks, but of which the success offers results so enormous, I wait for the scheme you have mentioned to me, and which you will send me by return of the courier. You must embark as many provisions as possible, so that under any circumstances you may have nothing to hinder you."

It is the weakness as well as the honor of human enterprises to depend upon the life and force of a man. Before Admiral Latouche-Tréville had been able to profit by the occurrence of the mistral to get out of Toulon and deceive Nelson, he himself succumbed to the illness that had preyed upon him since the expedition of San Domingo (20th August, 1804), and the projected expedition against the coast of England was indefinitely postponed. "The flotilla has been looked upon as temporary," wrote the Emperor to Decrès, the Minister of Marine; "it will be necessary henceforth to look upon it as a fixed estab-

lishment, and from this moment to give the greatest attention
to all that is unchangeable, managing it by other regulations
than the squadron."

It was at the same time the plan of the emperor to try to turn
away the thoughts of the English from his schemes of invasion; in the midst of his arangements for the coronation, and
of the diplomatic negotiations, and whilst writing a private
letter to the King of England, pompously proposing peace, he
had formed other designs and prepared new plans in order at
last to carry out his great enterprise.

It was no longer on the coasts of France or of Spain, but far
away in the regions of the Antilles that the French squadrons
of Toulon, Brest, and Rochefort were to effect their junction
and concentrate their forces. The hope of Napoleon was to
see the English, deceived by their disappearance, dash off in
pursuit of them and rush to the succor of the Indies. The
emperor had for a moment thought of directing the blows of
his united navy against this distant and new formed empire.
Returning to the project of the descent on England, he had
made Admiral Villeneuve set out directly after the 30th of
March. He was to join at Cadiz the Spanish Admiral Gravina
and at Martinique, Admiral Missiessy, who had left Rochefort
on the 11th of January. Admiral Ganteaume, taking advantage of the first moment when the English should be obliged
by contrary winds to withdraw from Brest, was in his turn to
set sail for Martinique. The fleet, which would then be fifty
or sixty strong, assured of triumphing over all the English
forces if they should dare to face it, would return into the
channel to cover the departure of the flotilla. "The English
do not know what calamity awaits them," wrote Napoleon on
the 4th of August to the Admiral Decrès. "If we are masters
of the passage for twelve hours, England's day is done."

Racine has said by the mouth of Mithridates,—

> " Mais, pour être approuvés,
> De semblables projets veulent être achevés."

Villeneuve quoted it to the Minister of Marine when the plans
formed by the emperor were confided to him. This mournful
forecast haunted, no doubt, more than once the thoughts of
the admiral when he found himself at sea, discontented and
uneasy. "We have bad masts, bad sails, bad rigging, bad
officers, and bad sailors," said he. Arrived, on the 14th of
May, at Martinique, he found Missiessy no longer there, but
his orders obliged him to await the arrival of Ganteaume. A

continuous calm prevented the latter from leaving Brest, where he was blockaded by the English. At the two ends of the world, discouragement weighed upon the admirals consigned to in-action by unforeseen obstacles met with in the execution of a plan which took no account of accidents of wind or sea. In vain wrote Napoleon to Ganteaume, " You hold in your hands the destinies of the world." The unfortunate commander of the Brest squadron communicated his despair to the Minister of Marine: "I believe, my friend, that you share all my experience. Every day that passes is a day of torment for me; and I tremble lest at the end I should be obliged to commit some gross folly. The length of the days and the beauty of the season cause me to despair of the expedition." In the middle of May, Admiral Magon was despatched to Martinique to give Villeneuve orders to return with his squadron, to raise the blockade of Ferrol, to touch at Rochefort, and join Admiral Missiessy, and then to present themselves before Brest in order to force the blockade with the aid of Ganteaume. The united fleets were then to set sail towards the channel.

Upon land, and until the day when success and presumption disturbed the clearness of his judgment, and the penetrating light of his genius, Napoleon was accustomed to judge soberly of the obstacles he calculated on overcoming, and of his power to do so. Without maritime experience, and struggling against the recognized superiority of the English navy, he constantly committed the error of counting on the mistakes of the enemy and of looking on the chiefs of his squadrons as equal in talent to Nelson. No sooner had the latter learnt the direction of Villeneuve than he dashed off in pursuit, caring little as to the number of vessels he might have to confront. Napoleon had miscalculated the length of the voyage. "Nelson will have been first to Surinam, thence to Trinidad, and from that to Barbadoes," wrote he on the 28th of June to Admiral Decrès; "he will lose two days at Cape Verd; he will lose much time in collecting his ships, on account of the vessels and frigates to which he will give chase on his way. When he learns that Villeneuve is not in the Windward Islands he will go to Jamaica, and during the days lost in provisioning and waiting, great blows will be struck. This is my calculation. Nelson is in America and Collingwood in the East Indies. Nelson will not venture before Martinique; he will stay at Barbadoes in order to plan a junction with Cochrane."

VII.—8

Nelson had already quitted Barbadoes and was pursuing his adversary from anchorage to anchorage. Troubled by this formidable proximity, and pressed by the formal orders which enjoined him to transfer his efforts to the seas of Europe, Villeneuve crowded all sail to reach Ferrol. Nelson soon followed him, directing his course towards the Mediterranean, but careful to warn the Admirality, who sent Admiral Calder with fifteen vessels to the neighborhood of Cape Finisterre. It was in these waters that Villeneuve encountered Nelson on July 22nd, 1805. The weather was foggy, and the sea rough; the engagement ended without any important result, two Spanish vessels being captured by the English. Villeneuve set sail speedily towards Ferrol, without entering the Channel, the order having arrived to take his course to Brest immediately; but he lingered at Corunna, persuaded that Nelson had joined Admiral Calder, and that both would combine with Lord Cornwallis for his destruction. In again taking to sea, he let it be thought that he was setting out for Brest; General Lauriston, aide-de-camp to the emperor, and who had accompanied Villeneuve in his expedition, wrote so immediately to the emperor. But the discouragement of Villeneuve, more profound than ever, showed itself in a letter to his friend, Admiral Decrès. "They make me the arbiter of the highest interests," wrote he; "my despair doubles in proportion as more confidence is placed in me, because I cannot pretend to any success, whatever plan I adopt. It is perfectly plain to me that the fleets of France and Spain cannot be effective in large squadrons. Divisions of three or four, or five at the most, are all that we are capable of conducting. Let Ganteaume get out, and he will judge the point. Public opinion will be settled. I am about to set out, but I know not what I shall do. Eight vessels are in view of the coast at a few leagues' distance. They will follow us, but I shall not be able to join them, and they will go to unite with the other squadrons before Brest or Cadiz, according as I make my way to one or other of those ports. I am far from being in a position, in leaving this place with twenty-nine vessels, to be able to fight against a similar number; I do not fear to tell you that I should be hard put to it to encounter twenty."

For three weeks past the emperor had been at Boulogne, consumed with impatience, exercising the troops every day, repeating the manœuvres of embarkation, his attention fixed upon the sea, and ready to deliver his flotilla and his army to the mercy of the waves as soon as his squadrons should at last appear in the Channel. The days sped by; in vain ships after ships were hurried off to Admiral Villeneuve, bearing the most urgent orders. "If you run up here in three days, if only for twenty-four hours, your mission would be accomplished. The English are not so numerous as you think; they are everywhere detained by the wind. Never will a squadron have run a few risks with so great an end, and never will our soldiers have had the chance on land or sea to shed their blood for a grander or nobler result. For the great object of aiding a descent upon that power which for six centuries has oppressed France, we ought all to die without regret."

The Minister of Marine, clever and experienced in naval affairs, endowed with a cold and prudent spirit, had never approved the projects of Napoleon, and had constantly sought to turn him from them. The conviction which was firmly rooted in the mind of Decrès as to the impossibility of success, in connection with the sorrowful discouragement which impelled Villeneuve towards Cadiz instead of towards Brest, increased the uneasiness as well as the anger of the emperor. Located in barracks by the seashore, whilst Napoleon resided at the Chateau du Pont de Briques, Decrès wrote to his terrible master: "I throw myself at the feet of your Majesty, to beseech of you not to associate the Spanish vessels with the operations of the squadrons. Far from having gained anything in this respect, your Majesty hears that this association would add to the vessels of Cadiz and Carthagena. In this state of things, in which your Majesty counts as nothing my arguments and experience, I know of no situation that would be more painful than mine. I desire your Majesty to take seriously into consideration that I have no other interest than that of your banner and the honor of your arms: and if your fleet is at Cadiz, I beseech you to consider this event as an act of destiny which reserves it for other operations. I implore you not to cause it to come from Cadiz into the channel, because the attempt at this moment would only be attended by misfortunes. I reproach myself with not being able to persuade your Majesty. I doubt if a single man could succeed in doing so. Deign to form a council upon maritime affairs—an admiralty, of those who may suit your Majesty, but as for me, I perceive that in place of growing stronger, I grow weaker every day. And it cannot but be true that a Minister of Marine, overruled by your Majesty in naval affairs, becomes useless for the glory of your arms, if, indeed, not positively hurtful."

A single word from the emperor was the reply to the despairing letter of his minister:—"Raise yourself to the height of the circumstances and of the situation in which France and England now find themselves; never again write me a letter like that which you have written to me; it is not to the purpose. As for me, I have only need of one thing, and that is to succeed."

In the depth of his soul, and in his secret thoughts, Napoleon saw himself conquered by a concurrence of circumstances which he had not been willing to foresee. His anger continued violent against the instrument who had failed him in his imprudent designs; he asked Decrès, however, what should be his plans in case Admiral Villeneuve were found at Cadiz, which he still refused to believe. On August 13th he wrote to Talleyrand: "The more I reflect upon the state of Europe, the more I see how urgent it is to take a decisive part. I have in reality nothing to expect from the explanations of Austria. She will answer by fine phrases and gain time, in order that I may not be able to act this winter. Her treaty of subsidies and her act of coalition will be signed this winter under the pretext of an armed neutrality, and in April I shall find 100,000 Russians in Poland, provided by England with equipment of horses, artillery, etc., 15,000 to 20,000 English at Malta, and 15,000 Russians at Corfu. I shall find myself then in a critical situation. My decision is taken. My fleet left Ferrol on the 29th Thermidor with thirty-four vessels. It had no enemy in sight. If it followed its instructions, joined itself to the squadron at Brest and entered the Channel, there is yet time, and I am master of England. If, on the contrary, my admirals hesitate, manœuvre badly, and do not accomplish their purpose, I have no other resource than to wait for the winter to cross with the flotilla. The plan is a hazardous one. It would be more so if, pressed by circumstances, political events placed me under the obligation of passing over in the month of April. In this state of things I rush to the point where I am most needed; I raise my camps, and replace my war battalions with my third battalion, always an army sufficiently formidable for Boulogne; and on the 1st Vendemiaire I find myself with 200,000 men in Germany, and 25,000 men in the kingdom of Naples. I march upon Vienna, and I do not lay down my arms till I have taken Naples and Venice, and have so augmented the States of the Elector of Bavaria that I shall have nothing to fear from Austria. She will in this manner be certainly pacified for the winter. I return to Paris, but to be off again immediately."

It was always one of the sources of power of the Emperor Napoleon, and perhaps the rarest among them, that the marvellous fecundity of his mind, and the inexhaustible variety of the projects and conceptions which he was constantly turning over, reciprocally sustained and complemented each other. This characteristic of his genius has been ignored; and little honor has been done to his foresight when he has been depicted as taken in some degree unawares by the failure of his maritime plans, and constrained to improvise by a supreme effort the direction of his campaign in Germany. In the last days of August, whilst he was still uncertain as to the movements of his squadrons, all the orders were already given for the concentration of his armies. Bernadotte was to proceed to Göttingen with the army of Hanover; Prince Eugène was collecting his forces on the Adige; Gouvion St. Cyr was ready to march upon Naples; and Marmont to advance from the Texel upon Mayence. General Duroc had set out for Berlin, commissioned to propose an alliance. "My intention is not to leave Austria and Russia to combine with England," said Napoleon. "My conduct in that event would be that of the great Frederic in his first war." He wrote to Marshal Berthier on August 25th: "The decisive moment has arrived; you know how important a day is in this affair. Austria restrains herself no longer; she believes, without doubt, that we are all drowned in the ocean."

Doubt was no longer possible; time was flying, and no news arrived of the squadron. Villeneuve had evidently retired to Cadiz. The violence and injustice of the emperor's utterances vexed Decrès beyond expression. "Villeneuve is a wretch, who ought to be ignominiously discharged," cried he; "he has neither contrivance, nor courage, nor public interest; he would sacrifice everything provided that he could save his skin." He broke out thus before Monge, for whom he had retained a true friendship, notwithstanding the known opinions of the savant, who had remained republican. Troubled by the anger of Napoleon, Monge went to apprise Daru, then principal Secretary of War, who presented himself before the emperor. Badly informed as to the intentions of the master and the causes of his discontent, he waited silently. The emperor, coming up to

him, exclaimed, "Do you know where Villeneuve is? He is at
Cadiz." And, unfolding before Daru all the projects he had
been cherishing for six months, and attributing their failure to
the cowardice and incapacity of the men he had employed, he
launched out into invectives and recriminations. All of a sudden, and as if he had relieved his soul by the outburst of his
passion, "Sit down there," said he to Daru, "and write!" A
powerful effort, and the natural play of a fruitful imagination,
had recalled him to the combinations which were to make his
enemies tremble, and to assure him of the triumph over Austria of which he had been baulked as regards England. The
plan of his campaign was fixed; all his thoughts turned towards
a dreadful execution of his will.

The secret had been carefully guarded, and already, on all
sides, the French armies were threatening the enemy, when,
on the 1st Vendemiaire, the emperor opened the session of the
Senate. "The wishes of the eternal enemies of the Continent
are fulfilled," said he. "War has broken out in the centre of
Germany; Austria and Russia are leagued with England; and
our generation is dragged once more into all the calamities of
war. A few days ago I still hoped that peace might not be
broken; menaces and outrages found me impassive; but the
Austrian army has passed the Inn, Munich is invaded, the
Elector of Bavaria is driven from his capital, all my hopes
have vanished. Senators, when, at your desire, at the call of
the entire French people, I placed upon my head the imperial
crown, I received from you, and from all citizens, the promise
to maintain it pure and without blemish. All the promises I
have made to you I have kept; the French people in their turn
have made no engagement with me which they have not even
surpassed. Frenchmen, your emperor will do his duty; my
soldiers will do theirs; you will do yours."

General Mack had entered Ulm, and the emperor was still at
Saint-Cloud. The movements of our troops were quietly going
forward, when Napoleon conceived the idea of surrounding the
enemy in Suabia by cutting off his communications with Austria. A note in his own handwriting, written on the 22nd of
September, indicates beforehand the positions of all the corps
of the army. On the 27th he arrived at Strasburg, prolonging
his residence there in order to deceive the Austrian general,
who kept his attention constantly fixed upon the Black Forest.
On the 30th, at Strasburg, the emperor addressed to his troops
a simple and firm proclamation, animated by that martial

DUROC.

DUC DE FRIOUL.

spirit which always inspired the army when he addressed it. "Soldiers, the war of the third coalition has commenced. The Austrian army has passed the Inn, broken the treaties, attacked our ally, and sent him from his capital. You yourselves have been compelled to hasten, by forced marches, to the defence of our frontiers. But already you have passed the Rhine. We will not stay our progress until we have assured the independence of the Germanic state, succored our allies, and confounded the pride of the unjust aggressors. We will have no more peace without a guarantee. Our generosity shall not again deceive our policy. Soldiers, your emperor is in the midst of you; you are only the vanguard of the great people. If it is necessary, they will rise as one man, to confound and dissolve this new league woven by the hatred and the gold of England. But, soldiers, we have forced marches to make, fatigues and privations of every kind to endure. Whatever obstacles may be opposed to us we shall be victorious, and we will take no rest till we have planted our eagles upon the territory of our enemies."

Napoleon had said, "I reckon on making more use of the legs of my soldiers than even of their bayonets." The fatal circle was narrowing round General Mack by the rapid movements of the French troops, without his appearing to comprehend their aim, or divine the danger which threatened him. On the 8th of October he still wrote, that never had an army been posted in a manner more fitted to assure its superiority. On the same day, advancing upon Günzburg, Marshals Lannes and Murat encountered at Wutingen an Austrian corps, which was tardily marching to the succor of General Kienmayer, already dislodged from the bridges of the Danube and the Lech. The engagement was short and brilliant; the fugitives bore at length to Ulm the conviction of the overwhelming forces which menaced the Austrian army. The Emperor Napoleon had arrived at Donauwerth. The first bulletin from the Grand Army was dated October 7th, explaining all the military operations: "This grand and vast movement has carried us in a few days to Bavaria; has enabled us to avoid the Black Mountains, the line of parallel rivers which fall into the Danube, and the inconvenience of a system of operations which would have always had the defiles of the Tyrol on the flank; and lastly, has placed us several marches in the rear of the enemy, who has no time to lose to avoid his entire destruction."

Napoleon was particularly watchful with respect to the

Tyrol, for he had settled in his own mind that General Mack
would seek an outlet on this side, to escape from the blockade
with which he was menaced.   The little German princes, terrified or won over, had submitted to the yoke of Napoleon, and
accepted his alliance; the French troops had violated neutral
territories with impunity; the Russian armies were at last
making forced marches, and had just entered into Germany.
At one moment Mack appeared to discover the feeble point in
the enemy's line; the left bank of the Danube at Albech, was
occupied by the divisions of Dupont and Baraguey d'Hilliers,
insufficient for resisting a violent attack.   Murat, who commanded the three divisions posted near Ulm, ordered Ney to
recall all the troops posted on the left bank.   The marshal was
indignant and furious, but obeyed; but General Dupont had
not accomplished his movement when he was assailed by a
corps of 25,000 Austrians, commanded by the Archduke Ferdinand.   The heroic resistance of the French troops enabled
them to fall back upon Albech with 1500 prisoners.   The enemy
contented themselves with occupying the little town of Elchingen, and burning the bridge.

Napoleon had quitted Augsburg, and Marshal Soult had just
effected the capitulation of Meiningen.   The emperor ordered
Ney to retake the positions of Elchingen.   The piles of the
bridge had not been burnt, and under the fire of the Austrians
the platform was replaced, and the troops rushed forward to
the attack on the village.   The convent which crowned the
height was taken at the bayonet's point.   Always pushing the
enemy before him, Ney seized upon the heights of Michelsberg;
the fire of his cannons commanded the grand square in Ulm.
The emperor in person had just arrived at the camp.

The Archduke Ferdinand had succeeded in escaping during
the night.   In spite of a frightful tempest he gained Biberach,
and rejoined Wernek in Bohemia.   Murat pursued him, while
Marshal Soult occupied Biberach.

Henceforth Mack found himself without resources.   "The
general-in-chief was in the city," said the sixth bulletin of the
grand army.   "It is the destiny of generals opposed to the
emperor to be taken in town.   It will be remembered that
after the splendid manœuvres of the Brenta, the old Field-
Marshal Wurmser was made prisoner at Mantua; Melas was
taken in Alexandria; so is Mack in Ulm."

The emperor caused the Prince of Lichtenstein, major-general of the Austrian army, to be summoned.   "I desire" said

he "that the place capitulate; if I take it by assault, I shall be compelled to do what I did at Jaffa, where the garrison was put to the sword. It is the sad law of war. I desire that the necessity for such a frightful act should be spared to me, as well as to the brave Austrian nation. The place is not tenable."

Mack consented to surrender if he was not succored before the 25th of October. The rain fell in torrents. For eight days the emperor had not taken off his boots. The Austrian prisoners were astonished to see him, "soaked, covered with mud, as much fatigued as the lowest drummer in his army, and even more so." An aide-de-camp repeated to Napoleon the remarks of the enemy's officers. Napoleon replied quickly, "Your master has been desirous of making me remember that I am a soldier," said he. "I hope he will be convinced that the throne and the imperial purple have not made me forget my first business."

Wernek had laid down his arms at Nordlingen; the archduke was fleeing into Bohemia before the cavalry of Murat: the corps of Jellachich in the Tyrol, and that of Kienmayer beyond the Inn, could send no succors to General Mack. Urged to escape the horror of the situation, he forestalled the day fixed for the capitulation: on the 20th of October, 1805, the garrison at Ulm, which still counted 24,000 or 25,000 men, defiled slowly before the conqueror. The troops were prisoners of war, the cannons and flags had been abandoned; seven lieutenant-generals, eight generals, and the general-in-chief, Mack, kept at the emperor's side, were present with death in their souls at the ceremonial which proved their defeat. "In fifteen days we have finished a campaign," said the proclamation of Napoleon to his soldiers. "That which we proposed is completed. We have driven the troops of the House of Austria from Bavaria, and re-established our ally in the sovereignty of his States. That army which, with as much ostentation as imprudence, came forward to place itself on our frontiers, is annihilated. But what matters it to England? Her purpose is answered; we are not at Boulogne, and the subsidy which she grants to Austria will be neither larger nor smaller."

England resented the defeat of her ally more keenly than Napoleon acknowledged in the bitterness of his hate. The rumor of the capitulation of Ulm had reached London. On November 2nd, Lord Malmesbury was seated at table beside Pitt, and spoke to him of the rumors he had heard. "Don't believe a word of it; it is simply a lie," said Pitt, roughly, raising his voice so as to make himself heard by those around him. "But the next day, Sunday, the 3rd," continues Lord Malmesbury in his journal, "he entered my house with Lord Mulgrave, about one o'clock, and they brought with them a Dutch journal which contained at full length the capitulation of Ulm. Neither of them knew that language, and all the officials were away. I translated the article as well as I could, and I saw very clearly the effect that it produced upon Pitt, in spite of the efforts he made to hide it. This was the last time that I saw him. This visit left upon me a profound impression, his manners and countenance were so altered; I conceived from it, in spite of myself, the sad presentiment of the misfortune which threatened us."

Pitt was again, for one day only, to taste for an instant of patriotic joy, bitterly mingled with regret. In spite of the bravery to which Napoleon did not always render justice, the French sailors, inexperienced and badly commanded, had alone failed in the great projects confided to them, and thwarted the hopes of the emperor. Before setting out for Strasburg he had ordered the fleet at Brest to make several cruises, and the fleet at Cadiz to take the soldiers it had on board to the support of the movement of Gouvion St. Cyr in the Bay of Naples. "It might seize an English vessel and a Russian frigate which are to be found there: it could remain in the waters near Naples all the time necessary to do the greatest possible harm to the enemy and intercept the convoy which he is projecting to send to Malta. After this expedition it will return to Toulon, where it will effect for me a powerful diversion. I estimate then that it is necessary to do two things, first to send a special message to Admiral Villeneuve, ordering him to effect this manœuvre; second, as his excessive pusillanimity will hinder him from undertaking it, you will send Admiral Rosily to replace him. He will be the bearer of letters enjoining upon Admiral Villeneuve to return to France, to render an account of his conduct."

The minister of Marine was a friend of Villeneuve, and in announcing to him the departure of Admiral Rosily, he did not make him acquainted with his own disgrace. Leaving the consequences to chance, he had given up the endeavor to influence the imperious will of Napoleon with regard to the squadrons, and he dared not give instructions to Villeneuve. Villeneuve divined what his friend hid from him. "The sailors of Paris and the departments will be very unworthy and very foolish if they cast a stone at me," wrote he to Decrès. "They will have themselves prepared the condemnation which will strike them later on. Let them come on board the squadrons, and they will see against what elements they are exposed to fight. For the rest, if the French marine, as is maintained, has only failed in daring, the emperor will shortly be satisfied, and may count upon the most brilliant successes."

In the middle of October, without having united with the Spanish squadron of Carthagena, nor the vessels which he had formerly imprudently detached under the orders of Captain Allemand, Villeneuve left Cadiz in company with Admiral Gravina and some Spanish vessels. The latter were large and heavy, difficult to manoeuvre, and fitted with very second-rate crews. The squadron of battle, commanded by Admiral Villeneuve and the Spanish Vice-Admiral Alava, numbered twenty-one vessels. The squadron of reserve, composed of twelve vessels, had been placed under the orders of Admiral Gravina.

The forces of Nelson numerically equalled those of Villeneuve, but they were infinitely superior to his in the quality of the vessels and their crews. The illustrious English admiral was ill; for several weeks he had sought repose in England. When he offered to resume the command of the fleet, he was impressed with the idea that he should not again see his country. He called upon the workman entrusted with making a coffin, which Captain Hollowell had ordered to be made from a fragment of the keel of the French vessel *L'Orient.** "Engrave the history of this coffin on the plate," said he; "I shall probably have need of it before long." When at length he appeared on board, the sailors cheered him as the assurance of victory. The English admiral had carefully concealed the number of his vessels, fearing Villeneuve might hesitate in view of his forces. On the 21st the Franco-Spanish fleet was entirely at sea, sailing in order of battle. The English had formed in two lines; Admiral Collingwood, upon the *Royal Sovereign*, commanded the first; Nelson, on board the *Victory*, directed the second. He had given orders to bear down upon the French lines in order to cut them. "The part of the enemy's fleet that you leave out of the fight," said he, "will come with difficulty to the assistance of the part attacked, and you will have conquered before it arrives." The same signal was hoisted all over the fleet, "England expects that every man will do his

---

* *L'Orient*, commanded by Admiral Brueys, foundered at Aboukir.

duty." Villeneuve had not less nobly announced his intentions to his officers. " You need not wait for signals from the admiral," were his orders : " in the confusion of a naval battle it is often impossible to see what is going forward, or to give orders, or above all to get them understood. Each one ought to listen only to the voice of honor, and throw himself into the place of greatest danger. Every captain is at his post if he is under fire." It was the misfortune of Admiral Villeneuve in the battle of Trafalgar, that he did not adhere to his original instructions. Gravina asked for authority to manœuvre in an independent manner. Villeneuve objected, and ordered him to place himself in line. Already at midday Admiral Collingwood, separated from his column by the superior swiftness of the *Royal Sovereign*, engaged so hotly in battle with the *Santa Anna*, the flag-ship of the Spaniard Alava, that he soon found himself in the midst of the enemy. " See how that brave Collingwood hurls himself into action," said Nelson to his flag-officers ; whilst on his own deck, in the midst of the bullets that rained around him, Collingwood cried, " Nelson would give all the world to be here." The greater number of the Spanish captains offered a feeble resistance, and Collingwood had already cut the line of battle. Gravina, upon the *Prince-des-Asturies*, was surrounded by English vessels. The *Fougueux*, the *Pluton*, the *Algésiras*, commanded by Rear-Admiral Magon, heroically resisted overwhelming attacks. The *Redoutable*, the *Santissima-Trinidad,* and the Frenchflag-ship the *Bucentaure*, crowded in upon each other, waited for the assault of the second column, which Nelson brought against them. Like Collingwood, he had got in advance of his squadron. The officers had begged of him to leave the vanguard to the *Temeraire*. " I am quite willing," said Nelson, " that the *Temeraire* should get in front if it can ;" and spreading all sail on board the *Victory*, he advanced first against the enemy. Already his topmast had been struck, and fifty men placed *hors de combat*. The English admiral had given orders to separate the *Redoutable* from the *Bucentaure* ; but Captain Lucas, who commanded the former vessel, profited by a slight breath of wind, and his bowsprit touched the stern of the *Bucentaure*. Nelson then engaged the *Redoutable*, dashing against it with a shock so violent that both vessels were thrown out of the line ; the *Bucentaure* and the *Santissima-Trinidad* were also surrounded by the English. The struggle continued between Nelson and his courageous adversary ; the flames were breaking out every moment upon the French vessel. "Hardy, this is too hot to last long," said Nelson to his flag-captain. Presently a ball from the topmast of the *Redoutable* struck the illustrious sailor in the loins. He fell, still supporting himself by one hand. "Hardy, they have done for me now," said he. "No! not yet," cried the captain, who sought to raise him up. "Yes," replied Nelson, "the spine is hit;" and drawing his handkerchief from his pocket, he himself covered his face and his decorations, in order to hide his fall from his crew. "Take care!" said he, as they carried him down; "the cable of the helm is cut." Between decks was crowded with the wounded and the dying. "Attend to those whom you can save," said he to the surgeon; "as for me, there is nothing to be done." Meanwhile he listened anxiously, noticing the discharges of artillery, seeking to divine the issue of the combat. The *Redoutable* had been attacked by the *Temeraire* and the *Neptune* at the moment when the French sailors were preparing to board the *Victory*. Captain Lucas was compelled to haul down his flag; of the 660 men of his crew, 522 were *hors de combat*. The *Bucentaure*, caught by its bowsprit in the gallery of the *Santissima-Trinidad*, was overwhelmed by the enemy, and, held in its position by the Spanish vessel, completely dismasted. Already the flag-officer and two lieutenants had been wounded by the side of Admiral Villeneuve, who courted death in vain. The *Bucentaure* was cut down close like a pontoon. The admiral wished to pass on to another vessel. Not a single boat was left him. When he at last pulled down his flag he could not reply with a single cannon-shot to the English vessels that were bent on his destruction.

Nelson still breathed. "Where is Hardy?" he repeated; "if he does not come to me, it is because he is dead." The captain presently came down, too much moved to utter a word. "How is it now with us?" said the dying man. "All goes well," said Hardy; "ten vessels have already lowered their flag. I see that the French are signalling to the vanguard to tack about. If they come against the *Victory* we will call for aid, and give them a beating." "I hope none of our ships have surrendered," said Nelson. "There is no danger," replied Hardy, who returned to his post. When he reappeared, Nelson's eyes were closed. The captain stooped over him. "We have fifteen prizes," said he. "I counted upon twenty," murmured the dying man. Then rousing himself, "Anchor,

Hardy, anchor; give the signal! Kiss me . . . I am satisfied. Thank God, I have done my duty." He expired,—just forty-seven years of age.

The French Admiral Magon was still defending the *Algesiras*, attacked by the *Tonnant ;* he wanted to board her, but his deck was swept by the grape shot of fresh assailants. Himself threatened with being boarded, the admiral repulsed the English, axe in hand, at the head of his sailors. He was covered with wounds. Bretonnière, become flag officer by the death of his seniors, implored Magon to have his wounds dressed; as he yielded to the request, a cannon-shot penetrating between decks struck him in the chest, and he was dead. The *Algesiras* at last hauled down her flag, at the moment when the *Achille*, for some time already the prey of flames which the crew had no time to extinguish, blew up with a terrific explosion. Thus ended the battle. Admiral Gravina rallied round him eleven vessels; a few had at an early period withdrawn from the combat. Admiral Dumanoir, who had not succeeded in engaging his vanguard, had already retired. The English carried off seventeen vessels, for the most part too shattered to be of service. The unfortunate French admiral was received by the conquerors with the honor due to his bravery. A few months later, when released by the enemy, Villeneuve in despair was to die by his own hand in an inn at Rennes, writing in the last moment these heartrending words: "What a blessing that I have no child to receive my horrible inheritance, and live under the weight of my name!"

The last orders of Nelson in dying, recommended the fleet to be anchored; Collingwood judged otherwise, and waited till daylight. Already Admiral Gravina had taken his vessels into the port of Cadiz, when a furious tempest broke forth, irresistible by the ships so dreadfully damaged in the conflict. The English had so much to do in looking after their own safety that they could not attend to their prizes, and the officer having charge of the *Bucentaure* resigned it to the French commanders: the unfortunate vessel perished on the coast, opposite Cape Diamant.

Indomitable in defeat as in battle, the officers and sailors of the *Algesiras* forced their guardians to surrender the vessel. They at last escaped death, after two nights of anguish and struggle. At their side the *Indomptable*, all hung with lanterns, its deck crowded with a despairing crew, was forced from its anchors by the hurricane, and shattered against the rocks. The English lost all their prizes but four; they were compelled to sink the *Swiftsure,* captured by Admiral Ganteaume and which they were intent on recapturing from us.

Nelson had made the request in dying, "Do not cast my poor body into the sea." The most extraordinary honors awaited in England the remains of this great seaman: the broken mast of his flag-ship, and one of the French bullets which struck him, still attract attention in a room at Windsor. The whole nation put on mourning; the politicians forgot the embarrassment which he had more than once caused them, and which had drawn from one of them the expression, "He is an heroic cockney." The splendor of his military genius, his devotion to his country, the noble simplicity of his character, inspired all minds with respect. The hero of the struggle against France, he fell at the height of his glory. He had taken part in nearly all the maritime victories which had signalized the war: the names of Aboukir, Copenhagen, and Trafalgar render his memory glorious.

The emperor bore the blow of his defeat without showing despondency or anger. "All this makes no change in my cruising projects," wrote he on the 18th November, to Admiral Decrès; "I am even annoyed that all is not ready. They must set out without delay. Cause all the troops that are on board the squadron to come to me by land. They will wait my orders at the first town in France."

Napoleon was then at Znaïm in Moravia, and the date of his letter told the story of his astonishing successes. Abandoned by the King of Prussia, with whom the Austrians and the Russians had turned to account the violation of his territory, Napoleon prepared to dispute Hanover with new enemies, without modifying his general plan, and without renouncing his march upon Vienna. The Russian army of Kutuzof alone barred his way; but already it was commencing a clever movement of retreat, never fighting without necessity, firm and resolute, however, when attacked. The Russians passed the Danube at Krems, destroying the bridges behind them. They committed great ravages during their march, and had gained the ill-will of the Austrian corps who went with them, and who fell back upon Vienna. With great imprudence General Mortier had been detached on the left bank of the Danube, where he was attacked by the larger portion of the Russian army at the very moment when he found himself separated from the division of Dupont. In spite of the heroic resistance of the French soldiers the danger was imminent. Mortier was urged to take to a boat, and not deliver to the enemy a marshal of France. "Who would leave such brave men?" replied Mortier; "we will be saved or perish together." A road lay open across the ground occupied by the Russians, to the village of Dernstein; the soldiers of General Dupont entered it at the same time from another direction. They hastened by forced marches to the succor of the marshal. Napoleon's anger fell heavily on Murat, whom he accused, not without reason, of vainglorious levity. Already the brilliant general of cavalry had presented himself at the gates of Vienna. The Emperor Francis had not wished to expose his capital to the horrors of a siege; when he saw the proposals for an armistice rejected which he had addressed to Napoleon (November 8th) he prepared to quit Vienna. Less menacing than at Ulm, the conqueror no longer invited the Emperor of Austria to meditate upon the fall of empires: he reminded him that the present war was for Russia only a fancy war; "for your Majesty and myself it is a war that absorbs all our means, all our sentiments, all our faculties." Fifteen days later Napoleon entered the palace of Schœnbrunn. Thanks to a ruse, more daring than fair, Murat had succeeded in carrying the bridges of Vienna at the moment when the workmen were preparing to blow them up; he was on the march for Moravia, pursuing the Russians, with the co-operation of Mortier and Bernadotte.

By his superior ability Napoleon struck his enemies at once with terror and astonishment, paralyzing their forces by their anxiety at the unforeseen blows he dealt them. The Archduke Charles had long remained immovable on the Adige; when he at last commenced his retreat he marched to the assistance of the threatened empire, and was pursued by Masséna. The marshal attacked the archduke in his camp of Caldiero after having seized Verona by night, and had fought him on the shores of the Tagliamento; he was now approaching Marmont, who occupied the Styrian Alps. The Archduke Charles rallying the remains of the army of his brother, the Archduke John, was engaged with him in Hungary, in order to rejoin the Russian army in Moravia. Before the two masses of the enemy could reach Brünn, and in spite of the clever manœuvre of Kutuzof, who succeeded before Hollabrunn in concealing from Murat and Lannes the great bulk of his army, the French were, on the 19th of November, in possession of the capital of Moravia. Napoleon entered it next day.

The Emperor Alexander joined the Emperor of Austria at Olmütz. Proud of his diplomatic successes at Berlin, and convinced that his visit to the King of Prussia had alone decided him to attach himself to the coalition, he nursed a military ambition, assiduously encouraged by his young favorites. The Emperor Francis sent Stadion and Giulay to Brünn, commissioned to treat for conditions of peace. Napoleon referred them to Talleyrand, whom he had sent to Vienna. "They know the state of the question by what I have said to them in a few words," wrote he; "but you have to treat it smoothly and at full length. My intention is absolutely to have the State of Venice, and to reunite it to the kingdom of Italy. I have good cause to think that the court of Vienna has taken its resolution on that point."

Napoleon was wishing for peace—immediate, glorious, and fruitful. He had vainly sought to separate the Austrians from the Russians; he could not doubt the hostile intentions of Prussia. The very explanations that Haugwitz had just given him as to the motives for the entry of a Prussian army into Hanover foreshadowed plenty of approaching hostilities: a brilliant victory, forestalling the union of the German and Russian forces, became necessary. For a few days the soldiers rested, recruiting their forces after their long and perilous marches. The impatience of the Emperor Alexander had already carried the general quarters of the allies to Wischau. It was there that General Savary presented himself, intrusted with aimless negotiations, which gave him opportunity to examine the condition of the Austro-Russian army. Prince Dolgorouki, sent from Brünn with the reply of the Emperor Alexander, was received at the advanced posts. The young favorite was thoughtless and proud. "What do they want of me?" said Napoleon. "Why does the Emperor Alexander make war on me? Is he jealous of the growth of France? Well, let him extend his frontiers at the expense of his neighbors on the side of Turkey, and all quarrels will be at an end." Dolgorouki protested the disinterestedness of his master. "The emperor wishes," said he "for the independence of Europe, the evacuation of Holland and Switzerland, an indemnity for the King of Sardinia, and barriers round France for the protection of its neighbors." Napoleon broke out in a passion: "I will never yield anything in Italy, even if the Russians should camp upon the heights of Montmartre." He sent back the negotiator, who had perceived the movements of

troops falling back around Brünn. Ignorant of the great
principle which directed the campaigns of Napoleon—" divide
in order to subsist, concentrate in order to fight"—he thought
he divined the preparations for retreat. The ardor of the
Russian army grew more intense. It advanced towards the
position long studied by Napoleon, and which he destined for
his field of battle. In accordance with the plan of the Austrian
general, Weirother, who was in great favor with the Emperor
Alexander, the allies had resolved to turn the right of the
French army, in order to cut off the road to Vienna by isolating numerous corps dispersed in Austria and Styria. Already
the two emperors and their staff-officers occupied the castle
and village of Austerlitz. On December 1st, 1805, the allies
established themselves upon the plateau of Platzen; Napoleon
had by design left it free. Divining, with the sure instinct of
superior genius, the manœuvres of his enemy, he had cleverly
drawn them into the snare. His proclamation to the troops
announced all the plan of the battle.

"Soldiers," said he, "the Russian army presents itself before you to avenge the Austrian army of Ulm. These are the
same battalions which you have beaten at Hollabrunn, and
that you have constantly pursued to this place.

"The positions that we occupy are formidable, and whilst
they march to turn my right they will present me their flank.

"Soldiers, I will myself direct your battalions. I will keep
myself away from the firing if, with your accustomed bravery,
you carry disorder and confusion into the enemy's ranks. But
if the victory were for a moment uncertain you would see your
emperor expose himself to the brunt of the attack; for this
victory will finish the campaign, and we shall be able to resume our winter quarters, where we shall be joined by new
armies which are forming in France. Then the peace I shall
make will be worthy of my people, of you, and of me."

It was late, and the emperor had just dismissed Haugwitz,
whom he had sent back to Vienna. "I shall see you again if
I am not carried off to-morrow by a cannon-ball. It will be
time then to understand each other." Napoleon went out to
visit the soldiers at the bivouac. A great ardor animated the
troops; it was remembered that the 2nd December was the
anniversary of the coronation of the emperor. The soldiers
gathered up the straw upon which they were stretched,
making it into bundles, which they lit at the end of poles; a
sudden illumination lit up the camp. "Be assured," said an

old grenadier, advancing towards the chief who had so many times led his comrades to victory, "I promise thee that we will bring thee to-morrow the flags and the cannon of the Russian army to signalize the anniversary of the 2nd December."

The fires were extinguished, and the enemies thought they saw in it the indication of a nocturnal retreat. Gathered around a map, the allied generals listened to Weirother, who developed his plan of battle "with a boasting air, which displayed in him a clear persuasion of his own merit and of our incapacity," says General Langeron, a French emigrant officer in the Russian army. Old Kutuzof slept. "If Bonaparte had been able to attack us, he would have done it to-day," was the assurance of Weirother. "You do not then think him strong?" "If he has 40,000 men, it is all." "He has extinguished his fires; a good deal of noise comes from his camp." "He is either retreating or else he is changing his position; if he takes that of Turas, he will spare us a good deal of trouble, and the dispositions of the troops will remain the same." The day was scarcely begun (2nd December, 1805) when the allied army was on the march. The noise of the preparations in the camps had reassured Napoleon as to the direction the enemy would take. On the previous evening, whilst listening to the learned lecture of Weirother, Prince Bagration, formerly the heroic defender of the positions of Hollabrunn, had uttered under his long moustache, "The battle is lost!" In seeing his enemies advance towards the right, as he had himself announced to his soldiers, Napoleon could not withhold the signs of his joy. He held the victory in his own hands. He waited patiently until his enemies had deployed their line. The sun had just risen, shining through the midst of a fog, which it dispersed with its brilliant rays. The plateau of Pratzen was in part abandoned; the emperor gave the signal, and the whole French army moved forward, forming an enormous and compact mass, eager to hurl itself on the enemy. "See how the French climb the height without staying to respond to our fire!" said Prince Czartoriski, who watched the battle near the two emperors. He was still speaking when already the allied columns, thrown out one after another on the slope, found themselves arrested in their movement and separated from the two wings of the army. Old Kutuzof, badly wounded, strove in vain to send aid to the disordered centre. "See, see, a mortal wound!" he cried, extending his arms towards Pratzen.

During this time the right, commanded by Marshal Davout, disputed with the Russians the line of Goldbach, extricating with the division of Friant General Legrand for a moment outflanked. Murat and Lannes attacked on the left eighty-two Russian and Austrian squadrons, under the orders of Prince John of Lichtenstein. The infantry advanced in quick time against the Uhlans sent against them, soon dispersed by the light cavalry of Kellermann. The Russian batteries drowned the sound of all the drums of the first regiment of the division of Cafarelli. General Valhubert had his thigh fractured, and his soldiers wished to carry him away. "Remain at your posts," said he calmly. "I know well how to die alone. We must not for one man lose six." The Russian guard at last turned towards Pratzen. A French battalion, which had let itself be drawn in pursuit, was in danger. Napoleon, stationed at the centre with the infantry of the guard, and the corps of Bernadotte, perceived the disorder. "Take there the Mamelukes and the chasseurs of the guard," said he to Rapp. When the latter returned to the emperor he was wounded, but the Russians, were repulsed, and Prince Repnin prisoner. A Russian division, isolated at Sokolnitz, had just surrendered; two columns had been thrown back beyond the marshes. The bridge broke under the weight of the artillery. The cold was intense; and the soldiers thought to save themselves by springing upon the ice, but already the French cannon-balls were breaking it under their feet. With cries of despair they were engulfed in the waters of the lake. Generals Doctoroff and Keinmayer effected their painful retreat, under the fire of our batteries, by a narrow embankment, separating the two lakes of Melnitz and Falnitz. Only the corps of Prince Bagration still kept in order of battle, Marshal Lannes having restrained his troops which were rushing forward in pursuit.

The day had come to a close; the two emperors had abandoned the terrible battle-field. Behind them resounded the French shouts of victory; around them, before them, they heard the imprecations of the fugitives, the groans of the wounded, unable any longer to keep on their way, the complaints of the peasants ravaged by the furious soldiery. They arrived thus at the imperial castle of Halitsch, where they found themselves next day pressed by Marshal Davout. Austerlitz became the headquarters of the conqueror.

Before even having reached a place of safety the Emperor Francis, gloomy and calm, had in his own mind taken his de-

cision.   Prince John of Lichtenstein was sent to ask from
Napoleon an armistice and an interview.   The conqueror was
still traversing the field of battle, attentive in procuring for his
soldiers the care that their bravery merited.   "The interview,
when the emperor will, the day after to-morrow, at our advanced posts," said he to the Austrian envoy; "until then, no
armistice."   Whilst Napoleon was speaking to his army and to
Europe, Marshal Lannes and the cavalry were already pursuing the vanquished enemy.

"Soldiers, I am satisfied with you," said he in his proclamation of the 3rd December, 1805.   "You have upon the day of
Austerlitz justified all that I expected from your intrepidity.
An army of 100,000 men, commanded by the Emperors of Russia and Austria, has been in less than four hours either cut up
or dispersed, and what escaped from your steel is drowned in
the lakes.   Forty flags, the standards of the Imperial Guard of
Russia, a hundred and twenty pieces of cannon, twenty generals, and more than thirty thousand prisoners are the results
of this ever-memorable day.   In three months this third coalition has been vanquished and dissolved.   Soldiers, when all
that is necessary in order to assure the happiness and prosperity of France shall be accomplished, I will lead you back
into France; there you will be the object of my most tender
solicitude.   My people will see you again with joy, and it will
suffice for you to say, 'I was at the battle of Austerlitz,' to receive the reply, 'There is a hero!'"

The army rested, intoxicated with pride and joy.   The
losses, considerable in themselves, were small in comparison
with the disasters inflicted on the coalition; the arrogance of
the Russians had undergone a most painful check; the youthful
illusions of their Czar cruelly dissipated.   The Emperor of
Austria informed him of his pacific intentions, and Alexander
hastened to release his allies from their engagements; he was
in a hurry to retire and disengage himself from a war which
could procure for him no other advantage than a vain hope of
glory.

Napoleon repeated his former sentiments to the Emperor
Francis when he met him next day at the mill of Paleny, between Nasiedlowitz and Urschitz.   "Do not confound your
cause with that of the Emperor Alexander.   Russia can to-day
only make a fancy war (*une guerre de fantaisie*).   Conquered,
she retires into her deserts, and you pay all the costs of the
war."   Then, gracefully returning to the courtesies of society,

the all-powerful conqueror made excuses for the poor place in which he was compelled to receive his illustrious host.

"These are the palaces," said he, "which your Majesty has compelled me to inhabit for three months past." "Your visit has succeeded sufficiently well for you to have no right to bear me any grudge," replied the Emperor Francis. The two monarchs embraced, and the armistice was concluded. The Russians were to retire by stages, and the seat of negotiations was fixed at Brünn. A formal order from Napoleon was necessary in order to stop the march of Marshal Davout in pursuit of the Russian army. General Savary was entrusted with this order; he brought to the Czar the conditions of the armistice. "I am satisfied, since my ally is," replied Alexander, and he allowed to escape from him the expression of an admiration which was long to exercise over him a profound influence. " Your master has shown himself very great," said he to Savary.

Napoleon left Talleyrand at Brünn exchanging arguments with Stadion and Giulay; he himself repaired to Vienna, where Haugwitz awaited him. Imperfectly instructed as to the alliance concluded on the 3rd of November at Potsdam between the King of Prussia and the allies, he knew enough of it to break forth in violent reproaches against the perfidy of the Prussian Government. And as Haugwitz made excuses and protests, the Emperor proposed to him all of a sudden that union with France which had been so often discussed. Hanover was to be the price of it. Prussia was uneasy, frightened, divided in her councils, but she accepted; the Marquisate of Anspach, the Principality of Neufchâtel, and the Duchy of Clèves were ceded to France, and the treaty was signed at Schönbrunn on the 15th December, 1805. Prussia recognized all the conquests of Napoleon; the two sovereigns reciprocally guaranteed each other's possessions.

Talleyrand had just quitted Brünn, which had become unhealthy through the overcrowding of the hospitals; the negotiations were being carried on at Presburg. In spite of the wise and prudent counsels of his minister, Napoleon was resolved on exacting from Austria still more than he had declared before Ulm. The defection of Prussia had thoroughly disheartened the plenipotentiaries of the Emperor Francis. The French armies concentrated afresh around Vienna. Napoleon was doubly imperious, threatening to recommence the war; the negotiators at length yielded to necessity. On the 26th of December, 1805, peace was signed at Presburg between France

and Austria. The Emperor Francis abandoned to the conqueror Venice, Istria, Frioul, and Dalmatia, which were to become part of the kingdom of Italy; the Tyrol and Vorarlberg,
of which Napoleon made a present to Bavaria; the outlying
territories of Suabia, handed over to Wurtemberg; the Brisgau,
Ortenau, and the city of Constance, which were added to the
territories of the Elector of Baden. Napoleon ceded to the
Emperor the Principality of Wurtzburg for one of the archdukes; the secularization of the Teutonic Order was agreed
upon to the profit of Austria; the latter power was to pay a
war indemnity of forty millions.

The small German princes, who beheld their possessions increased and their titles made more glorious by the powerful
hand of the conqueror, were in their turn to pay the price of
the terrible alliance which weighed upon them. The new Kings
of Wurtemberg and Bavaria found themselves obliged to give
their daughters to Jerome Bonaparte and to Eugène de Beauharnais; the marriage that the former had contracted in
America, and the betrothal of the Princess of Bavaria to the
son of the Elector of Baden, weighed nothing in the balance in
comparison with the iron will of Napoleon. Intimidated and
restless, the Elector of Baden himself broke off the marriage of
his son, accepting for him the hand of Stéphani de Beauharnais, niece of the Empress Josephine. Before taking the road
to France, the Emperor was present at the marriage of the
vice-King of Italy with the princess whose portrait he had seen
a few days before upon a porcelain cup. Everything had
yielded to his power,—sovereigns, families, and hearts. Russia and England alone remained openly enemies. "Rest
awhile, my children," said the Archduke Charles in disbanding
his army; "rest awhile, until we begin again."

I have been desirous of conducting General Bonaparte, now
become the Emperor Napoleon, up to the popular summit of his
glory. He had already tainted it by many acts of violence,
and by an exclusive devotion to personal ends, in defiance of
justice and liberty. Henceforward and under the disastrous
inspirations of a mad ambition, victory itself was to become a
fatal seduction which by inevitable degrees draws us on to ruin.
Great and terrible lesson of Divine justice on the morality of
nations! Starting from the violation of the peace of Amiens,
and in spite of the glory of the sun of Austerlitz, the history of
the glory of the conqueror includes in germ the history of his
fall, and of the ever-increasing misfortunes of France.

CHAPTER IX.

GLORY AND CONQUEST (1805—1808).

GUIZOT has said at the commencement of his essay on Washington: "There is a spectacle as fine as that of a virtuous man struggling with adversity, and not less salutary to contemplate; it is the spectacle of a virtuous man at the head of a good cause and assuring his triumph."

There is a spectacle, sorrowful and sad, also salutary to contemplate in its austere teachings: it is that of a man of genius bearing along in his train an enthusiastic nation, and squandering all the living forces of his genius and his country in the service of a senseless ambition, as fatal to the sovereign as the people, both foolishly dragged along by a vision of glory towards injustices and crimes not at first foreseen. Such is the spectacle offered to us by the history of the Emperor Napoleon, and of France, after the battle of Austerlitz and the Peace of Presburg.

For the moment a stupor seemed to oppress the whole of Europe. Prussia, humiliated and indignant, had, however, just ratified the treaty of Schönbrunn; Austria was panting and conquered; England had lost her great minister: William Pitt died 23rd January, 1806, struck to the heart in his patriotic passion, by the new victory of the conqueror whom he dreaded for the liberty of the world. "Roll up this map of Europe," said he when the news was brought to him as he lay dying in his little house at Putney, "in ten years time there will be no further need for it." Already his rival had succeeded him in office, and Fox did not yet foresee that he would presently be inevitably brought to adopt the policy of resistance to the long increasing power of Napoleon. He was then making cordial advances towards him. The Emperor Alexander had not disarmed, but the appeals to him from the Court of Naples found him immovable. Already the Bourbons were trembling on the thrones they still occupied.

Napoleon announced it in his thirty-seventh bulletin, dated from Vienna. "General Saint Cyr marches by long stages towards Naples, to punish the treason of the queen, and hurl from the throne this criminal woman who has violated everything that is held sacred among men." Intercession was attempted for her with the Emperor. He replied, "Ought hostilities to recommence, and the nation to sustain a war of thirty years, a perfidy so atrocious cannot be pardoned."

In this struggle between violence and treason the issue could not remain long doubtful. In the name of Joseph Bonaparte, Masséna commanded the army which came to take possession of the kingdom of Naples. For the second time, King Ferdinand and Queen Charlotte took refuge in Sicily. "It is the interest of France to make sure of the kingdom of Naples by a useful and easy conquest," the *Moniteur* had formerly declared, in publishing the treaty of neutrality agreed to by the House of Bourbon. The work was accomplished; on the 30th of March, Joseph Bonaparte was proclaimed King of the Two Sicilies. The city of Gaëta alone was to prolong its resistance.

Two months later, with the appearance of the national consent, Napoleon elevated his brother Louis to the throne which he had instituted for him in Holland. The prince had been ordered to protect this country, threatened by the Anglo-Swedish army. After the battle of Austerlitz he presented himself before the Emperor. "Why have you quitted Holland?" demanded the latter brusquely, "we saw you there with pleasure, and you should have remained there." "Sounds of a monarchical transformation circulate in Holland," replied Louis Bonaparte, "they are not agreeable to this free and worthy nation, nor are they any more pleasant to me."

Napoleon broke out into a passion. "He gave me to understand," says Prince Louis in his *Mémoires*, "that if I had not been more consulted over this affair, it was for a subject only to obey." At the same time the Emperor wrote to Talleyrand, "I have seen this evening Admiral Verhuell. In two words hear what this question amounts to. Holland is without executive power. It requires that power, and I will give it Prince Louis. In place of the Grand Pensionary Schimmelpenninck, there shall be a king. The argument is that without that I shall not be able to give peace a firm settlement. Prince Louis must make his entry into Amsterdam within twenty days." The accession to the throne of the new monarch was celebrated on the 5th June, 1806.

Napoleon disposed at his will of crowns and appanages, elevating or dethroning kings, magnificently dowering the com-

panions of his military life and the servants of his policy. He
had at the same time conceived the idea of forming beyond his
States a barrier which should separate them from the great
German powers, always secretly hostile. The dukes and the
electors whom he had made kings, the princes whose domains
he had aggrandized, were to unite in a confederation for the
protection of the new State of Germany. The seat of government was established at Frankfort. The town of Ratisbon,
formerly honored by the assemblies of the Diet, had been ceded
to Bavaria. The Diet was officially informed that Prussia received a decisive authorization to form in its turn a confederation of the North. Most of the German States having been
forcibly taken from him, Francis II. voluntarily resigned the
vain title he still bore; he ceased to be Emperor of Germany,
and became Emperor of Austria.

Meanwhile the overtures of Fox towards France had until
now remained without result. England refused to treat without Russia, whom the Emperor would not admit to a common
negotiation. "Regrets are useless," wrote Fox to Talleyrand
on the 10th April, 1806; "but if the great man whom you serve,
could see with the same eye with which I behold it, the true
glory which would accrue to him from a moderate and just
peace, what good fortune would not result from it for France
and for all Europe?"

In the depth of his soul and in his secret thoughts Napoleon
now desired peace. Amongst the English prisoners detained in
France after the rupture of the treaty of Amiens, a few had
been exchanged since the advent of Fox to the ministry; one of
them, Lord Yarmouth (afterwards Lord Hertford), elegant and
dissipated, had been commissioned by his government to talk
over familiarly with Talleyrand the chances of peace that ex·
isted between the two nations. Napoleon had conceded Hanover to Prussia as the price of peace; he was ready to retrocede
it to England, free to idemnify Prussia at the expense of Germany. The negotiation was carried on secretly, the negotiators
meeting as men of the world rather than diplomats. Oubril,
an envoy from the Emperor Alexander, had just arrived in
Paris, charged with reassuring France on the subject of a circumstance which had recently taken place in Dalmatia. The
Russian admiral, Sinavin, animated with unseasonable zeal,
with the aid of the Montenegrins had seized the mouths of the
Cattaro. The Austrian officers, appointed to hand over the
territory to the French, had not opposed any resistance to the

Russians. The two Emperors of Austria and Russia hastened to disavow their agents; on 20th July Oubril signed with France a separate peace.

This was failing in loyalty towards England, who had refused to treat without its ally. The Emperor of Russia perceived it; he had thought the cabinet of London more inclined to conclude peace at any cost. The health of Fox was giving way, and his successors were likely to be less favorable to the demands of Napoleon. Alexander declared that he would not ratify the treaty negotiated by Oubril. This news arrived at Paris on the 3rd of September, 1806. On the 13th of the same month Fox expired in London, amiable and beloved to the last day of his life; ardently devoted to his friends, to freedom, to all noble and generous causes; a great orator and a great debater; feeble in his political conduct even in opposition, incapable of governing and of sustaining the great struggle which for so long agitated Europe. At his death the party of resistance resumed power in England. In Germany the secret of the negotiations with regard to Hanover had transpired; the disregard of sworn faith which Prussia had more than once practised during the war fell back upon herself with crushing weight. Napoleon thought nothing of his engagements; he had detached King Frederick William from his natural allies, and showed himself disposed to snatch from him the price of his compliance. The nation and the king had with great difficulty accepted the treaty negotiated by Haugwitz; indignation broke forth on every side. It had already betrayed itself for a few weeks past by numerous and violent pamphlets against the Emperor of the French and against the armies of occupation. Napoleon responded to them by a despotic and cruel act which was to bear bitter fruits. On the 5th August he wrote to Marshal Berthier:—

"My cousin,—I imagine that you have had the booksellers of Augsburg and Nuremberg arrested. My intention is that they should be indicted before a military tribunal, and shot within twenty-four hours. It is no ordinary crime to spread libels in places where the French army is stationed, in order to excite the inhabitants against it. It is a crime of high treason. The sentence shall set forth that wherever there is an army, the duty of the commander being to watch over its safety, such and such individuals convicted of having attempted to stir up the inhabitants of Suabia against the French army are condemned to death. You will place the criminals in the midst of a division, and you will appoint seven colonels to try them. You will have the sentence published throughout Germany." Only one bookseller of Nuremberg, named Palm, was arrested, and suffered the terrible sentence. Berthier never forgot the cruel necessity to which he had been subjected in ordering this odious procedure. "He makes us condemn under the penalty of being condemned ourselves," said General Hullin, in reporting the murder of the Duc d'Enghien.

The growing irritation of Germany only awaited an excuse for bursting forth. A despatch of the Marquis of Lucchesini, then minister of Prussia at Paris, gave the protracted irritation of the court of Berlin its opportunity. According to the information received from this diplomatist, the French government was putting pressure upon the German Princes of the North, to prevent them from entering the Confederation projected by Prussia. A letter from King Frederick William and a diplomatic note demanded peremptorily the evacuation of Germany by the French troops, and liberty of action for the German Princes. At the same time the armaments of Prussia, for a long time prepared in secret, became public. Already the Emperor Napoleon had quitted Paris, without Laforest, his minister at Berlin, having been authorized to reply to the demands of the Prussians. "We have been deceived three times," said Napoleon. "We must have facts; let Prussia disarm, and France will re-cross the Rhine, and not before." It was to the Senate and to the soldiers alone that Napoleon now addressed the explanation of his aggressive movements against Prussia.

"Soldiers, the order for your re-entry into France was issued; you had already approached it by several marches. Triumphant fêtes awaited you, and the preparations to receive you had already commenced in the capital.

"But whilst we abandon ourselves to this too confident security, new plots are hatched under the mask of friendship and alliance. War cries have made themselves heard from Berlin. For two months we have been provoked more and more every day.

"The same faction, the same spirit of giddiness which, under favor of our internal dissensions, conducted the Prussians fourteen years ago into the midst of the plains of Champagne, rules in their councils; if it is no longer Paris that they wish to burn and overthrow to its foundations, it is to-day their flag that they wish to plant in the capitals of our allies; it is Saxony that they wish to compel by a shameful transaction to renounce its independence by ranging it in the number of their provinces ; it is, in fine, your laurels that they wish to snatch from your foreheads. They wish us to evacuate Germany at the sight of their arms. Fools ! What ? Shall we then have braved the seasons, the seas, the deserts, conquered Europe several times allied against us, carried our glory from the east to the west, in order to return to-day into our country like fugitives who have abandoned their allies ; to hear it said that the French eagle fled in fear at the mere sight of the Prussian armies ? "

It was, in fact, a fourth continental coalition which was beginning to be formed against France. Prussia alone was then on the scene ; long prudent and circumspect in its conduct, it had been drawn in this time, in spite of its weakness, by irresistible anger and indignation. Napoleon did not dread the war. " I have nearly 150,000 men in Germany," wrote he to King Joseph ; " with them I can subdue Vienna, Berlin, St. Petersburg." The reply that he at last deigned to address to the King of Prussia from the camp of Gera breathed the most haughty confidence. A few engagements had already taken place. " Monsieur my brother," wrote Napoleon to Frederick William, " I only received on the 7th the letter of your Majesty of the 25th of September. I am vexed that you have been induced to sign this sort of thing. You appoint a meeting with me on the 8th. Like a good knight, I keep faith with you, I am in the middle of Saxony ; believe me I have such forces with me that all your forces cannot long prevent my victory. But why spill so much blood ? To what end ? Sire, I have been your friend for six years past. I do not wish to profit by that species of giddiness which animates your council, and has caused you to commit political errors, at which Europe is still astonished, and military errors of such an enormity that Europe will soon ring with them. If in your note you had asked possible things from me, I would have granted them to you ; you have asked for my dishonor : you ought to have been certain of my reply. War is then made between us, the alliance broken forever ; but why make our subjects kill each other ? Sire, your Majesty will be conquered ; you will have compromised the peace of your days and the existence of your subjects without the shadow of a pretext. I have nothing to gain against your Majesty. I want nothing, and I have wanted nothing from you. The present war is an impolitic war."

Napoleon had well estimated the forces of the enemy he was preparing to crush; he had concentrated under his hand a power superior to all the resources of the Prussians, whose soldiers were courageous and well disciplined, but for a long time little exercised in war. Napoleon's precautions were taken at every point of his vast territory; he had called new troops under his banners; everywhere he held in check his enemies, either secret or avowed. At one moment he thought of tendering his hand to Austria; he wrote to his ambassador at Vienna, M. de la Rochefoucauld: "My position and my forces are such that I have no cause to fear any one; but at length all these efforts are burdensome to my people. Of the three powers, Russia, Prussia, and Austria, I must have one for an ally. In any case one cannot rely on Prussia: there remains only Austria. The navy of France formerly flourished through the benefit resulting from an alliance with Austria. This power also feels the need of remaining quiet, a sentiment that I partake with all my heart. The house of Austria having often caused hints to be thrown out to me, the present moment, if it knows how to profit by it, is the most favorable.

Austria remained immovable, the uneasy spectator of the events that were preparing. The Russians had not quitted their positions on the Vistula; already the Prussians had invaded Saxony, compelling that little power to furnish them with an army of 20,000 men. The old Duke of Brunswick collected at the same time the contingent of the Elector of Hesse-Cassel, who had sought in vain to maintain his neutrality. The French army occupied Franconia; it was across these mountainous defiles that Napoleon had resolved to march against the enemy divided into two corps, under the orders of the Duke of Brunswick and the Prince of Hohenlohe. Already Marshals Davout and Bernadotte were established upon the left bank of the Saale. The troops of the Prince of Hohenlohe occupied the road from Weimar to Jena. Marshal Lannes had taken possession of the heights which commanded this last town. On the morning of the 14th October, the combat was opened against the corps of the Prince of Hohenlohe; superior in number to the troops employed by the Emperor Napoleon, but surprised by an attack of which they had not foreseen the vigor, the Prussian soldiers were soon thrown into a panic terror. The two wings of the French army, commanded by Soult and Augereau, already enveloped the enemy when Napoleon sent forward the guard and the reserves. The centre of the Prussian army fell back before this enormous mass; the retreat changed into a rout. At the same moment Marshal Biechel arrived by forced marches to the aid of the Prince of Hohenlohe; he brought 20,000 men, but in vain did he struggle to rally and curb the fugitives; he was drawn along and repulsed by the conquered as well as by the conquerors. French and Germans entered at the same time into Weimar; already the crowd of prisoners hindered the march of the victorious army.

At the same hour on the same day, with forces less considerable, Marshal Davout struggled alone, near Auerstadt, against the enemy's corps, commanded by the Duke of Brunswick and by King Frederick William. Marshal Bernadotte had quitted him, obeying literally the orders of the Emperor, who had enjoined him to occupy Hamburg, little careful, perhaps, of the danger to which he exposed his companion-in-arms. Davout cut the road of the Prussians in the defile of Kœsen. The Duke of Brunswick, marching himself at the head of his troops, rushed upon him, violently attacking our immovable squares under a murderous fire. The old general fell, mortally wounded; the effort of Prince William and the king remained equally fruitless. Profiting by the trouble caused by his resistance, Davout threw his troops forward, and seized the heights of Eckartsberg; there, protected by his artillery, he could still defend his positions. The King of Prussia gave orders to retire on Weimar; he counted on joining the corps of the Prince of Hohenlohe, in order to renew the attack with all his forces. He had already travelled over half the distance without being harassed by Marshal Davout, whose troops were exhausted; but Bernadotte barred his passage; the confused waves of fugitives from Jena precipitated themselves into the ranks of their friends and compatriots. Behind them appeared the French soldiers, ardent in pursuit. The king turned off hastily, by way of Sommerda; the darkness was increasing, and the disorder increased with the darkness. In a single day the entire Prussian army was destroyed. "They can do nothing but gather up the *débris*," said Napoleon.

He took care to crush everywhere these sad remains of a generous and patriotic effort. Whilst his lieutenants were pursuing the wandering detachments of the Prussian army. the emperor imposed upon the nation he had just conquered a contribution of a hundred and fifty-nine millions. He sent the elector of Hesse to Metz, announcing in a letter to Marshal Mortier his intention that the house of Hesse should cease to reign, and would be effaced from the number of the powers. The Saxon prisoners, on the contrary, were sent back free to their sovereign. Everywhere the English merchandise found in the ports and warehouses was confiscated for the profit of the army. The Prussian commerce was ruined like the state.

Napoleon advanced upon Berlin; the King of Prussia sought to reach Magdeburg, constantly accompanied by the queen, whose warlike and patriotic ardor excited the rage and the insults of the emperor. "The Queen of Prussia has been many times in view of our posts," says the 8th bulletin of the grand army; "she is in continual fear and alarms. Last night she passed her regiment in review; she continually excited the king and the generals; she craves for blood. Blood the most precious has flowed; the most distinguished generals are those upon whom the first blows have fallen." Gross insinuations aggravated these rude allusions. "All the Prussians assign the misfortunes of Prussia to the journey of the Emperor Alexander. The change which has since then taken place in the spirit of the queen, who, from being a timid and modest woman, occupied with her home affairs, has become turbulent and warlike, is quite a sudden revolution. She desired all at once to have a regiment, to go to the Council, and she has led the monarchy so well that in a few days she has conducted it to the edge of a precipice."

A few battles finally opened everywhere the roads to the conqueror; Magdeburg was besieged, Erfurt had surrendered, Marshal Davout occupied Wittemberg, and Lannes occupied Dessau; Bernadotte had thrown himself against Halle, still defended by Prince Eugene of Wurtemberg. The resistance was severe; when the emperor came to visit the battle-field, he recognized among the corpses still scattered upon the ground the uniforms of the 32nd half-brigade. "Still the 32nd!" cried he. "I have had so many of them killed in Egypt, in Italy, everywhere, that there ought to be no more of them." It was with the same accent of indifferent and cold reflection that he was to say much later, in contemplating his sleeping son, "How long it takes to make a man! I have, however, seen fourteen of them cut off by a cannon-shot!"

Napoleon was at Potsdam, in the palace of the great Frederick, the military genius of this prince had for a long time excited his admiration. "At Potsdam has been found the sword of the great Frederick, the sash of a general, which he carried in the Seven Years' War, and his cordon of the Black Eagle," says the 19th bulletin.

The emperor siezed upon these trophies with eagerness, and said, "I prefer these to twenty millions." Then, thinking a moment to whom he should confide this precious trust, "I will send it," said he, "to my old soldiers of the Hanoverian War; I will make a present of it to the governor of the Invalides; it shall remain at the Hotel."

On the 27th, for the first time in his life, Napoleon entered in triumph into an enemy's capital. For two days Berlin had been occupied by Marshal Davout. A gloomy sadness rested on all faces, but order was everywhere respected. The Prussian nation had valiantly defended itself, and there was no shame mingled with its sorrow. The dying Duke of Brunswick recommended his subjects to the emperor. The latter, in a passion, recalled bitterly to the old general the wild manifesto published in his name at the commencement of the French Revolution. "If I had the city of Brunswick demolished, and if I did not leave of it one stone on another, what would your prince say? Does not the law of retaliation permit me to do to Brunswick what he wanted to do to my capital? It is the Duke of Brunswick whom France and Prussia can accuse of being the sole cause of this war. Tell the general that he will be treated with all the respect due to a Prussian officer, but that in a Prussian general I cannot recognize a sovereign."

The same harshness characterized the reception by the emperor of the great Prussian nobles. "Do not come into my presence," said he to the Prince of Hatzfeld, who brought before him the civil magistrates of Berlin. "I have no need of your services; retire to your own estates." A letter from the prince to the King of Prussia, giving an account of the entry of the emperor, was intercepted. Napoleon saw treason in this communication, and a decree was immediately sent to Marshal Davout. "The Prince of Hatzfeld, who presented himself at the head of the deputation from Berlin, as entrusted with the civil government of this capital, and who, notwithstanding this office, and the duties which are attached to it, has made use of the knowledge which his position afforded him as to the situation of the French army, to convey intelligence respecting it to the enemy, will be tried before a military commission, in order to be judged as a traitor and a spy.

VII.—10

"Marshal Davout is charged with the execution of this order.

"The military commission will be composed of seven colonels of the corps of Marshal Davout, by whom he will be tried."

In vain all the most faithful servants of the emperor wasted their entreaties in order to obtain mercy for the Prince of Hatzfeld; only the wife of the accused, far advanced in pregnancy, and overwhelmed with terror, succeeded in arresting the anger of the conqueror. "This is most certainly the writing of your husband," said he to the poor woman, who could scarcely support herself. And as she dared not deny it: "Throw this letter into the fire," added Napoleon, "and I shall no longer have any power to procure his death." It was Marshal Duroc who had taken upon himself the introduction of the Princess of Hatzfeld to the palace.

The prince of Hohenlohe, hard pushed by Murat and Marshal Lannes, had capitulated before Prenzlow, on the 28th of October; General Blucher, who had seized by force the free city of Lubeck, in the hope of finding there a place of support, was constrained, on November 7th, to follow his example. On the 8th, Magdeburg surrendered to Marshal Ney. Lannes occupied Stettin, and Davout occupied Custrin. "Sire," wrote Lannes to Napoleon, "I read your proclamation to the soldiers; they all began to cry 'Long live the Emperor of the West!' I beseech your Majesty to let me know if, for the future, you wish me to address my despatches to the Emperor of the West, and I ask it in the name of my *corps d'armée.*"

Napoleon did not reply; this dream of supreme glory, which he had had an idea of realizing in the footsteps of Charlemagne, doubtless appeared to him still beyond his reach. More than one sign, however, betrayed the undying hope, that he was never to realize. It is only by reason and the general good that genius is effectively sustained in extraordinary enterprises. From day to day, and from victory to victory, these great supports of the human mind became less and less visible in the conduct of the Emperor Napoleon.

Hanover and the Hanseatic towns were occupied by the French army; Prussia asked for a suspension of hostilities, in order to treat for peace. But the emperor had conceived a new project. In the ceaseless activity of his thoughts he reasonably enough looked on England as the implacable and invincible enemy who directed and excited against him the animosity of Europe. It was against England that he henceforth directed his efforts. " I am about to reconquer the colonies over the globe," he wrote to the King of Holland. It was in the same spirit that he made his declaration to the Senate: "We have unalterably determined not to evacuate Berlin or Warsaw, or the provinces which have fallen into our hands by force of arms, until a general peace be concluded, the Spanish, Dutch, and French colonies restored, the foundations of the Ottoman power confirmed, and the absolute independence of this vast empire, the first interest of our people, irrevocably secured."

These brilliant pledges of victory, which Napoleon kept in his hand as hostages for the purpose of enforcing submission on England, did not, however, appear to him sufficient; he resolved to strike at the wealth of his enemy a mortal blow, which should exhaust its resources at the fountain-head. On the 21st of November, 1806, he sent from Berlin to Talleyrand a decree, putting England in the Index Expurgatorius of Europe—at least, of that part of Europe which was in submission to his rule. The continental blockade was established and regulated in the following terms:—

"The British Isles are declared in a state of blockade.

"All commerce, and all correspondence, with the British Isles are forbidden. Consequently, letters or packets addressed to England, or to an Englishman, or written in the English language, will not pass through the post, and will be seized.

"Every individual English subject, whatever may be his state or condition, who shall be found in the countries occupied by our troops, or in the countries of our allies, shall be made prisoner of war.

"Every warehouse, all merchandise, all property of whatsoever nature it may be, belonging to an English subject, shall be deemed lawful prizes.

"Commerce in English merchandise is forbidden; any ships coming directly from England or from the English colonies, or having been there since the publication of the present decree, shall not be admitted into any port."

The Emperor Napoleon was right in recognizing, in his declaration to the Senate, that it was lamentable, after so many years of civilization, to recur to the principles, the barbarism, of the first ages of nations; and the pretexts which he adduced for this necessity were as insufficient as the consequences that flowed from his policy were odious. More than once the English had replied by violent and rude proceedings to the proceed-

ings of the same nature in which Napoleon had for a long time
been indulging on all seas. They had claimed to interdict
the commerce of neutrals by imprudent and unjust "Orders in
Council;" a still more inexcusable iniquity fettered at one
stroke the commerce of Europe in all its branches, carrying
annoyance into all families, and arbitrarily modifying the conditions of all existence. From henceforth, in the poorest house.
hold, no one could forget for a single day the power and the
vengeance of the Emperor Napoleon, as well as the death grap-
ple between him and England. It is a terrible undertaking for
the most powerful of men to change on all sides the habits of
life, and lay his hands upon the daily interests, of every one.
The continental blockade was in Napoleon's hands a redoubtable weapon against his enemy; the firmness of England and
the general distress, were yet cruelly to turn that weapon
against his own bosom.

He was not yet satisfied, and Napoleon resolved on making
an end of all his adversaries. Russia alone, silent and immovable, remained the ally of England, and its last support. Its
armies occupied Poland, always quivering under the hands of
its oppressors, ready to rise up against them at the first appeal.
It was upon the Vistula that the emperor had resolved to go
and seek the Russians, intoxicating the Poles beforehand with
the hope of the reconstitution of their country, and assured of
finding amongst them inexhaustible stores of provisions, ammunition, and soldiers. "A Pole is not a man," he was accustomed to say, "he is a sabre." He counted on all these sabres
being ready to leap from their scabbards at his voice, for the
service of Poland. To the disquietudes of the court of Vienna
on the subject of the insurrections which might be produced in
Galicia, Napoleon answered in advance by the promise of Silesia. "The insurrection in Poland is a consequence of my
war with Russia and Prussia," wrote he to General Andréossy,
recently sent to Vienna. "I have never recognized the partition of Poland; but, a faithful observer of treaties, in favoring
an insurrection in Russian and Prussian Poland, I will not mix
myself up with Austrian Poland. Does Austria wish to keep
Galicia? Would she cede a part of it? I am willing to give
her all the facilities she can desire. Does she wish to treat
openly or secretly? After these manifestations I ought to say
that I fear no one."

At the same time that he entered Poland, Napoleon excited
the hostile sentiment of the Porte against Russia. General Se-

bastiani was charged to say to Sultan Selim: "Prussia, who was leagued with Russia, has disappeared; I have destroyed its armies, and I am master of its fortified towns. My armies are on the Vistula, and Warsaw is in my power. Prussian and Russian Poland are rising, and forming armies to reconquer their independence; it is the moment for reconquering yours. I have given orders to my ambassador to enter into all necessary engagements with you. If you have been prudent up to this time, a longer forbearance towards Russia would be weakness, and cause the loss of your empire."

The King of Prussia had refused to accept the harsh conditions of the armistice; he had resolved to struggle to the end, and to join the remains of his forces to the army of the Emperor Alexander. "Your Majesty has had me informed that you are throwing yourself into the arms of the Russians," wrote Napoleon to King Frederick William. "The future will make it apparent whether you have chosen the best and most effective part. You have taken the dice-box and thrown the dice, and the dice will decide the question." Already the French armies had entered Poland, but they were not there alone; two Russian corps, under the orders of General Benningsen and General Buxhouden, had crossed the Niemen, and advanced towards the Vistula, and soon afterwards they entered Warsaw. Marshals Davout and Lannes sent reports, apparently contradictory, but in reality identical, as to popular feeling in Poland. Davout had found at Posen an extreme enthusiasm; he could scarcely furnish with arms those who pressed forward to ask for them; the same sentiment animated the population of Warsaw, when he made his entry in pursuit of the Russians, who fell back before him. Meanwhile he wrote to the emperor, on December 1st: "Levies of men are very easily made, but there is a want of persons who can direct their instruction and organization. There is also a want of guns. The feeling of Warsaw is excellent, but the upper class are making use of their influence to calm the ardor which is prevalent in the middle classes. The uncertainty of the future terrifies them, and they leave it to be sufficiently understood that they will only openly declare themselves when, with the declaration of their independence, they can also receive tacit guarantees for its maintenance." Lannes regretted the campaign in Poland; he recommended that they should establish themselves on the Oder, and pointed out the inconveniences and dangers of the enterprise they were about to attempt in a sterile and desert country. "They are always the same—frivolous, divided, anarchical; we shall uselessly waste our blood for their sakes, without founding anything durable."

Murat dreamed of seating himself on the throne of a restored Poland, and he was angry at the mistrust of the great nobles. Napoleon read in his correspondence a thought that the brilliant chief of the vanguard dared not express; he had said to Davout, at the beginning of the campaign, "When I shall see 40,000 Poles in the field I will declare their independence, not before." In their turn the Poles, long crushed down by harsh servitude, asked for guarantees from the conqueror, who had only delivered them in order to subjugate them afresh. "Those who show so much circumspection, and ask so many guarantees, are selfish persons, who are not warmed by the love of country," wrote the emperor to Murat, already Grand Duke of Berg for several months past. "I am experienced in the study of men. My greatness is not founded on the aid of a few thousand Poles. It is for them to profit, with enthusiasm, by present circumstances; it is not for me to take the first step. Let them display a firm resolution to render themselves independent—let them engage to uphold the king who will be given to them, and then I shall see what I shall next have to do. Let it be well understood that I do not come to beg a throne for any of my relations; I have no lack of thrones to give to my family."

In that conversation with the world which he kept up by bulletins from the grand army, Napoleon spoke of the Poles in other language; but he no longer laid bare the secret of his thoughts. "The army has entered into Warsaw," wrote he from Posen on December 1st. "It is difficult to paint the enthusiasm of the Poles. Our entry into this great city was a triumph, and the feelings that the Poles of all classes display since our arrival cannot be expressed. The love of country and the national sentiment is not only preserved in its entirety in the hearts of the people, but it has even gained new vigor from misfortune. Their first passion, their chief desire, is to become once more a nation. The richest leave their castles in order to come and demand, with loud cries, the re-establishment of the nation, and to offer their children, their fortunes, their influence. This spectacle is truly touching. Already they have everywhere resumed their ancient costume and their ancient customs.

"Shall the throne of Poland be re-established, and shall this great nation reassert its existence and its independence? From the depths of the tomb shall it be born again to life? God alone, who holds in His hands the results of all events, is the arbiter of this grand political problem."

Under the hand of God, which in the depths of his soul he often recognized, the Emperor Napoleon believed himself to be the arbiter of the grand problem of the independence of Poland. He remained personally indifferent to it, resolved on pursuing his own interest, either in aid of, or in contempt of, the interests and aspirations of the Poles.

In spite of the generous cordiality of the population, who lavished their resources upon those from whom they hoped for deliverance, Napoleon and his troops perceived that they had entered a desert. "Our soldiers find that the solitudes of Poland contrast with the smiling fields of their own country; but they add immediately, 'They are a fine people, these Poles!'" Before establishing himself for the winter in this savage country, under a frozen sky, and on a cold and damp soil, it was necessary to push back the enemy. Napoleon only went to Warsaw, and advanced towards the Russians entrenched behind the Narew and the Ukra. Already his lieutenants, Davout, Augereau, Ney, had taken up positions for attack. Furious battles at Czarnovo, at Pultusk, at Golymin, at Soldau, obliged the Russians to fall back upon the Pregel, without disaster to their *corps d'armée,* although they had been constantly beaten. The rigor of the season had prevented those grand concentrations of forces and those brilliant strokes in which Napoleon ordinarily delighted; the troops advanced with difficulty through impenetrable forests, soaked by the rain: the men fell in great numbers without a battle. In the month of January, 1807, the emperor at last took up his winter-quarters, carefully fortifying his positions, and laying siege to the towns which still resisted him in Silesia. Breslau, Glogau, Brieg successively succumbed. The old Marshal Lefebvre was charged with the siege of Dantzig.

Meanwhile the Russians, henceforth concentrated under the orders of General Benningsen, and less affected than the French by the inclemencies to which they were accustomed, had not suspended their military operations. Soon Marshal Ney, in one of those armed reconnoitering expeditions which he often risked without orders, was able to assure himself that the enemy was approaching us by a prolonged movement, which was to bring him to the shore of the Baltic. Already a few battles had taken place. The weather became cold; ice succeeded to the mud. Napoleon quitted Warsaw on January 30th, resolved to march against the enemy. "Since when have the conquered had the right of choosing the finest country for their winter-quarters?" said the proclamation to the army. Twice a great battle appeared imminent; twice a movement of the Russians in retreat enabled them to escape from the overwhelming forces which Napoleon had been able to collect; a few skirmishes, however, signalized the first days of February. On the seventh day's march General Benningsen entered Eylau.

The French entered in pursuit, and dislodged them. The Russians made their bivouac outside the city whilst the battle was preparing for the morrow. The weather was cold; one half of the country upon which the armies were camped was only a sheet of ice covering some small lakes. The snow lay thick upon the ground, and continued to fall in great flakes. The two armies were composed of nearly equal forces; several French corps, detached or delayed, were about to fail in the great effort which this rough winter campaign required. The troops were fatigued and hungry. "I have wherewith to nourish the army for a year," wrote Napoleon to Fouché, annoyed at the reports current in France as to the sufferings of the soldiers, "it is absurd to think one can want corn and wine, bread and meat, in Poland." The provisions remained, nevertheless, insufficient. "I can assure you," said the Duc de Fezensac in his military souvenirs, "that with all these orders so freely given in January, our *corps d'armée* was dying of hunger in March."

Long before the dawn of a slowly breaking and cloudy day Napoleon was already in the streets, establishing his guard in the cemetery of Eylau, and ordering his line of battle. The formidable artillery of the Russians covered their two lines; presently the shells fired the town of Eylau and the village of Rothenen, which protected a division of Marshal Soult's. The two armies remained immovable in a rain of cannon-balls. The Russians were the first to move forward, in order to attack the mill of Eylau; "they were impatient at suffering so much," says the 58th bulletin of the grand army. Nearly at the same moment the corps of Marshal Davout arrived; the emperor had him supported by Marshal Augereau. The snow fell in thick masses, obscuring the view of the soldiers; the troops of Augereau turned swiftly to the left, decimated by the

THE CHARGE OF THE CUIRASSIERS AT EYLAU.

Russian artillery. The marshal himself, already ill before the battle, was struck by a ball. The officers were nearly all wounded. The emperor called Murat: " Wilt thou let us be annihilated by these people?" The cavalry shot immediately in advance; only the imperial guard remained massed round Napoleon.

In a moment Murat had routed the Russian centre, but already the battalions were reforming. Marshal Soult defended with difficulty the positions of Eylau; Davout maintained a furious struggle against the left wing of the Russians: the Prussians, preceding by one hour Marshal Ney, who had been pursuing them for several days, made their appearance on the battle-field. The dead and dying formed round the emperor a ghastly rampart; gloomy and calm he contemplated the attack of the Prussians and Russians united, in great numbers, and pressing upon Marshal Davout. The latter glanced along the ranks of his troops: "The cowards will go to die in Siberia," said he, "the brave will die here like men of honor." The effort of the enemy died out against the heroic resistance of the French divisions, who maintained their positions.

The night was falling; the carnage was horrible. In spite of the serious advantage of the French troops, General Benningsen was preparing to attempt a new assault, when he learnt the approach of Marshal Ney, who was debouching towards Althof. The bad weather and the distance retarded the effect of the combinations of the emperor. He had caused much blood to be spilt; victory, however, remained with him; the Russians and Prussians were decidedly beating a retreat. The French remained masters of this most sanguinary battle-field, destitute of provisions, without shelter, in the wet and cold. Marshal Ney, who had taken no part in the action, to which, however, he assured success, surveyed the plain, covered with corpses and inundated with blood. "He turned away from the hideous spectacle," says M. de Fezensac, "crying, 'What a massacre, and without result!'" The Russians had retired behind the Pregel to cover Königsberg. Napoleon re-entered his cantonments. He established his headquarters at the little town of Osterode, directing from this advanced post the works of defence on the Vistula and Passarge, at the same time as the preparations for the siege of Dantzig. On arriving there he wrote to King Joseph: "Staff-officers, colonels, officers, have not undressed for two months, and a few of them not for four; I have myself been fifteen days without taking off my boots. We are in the midst of snow and mud, without wine, without brandy, without bread, eating potatoes and meat, making long marches and counter-marches, without anything to sweeten existence, and fighting at bayonet-point and under showers of grape-shot, the wounded very often obliged to be removed on a sledge for fifty leagues in the open air. After having destroyed the Prussian monarchy, we are making war against the remnants of Prussia, against the Russians, the Calmucs, the Cossacks, and the peoples of the north who formerly invaded the Roman Empire; we are making war in all its energy and all its horror." Such vigorous language was not permitted to all. "The gloomy pictures that have been drawn of our situation," wrote Napoleon to Fouché on April 13th, "have for authors a few gossips of Paris, who are simply blockheads. Never has the position of France been grander or finer. As to Eylau, I have said and resaid that the bulletin exaggerated the loss; and, for a great battle, what are 2000 men slain? There were none of the battles of Louis XIV. or Louis XV. which did not cost more. When I lead back my army to France and across the Rhine, it will be seen that there are not many wanting at the roll-call."

It was against Russia and against the vigor of its resistance that Napoleon now concentrated all his efforts. Tardy hostilities had at length commenced between the Porte and Russia. For a moment the Sultan had appeared to hesitate before the demands of the English, united to those of the Russians: Admiral Duckworth forced the Dardanelles at the head of a squadron, and destroyed the Turkish division anchored at Cape Nagara. In spite of the terror which reigned in Constantinople, the energetic influence of General Sebastiani carried the day. The overtures of the English Legation were repulsed; the capital was armed all of a sudden, under the direction of French officers. When Admiral Duckworth appeared before the place, he found it in good condition of defence; thus the English squadron could not leave the Straits of the Dardanelles without sustaining serious damage. For the British navy the evil was small; the moral effect could not but have some influence.

The Emperor Napoleon sought to profit by this circumstance to enter afresh into negotiations with Austria. On the day after the battle of Eylau he sent General Bertrand to the King of Prussia, offering to surrender him his States as far as the

Elbe. The messenger was charged with the significant insin-uation: "You will give just a hint that as to Poland, since the emperor has become acquainted with it, he attaches to it no value." The sacrifice of a fourth of the Prussian monarchy seemed too bitter for King Frederick William; he replied to the envoy with evasive answers. Napoleon became disdainful as regards the Prussians. It was with Austria that he deter-mined henceforth to treat concerning the affairs of Prussia. "See now my plan, and what you must say to M. de Vincent," wrote he on March 9, 1807, to Talleyrand: "To restore to the King of Prussia his throne and his estates, and to maintain the integrity of the Porte. As to Poland, that will be found included in the first part of the sentence. If these bases of peace suit Austria, we shall be able to understand each other. As for the remark of M. de Vincent, that Prussia is too thoroughly humiliated to hope for recovery, that is reason-able. The end of all this will be an arrangement between France and Austria, or between France and Russia; for there will be no repose for the people, who need it so much, except by this union."

Austria responded to these propositions of alliance by offer of mediation; at the same time, and without ostentation, as a precautionary measure, she was getting ready for war, and was secretly preparing her armaments. The small places in the north of Prussia had fallen, one after another; Dantzig alone was still waiting for the army which was to besiege it. The Prussians had profited by this delay to put the place into a good state of defence. On all sides Napoleon collected fresh forces, as if resolved upon terrifying his secret enemies and crushing his declared ones. The conscription for 1808 was en-forced in France by an anticipation of nearly two years; the Italian regiments and the auxiliary German corps were con-centrated on the Vistula; the emperor even went so far as to demand from Spain the contingent which the Prince de la Paix had offered him on the day after the battle of Jena. Formerly the Spanish minister had nursed other ideas, and had counted on serving the Prussians; he, however, hastened to despatch 10,000 men to the all-powerful conqueror. An army of reserve had just been created on the Elbe; by the middle of March the town of Dantzig was completely invested.

I do not care to recount the incidents of a siege which lasted more than two months, and which was conducted in a mas-terly manner by Chasseloup and Lariboisière. Marshal Lefebvre grew weary of the long and able preparations of his colleagues, and wished to begin the actual assault. Authorization for this step was asked of the emperor. "You only know how to grumble, to abuse your allies, and change your opinion at the will of the first comer," wrote Napoleon to the old warrior. "You treat the allies without any consideration; they are not accustomed to be under fire, but that will come. Do you think that we were as brave in '92 as we are to-day, after fifteen years of warfare? The chests of your grenadiers that you wish to push everywhere will not overturn walls; you must let your engineers work, and whilst waiting learn to have patience. The loss of a few days, which I should not just now know how to employ, does not require you to get several thousand men killed whose lives it is possible to economize. You will have the glory of taking Dantzig; when that is accomplished, you will be satisfied with me."

Meanwhile, the Russians and Prussians had resolved upon an attempt to raise the siege of Dantzig: a considerable body came to attack the French camp before the fort of Weichelsmunde. They were repulsed, after a furious combat, by the aid of the reinforcements which had arrived to succor Marshal Lefebvre; and the attempts of the English corvettes to revictual the town were equally unsuccessful. A previous attack of the Swedes upon Stralsund had brought about no definite result, and their general, Essen, had been constrained to conclude an armistice. Dantzig capitulated at last, on the 26th of May, without having undergone the assault which the French soldiers loudly demanded. As early as the 22nd, Napoleon had written to Marshal Lefebvre: "I authorize Marshal Kalbreuth to go out under the ordinary regulations, wishing to give this general an especial proof of esteem; however, the capitulation of Mayence cannot be taken as a basis, as the siege was less advanced than that of Dantzig now is. I allowed, at the time, an honorable capitulation for General Wurmser, shut up in Mantua; I wish to accord one more advantageous to General Kalbreuth, taking a middle position between that of Mayence and that of Mantua."

All the French *corps d'armée* occupied entrenched camps, prudently defended against the attacks of enemies; they were suffering from the rigors of the winter, and the large stores of wine found in Dantzig were an important resource for the soldiers. The attempts at mediation by Austria had failed; the campaign of 1809 was being prepared; everywhere the grass was springing up in the fields, affording necessary sustenance for the horses; the wild swans were reappearing in flocks upon the shores of the Passarge. The Emperor Napoleon had fixed upon the 10th of June for the resumption of hostilities.

The Russians forestalled it: Alexander had sent his guard to General Benningsen. "Brothers, uphold honor!" said the young emperor to his soldiers as they began the march. "We will do everything that is possible," cried the troops: "adieu, master!" Already Benningsen was advancing against the corps of Ney, who occupied the advanced posts, but the clever and prudent arrangements of Napoleon had prepared the retreat of his lieutenants; without disorder and without weakness, always victoriously fighting, Marshal Ney fell back upon Deppen; two other attacks upon the bridges of Lanutten and Spanden were likewise repulsed. The concentration of the French *corps d'armée* began to be effected near Saafeldt, when General Benningsen changed all of a sudden his plan of campaign: passing from the offensive to the defensive, he decided to repass the Alle, in order to protect the entrenched camp of Heilsberg, and by the same movement the town of Königsberg, the last refuge of the resources of Prussia. The retreat of the Russians commenced on the evening of the 7th of June.

Napoleon followed them with almost the whole of his army; the detachments of the vanguard and rearguard had more than once been engaged in partial combats when, on the evening of the 10th of June, the French army debouched before the entrenched camp of Heilsberg strongly supported by the banks of the Alle. Napoleon followed the left bank, seeking to forestall the enemy at the confluence of the Allo and the Pregel, in the hope of seizing Königsberg before the place could be succored. Murat and Davout were already threatening the city.

It was the supreme feature in the genius of Napoleon, that an indomitable perseverance in wisely calculated projects did not exclude the thunderbolts of a marvellous promptitude in resolution and combinations. Uncertainty and want of foresight reigned, on the contrary, in the military councils of the Russians. General Benningsen, formerly in the attitude of attack, now compelled to engage in a defensive march, and projecting the defence of Königsberg, thought it all of a sudden necessary to protect himself against an attack in flank. He crossed the Alle under the eyes of the French, and meeting them on the left bank of the river, he advanced towards the corps of Marshal Lannes, whom the emperor had sent against Domnau; a strong Russian detachment drove from Friedland the regiment of French hussars, who had established themselves there. The whole Russian army attacked Marshal Lannes, who had just collected a few reinforcements. It was to judge badly of the able prudence of the Emperor Napoleon, to hope to encounter a single corps of his grand army: Lannes held out till mid-day upon the field of battle with heroic skill; he sent meanwhile express after express to the emperor, who arrived at a gallop, his face radiant with the anticipation of the joys of victory. "It is the 14th of June," said he, "the anniversary of Marengo; it is a lucky day for us."

Napoleon and his staff had preceded the march of the troops; Lannes and his soldiers recovered their forces in the presence of the invincible chief who had so many times led them to victory. "Give me only a reinforcement, sire," cried Oudinot, whose coat was pierced with bullets, "and although my grenadiers can do no more, we will cast all the Russians into the water."

This was the aim of the emperor as well as of his soldiers; and the positions which General Benningsen had taken, concentred in a bend of the river, rendered the enterprise practicable. The day was advanced, and a few of the generals had been wishing to put off the battle till the morrow. "No!" said Napoleon; "one does not surprise the enemy twice in such a blunder." Then sweeping with his telescope the masses of the enemy grouped before him, he quickly seized the arm of Marshal Ney. "You see the Russians and Friedland," said he; "the bridges are there—there only. March right on before you; enter into Friedland; take the bridges, whatever it may cost, and do not disquiet yourself about what shall take place on your right, or your left, or in your rear. That concerns us—the army and me."

When Marshal Ney had set out, marching to danger as to a festival, the emperor turned towards Marshal Mortier and said, "That man is a lion."

Upon the field of battle, where he had just arrived in face of the enemy, who appeared hesitating and troubled, Napoleon dictated his orders, which he caused to be delivered to all his lieutenants. The troops continued to arrive; all the corps formed again at the posts which had been assigned to them.

The emperor checked the impatience of his generals. "The action," he told them, "will commence when the battery posted in the village of Posthenen shall commence to fire." It was half-past five when the cannon at last sounded.

Ney advanced towards Friedland under a terrible fire from the Russians; extricated by the cavalry of Latour-Marbourg, and protected by the artillery of General Victor, suddenly thrown in advance, the French columns had reached a stream defended by the imperial Russian guard. The resistance of these picked troops for a moment threw disorder into our lines, who fell back; when General Dupont, arriving with his division, broke the Russian guard. The French in pursuit of their enemies penetrated into Friedland. The city was in flames; the fugitives fled towards the bridges; a very small number had succeeded in reaching them when this only means of safety was snatched from them; the bridges were cut and set on fire when Marshal Ney took possession of the burning remains of Friedland. At the same moment the corps of General Gortschakoff, pressed by Marshals Lannes and Mortier, fighting valiantly in a position without egress, sought in vain to reconquer the city, and afterwards redescended the length of the river in the hope of finding fordable passages. Many soldiers were drowned, others succeeded in regaining the right shore. Almost the entire column of General Lambert succeeded in escaping. Night at length followed the long twilight; it was ten o'clock in the evening when the combat ceased. The victory was complete; the remains of the Russian army retired upon the Pregel without Napoleon being able again to encounter them. They soon afterwards gained the Niemen. Meanwhile Marshal Soult had occupied Königsberg, evacuated by Generals Lestocq and Kaminsky. The King of Prussia possessed nothing more than the little town of Memel.

The Emperor Alexander had rejoined his troops, vanquished and decimated in spite of their courage; the King Frederick William placed himself close to his ally, at Tilsit. Peace had become necessary for the Russians; for the Prussians it had long been so. Napoleon resolved on negotiating for himself. In response to the request for an armistice, he proposed an interview, with the Emperor Alexander. It was in the middle of the Niemen, upon a raft constructed for this purpose, that the two emperors met.

Alexander was young, amiable, winning, drawn along at

times by chivalrous or mystical sentiments and enthusiasms, at other times under the dominion of Oriental tastes and passions. No one could be more. capable of being influenced by the charm of a superior genius and an extraordinary destiny, and the personal ascendancy of a man who knew at once how to please and how to vex.

Napoleon wished to captivate his vanquished enemy, whom he desired to make his ally; he succeeded in doing so with ease. Master of the destinies of the world—in his own idea more so than he even was in reality—he had resolved upon offering to Alexander compensations which might satisfy him, whilst distracting his attention from the conquests and encroachments which Napoleon reserved for himself. On the eve of Austerlitz, Napoleon had said to Prince Dolgorouki: "Ah well! let Russia extend herself at the expense of her neighbors!" It was the same thought that he was about to present to the young monarch, humiliated and conquered, wishing to display it before his eyes in order to blind him more completely.

The Russians and Prussians were equally irritated against England. She had granted them money, but her military efforts had not corresponded with her promises; and it was to her obstinate hatred of France that the two monarchs attributed the origin of their defeats. "If you have a grudge against England," said Alexander, "we shall easily understand each other, for I have myself to complain of her as much as you have." It was in this first interview the sole effort of Napoleon to develop in the mind of Alexander the sentiments of anger and weariness by which. he had been inspired by the selfishness which he imputed to Great Britain and the inability and weakness which he recognized in Prussia, and to engage the Russian emperor to become friendly with the only power which could offer him a glorious and profitable alliance. In the mind of the emperor, we have already said, the necessity for a continental alliance had long since made itself felt. "Austria or Russia," he had said to Talleyrand. Napoleon offered his hand to the Emperor Alexander.

The city of Tilsit was neutralized, and the two emperors established their quarters there. Before quitting the opposite shore of the Niemen, Alexander presented the King of Prussia to Napoleon in that floating pavilion on the river which flowed between the two nations. Honest, moderate, and dignified even in his profound abasement, Frederick William neither experienced nor exercised in any degree the seductiveness to which the Emperor Alexander succumbed, and which he was in his turn capable of displaying. He entreated his ally to make constant and persevering efforts in his behalf, which Alexander felt himself compelled to do not without a secret ill feeling. It was with an ostentatious display of graciousness and condescension that Napoleon ceaselessly reminded the young Czar that he accorded no favor to the King of Prussia except out of regard for his entreaties.

" In the midst of the war in which Russia and France have been engaged," wrote Napoleon, on the 4th of July, 1807, " both sovereigns, enlightened as to the situation and the true policy of their empires, have desired the re-establishment not only of peace, but of a common accord, and by the force of reason and truth have wished to form an alliance, and to pass in a single instant from open war to the most intimate relations. The boundless amity and confidence which the high qualities of the Emperor Alexander have inspired in the Emperor Napoleon have caused his heart to seal that which his reason had already approved and ratified. The protection of the emperor will result in the King of Prussia being allowed to re-enter into the possession of all the countries which border on the two Haffs, extending from the sources of the Oder to the sea. Solely with a desire of pleasing the Emperor Alexander, a large number of fortified towns will be restored to the King of Prussia. The policy of the Emperor Napoleon is that his immediate influence should be bounded by the Elbe; and he has adopted this policy because it is the only one which can be reconciled with the system of sincere and constant amity which he wishes to maintain with the great empire of the north."

Under the veil of this apparent moderation the pretensions or resolutions of the Emperor Napoleon were thus summed up: King Frederick William recovered Old Prussia, Pomerania, Brandenburg, Upper and Lower Silesia; he would abandon all the provinces to the left of the Elbe, which were to constitute, with the Grand Duchy of Hesse, a kingdom of Westphalia, destined for Joseph Bonaparte. The Duchies of Posen and Warsaw, snatched from Russian Poland, were to form a Polish State under the title of the Grand Duchy of Warsaw, of which the Elector of Saxony, recently elevated to the royal dignity, received the gift, on condition of maintaining a military road

VII.—11

across Silesia. All the States founded by Napoleon were to be recognized. Russia was charged with the mediation between France and England; France became arbitrator between Russia and the Porte.

It was much, and indeed too much, for Prussia, torn asunder without being completely destroyed, reduced to the half of its territory, and deprived of its most important towns—for Dantzig became a free city, and Magdeburg formed part of the new kingdom of Westphalia. When these hard conditions were revealed to Frederick William by the Emperor Alexander, the unfortunate king protested against a ruin so complete. He conceived, for a moment, the vain hope of obtaining from Napoleon some concessions, by bringing to bear on him the influence of the genius and beauty of Queen Louisa. This princess quitted Memel to present herself at Tilsit. " She is charming," wrote Napoleon to the Empress Josephine; but this cold appreciation of the accomplishments of the woman exercised no influence upon the resolutions of the conqueror and the politician. The queen in vain brought into play all the resources of her intellect and her charming graces; in vain presenting to the conqueror a rose which she had just plucked, she ventured to ask for Magdeburg in exchange for her flower. "It is you who have offered it to me, madame," said Napoleon, roughly. Queen Louisa quitted Memel, humiliated and sorrowful down to the very depths of her soul. Her children and her people were never to pardon us for their wrongs.

Alexander had loyally defended his friend, and felt assured of having obtained for him all that it was possible to obtain; in his secret thoughts he consoled himself for the concessions he had been constrained to make for others as well as for himself, by the dazzling prospects which Napoleon knew so well how to open brightly to his view. To the north and south the young Czar believed himself master of new territories, long objects of ambition to the Russian Empire. The Sultan Selim had just fallen at Constantinople before a revolt of the Janissaries; he was a prisoner in his own palace, and the government which was about to succeed him would naturally be hostile to French influence. Napoleon then found himself free to abandon to Russia a large part of that Ottoman Empire always coveted by her. " Constantinople! never!" Napoleon had said, in exclamation to himself, heard by one of his secretaries; "the empire of the world is at Constantinople!" But the *débris* of the Turkish power were of a character to satisfy all the claimants; and in case Turkey should not accept the peace, the secret treaty concluded between France and Russia assured to the Czar all the European provinces, with the exception of Constantinople and Roumelia. In case of the cabinet of London refusing the mediation of Russia, Alexander engaged himself to declare war against England. Should Portugal and Sweden, equally subject to European influence, participate in the same refusal, it was agreed that the Emperor Napoleon should send an army into Portugal, and that the Emperor Alexander should enter Sweden. Finland lay very convenient for the Russian Empire. "The King of Sweden is in truth your brother-in-law and your ally," said Napoleon; "let him follow the changes in your policy, or let him undergo the consequences of his ill-will. Sweden is the geographical enemy of Russia. St. Petersburg finds itself too near to Finland. The good Russians must no longer hear from their palaces at St. Petersburg the cannon of the Swedes."

The treaty of Tilsit was concluded on the 7th of July, 1807, and was signed on the 8th. The King and Queen of Prussia departed immediately, full of bitter sorrow and discouragement. The two emperors separated on the 9th, with a cordiality at that time sincere in its ostentatious display. More than once they had together passed their troops in review; yet once again they showed themselves to the two armies. Napoleon decorated, with his own hand, a soldier of the Russian army, who had been pointed out to him by the Czar. At last he accompanied Alexander to the shores of the Niemen, waiting upon the bank until his friend and ally had reached the farther shore. Then entering his carriage, he took the road to Königsberg, and immediately afterwards that to France, charging Berthier and Marshal Kalbreuth with the regulation of the details of the evacuation of Prussia, and the payment of the war contributions with which the conquered countries were to be crushed down. On the 27th of July, at six o'clock in the morning, the emperor re-entered Paris, which he had quitted the preceding year, and which, since then, he had so many times intoxicated with the report of his victories. The military glory was brilliant and even dazzling; the political work remained precarious, by its nature as well as by its immensity. Empires founded upon conquest are necessarily fragile, even when the war has been undertaken from serious and legitimate motives. When the war is carried on through the ambition of a man or a people, in scorn of right or justice

—when it injures at once the interests, the pride, and the repose of all nations—no genius or brightness of glory can succeed in assuring its duration, or legitimatizing its success.
France perceived this in the midst of the enthusiasm of victory. England repeated it with malicious confidence, in the
hope of confirming the courage of its people. Once more the
latter power found itself alone, in face of the ever-increasing
might of France and the incomparable genius of its sovereign.

It is the mournful effect of a weakening of the moral sense
in the chief of a state, to enfeeble that moral sense at the same
time, and by an inevitable contagion, amongst his rivals and
adversaries. In presence of the continental blockade, and of
the resolution which the Emperor Napoleon had announced of
imposing it upon the whole of Europe, the English cabinet,
henceforth directed by the inheritors of the policy of Pitt, by
Canning and Lord Castlereagh, resolved upon using violence
in its turn. Fearful of seeing the maritime forces of Denmark
pass into the power of Napoleon, England violated the neutrality of this little kingdom, and forestalled the secret conditions of the treaty of Tilsit. Lord Cathcart, at the head of a
considerable squadron, was charged with the duty of summoning the Prince Regent to deliver to him the Danish fleet, as a
pledge of the loyal intentions of his country; he offered at the
same time to defend the Danish territory and all its colonies.
The prince responded with bitter irony, "Your protection?
Have we not seen your allies waiting for succor more than a
year, without receiving it?" Copenhagen was bombarded;
Sir Arthur Wellesley, whose name, for the first time, became
known in Europe, effected his disembarkation with a corps of
10,000 men. The prince saw himself compelled to capitulate,
and deliver to the English his fleet, with all the matériel of his
arsenals. Vehemently did Europe reprobate this act of violence. The English cabinet made public the article of the
Treaty of Tilsit, which had furnished the motive for its agres-
sion. But any effort at mediation was now ridiculous. The
Emperor Alexander perceived it to be so. On the 11th of
November, Lord Leveson Gower, then Ambassador of England
at St. Petersburg, received his passports, and the Czar haughtily
adhered to the French alliance. "I deem it prudent to close
one's eyes against the orders which English mercantile vessels
have received to quit Russian ports," said General Savary,
whom Napoleon had accredited to the Emperor Alexander.
The latter treated the French envoy with distinction, but the

court and world of St. Petersburg had not forgotten the part that Savary had taken in the murder of the Duke d'Enghien; he remained isolated in his palace, and even in the saloons of the emperor. The Russian declaration of war was responded to by the manifesto of England. "Publish the treaty of Tilsit, with the secret articles," said Canning; "they have not been communicated to England, but we are acquainted with them, nevertheless; they will explain to Europe our conduct and our fears, as well as the change of attitude on the part of Russia." The Emperor Napoleon was already regretting the magnificent prospect which he had opened before the Czar on the side of Turkey; the government of the Sublime Porte had adroitly accepted the mediation of France. Napoleon sought to excite the covetousness of the Russians towards the north; M. de Caulaincourt, who had replaced Savary at St. Petersburg, pushed forward with ardor the war against Sweden, and the conquest of Finland. As a consequence of the English aggression, Denmark had cast itself into the arms of France; it accordingly became easy to close against England the passage of the Sound. The Czar and his favorite counsellor, M. de Romanzoff, returned ceaselessly to the hopes that Napoleon had led them to conceive. "The ancient Ottoman Empire is played out," said the Russian minister; "unless the Czar lays his hand on it, the Emperor Napoleon will be soon obliged to announce in the *Moniteur* that the succession of the Sultans is open, and the natural heirs have only to present themselves."

In the meantime, and as a constant menace against an ally whom he was not completely satisfying, Napoleon was prolonging his occupation of the Prussian territory, under the pretext of the alleged slowness of payment of the war contributions; he was organizing provisionally the government of Hanover, which he had reserved as a future bait for the English government; and he was treating with Spain for the passage of troops necessary for the invasion of Portugal. This power, constantly faithful to the English alliance, having refused to give in its adhesion to the continental blockade, the emperor had sent against it General Junot with 26,000 men. The negotiations with Madrid had not been completed, and the French soldiers had already entered Spanish territory. A second army was preparing to follow them. Austria remained disquieted, and ready to take offence; a convention favorable to her was signed at Fontainebleau, on October 10th. On the 27th the eventual and provisional partition of Portugal was

accepted by the Spanish envoy, Yzquierdo. A kingdom of
Southern Lusitania was assigned to the Queen of Etruria, who
renounced her Italian possessions; the independent principality
of Algarve was to be constituted for the Prince de la Paix; the
emperor reserved for himself the centre of the country, conquered by anticipation. A Spanish corps was to join the
French troops for the invasion of Portugal. General Junot
marched upon Lisbon. Vast projects, unjustifiable in their
nature, were linked with this invasion of the Peninsula, necessarily entailing blunders and crimes as dangerous as lamentable. Napoleon had resolved upon driving the Bourbons from
all the thrones of Europe, in order to replace them with Bonapartes. He set out for Italy with the view of completing one
part of his work before laying his hand on Spain.

Quitting Paris on November 16th, the Emperor surprised
Eugene Beauharnais (whom he was about solemnly to adopt)
by assuring to him the succession of the crown of Italy. He
ran through the north of the Italian peninsula, reorganizing at
Venice the public services, which had fallen into desuetude;
decreeing the creation of a commune on Mont Cenis; and providing for the needs of travellers by the new route which he
had opened. At Mantua he had an interview with his brother
Lucien, whom he would have wished to place upon the throne
of Portugal, but that the latter remained obstinately rebellious
against the authority of his all-powerful brother, who required
of him the rupture of an already old union with Madame Jou-
berthon. Having returned to Milan on the 13th of December,
Napoleon published there, on the 17th, a decree destined to
aggravate the rigors of the continental blockade. By reprisals
as unjust as awkward, directed against decree of Berlin, the
English Cabinet had promulgated, on the 11th of November,
1807, an Order in Council which compelled the ships of all
neutral nations to touch at an English port to import or export
merchandise, paying custom-house dues averaging 25 per cent.
The ships which neglected this precaution were to be declared
lawful prizes. In response, the Emperor Napoleon decreed
that any vessel touching at an English port, or submitting to
inspection from an English ship, should be by that very fact
deneutralized, and become in its turn a lawful prize. In this
insensate rivalry, which ruined at the same time the commerce
of England and of the world, the Cabinet of London had taken
no care to modify, in favor of the United States, the rigor of
its ordinances. This was for England the occasion of grave

difficulties, and of a war at one time dangerous.   Arbitrary interference and violence were the rule on all the seas.

Through difficulties and sufferings which threatened to destroy the army placed under his orders, General Junot arrived at the gates of Lisbon.   He had to struggle with no other enemy than the bad roads and the want of provisions.   Terror had seized upon the royal house of Portugal.   The *Moniteur* of November 13th already contained an article upon the fall of the illustrious house of Braganza.   "The Prince Regent of Portugal loses his throne," said the official journal; " he loses it influenced by the intrigues of the English; he loses it for not having been willing to seize the English merchandise at Lisbon.   What does England do,—this ally so powerful?   She regards with indifference all that is passing in Portugal.   What will she do when Portugal shall be taken?   Will she go to seize Brazil?   No; if the English make this attempt the Catholics will drive them out.   The fall of the House of Braganza will remain another proof that the fall of whatever attaches itself to the English is inevitable."

The Prince Regent of Portugal had thought it possible to arrest the march of General Junot by sending to him emissaries charged to make all the submissions required by Napoleon. The envoys had not been able to meet the French army, scattered and decimated by the ills it had undergone; it advanced, however, and the news of its approach drove the Court of Portugal on board the ships which were still to be found at the mouth of the Tagus.   On November 27th the mad queen, her son the prince regent, her daughters, and nearly all the families of distinction in Lisbon, accompanied by their servants, crowded on board the Portuguese fleet, resolved to take their flight to Brazil.   From seven to eight thousand persons, with all their portable property, thus obstructed the mouth of the Tagus, protected by the English fleet; on the 28th a favorable wind permitted them to sail.   When General Junot entered Lisbon, on the 30th of November, at eight o'clock in the morning, the treasures which he was charged to seize were beyond his reach.   He established himself without resistance in the capital, soon overwhelmed with confiscations and war contributions.   "Everything is more easy in the first moment than afterwards," wrote the Emperor to Junot on the 13th of December, 1807.   "Do not seek for popularity at Lisbon, nor for the means of pleasing the nation; that would be failing in your aim, emboldening the people, and preparing misfortunes for yourself. The hope that you conceive of commerce and prosperity, is a chimera with which one is lulled asleep."

Jerome Bonaparte had been declared King of Westphalia on the 8th of December. On the 10th the act announced by the treaty of Fontainebleau was consummated. The Queen Regent of Etruria, Maria Louisa of Bourbon, declared to her subjects, in the name of her son, that she was called upon to reign over a new kingdom. Tuscany then fell directly into the hands of the Emperor Napoleon, who confided its government to his sister, Eliza Baciocchi, to whom he had already given the principality of Lucca and Piombino.

Submission or flight! such was the only alternative that seemed to remain to continental sovereigns in presence of the exactions and the imperious will of Napoleon. The Pope alone, as already for two years past, was still resisting his demands, and was evincing an independence with regard to him which was every day irritating more and more the all-powerful master of Europe. Sadly disabused of the illusions and the hopes which had drawn him to Paris for the coronation of Napoleon, Pius VII. had preserved in his personal communications with the emperor a paternal and tender graciousness. He had much to obtain and much to fear on the part of the conqueror. Returning to Italy in the month of June, 1805, he said, in his allocution to the cardinals: "We have clasped in our arms at Fontainebleau this prince, so powerful and so full of love for us. Many things have already been done, and are only the earnest of that which is yet to be accomplished."

Meanwhile, the Code Napoleon had been applied to Italy, authorizing divorce, and taking the place of the Italian Concordat, which declared the Catholic religion to be the religion of the State. The Pope had complained of it, not without warmth, and had received on the part of the emperor assurances which were as vain as they were futile. But already the conflict was becoming personal and more pressing; the refusal of the Holy Father to dissolve the marriage of Jerome Bonaparte with Miss Paterson (June, 1805), at once produced antagonism between the conscience of the Pope and the views of Napoleon as to the elevation of his family to the new or ancient thrones which he destined for them in Europe. Pius VII. had long studied canonical interdictions; he consulted neither his ministers nor his doctors; it was a personal reply which he addressed to the emperor. "It is out of our power," said he, " to pronounce the judgment of nullity; if we were to usurp such an authority that we have not, we should render ourselves culpable of an abominable abuse before the tribunal of God; and your Majesty yourself, in your justice, would blame us for pronouncing a sentence contrary to the testimony of our conscience and to the invariable principles of our Church."

Napoleon's anger remained warm, but he had surmounted the difficulty by dissolving by an imperial decree the marriage of his brother, and by causing him soon after to marry a princess of Wurtemberg. The disagreement with the Court of Rome, which was soon to break forth, depended on his all-powerful will, and caused him no care. In the movement of the troops, necessitated in October, 1805, by his campaign against Austria, the emperor had charged General Gouvion St. Cyr to traverse the States of the Church in order to take up a position in Lombardy. Upon the route lay the town of Ancona. The French troops received an order to seize the place and establish a garrison there, an order which was immediately executed.

In spite of the difficulties which had recently arisen between the emperor and himself, the Pope thought that Napoleon and the French Revolution were much indebted to him personally. Europe took this view, and frequent reproaches had been addressed to the Court of Rome by the powers who were enemies or rivals of France. It was, then, with astonishment, mingled with indignation, that Pius VII. learnt the news of the occupation of Ancona; he wrote, on the 13th November, 1805, a personal and secret letter to the emperor:—"We avow frankly to your Majesty the keen chagrin that we experience in seeing ourselves treated in a way that we do not think we have in any degree merited. Our neutrality has been recognized by your Majesty, as by all other powers. The latter have fully respected it, and we had especial motives for thinking that the sentiments of amity which your Majesty professed with regard to us would have preserved us from such a cruel affront. We will tell you frankly, since our return from Paris we have experienced only bitterness and trouble, and we do not find in your Majesty a return of those sentiments which we think ourselves warranted in justly expecting from you. That which we owe to ourselves is to ask from your Majesty the evacuation of Ancona, and, if met with a refusal, we should not see how to reconcile therewith a continuation of a good understanding with the French minister."

It was from Munich, on the morrow of the battle of Austerlitz and of the peace of Presburg, that Napoleon at length responded, on the 7th of January, 1806, to the letter of the Pope,
in the midst of the concert of adulations and transports which
were lavished on him by the vanquished as well as by his courtiers.   The protest of Pius VII. recalled to him the disagreeable
remembrance of an independent authority, and one which he
had not been always able to submit to his will; the anger of the
despot broke forth with violence at once spontaneous and
measured: " Your Holiness complains that since your return
from Paris you have had nothing but causes of sorrow.   The
reason is, that since then all those who were fearing my power
and testifying their friendship have changed their sentiments,
thinking themselves authorized to do so by the power of the
coalition; and that since the return of your Holiness to Rome
I have experienced nothing but refusals to all my designs, even
those that were of the utmost importance to religion; as, for
example, when it was a question of hindering Protestantism
from raising its head in France.   I look upon myself as the
protector of the Holy See, and by this title I have occupied
Ancona.   I look upon myself, like my predecessors of the
second and third dynasty, as the eldest son of the Church, as
alone bearing the sword to protect it and to shelter it from being defiled by Greeks and Mussulmans.   I should ever be the
friend of your Holiness, if you would only consult your heart
and the true friends of religion.   If your Holiness wishes to
send away my minister, you are free to do so.   You are free to
receive in preference the English and the Caliph of Constantinople.   God is the judge who has done most for the religion of
all the princes who reign."

Napoleon had excluded his brother Jerome from the succession to the Empire, but he affected to dread for France the possibility of a Protestant sovereign.   It was with an increase of
coarse violence that he wrote on the same day to his uncle,
Cardinal Fesch: " Since these imbeciles think there will be no
inconvenience in a Protestant occupying the throne of France,
I will send them a Protestant ambassador.   I am religious, but
I am not a bigot.   Constantine separated the civil from the
military, and I also may appoint a senator to command in my
name at Rome.   Tell Consalvi—tell even the Pope himself—
that since he wishes to drive my minister from Rome, I should
be well able to re-establish him there.   For the Pope, I am
Charlemagne, because, like Charlemagne, I unite the crown of

France with that of the Lombards, and my empire borders on that of the East. I expect then that his conduct towards me shall be regulated from this point of view. Otherwise I shall reduce the Pope to the position of Bishop of Rome."

The French troops did not evacuate Ancona, and the French minister remained at Rome. But soon new subjects of disagreement arose between Napoleon and the Pope, always a scrupulous observer of the neutrality which he thought due from him to all the powers. The emperor had already required that all the ports of his allies should be closed against English commerce; in proportion as his enemies became more numerous and his arbitrary power more oppressive, he extended his pretensions even over the countries neutral by situation and by state obligations. Joseph Bonaparte had just been proclaimed King of Naples; the house of Bourbon occupied in Italy only the ridiculous throne of Etruria, already on the point of being taken from them. Napoleon wished to exact from the Pope an interdiction of his ports and his territory to the exiles or the refugees who had from time immemorial been accustomed to seek an asylum in Rome. "Your Holiness would be able to avoid all these embarrassments by going forward in a straight road," wrote Napoleon to Pius VII., on February 22, 1806. "All Italy will be subject to my laws. I will not touch in any way the independence of the Holy See; I will even repay it for the injuries which the movements of my armies may occasion to it; but it must be on the condition that your Holiness will show the same regard for me in temporal affairs as I show for you in spiritual ones, and that you will cease your useless consideration for the heretical enemies of the Church, and for the powers who can do nothing for you. Your Holiness is sovereign of Rome, but I am its emperor. All my enemies ought to be yours. It is not proper then that any agent of the King of Sardinia, any Englishman, Russian, or Swede, should reside at Rome or in your states, neither that any ship belonging to these powers should enter your ports. Those who speak any other language to your Holiness deceive you, and will end by drawing down upon you misfortunes that will be disastrous." He added in his letter to Cardinal Fesch: "Say plainly that I have my eyes open, that I am not deceived any more than I choose to be; that I am Charlemagne, the sword of the Church, the emperor; and that they ought not to know that there is an empire of Russia. I make the Pope acquainted with my intentions in a few words. If he does not agree, I shall reduce

him to the same position which he occupied before Charlemagne."

It was against Cardinal Consalvi, formerly the clever and
firm negotiator of the Concordat, that the emperor, assisted by
Cardinal Fesch, nursed his suspicions and his anger; he regarded him as systematically hostile to France; but the
attachment of the Pope for his minister remained unshakable;
it was from Consalvi alone that a voluntary submission
might be hoped for. "If he loves his religion and his country,
tell Consalvi, plainly," wrote the emperor to his uncle, "that
there are only two courses to select from—either to do always
what I wish, or to quit the ministry."

The moderation and prudent resolutions of the Roman ministry showed itself in the response of the Pope to the requirements of Napoleon. Already an obscure Englishman—Mr.
Jackson, for a long time accredited to the King of Sardinia—
had excited the mistrust of Napoleon, who insulted him in
official documents. "An English minister, the disgrace of his
country, found in Rome an asylum. There he organized con-
spiracies, subsidized brigands, hatched perfidies, bribed assassins; and Rome protected the traitor and his agents—becoming
a theatre of scandal, a manufactory of libels, and an asylum
of brigandage." The only crime of Jackson had been to keep
his court *au courant* with the state of affairs in Rome.
Quietly, and with all the respect his character merited, Cardinal Consalvi prevailed on Mr Jackson to quit Rome. The
cardinals were assembled in secret Consistory. Cardinal Fesch
was not summoned; he was informed that they were aware of
his opinions, and that his station as ambassador disqualified
him for the Council of the holy father.

The Consistory did not deceive itself for a single instant as
to the consequences that the concessions demanded by Napoleon would forcibly draw in their train. "We all saw," says
Cardinal Consalvi in his memoirs, "that far from admitting
the neutrality of the Holy See, Bonaparte expected it in the
capacity of feudatory and vassal to take up the quarrels of
France in no matter what war the latter might subsequently
be engaged. The Holy See might then see itself, any morning
or evening, attacked by Austria or Spain, or by all the Catholic or non-Catholic powers. What! the sole ambition or
greed of France was to have the right of despoiling the holy
father of his title of the common father of the faithful, and of
compelling the representative of a God of Peace and the head

of the religious world, to sow everywhere desolation and ruin, by keeping in a perpetual state of war the nations owing fealty to the tiara."

So many reasons, human and divine, as evident to common sense as to conscience, decided the response of the Pope. He was moderate, tender, prudent; but he replied categorically to the requirements of the emperor. Pius VII. wished to remain neuter, and not to drive from his states the English or the Russians; he did not admit the claim of the emperor to exercise over Rome a supreme protectorate. "The Pope does not recognize, and never has recognized, any power superior to himself. Your Majesty is infinitely great; you have been elected, crowned, consecrated, recognized emperor of the French, but not emperor of Rome. There exists no emperor of Rome."

There was a good deal of boldness in repelling so haughtily the imperial pretensions; the Pope and Cardinal Consalvi were soon involved in a still more dangerous course. The accession of the new King of Naples had been announced to the court of Rome, by Cardinal Fesch, in arrogant terms: "The throne of Naples being vacant by a penalty incurred by the most scandalous perfidy of which the annals of nations have ever made mention, and his Majesty having found himself under the necessity of shielding this country, and the whole of Italy, from the madness of an insensate court, has judged it suitable to his dignity to confide the destinies of this country, which he loves, to a prince of his own house. The undersigned doubts not but that the Pontifical Government will see in this happy event a new guarantee of the system of order, justice, and consistency, which he has always had at heart to establish in all the places which have submitted to his influence."

To this circuitous demand for the recognition of Joseph Bonaparte, the Pope replied by urging his ancient feudal rights over the kingdom of Naples—"agreements," said Cardinal Consalvi, "which have always been observed, especially in the case of conquests; not only at the establishment of a new dynasty, but also at the commencement of each new reign."

It was going very far back into history to reclaim doubtful rights. Napoleon keenly criticised the pretension: "His Majesty needs to make no researches to become aware of the fact that in times of ignorance the court of Rome usurped the right of giving away crowns and temporal rights to the princes

of the earth; but if we found that in other ages the court of
Rome dethroned sovereigns, preached crusades, and laid entire
kingdoms under interdict, we should also discover that the
Popes have always considered their temporal power as springing from the French emperors; and the court of Rome, without doubt, does not claim that Charlemagne received from it
the investiture of his kingdom. If this is to go on,'"added
Napoleon, brusquely abandoning his historic researches, "I
shall cause Consalvi to quit Rome, and make him responsible
for what he is trying to do, because he is evidently bought by
the English. He will see whether or not I have the power to
maintain my imperial crown. Lay stress on that word
imperial, and not royal, and upon the fact that the relations
of the Pope with me must be those of his predecessors with the
emperors of the west." *

At the same time, and as the thunder follows the lightning,
the court of Rome learnt that the threat had been followed by
performance. Upon the express order of the Emperor Napoleon, Civita Vecchia had been occupied by two regiments of the
Neapolitan army. The districts of Benevento and Ponte-Corvo,
surrounded by the kingdom of Naples, and belonging to the
Holy See, were erected into principalities in favor of Talleyrand and Marshal Bernadotte. Cardinal Fesch was recalled.
He quitted Rome after a warm altercation with the Pope. A
few days later, and in the vain hope of ameliorating political
relations becoming more and more difficult, Cardinal Consalvi
gave in his resignation. He wrote to Cardinal Caprara, perpetual papal legate at Paris and completely subject to
the imperial authority: " If any one had told me when I was
negotiating the Concordat that in a short time I should appear
to the French Government in the light of an enemy, I should
have thought I was dreaming. But I am too much attached
to the Holy See, to my sovereign, to my benefactor, and to my
country, not to consider myself as compelled to dispel by my
retirement the evils which might result from my presence.
His Holiness consents to my resignation. His object has been
to satisfy the emperor, and give him a proof of his desire to
preserve harmony with his government by removing everything that might compromise it."

The sacrifice of Cardinal Consalvi was useless, and passed
unnoticed. Napoleon required from the Holy See not only sub-

---

* **Draft of a** note sent to Talleyrand by the emperor.

mission to his will, but the acceptance of his principles. The caution of the court of Rome irritated him more and more. He frightened Cardinal Caprara with a violent scene: "Write that I demand from his Holiness a declaration without ambiguity, stating that during the present war, and any other future war, all the ports of the pontifical states shall be closed to all English vessels, either of war or commerce. Without this I shall cause all the rest of the pontifical states to be occupied, I will have the eagles fixed up over the gates of all its cities and domains, and, as I have done for Benevento and Ponte Corvo, I shall divide the provinces possessed by the Pope into so many duchies and principalities, which I shall confer upon whomsoever I please. If the Pope persists in his refusal, I will establish a senate at Rome; and when once Rome and the pontifical states shall be in my hands, they will never be out of them again." Already the revenues of Civita Vecchia had been seized by Generals Lemarrois and Duhesme. "By what right do you do this?" demanded an employé of the pontifical treasury. "You serve a little prince and I serve a great sovereign," replied the officer; "in that you can see all my right." Such was throughout Europe the foundation of the right of the Emperor Napoleon. The governor of Civita Vecchia, Mgr. Negreta, had been seized by force in his residence, and sent back to Rome without an escort. Personal communication no longer existed between the Pope and the emperor. The letter of Pius VII., sent by the hands of Cardinal Caprara, remained unanswered. Alquier alone, who had succeeded Cardinal Fesch at Rome, still informed Napoleon as to the state of feeling there. An old Conventional, intelligent and moderate, the Minister of France, reported to Talleyrand, then Minister of Foreign Affairs, "People are strangely mistaken as to the character of the sovereign pontiff, if they have thought his apparent flexibility was yielding to all that they were striving to impress upon him. In all that pertains to the authority of the head of the Church, he takes counsel with himself alone. The Pope has a mild character, but very irritable, and susceptible of displaying a firmness proof against any trial; already they are openly saying, 'If the emperor overturns us, his successor will re-establish us.'"

On the morrow of the battle of Jena, when the ruin of the Prussian monarchy had added new lustre to the splendor of Napoleon's victories, the emperor wished to make one last effort in order to establish an absolute dominion over that little corner of Italy which still preserved an independent sovereignty. For more than a year he had not accepted any direct communication with the court of Rome: he commanded the attendance of Mgr. Arezzo, Bishop *in partibus* of Seleucia, formerly papal nuncio in Russia, and who then happened to be at Dresden. The prelate was admitted to the emperor at Berlin, in the cabinet of the great Frederick: he has preserved a textual account of his conversation with Napoleon. "What did you have to do with Russia?" "Your Majesty is aware that there are in Russia 4,000,000 of Catholics. It is for that reason that the Pope maintains a representative there." "The Pope ought not to have a minister at St. Petersburg; the Greeks have always been the enemies of Rome, and I do not know by what spirit of madness Rome can be possessed to desire the good of its enemies rather than of its friends. You are about to quit Dresden, and repair to Rome. You are my enemy. In the first place, you are not a Sicilian for nothing. I do not mean by that that you have spoken abusively of me, but you have desired that I should come to nothing, that my armies should be beaten, and that my enemies should triumph. You are not the only one to wish me evil; at Rome people think no better than elsewhere. The Pope is a holy man, whom they make believe whatever they please. They represent my demands to him under a false aspect, as Cardinal Consalvi has done, and then the good Pope is roused up to say that he will be killed rather than yield. Who thinks of killing him, *bon Dieu?* If he will not take the course I wish, I will certainly deprive him of his temporal power at Rome, but I shall always respect him as the head of the Church. There is no necessity that the Pope should be sovereign of Rome. The most holy Popes were not so. I shall secure him a good appanage of three millions, upon which he can properly keep up his position; and I shall place at Rome a king or a senator, and I shall divide his states into so many duchies. In reality, the main point of the matter is, that I wish the Pope to accede to the confederation; I expect him to be the friend of my friends, and the enemy of my enemies. In fifteen days you will be at Rome, and will peremptorily signify this to him." "Your Majesty will permit me to repeat to him that which has been already said to him so many times: that the Pope, being the common father of the faithful, cannot separate himself from some to attach himself to others; and his ministry being a ministry of peace, he cannot make war against anybody, nor declare himself the enemy of any one whatever without failing in his duties and compromising his sacred character." "But I do not claim at all that he should make war against anybody. I wish him to shut his ports against the English, and that he should not receive them into his states, and that not being able to defend his ports and fortresses he should permit me to defend them. Rest assured that at Rome they have lost their heads. They have no longer there the great men of the time of Leo X. Ganganelli would not have conducted himself in this style. I wish to be in safety in my own house. The whole of Italy belongs to me by right of conquest. Let the Pope do what I wish, and he will be recompensed for the past and for the future. I only forewarn you that all must be completed before the 1st of January: if the Pope will consent, he will lose nothing; if he will refuse, then I shall take away his states. Excommunications are no longer in fashion, and my soldiers will not refuse to march wherever I send them. Call to mind Charles V., who kept the Pope prisoner, and who made him recite prayers for him at Madrid. I shall take the same course if I am brought to bay."

Mgr. Arezzo having asked for some prolongation of the delay: "Ah well! I give you till February," replied the emperor; "but let everything be finished before February." "And where will it be necessary to send the ambassador of the Pope? to Berlin, to Warsaw, to St. Petersburg? Your Majesty moves so quickly!" Napoleon began to laugh. "No, to Paris," said he.

It was in fact at Paris, in the month of October, 1807, when the victory of Friedland had delivered Russia, like Prussia, to the influence of Napoleon, that the envoy of the Pope succeeded in obtaining an audience—not of the emperor, but of Champagny, his new Minister of Foreign Affairs. New difficulties had aggravated the bitterness of the relations between France and Rome. Pius VII., however, had perceived that the requirements of the emperor, so absolute in their harshness, would not yield to his moderate and passive resistance. He had authorized his French representative, the Cardinal de Bayanne, to make an important concession. "The last demands of his Imperial Majesty," wrote Cardinal Casoni, Minister of State, on the 14th of October, "are limited as regards the English to the closure of the ports. The holy father has every reason to think that his adherence ought to be limited to this closure; but if anything else is required of him he will consent to it, provided that it does not compel him to engage in actual war, and that it does not injure the independence of the pontifical sovereignty. It will be desirable then that your Eminence and the cardinal legate, to whom this despatch is common, should be on your guard, to concert the explanation and import of these words in order to satisfy his Imperial Majesty as the holy father desires, but at the same time not to impose upon his Holiness an obligation opposed to his duties and his honor."

This was a good deal to grant, and it curtailed considerably the formal declarations of neutrality so often repeated by the court of Rome. Napoleon required still more, and his secret thoughts were not in accord with his public declarations. The obstacles to the free choice of an ambassador; the requirements with regard to the full powers which were to be conferred on Cardinal de Bayanne; the forcible hindrance to the journey of the latter, arbitrarily detained at Milan; the systematic neglect of his requests for an audience—clearly proved the decision taken to obtain all or nothing—to subjugate or break the pontifical power. The last offers of the Pope fully satisfied the demands of the emperor, as expressed by Cardinal Fesch, Talleyrand, and Napoleon himself again and again. Champagny declared that these concessions were no longer sufficient. The Pope was to engage himself to make common cause with the Emperor Napoleon, and to unite his land and sea forces with those of France in all wars against England. The ports closed against the English; the care of the ports of Ostia, Ancona, and Civita Vecchia confided to France; 2000 men of the French troops maintained at Ancona at the cost of the Holy See; and concessions without reserve on the subject of the number of French cardinals, as of the consecration of Italian bishops— such were the conditions of the convention presented to the Cardinal de Bayanne by Champagny. A few other articles, treating of the spiritual power, and which had been abandoned at the request of Cardinal Fesch, remained as a menace suspended over the head of the negotiator, in case his submission should not be sufficiently prompt and complete. General Lemarrois had already taken possession of the duchy of Urbino, of the province of Macerata, of Fermo, and Spoleto. The Cardinal de Bayanne was still negotiating, but the order for his recall had been sent from Rome (9th of November, 1807). "God and the world will do us justice against the proceedings of the emperor, let them be what they may," wrote Pius VII.

The exactions of Champagny had heaped up a measure which was already overflowing.   In full Consistory, and without any hesitation on the part of either Pope or cardinals, the proposals were unanimously rejected.   "This is the fruit of our journey to Paris, of our patience, of the forbearance which has led us to make so many sacrifices, to suffer so many humiliations.   If such pretensions are persisted in, you must immediately demand your passport, and come away."   Such were the instructions sent on the 2nd of December to the Cardinal de Bayanne by the holy father.   The orders sent by the emperor to his agents did not wait long for a response. Already for some time past very considerable forces had been grouped to the north and south of the pontifical states, under the orders of General Miollis.   Six thousand Frenchmen were destined for this expedition.   A Neapolitan column of 3000 men was to occupy Terracina.   All the movements of the troops had been carefully calculated and foreseen; the care of watching over their execution was confided to Prince Eugene and the King of Naples.   The emperor wrote to Champagny on the 22nd of January, 1808:

"On the 25th of January the French army will be at Perugia; on the 3rd of February it will be at Rome.   The express, setting out on the 25th, will arrive at Rome on the 1st of February, and will thus carry your orders to Signor Alquier two days before the troops arrive.   You ought to make known to Signor Alquier that General Miollis, who commands my troops, and who appears to be directing his course towards Naples, will stay at Rome and take possession of the castle of St. Angelo. When Signor Alquier shall become aware that the troops are at the gate of Rome, he shall present to the Cardinal Secretary of State the subjoined note: 'The arrival of General Miollis has for its aim the protection of the rearguard of the army of Naples.   On his way, he presents himself at Rome to give force to the measures which the emperor has resolved on taking to purge this city of the scoundrels to whom it has given asylum, and consequently to all the enemies of France."   You will put in cipher in your despatch the following paragraph: ' The intention of the emperor is to accustom by this note, and by these proceedings, the people of Rome and the French troops to live together, in order that if the court of Rome should continue to show itself as insensate as it now is, it might insensibly cease to exist as a temporal power without any notice being taken of it.'   Nevertheless, whilst desiring to

avoid disturbance, and to leave things *in statu quo*, I am prepared to take strong measures the first time the Pope indulges
in any bull or manifesto; for a decree shall be immediately
published, revoking the gift of Charlemagne, and reuniting the
states of the Church to the kingdom of Italy, furnishing proofs
of the evils that religion has suffered through the sovereignty
of Rome, and making apparent the contrast between Jesus
Christ dying on the cross and His successor making himself a
king!"

It was not without a certain uneasiness that the emperor was
preparing thus to use violence against an unarmed sovereign,
and historical decrees were not the only arms on which he expected to rely. "The slightest insurrection that may break
out," wrote he to Prince Eugene (February 7th, 1808), "must
be repressed with grape-shot, if necessary, and severe examples
must be made."

No insurrection broke out; the Pope and his followers had
resolved upon giving to the world a startling demonstration of
the material powerlessness of the Holy See in presence of brute
force. Whilst General Miollis was entering Rome, on February 2nd, 1808, at eight o'clock in the morning, disarming
the pontifical troops in order to seize upon the Castle of St.
Angelo, the Pope was officiating in the chapel of the Quirinal,
surrounded by the Sacred College. The palace was invested
by the troops, and cannon were pointed at the walls; the cardinals went forth without tumult or protest. The French
officers were not a little surprised to see them get into their
carriages and retire without letting any trace of annoyance
be visible on their countenances.*

Only a protest by the holy father, conceived in the most
moderate terms, was affixed to the walls of Rome: "Not having been able to comply with all the demands which have been
made to him on the part of the French Government, because
the voice of his conscience and his sacred duties forbade it, his
Holiness Pius VII. has believed it his duty to submit to the
disastrous consequences with which he has been threatened as
the result of his refusal, and even the military occupation of
his capital. Resigned in the humility of his heart to the un-
searchable judgments of heaven, he commits his cause into the
hands of God; but at the same time, unwilling to fail in his
essential obligations to guarantee the rights of his sovereignty,

---

* Memoirs of Cardinal Pacca.

he has given orders to protest, as he protests daily, against every usurpation of his dominions, his will being that the rights of the Holy See should be and remain always intact."

The times of supreme violence had not yet come, and the emperor himself had not perhaps foreseen to what extremities he would be led, by the aggression he had just committed, and the underhand struggle he had been maintaining for three years against the conscientious will of an unarmed old man. However, the habitual roughness of his arbitrary proceedings did not fail to manifest themselves from the beginning. Champagny had been ordered to declare to the Cardinal de Bayanne that the French soldiers established at Rome would remain there until the Pope should have entered into the Italian Confederation, and should have consented to make common cause with the powers composing it, in every case and against all enemies. "This condition is the *sine qua non* of his Majesty's proposal. If the Pope does not accept it, his Majesty will not know how to recognize his temporal sovereignty. He has decided to transfer the power of Rome into secular hands."

At the same time, and as a necessary commentary on these imperious injunctions, the foreign cardinals in the pontifical states received orders from Napoleon to quit Rome. The Neapolitan cardinals, to the number of seven, had up to that time refused to take an oath to King Joseph. At the first news of the measure which threatened them, the Pope ordered them to remain near himself, "for the service of the Holy See;" they were seized in their houses, and conducted to the frontiers of the kingdom of Naples by gendarmes. On March 10th the same order was addressed by the emperor to the vice-King of Italy for fourteen new members of the Sacred College. "Let Litta return to Milan; let the Genoese return to Genoa, the Italians to the kingdom of Italy, the Piedmontese to Piedmont, the Neapolitans to Naples. This measure is to be executed by fair means or foul. Since it is the cardinals who have lost the states of the Church by their evil counsels, let them return every one to his own place." Cardinal Casoni, till recently Secretary of State to the Pope, and Cardinal Doria Pamphili, now officiating—the one born at Sarzana, the other a Genoese—were prevented by this interdiction from living in the Roman States. Alquier, the minister of France, was quietly recalled to Paris; a simple secretary of legation remained at Rome to represent the diplomatic service. General

Miollis well seconded the intentions of the emperor with re gard to the Holy See. Against the advice of his counsellors, the Pope sent to Cardinal Caprara an order to quit Paris. " Violence has been resorted to," wrote Pius VII. to his easy-going legate, " even to laying hands on four of our cardinals and conducting them to Naples in the midst of an armed force; an excess which only requires the violation of our own personal freedom for the scandal to be complete. We cannot, by the residence of our representative with the French Government, give occasion for thinking any longer that we are not deeply wounded by the persecution we have been made to suffer, and the oppression manifested towards the Holy See. Our intention is, then, if our capital is not without delay evacuated by the French troops, that you should demand your passports, and that you should set out with the Cardinal de Bayanne, our legate extraordinary, in order to come and share with us and your brothers the lot which is reserved for us."

I wished to tell in some detail the relations of Napoleon with the court of Rome, because they clearly point out the first steps decidedly taken along a path that grew more and more daring. Conquest had for a long time borne its bitter fruits. Conquered sovereigns had submitted to the yoke and to the haughty requirements of the conqueror; such was the absolute right of victory, and those who suffered from it recognized a power which in all time had belonged to the conqueror. The emperor henceforth went much further tha.. this; he did not confine himself to fighting, conquering, and dispossessing those he had vanquished, and dividing their spoils He began at Rome to impose his arbitrary caprices up n a prince who had never taken up arms against him. At the same time, and by a manœuvre concocted in the most masterly m ner, and yet most inexcusable, he was about to dethrone king, his lly, humbly submissive to his power and I is exactions. The throne of Spain was the only one still occupie by a prince f the house of Bourbon. Napoleon had resolved upon seating a Bonaparte upon it. Already the troops destined for this enterprise were quitting Paris, marching, without knowing it, towards long disasters. Yielding to the irresistible impulses of absolute power without limits and without a curb, Napoleon was led into having recourse to every description of violence, and making use of every kind of perfidy. He wished to be everywhere and always obeyed. For six years past no one had resisted his will without being crushed; he was at last about to meet with a check—at Rome, in the conscience of the Pope; in Spain, in the passions of an aroused people.

The situation of Spain had for a long time been sad and wretched. Governed by a favorite, whose crimes he ignored, King Charles IV. had abandoned power into the hands of the Prince de la Paix. At his side, and in a condition of suspicion which resembled captivity, the heir to the throne, Ferdinand, Prince of Asturias, had become the idol of the people, as a consequence of the scorn and aversion inspired by the favorite. The young prince, weak and cunning, submissive in his turn to his old tutor, the Canon Escoiquiz, was carrying on underhand intrigues with a few great lords who were devoted to him. He had attached to himself Beauharnais, the ambassador of France, an upright and sincere man, with no great political penetration. The little council of the prince had thought themselves capable of concluding an alliance between Ferdinand and the all-powerful sovereign of France. On the 11th of October, 1807, the Prince of Asturias sent by Beauharnais a letter addressed to the " hero who threw into the shade all those who had preceded him;" Ferdinand solicited the hand of a princess of the imperial house.

It was the moment of the negotiation of the treaty of Fontainebleau and the anticipated partition of Portugal. On the same day on which the signatures were exchanged (October 27th, 1807) the Prince of Asturias, for a long time suspected of criminal intrigues, was arrested at Madrid, as well as his accomplices. On the 29th, King Charles IV. wrote to the emperor, in order to make him acquainted with the sad discovery which had just wounded all his paternal sentiments. "I pray your Majesty," added the unfortunate monarch, "to aid me with your knowledge and advice."

The troops that were to enter Spain were ready, and the first movement of Napoleon was to march them forward immediately. The trouble existing in the royal house afforded a ready excuse for an intervention entreated at once by both father and son. The King of Spain himself invoked assistance. The army of the Gironde was immediately reinforced and provisioned. A second corps was already preparing, but the Prince de la Paix discovered in the correspondence of Ferdinand the proof of his relations with Beauharnais. He did not wish to compromise his principality of Algarve by exciting the anger of Napoleon: the Prince of Asturias was exempted from the law, and his pardon solemnly proclaimed in an official decree

by Charles IV. Only his accomplices were prosecuted, but the
tribunals acquitted them. Meanwhile the army of the Gironde, under General Dupont, had entered Spain. The corps
for watching the sea coasts, commanded by Marshal Moncey,
followed in the same direction. Other detachments seized
upon the fortresses of the frontiers. "On arriving at Pampeluna, General Duhesme will take possession of the town," wrote
the emperor to General Clarke, Minister of War (January 28th,
1808), and without making any show he will occupy the citadel
and the fortifications, treating the commandants and the inhabitants with the greatest courtesy, making no movement,
and saying that he is expecting further orders."

The orders were not long in arriving; 100,000 men of the
grand army were effecting a backward movement, approaching France, and consequently Spain. At the same time, Joachim Murat, the living hero of hazardous and doubtful enterprises, had just been appointed general-in-chief of the armies
in Spain. His instructions were all military. "Do not disturb
in any manner the division of Duhesme," wrote the emperor to
his lieutenant, on the 16th of March, 1808; "leave that where
it is. It guards Barcelona and holds that province, and fulfils
its purpose sufficiently. When the 3000 men of the reinforcement who are about to rejoin this division, and who will be at
Barcelona towards the 5th or 6th of April, shall have arrived,
it will be another thing. Then he will have an army capable
of carrying him anywhere. At the moment when you receive
this letter, the head of General Verdier's corps will touch the
borders of Spain, and General Merle ought to find himself at
Burgos. Continue to speak smooth words. Reassure the king,
the Prince de la Paix, the Prince of Asturias, and the queen.
The great thing is to arrive at Madrid, and there let your
troops rest, and replenish their stores of provisions. Say that
I am soon coming in order to reconcile and arrange matters;
above all, do not commit any hostilities, if it can possibly be
helped. I hope that everything may be arranged, and it would
be dangerous to scare these folks too much."

Murat had conceived intoxicating hopes which did not tend
to the tranquillity of the Spanish court. He had asked for political instructions, which were refused to him. "What I do
not tell you is what you ought not to know," wrote Napoleon
to his lieutenant. Uneasiness and fear reigned in the household of the king, under the outside show of welcome lavished
on the French soldiers. Already the Prince de la Paix was

preparing for the flight of the royal family. That which the house of Braganza had done by setting out for Brazil, the house of Bourbon could do by taking refuge in Peru. The departure of the court for Seville was announced; it was the first step in a longer journey, of which the project had not yet been revealed to Charles IV. The royal family were besides profoundly divided. The Prince of Asturias swore that he would not quit Aranjuez; his uncle Don Antonio supported him in resistance. A few of the ministers were seemingly throwing off the yoke of the Prince de la Paix. The Marquis of Caballero, the Minister of Justice, refused to sign the orders necessary for the departure. "I command it," said the Prince de la Paix imperiously. "I only receive orders from the king," said the Spanish nobleman in a tone to which the favorite was not accustomed.

Meanwhile the population of Madrid, and the peasants in the environs of Aranjuez, were stirred up by the reports of the departure which circulated in the country; the preparations carried on by the confidants of the Prince de la Paix, excited much anger and uneasiness. An agitated and inquisitive crowd ceaselessly surrounded the palace, carefully watching all the movements of the inmates: a proclamation of the King, promising not to withdraw, did not suffice to allay suspicion. On the night of March 17th, a veiled lady came forth from the house of the Prince de la Paix to a carriage which was waiting for her. The multitude thought they had discovered a prelude to the departure; all hands were extended to stay the fugitive. In the struggle a shot was fired; the crowd immediately rushed forward, forcing the gates, and overturning the guards who protected the palace of the favorite. In an instant his dwelling was pillaged, his art treasures destroyed, his tapestries torn up and scattered to the winds. We have been witnesses of the sorrowful results of popular fury. The Princess de la Paix alone, trembling for her life in the palace where her just pride had so often suffered, was spared by the vengeance of the multitude; they brought her in triumph to the house of the king. "Behold innocence!" cried the people. The Prince de la Paix had disappeared.

They were seeking for him thirty-six hours, and the anxiety of the king and queen was becoming insupportable; both loudly demanded their favorite. With a view of turning away the anger of the people from his head, Charles IV. issued an edict depriving Emanuel Godoy, Prince de la Paix, of all his offices and dignities, and authorizing him to choose for himself the place of his retreat. The favorite had more correctly estimated the hatred excited against himself; he had sought no other retreat than a loft in his palace. There, rolled up in a mat, with a few pieces of gold in his hands, he waited for the moment to take his flight. On March 19th, at ten o'clock in the morning, as he attempted to escape secretly, he was perceived by a sol dier of that guard to which he had formerly belonged; immediately arrested, he was dragged to a guard-house. When he at length reached this sad refuge he was bruised and bleeding, from the blows showered upon him by all those who could reach him through the crowding ranks of the multitude and the barriers formed by the soldiers. At the barracks where the Prince de la Paix lay on the straw, the Prince of Asturias came to seek him out in the name of his parents, and to promise him his life. " Art thou already king, that thou canst thus dispense pardon?" asked Godoy, with a bitter perception of the change which had been effected in the position of the prince as in his own. " No," replied Ferdinand, " but I soon shall be."

The royal uneasiness did not permit them long to leave the favorite in a guard-house, a prey to the insults and ill-usage of the populace; the king and queen remained obstinately faithful to their friend. A coach was got ready to take him away to a place of safety; as soon as it appeared, the people threw themselves upon the carriage and broke it up. When the noise reached the palace the old king burst into tears: " My people no longer love me!" cried he; "I will no longer reign over them. I shall abdicate in favor of my son." The queen's mind was occupied with no other thought than the safety of Godoy; she thought it assured by this renunciation of the throne, and willingly set her hands to it. The act of abdication was immediately made public, and saluted, at Madrid as at Aranjuez, by the transports of the multitude. Henceforth King Ferdinand VII. was alone surrounded by the courtiers; his aged father remained abandoned in the palace of Aranjuez. Murat was already approaching Madrid, and all eyes were turned towards him as towards the forerunner of the supreme arbiter. Ferdinand VII. hastened to send emissaries to him. The Queen of Etruria, who had only just reached her parents, wrote to him conjuring him to come to Aranjuez, to judge for himself of the situation. On March 25th, 1808, the French army made its entry into the capital.

The popular insurrection which had overthrown the Prince

de la Paix and provoked the abdication of Charles IV., had thwarted the plans of Napoleon so far as his lieutenant was able to divine them. The flight of the royal family would have left the throne of Spain vacant, and Murat had cherished the hope of posing as a liberator of the Spanish nation, delivered from the yoke so long imposed on it by a miserable favorite. In the presence of a new and popular royalty, born of a patriotic sentiment, Murat comprehended for the first time the necessity of reserve and prudence. The distrust of the new monarch as regards fallen royalty, the anger and ill-will of the parents as regards the son who had dethroned them, were to bring both parties before the powerful protector who had been wise enough beforehand to effect a military occupation of their country. It was important to remain free, and to prepare for war with King Ferdinand VII. The popular passion naturally offered a point of support against Charles IV., his wife, and his favorite. Montyon, aide-de-camp to Murat, repaired to Aranjuez, counselling the old king to draw up a protest against the violence of which he had been the victim. Until then, the queen in the letters which she had addressed to Napoleon and to Murat, had only asked for a place in which to lay her head: " Let the grand duke prevail upon the emperor to give to the king my husband, to myself, and to the Prince de la Paix, sufficient for all three to subsist upon in a place good for our health, free from oppression or intrigues." At the instigation of Murat, and not without some hesitation, Charles IV. declared that he had only abdicated in order to avoid greater evils, and to prevent the effusion of the blood of his subjects, " which rendered the act null and of no effect." Murat at the same time made use of the friendship and confidence which had long existed between Beauharnais and Ferdinand VII., to suggest to this prince the idea of presenting himself before the emperor and asking sanction for his royal authority. The Spanish troops received orders to effect a retrograde movement, and the new monarch solemnly entered into Madrid on the 24th of March, amidst impassioned cries of joy from the populace.

The lieutenant had well divined the idea of the imperious master from whom he was separated by a distance that perilously retarded his orders. The emperor had heard the news of the royal departure for Seville and for America. He had written, on March 23rd, the same day upon which Murat had entered Madrid in the footprints of the revolution: "I suppose

I am about to receive the news of all that will have taken place at Madrid on the 17th and 18th of March." Unforeseen events having occurred, he wrote to Murat on the 27th: "You are to prevent any harm from being done, either to the king or queen or to the Prince de la Paix. If the latter is brought to trial, I imagine that I shall be consulted. You are to tell M. de Beauharnais that I desire him to intervene, and that this affair should be hushed up. Until the new king is recognized by me you are to act as if the old king was still reigning; on that point you are to await my orders. As I have already commanded you, maintain good order at Madrid; prevent any extraordinary warlike preparations. Employ M. de Beauharnais in all this until my arrival, which you are to declare to be imminent. You are always saying that you have no instructions; I give you them every time; I tell you to keep your troops well rested, to replenish your commissariat, and not to prejudice the question in any way. It seems to me that you have no need to know anything more."

The political instructions were to reach Murat through the agency of General Savary, often charged by the emperor with delicate missions requiring absolute and unscrupulous devotion. On seizing by stratagem the fortress of Pampeluna, General Darmagnac had frankly said, "This is dirty work." General Savary obeyed without reserve, always absorbed in the enterprise confided to him, and never letting himself be turned aside by any obstacle. The emperor wrote on the 30th of March to the Grand Duke of Berg:—

"I received your letters with those of the King of Spain. Snatch the Prince de la Paix from the hands of these people. My intention is that no harm shall be done to him, since he is two leagues from Madrid and almost in your reach; I shall be much vexed to hear that any evil has happened to him.

"The king says that he will repair to your camp; I wait to know that he is in safety, in order to make known to you my intentions.

"You have done well in not recognizing the Prince of Asturias.

"You are to place King Charles IV. at the Escurial, to treat him with the greatest respect, to declare that he continues always to rule in Spain, until I shall have recognized the revolution.

"I strongly approve your conduct in these unforeseen circumstances. I suppose you will not have allowed the Prince de la Paix to perish, and that you will not have permitted King Charles to go Badajoz. If he is still in your hands, you must dissemble with Beauharnais, and say that you cannot recognize the Prince of Asturias, whom I have not recognized; that it is necessary to let King Charles come to the Escurial; that the first thing I shall require on my arrival will be to see him. Take all measures not to have his life in jeopardy. I hope the position in which you find yourself will have led you to adopt a sound policy."

On the 27th of March, three days before ordering Murat to hold the balance suspended between father and son, Napoleon had written to the King of Holland, Louis Bonaparte: " My brother, the King of Spain has just abdicated; the Prince de la Paix has been thrown into prison. The commencement of an insurrection has broken forth at Madrid. On that occasion my troops were forty leagues away from Madrid. The Grand Duke of Berg was to enter on the 23rd with 40,000 men. Up to this time the people loudly call for me. Certain that I should have no solid peace with England except by effecting a great change on the continent, I have resolved to place a French prince upon the throne of Spain. The climate of Holland does not suit you. Besides, Holland would never know how to emerge from its ruins. In this whirlwind of the world, whether we have peace or not, there are no means by which Holland can sustain herself. In this state of things, I think of you for the throne of Spain. You will be the sovereign of a generous nation, of 11,000,000 of men, and of important colonies. With economy and activity, Spain could have 60,000 men under arms and fifty vessels in her ports. You perceive that this is still only a project, and that, although I have 100,000 men in Spain, it is possible, according to the circumstances that may arise, either tha I may march directly, and that all may be accomplished in a fortnight, or that I may march more slowly, and that this may be a secret during several months of operations. Answer me categorically. If I appoint you King of Spain, do you agree? Can I count upon you? Answer me only these two words: ' I have received your letter of such date; I answer Yes;' and then I shall conclude that you will do what I wish; or, otherwise, 'No,' which will give me to understand that you do not agree to my proposition. Do not take anyone into your confidence, and do not speak to anyone whatever as to the purport of this letter, for a thing must be done before we confess to having thought of it."

Full of these resolves, which he had not yet completely revealed to his most intimate confidants, the emperor quitted Paris on the 2nd of April. He was expected in Spain, and he had announced his arrival over and over again, but his purpose was not to push forward his journey so far. Already, at the instigation of General Savary, who knowingly seconded the advice innocently given by Beauharnais, the new king had resolved upon presenting himself before Napoleon. The latter was equally expecting the arrival of the Prince de la Paix, the bearer of messages from the king, Charles IV., and the queen. The emperor had written on his behalf to Marshal Bessières, recommending him to protect the progress of the formerly all-powerful favorite. "I have not to complain of him in any way," said he; "he is only sent into France for his safety; reassure him by all means." The counsellors of Ferdinand VII. refused to allow the Prince de la Paix to set out; he was regarded as a hostage. The young king had vainly solicited from his father a letter of introduction to Napoleon. "In this letter," said he, "you will felicitate the emperor on his arrival, and you bear witness that I have the same sentiments with regard to him that you have always shown." Anger and distrust remained very powerful in the little court of Aranjuez. Ferdinand VII. set out on the 10th of April, accompanied by General Savary, who lavished upon him the royal titles rigorously refused by Murat. The emperor had given similar instructions to Bessières. "Without entering into the political question, on those occasions on which you will be compelled to speak of the Prince of Asturias do not call him Ferdinand VII.; evade the difficulty by calling those who rule at Madrid the government." A junta, or Council of State, had been formed at Madrid, under the presidency of the Infanta Don Antonio, in order to direct affairs in the absence of the new monarch. The latter had already arrived at Burgos.

Napoleon had not yet passed Bordeaux, where he remained a few days, designedly vying in delay with the Spanish court. He wrote on the 10th of April to Murat: "If the Prince of Asturias presents himself at Burgos and at Bayonne, he will have kept his word. When the end that I propose to myself, and with which Savary will have made you acquainted, is accomplished, you will be able to declare verbally and in all conversations that my intention is not only to preserve the integrity of the provinces and the independence of the country, but also the privileges of all classes, and that I will pledge myself to do that; that I am desirous of seeing Spain happy, and in such circumstances that I may never see it an object of dread to France.   Those who wish for a liberal government and the regeneration of Spain will find them in my plan; those who fear the return of the queen and the Prince de la Paix may be reassured, since those individuals will have no influence and no credit.   The nobles who wish for consideration and honors which they did not have in the past administration, will find them.   Good Spaniards who wish for tranquillity and a wise administration, will find these advantages in a system which will maintain the integrity and independence of the Spanish monarchy."

Perhaps some provision of the *system* that the Emperor Napoleon was projecting had crossed the mind of Ferdinand VII. and of his counsellors; perhaps the Spanish pride was wounded by the little eagerness to set foot in Spain shown by the all-powerful sovereign of the French.   Certain it is that General Savary, who had had much difficulty in persuading Ferdinand VII. to decide on pursuing his journey beyond Burgos, failed in his efforts to induce him to quit Vittoria.   The behavior of the general became rude and haughty.   "I set out for Bayonne," said he; "you will have occasion to regret your decision."   Napoleon arrived, in fact, at Bayonne a few hours after his envoy.

Two days later General Savary retook the road to Vittoria, the bearer of a letter from the emperor for the *Prince of Asturias.*

"My brother, I have received the letter of your Royal Highness.   You ought to have found proof, by the papers which you have had from the king your father, of the interest I have always taken in him.   You will permit me, under the circumstances, to speak to you freely and faithfully.   On arriving at Madrid I was hoping to induce my illustrious friend to accept a few reforms necessary in his states, and to give some satisfaction to public opinion.   The dismissal of the Prince de la Paix appeared to me necessary for his happiness and that of his subjects.   The affairs of the north have retarded my journey.   The events of Aranjuez have taken place. I am not the judge of what has passed, and of the conduct of the Prince de la Paix; but I know well that it is dangerous for kings to accustom their people to shed blood and do justice for themselves.   I pray God that your Royal Highness may not one day have to make the experiment.   How could you bring the Prince de la Paix to trial without including with him the queen, and your father the king? He has no longer any friends. Your Royal Highness will have none if ever you are unfortunate. The people willingly avenge themselves for the honor they render to us. I have often manifested a desire that the Prince de la Paix should be withdrawn from affairs; the friendship of King Charles has as often induced me to hold my tongue and turn away my eyes from the weakness of his attachment. Miserable men that we are! feebleness and error are our mottoes. But all this can be set right. Let the Prince de la Paix be exiled from Spain, and I will offer him a refuge in France. As to the abdication of Charles IV., it took place at a moment when my armies covered Spain, and in the eyes of Europe and of posterity I should appear to have despatched so many troops only to precipitate from the throne my ally and friend. As a neighboring sovereign it is permitted me to wish to become fully acquainted with this abdication before recognizing it. I say to your Royal Highness, to the Spaniards, to the entire world, If the abdication of King Charles is a spontaneous movement, if it has not been forced upon him by the insurrection and the mob of Aranjuez, I make no difficulty about admitting it, and I recognize your Royal Highness as King of Spain. I desire then to talk with you on this point. When King Charles informed me of the occurrence of October last I was sorrowfully affected by it.

" Your Royal Highness has been much in the wrong: I did not require as a proof of it the letter you wrote to me, and which I have always wished to ignore. Should you be a king in your turn you would know how sacred are the rights of the throne; any application to a foreign sovereign on the part of an hereditary prince is criminal. As regards the marriage of a French princess with your Royal Highness, I hold it would be conformable to the interests of my people, and above all a circumstance which would attach me by new bonds to a family that has won nothing but praises from me since I ascended the throne. Your Royal Highness ought to mistrust the outbreaks of popular emotions; they may be able to commit a few murders on my isolated soldiers, but the ruin of Spain would be the result of it. Your Highness understands my thoughts fully; you see that I am floating between diverse ideas, that require to be fixed. You may be certain that in any case I shall comport myself towards you as towards the king your father."

On receiving this letter, by turns menacing and caressing, and on listening to the commentaries with which General Savary accompanied it, the prince and his followers still hesitated to advance beyond the frontiers. The repugnance manifested by the population became every day more intense. Urquijo, one of the oldest and wisest counsellors of King Charles IV., insisted upon the advantages that Napoleon would realize by counterbalancing the claims of the son by those of the father, and by thus placing the peninsula under the laws of the general system of the French Empire. He asserted that the intention was already apparent under the words used, official and private, and that Ferdinand would lose himself, and lose Spain, in repairing to Bayonne. "What!" cried the Duc de l'Infantado, for a long time an accomplice in all the intrigues of the Prince of Asturias, "what! would a hero surrounded with so much glory descend to the basest of perfidies?" "You do not understand heroes," replied Urquijo, bitterly. "You have not read Plutarch. The greatest amongst them have raised their greatness upon heaps of corpses. What did our own Charles V. do in Germany and Italy, and in Spain itself? I do not go back to the most wicked of our princes. Posterity takes no account of means."

This counsel was too prudent and wise to prevail with minds at once headstrong and feeble. Ferdinand resolved to trust to the hopes that Napoleon caused to gleam before his eyes; he knew not that his retreat was cut off. "If the prince comes to Bayonne," the emperor had written to Marshal Bessières, "it is very well; if he retires to Burgos, you will have him arrested, and conducted to Bayonne. You will inform the Grand Duke of Berg of this occurrence; and you will make it known at Burgos that King Charles has protested, and that the Prince of Asturias is not king. If he refuses the interview that I propose, it is a sign of his belonging to the English party, and then there will be nothing more to arrange." On the 20th of April the prince and his suite crossed the little river of the Bidassoa. As he was leaving Vittoria, the crowd assembled in the streets became violent, and cut the traces of the horses. In order to avoid a popular riot, the squadrons of the imperial guard had to surround the carriage of the prince; he set out from his states as if already a prisoner.

It was as a suppliant that he arrived at Bayonne, and the sorrowful impression he had experienced on passing the frontier increased as he drew nigh to the end of his journey.

VII.—13

There was no one on his road to meet him or compliment him,
save the three Spanish noblemen whom he had himself sent to
Napoleon, and who returned to their prince troubled with the
gloomiest presentiments. Marshals Duroc and Berthier received him, however, with courtesy when he arrived at
Bayonne, and the emperor soon had him brought to the
chateau of Marac, in which he himself was installed. Carrying out his previous declaration, Napoleon would give to his
visitor no other title than that of Prince of Asturias. At the
end of the day, General Savary escorted Ferdinand to his
apartment; the emperor kept beside himself Canon Escoiquiz.

The hour for revelations had arrived. Napoleon took the
trouble to develop to the canon preceptor his reasons for depriving the house of Bourbon of the throne, and for placing
upon it a prince of the Bonaparte family. "I will give
Etruria to Prince Ferdinand in exchange," said he; "it is a
fine country; he will be happy and tranquil. The populace
will perhaps rebel on a few points, but I have on my side religion and the monks. I have had experience of it, and the
countries where there are plenty of monks are easy to subjugate."

Napoleon paced to and fro in his room, sometimes stopping
in front of the canon, whom he terrified by his flashing
glances and by the extreme animation of his language, sometimes according to him one of those familiar and waggish
gestures which were the signs of his favor. The unfortunate
Escoiquiz sought in vain to defend the cause of his prince,
making the most of his merits and his personal attachment to
the emperor, and pledging his submission if he became sovereign of Spain and an ally of the imperial family. "You are
telling me stories, canon," replied Napoleon. "You are too
well informed to be ignorant of the fact that a woman is too
feeble a bond to determine the political conduct of a prince:
and who will guarantee that you will be near him in six
months' time. All this is only bad politics. Your Bourbons
have never served me except against their will. They have
always been ready to betray me. A brother will be worth
more to me, whatever you say about it. The regeneration of
Spain is impossible in their hands; they will be always, in
spite of themselves, the support of ancient abuses. My part
is decided on; the revolution must be accomplished. Spain
will not lose a village, and I have taken my precautions as to
the colonies. Let your prince decide before the arrival of

King Charles relative to the exchange of his rights against Tuscany. If he accepts, the treaty will be concluded; if he refuses, it is of little consequence, for I shall obtain from his father the cession that I require, Tuscany will remain in possession of France, and his royal highness will receive no indemnity."

The canon covered his face with his hands. "Alas!" cried he, "what will be said of us who counselled our prince to come hither?" The emperor again reassured him. "Do not annoy yourself, canon," said he; "neither you nor the others have any cause to afflict yourselves. You could not divine my intentions, for nobody was acquainted with them. Go and find your prince."

General Savary displayed less eloquence and power of persuasion in announcing to the unfortunate Ferdinand the intentions of the emperor, whom he had on his part so adroitly served. The prince was utterly astounded when his old preceptor entered his room. The intimate counsellors were convoked; they persisted in seeing in the declaration of Napoleon a daring manœuvre intended to terrify the house of Spain into some important cession of territory. The prince formally refused to accept the kingdom of Etruria: he maintained that the rights of the crown of Spain were unalienable; he possessed them by consent of his father Charles IV., who alone could dispute the throne with him. Two negotiators were successively commissioned to carry this reply to Champagny, the Minister for Foreign Affairs.

The latter had just drawn up a report for the emperor, deciding upon taking possession of Spain. "We must recommence the work of Louis XIV.," it said. "That which policy counsels, justice authorizes. The present circumstances do not permit your Majesty to refrain from intervention in the affairs of this kingdom. The King of Spain has been precipitated from his throne. Your Majesty is called upon to judge between the father and son: which part will you take? Would you sacrifice the cause of sovereigns and of all fathers, and permit an outrage to be done to the majesty of the throne? Would you leave upon the throne of Spain a prince who will not be able to preserve himself from the yoke of the English, so that your Majesty will have constantly to maintain a large army in Spain? If, on the contrary, your Majesty is determined to replace Charles IV. on the throne, you know that it could not be done without having to overcome great resistance, nor without causing French blood to flow. Lastly, could your Majesty, taking no interest in these great differences, abandon the Spanish nation to its doom, when already a violent fermentation is agitating it, and England is sowing there the seeds of trouble and anarchy? Ought your Majesty then to leave this new prey to be devoured by the English? Certainly not. Thus your Majesty, compelled to undertake the regeneration of Spain, in a manner useful for her and useful for France, ought neither to re-establish at the price of much blood a dethroned king, nor to sanction the revolt of his son, nor to abandon Spain to itself; for in these two last cases it would be to deliver it to the English, who by their gold and their intrigues have succeeded in tearing and rending this country, and thus you would assure their triumph.

"I have set forth to your Majesty the circumstances which compel you to come to a great determination. Policy counsels it, justice authorizes it, the troubles of Spain impose it as a necessity. Your Majesty has to provide for the safety of your empire, and save Spain from the influence of the English."

Even the most resolute and scrupulous men love to be bolstered up with words, and to surround themselves with vain pretexts. The Emperor Napoleon, resolved on robbing the house of Bourbon of a throne which had become suspected by him, had asked from Champagny an explanatory memoir, and took care to pose as an arbitrator between King Charles IV. and his son, in order to cover his perfidy with a mantle of distributive justice. He had already apprised Murat of his desire to see the old sovereign of Spain before him: the request of Charles IV. and his queen forestalled this proposal. The lieutenant-general had at last snatched away the Prince de la Paix from the hands which detained him. The favorite had taken refuge under the wing of Murat, in the most pitiable condition. "The Prince de la Paix arrives this evening," wrote Napoleon to Talleyrand on the 25th of April; "he has been for a month between life and death, always menaced with the latter. Would you believe it that, in this interval, he has never changed his shirt, and has a beard seven inches long? The most absurd calumnies have been laid to his charge. Cause articles to be written, not justifying the Prince de la Paix, but depicting in characters of fire the evils of popular insurrections, and drawing forth pity for this unfortunate man. It will be as well for him not to delay his arrival in Paris." On the 1st of May, after the arrival of the entire royal family: "The Prince de la Paix is here. King Charles is a brave man. I know not whether it is his position or circumstances, but he has the air of a frank and good patriarch. The queen has her heart and history on her countenance; that is enough to say to you; it surpasses everything that it is permitted to imagine. The Prince de la Paix has the air of a bull. He is beginning to feel himself again; he has been treated with unexampled barbarity. It will be well for him to be discharged from all false imputations, but it will be necessary to leave him covered by a slight touch of contempt.

"The Prince of Asturias is very stupid, very evilly disposed, very much the enemy of the French. You readily perceive that with my practice in managing men his experience of twenty-four years has not been able to impose upon me; and this is so evident to me, that it would take a long war to bring me to recognize him as King of Spain. Moreover, I have had it notified to him that I ought not to hold communications with him, King Charles being upon my frontiers. I have consequently had his couriers arrested. One of them was the bearer of a letter to Don Antonio: 'I forewarn you that the emperor has in his hands a letter from Maria Louisa (the Queen of Etruria, his sister), which states that the abdication of my father was forced. Act as if you did not know this, but conduct yourself accordingly, and strive to prevent these accursed Frenchmen from gaining any advantage by their wickedness.'" All the correspondence of the Prince of Asturias passed under the eyes of Napoleon.

On their arrival at Bayonne on the 30th of April, King Charles IV. and his queen were received with all royal honors. The emperor had himself regulated the ceremonial. "All who are here, even the Infantado and Escoiquiz, came to kiss the hand of the king and queen, kneeling," wrote Napoleon to Murat on May 1st. "This scene roused the indignation of the king and queen, who all the time regarded them with contempt. They proceeded to their apartments ushered by Marshal Duroc, when the two princes wished to follow them; but the king turning towards them, thus addressed them: 'Princes, you have covered my gray hairs with shame and sorrow; you come to add derision also. Depart, that I may never see you again.' Since this occurrence the princes appear considerably stunned and astonished. I know not yet upon what they have resolved."

On arriving at the gate of the chateau of Marac the old

king, Charles IV., fell weeping into the arms of Napoleon. "Lean upon me," said the emperor; "I have strength enough for both." "I know it well!" replied Charles: it was the genuine expression of his thoughts. The Prince de la Paix was not long in coming to the conclusion that all hope of his master's restoration was lost. Repose, with an ample competency, was promised to him; Napoleon also enabled him to get a taste of the pleasure of vengeance. Charles IV. had given command to his son, requiring from him a pure and simple renunciation of the crown which he had usurped: the prince peremptorily refused. The old king rose up with difficulty, brandishing his cane above his head: "I will have you treated like the rebel emigrants," cried he, "as an unnatural son who wished to snatch away my life and my crown." They had to restrict themselves to written communications. A letter from Charles IV. reclaimed the crown, and presented to his son's notice a mournful picture of his proceedings. "I have had recourse to the Emperor of the French," said he, "no longer as a king, at the head of his army and surrounded with the splendor of a throne, but as an unfortunate and forsaken monarch. I have found protection and refuge in the midst of his camp. I owe him my life and that of my queen and of my First Minister. All now depends on the mediation and protection of this great prince. I have reigned for the happiness of my subjects; I do not wish to bequeath them civil war, rebellions, and the popular assemblies of revolution. Everything ought to be done for the people, and nothing for one's self. All my life I have sacrificed myself for my people; and it is not at the age at which I have now arrived that I should do anything contrary to their religion, their tranquillity, and their happiness. When I shall be assured that the religion of Spain, the integrity of my provinces, their independence and their privileges, will be maintained, I shall descend into the tomb pardoning you the bitterness of my last years."

The king had already invested Murat with supreme power in the capacity of Lieutenant-General of the Kingdom. Ferdinand continually resisted—proposing, indeed, to make an act of renunciation, but only at Madrid, in presence of the Cortes, and under the condition that the king, Charles IV., should himself resume possession of the throne. The preliminary negotiations became each day more bitter. Napoleon pursued his aim without disturbing himself at the refusals of the prince, who, however, provoked in him some ill-humor. He

had by a single stroke destroyed the illusions and hopes of
Murat by writing to him on the 2nd of May, "I intend the
King of Naples to reign at Madrid. I wish to give you the
kingdom of Naples, or that of Portugal. Answer me imme
diately what you think of it, for it is necessary for this to be
done in a day." The very day on which Napoleon thus inflicted on his brother-in-law a stroke for which Murat never
consoled himself, the insurrection which broke out at Madrid
rendered impossible the elevation to the throne of Spain of the
man whose duty it was so roughly to repress it. For a fortnight the excitement in the capital had been intense, carefully
kept up by the reports which Ferdinand and his friends found
the means of freely spreading amongst the population. An
order had been sent to Murat to make all those princes of the
royal house who were still at Madrid set out for Bayonne;
when the Junta had been induced with great difficulty to give
its consent to this measure, the populace opposed the departure. A certain number of soldiers were massacred, an
aide-de-camp of Murat escaping by a miracle from the popular
anger. The troops had for a long time been posted as a precaution against an insurrection, and all the streets were soon
swept by charges of cavalry; cannon resounded in all directions. The Spanish troops, consigned to their quarters, only
took part in the struggle at one point; a company of artillery
gave up its pieces to the people. When the insurrection was
suppressed a hundred insurgents were shot without any form
of trial.

This was, in the capital, the last and feeble effort of a resist-
ance which had not yet had time to become a patriotic passion.
Henceforth Murat felt himself master of Madrid; he became
President of the Junta. Don Antonio had accompanied to
Bayonne his nephew, François de Paule, and his niece, the
Queen of Etruria.

"Your Majesty has nothing more to do than to designate
the king whom you destine for Spain," mornfully wrote the
lieutenant-general on the morning of the 3rd; "this king will
reign without obstacle." But lately he had repeated this proposal, heard on several occasions amongst the inhabitants of
Madrid: "Let us run to the house of the Grand Duc de Berg,
and proclaim him king."

The news of the insurrection of Madrid precipitated at Bayonne the *denoûment* of the tragi-comedy in which for several
days the illustrious actors had been playing their parts. The

emperor feigned great anger, and the terror of the old Spanish sovereigns was real.

It is thou who art the cause of all this!" cried the king, Charles IV., violently apostrophizing his son. "Thou hast caused the blood of our subjects and of our allies to flow, in order to hasten by a few days the moment of bearing a crown too heavy for thee. Restore it to him who can sustain it." The prince remained taciturn and sombre, limiting himself to protesting his innocence. His mother threw herself upon him. "Thou hast always been a bad son," she cried with violence; "thou hast wished to dethrone thy father, to cause thy mother's death; and thou art standing there before us insensible, without replying either to us or to our friend the great Napoleon: speak, justify thyself, if thou canst." The emperor, who was present at this sorrowful scene, intervened: "If between this and midnight you have not recognized your father as the lawful king, and have not sent word to Madrid to that effect, you shall be treated as a rebel."

This was too much for the courage of Ferdinand; he was in the hands of an irritated master, who had drawn him and his into a snare which was at this time impossible to be broken through. Weakness and cowardice in the present did not forbid far-off hopes; the prince yielded, counting on the future. "For any one who can see it, his character is depicted by a single word," Napoleon had said; "he is a sneak."

The treaty was concluded the same evening, through the mediation of the Prince de la Paix. King Charles IV., recognizing that he and his family were incapable of assuring the repose of Spain, of which he was the sole lawful sovereign, surrendered the crown to the Emperor of the French, for him to dispose of it at his will. Spain and her colonies were to form an independent state. The Catholic religion was to remain dominant, to the exclusion of all others. King Charles IV. was to enjoy during life the castle and forest of Compiègne; the castle of Chambord was to belong to him in perpetuity; a civil list of 7,500,000 francs was assured to him from the French Treasury. A particular convention accorded the absolute property of the castle of Navarre to Prince Ferdinand, with a revenue of 1,000,000 francs, and 400,000 livres income for each of the Infantas. When the emperor notified to Count Mollien, then Minister of the Treasury, the tenor of the treaty, he added: "That will make 10,000,000. All these sums will be reimbursed by Spain." The Spanish nation was to pay for

the fall of its dynasty and the pacific conquest upon which
Napoleon counted. She reserved for him another price for his
perfidious manœuvres.

Already the Spanish princes were on the way to their re-
treats. Compiègne and Navarre not being ready for their reception, the old king was to inhabit Fontainebleau provisionally. The emperor ordered Talleyrand to receive the Infantas
at Valençay, thus confiding to his vice-grand-elector the honorable functions of a jailer. " I desire," he wrote to him on the
9th of May, "that the princes may be received with no external ceremony, but with respect and care, and that you do
everything possible to amuse them. Be on Monday evening at
Valençay. If you have a theatre there, and could get a few
comedians to come, it would not be a bad idea; you might bring
Madame de Talleyrand there, with four or five ladies. I have
the greatest interest in the Prince of Asturias being prevented
from taking any false steps. I desire, then, that he may be
amused and occupied. Harsh policy would lead one to put
him in the Bicêtre, or in some strong castle; but as he has
thrown himself into my arms, and has promised me to do
nothing without my orders, and as all goes on in Spain as I desire, I have decided to send him into a country place, surrounding him at the same time with pleasures and keeping him under
strict surveillance. Let this last during the month of May and
part of June; the affairs of Spain will have taken a turn, and I
shall then see what part I shall take.

" As to you, your mission is honorable enough; to receive at
your house these three illustrious personages, in order to
amuse them, is altogether worthy of the nation and of your
rank."

The captivity of the Spanish princes was to be much longer
and less cheerful than the Emperor Napoleon was depicting it
beforehand. He had already provided for the government of
Spain. Sorrowfully and with great difficulty, Murat had prevailed upon the Grand Council of Castile and the Indies to
indicate a preference for the King of Naples. The Junta had
absolutely refused to take part in any manifestations of this
nature. On the 10th of May, Napoleon wrote to King Joseph,
" King Charles, by the treaty I have made with him, cedes to
me all the rights of the crown of Spain. The nation, through
the medium of the Supreme Council of Castile, asks from me a
king. It is for you that I destine this crown. Spain is not like
the kingdom of Naples: it has 11,000,000 of inhabitants, more

than a hundred and fifty millions of revenue, without counting the immense revenues and possessions of all the Americas. It is, besides, a crown which places you at Madrid, within three days of France, which entirely covers one of its frontiers. At Madrid you are in France; Naples is at the end of the world. I desire, then, that immediately you have received this letter you should confide the regency to whoever you will, and the command of the troops to Marshal Jourdan, and that you should set out for Bayonne by way of Turin, Mont Cenis, and Lyons. You will receive this letter on the 19th, you will set out on the 20th, and you will be here on the 1st of June. Withal, keep the matter secret; people will perhaps suspect something, but you can say that you have to go to Upper Italy in order to confer with me on important affairs."

Napoleon had said, the moment when he concluded the treaty which deprived the house of Bourbon of its last throne, "What I am doing is not well in a certain point of view, I know. But policy demands that I should not leave in my rear, so near Paris, a dynasty inimical to my own."

Justice and right possess lights of which the cleverest framers of human politics are at times ignorant. The Emperor Napoleon descended several steps towards his fall when he abused his power as regards Pope Pius VII., and used odious means to dethrone the feeble and ignorant princes who were ruling over Spain. Very slippery are the roads of universal power; in the steps of its master, France was rushing to disaster.

CHAPTER X.

THE HOME GOVERNMENT (1804—1808).

For more than twenty years the history of France was the history of Europe; for more than fifteen years the history of Napoleon was the history of France, but a history cruelly bloody and agitated, often adorned with so much glory and splendor, that the country might, and in fact did, indulge itself in long and fatal illusions which drew down bitter sufferings. All this life of our country, however, was not dissipated afar off in the train of its victorious armies, or its arrogant ambassadors; if old France was sometimes astonished to find herself so much increased that she ran the risk of becoming one of the provinces of the Empire, she always remained the centre, and her haughty master did not forget her. Carried beyond her territory by the wild instinct of ambition, he did not renounce the home government of his first and most famous conquest. Seconded by several capable and modest men to whom he transmitted peremptory orders, often modified by them in the execution, Napoleon founded again the French administration, formerly powerful in the hands of the great minister of Louis XIV., but destroyed and overthrown by the shocks of the Revolution. He established institutions, he raised monuments which have remained while all the dazzling trophies of his arms have disappeared, while all his conquests have been torn from us, after worn out France, bruised and bleeding, found herself smaller than at the end of the evil days of the French Revolution.

"Scarcely invested with a sovereignty, new both to France and to himself," said Count Mollien in his memoirs, "Napoleon imposed upon himself the task of ascertaining all the revenues and expenses of the state. He had acquired patience for the details from the fact that, in his campaigns, he depended entirely upon himself for the care of securing food, clothing and pay of his armies." On the eve of Austerlitz, after immense efforts made by the government as well as the public, to re-establish order and activity in a country so long agitated and weakened by incessant shocks, the measure of new enterprises had been exceeded; embarrassments extended from public to private fortunes, all the symptoms of a serious and impending crisis were already shown. Napoleon did not hide this from himself, but he saw and sought for no other remedy than victory. Passing before Mollien, when going to theatre, he said to him, "The finances are in a bad way, the Bank is embarrassed. I cannot put these matters right." For a long time the fortune as well as the repose of France was to depend upon the ever doubtful chances of victory; long she submitted to it with a constancy without example. The day came when victory was not sufficient for our country, she had not strength enough to support the price of her glory. The Emperor Napoleon was deceived in seeking the sources of public prosperity in conquest; the blood which flows in the veins of a nation is not restored as soon as another nation, humiliated and vanquished, shall in its turn give up drop by drop its blood, its children, and its treasures. Society is exhausted unless war contributions and exactions definitively fill the coffers of the victor. The long hostilities of Europe, and our alternate successes and reverses, have sufficiently taught us this hard lesson. Victor or vanquished, France has never completely crushed her enemies, she has never been crushed by them. All have suffered, all still suffer from this outrage on the welfare of society, which is called a war of conquest. In the beginning of his supreme power, Napoleon thought to find in victory an inexhaustible source of riches. " It was the ideas of the ancients which Napoleon applied to the right of conquest," said Mollien.

He learnt even on the morrow of the battle of Austerlitz that victory is not sufficient for the repose and prosperity of a state; the expenses necessitated by the preparations for war, the enormous sums which the treasury had had to pay, the general crisis in the commercial world had induced the minister of the treasury, Barbé Marbois, to have recourse to hazardous enterprises entrusted to unsafe hands. " You are a very honest man," the emperor wrote * to his minister, " but I cannot help believing that you are surrounded by rogues." Six weeks after the battle of Austerlitz, on the 26th January, 1806, Napoleon arrived at Paris in the night and summoned a council of finance for the following morning. The emperor scarcely permitted a few words to be addressed to him on a campaign so promptly and gloriously terminated. " We have," he said, " questions to deal with which are more serious; it appears that the greatest dangers of the state are not in Austria; listen to the report of the minister of the treasury."

" Barbé Marbois commenced the report with the calm of a conscience which has nothing to reproach itself," adds M. Mollien. He soon showed how the receipts, constantly inferior to the indispensable expenses, had obliged the treasury to borrow, first from the receivers-general, then from a new company of speculators at the head of whom was M. Ouvrard, a man of ability, but of doubtful reputation; the brokers as they were called, had in their turn engaged the state in perilous affairs with Spain, and the commissions upon the receivers-general, which had been conceded to them, enormously surpassed their advances. " The State is the sole creditor of the company," Marbois said at last. The emperor got in a passion. His prompt and penetrating mind, always

* The " Négociants réunis."

ready to distrust, discovered by instinct, and without penetrating into details, the fraud to which his minister was blind.
He called before him the brokers, the principal clerks at the
treasury, and confounding them all by the bursts of his anger,
he forgot at the same time the respect he owed to the age and
character of Marbois, who was suddenly dismissed, and immediately replaced by Mollien.

"I had no need to listen to the entire report to guess that
the brokers had converted to their own use more than sixty
millions," said Napoleon to his new minister; "the money
must be recovered."

The debts of the brokers to the public treasury were still
more considerable: Mollien had to find the proof and ward off
in a great measure the dangers resulting to the treasury from
this fatal association with a company of speculators.

Two years later the emperor placed Barbé Marbois at the
head of the Court of Accounts which he had just founded. He
did not admit the want of repose or a wish for retirement. For
a moment Mollien had hesitated to accept the post imposed upon
him by his master. He was director of the *caisse d'amortisse-
ment* (bank for redemption of rents), and was satisfied with
his place. " You cannot refuse a ministry," said the emperor,
suddenly, "this evening you will take the oath." Count
Mollien introduced important improvements into the management of the finances. The foundation of the bank of service,
in current account with the receivers-general, book-keeping by
double entry, formerly brought into France by Law, but which
had not been established at the treasury, the publication of
annual balance sheets, such were the improvements accomplished at that time by the minister of the treasury.

The public works had not been neglected in this whirlwind
of affairs which circled round Napoleon. He had ordered vast
contracts in road and canal-making; in the intervals of leisure
which he devoted to France and the home government, he
conceived the idea of monuments destined to immortalize his
glory and to fix in the spirit of the people the remembrance of
the past, on which the new master of France, set much value.
He repaired the basilica of St. Denis, built sepulchral chapels,
and instituted a chapter composed of former bishops. He
finished the Pantheon, restored to public worship under the
old name of Sainte-Geneviève, ordered the construction of the
arcs de triomphe (triumphal arches) of the Carrousel and
l'Etoile, and the erection of the column in the Place Vendôme.

He also decreed two new bridges over the Seine, those of Austerlitz and Jena. The termination of the Louvre, the construction of the Bourse, the erection of a temple consecrated to the memory of the exploits of the great army and which became the church of the Madeleine, were also decreed. In the great range of his thoughts, which constantly advanced before his epoch and the resources at his disposal, Napoleon prepared an enormous task for the governments succeeding him. All have laboriously contributed to the completion of the works which he had conceived.

At the same time that he constructed monuments and reorganized the public administration, Napoleon desired to found new social conditions. He had created kings and princes; he had raised around him his family and the companions of his glory, to unheard-of fortune; he wished to consolidate this aristocracy, which owed all its splendor to him, by extending it. He had magnificently endowed the great functionaries of the Empire; he wished to re-establish below and around them a hierarchy of subalterns, honored by public offices and henceforth, for this reason, to have themselves and families distinguished by hereditary titles. In the speech from the throne, by which he opened the session of the legislative body in 1807, Napoleon showed his intentions on this subject. "The nation," said he, "has experienced the most happy results from the establishment of the Legion of Honor. I have created several imperial titles to give new splendor to my principal subjects, to honor striking services by striking recompenses, and also to prevent the return of any feudal titles incompatible with our Constitution."

Thus it was that, by a child of the Revolution, still possessed by most of its doctrines, a nobility was to be created in France. The country was not deceived. The emperor could make dukes, marquises, counts, barons; he could not constitute an aristocracy, that slow product of ages in the history of nations. The new nobles remained functionaries when they were not soldiers, illustrious by themselves as well as by the incomparable lustre of the glory of their chief.

The emperor gained battles, concluded treaties, raised or overthrew thrones; he founded a new nobility, and decreed the erection of magnificent monuments by the simple effort of his all-powerful will; he imagined that his imperial action had no limit, and thought himself able to command the masterpieces of genius as well as the movements of his armies. He was not, and had never been, indifferent to the great beauties of intellect, and his taste was shocked when he was extolled at the opera in bad verses.

In his opinion, mind had its place in the social state, and should be everywhere regulated as a class of that institute which he had reconstituted and completed.   He had already laid the foundations of a great university corporation, which he was soon to establish, and which has since, in spite of some defects, rendered such important services to the national education and instruction.   In the session of 1806, a project of law, drawn up by M. Fourcroy, Director of Public Instruction, had made the fundamental principles known.   By the side of the clerical body, to whom Napoleon would not confide the public education, he had imagined the idea of a lay corporation, which should not be subject to permanent vows, while at the same time imbued with that *esprit de corps* which he had come to look on as one of the great moral forces of society.   Under the name of the Imperial University, a new body of teachers was to be entrusted with the public education throughout the empire; the members of this body of teachers were to undertake civil, special, and temporary obligations. The professional education of the men destined to this career, their examinations, their incorporation in the university, the government of this body, confided to a superior council, composed of men illustrious by their talents; all this vast and fertile scheme, due in a great measure to the aid of Fontanes, was afterwards to be developed in the midst of the storms which already commenced to gather around France.   Napoleon had long conceived the project, but deferred the details to another time, waiting until he had created the nursery which should furnish France with learned men, whose duty was to educate the rising generation.   The all-powerful conqueror, in the midst of his Polish campaign, and in his winter-quarters of Finkestein, prepared a minute on the establishment of Écouen, which had been recently founded for the education of poor girls belonging to members of the Legion of Honor.   I wish to quote this document, which, though blunt and insolent, shows much good sense, in order to show how this infinitely active and powerful mind pursued at once different enterprises and thoughts, stamping on all his works the seal of his character and his personal will.

"This establishment must be handsome in all that relates to building, and simple in all that relates to education.   Beware of following the example of the old establishment of St. Cyr, where they spent considerable sums and brought up the young ladies badly. The employment and distribution of time are objects which principally demand your attention. What shall be taught to the young ladies who are to be educated at Écouen? We must begin by religion in all its strictness. Do not admit on this point any modification. Religion is an important matter in a public institution for young ladies. It is, whatever may be said to the contrary, the surest guarantee for mothers and for husbands. Let us bring up believers, and not reasoners. The weakness of woman's brain, the uncertainty of their ideas, their destiny in society, the necessity of constant and perpetual resignation, and a sort of indulgent and easy charity; all this cannot be obtained, except by religion, by a religion charitable and mild. I attached but small importance to the religious institutions of the military school of Fontainebleau, and I have ordained only what is absolutely necessary for the lyceums. It is quite the reverse for the institution of Écouen. Nearly all the science taught there ought to be that of the Gospel. I desire that there may proceed from it not very charming women, but virtuous women; that their accomplishments may be those of manners and heart, not of wit and amusement.

"There must, therefore, be at Écouen a director, an intelligent man, of middle age and good morals. The pupils must each day say regular prayers, hear mass, and receive lessons on the catechism. This part of their education must be most carefully attended to.

"The pupils must then also be taught arithmetic, writing, and the principles of their mother tongue, so that they know orthography. They must be taught a little geography and history, but be careful not to teach them Latin or any foreign tongue. To the eldest may be taught a little botany, or a slight course of physics or natural history, and even that may have a bad effect. They must be limited in physics to what is necessary to prevent gross ignorance or stupid superstition, and must keep to facts, without reasonings which tend directly or indirectly to first causes.

"It will afterwards be considered if it would be useful to give to those who attain to a certain class a sum for their clothing. They might by that get accustomed to economy, to calculate the value of things, and to keep their own accounts. But, in general, they must all be occupied during three fourths of the day in manual work; they ought to know how to make stockings, chemises, embroidery—in fact, all kinds of women's work. These young girls ought to be considered as if they belonged to families who have in the provinces from fifteen to eighteen thousand francs a year, and be treated accordingly. You will therefore understand that hand-work in the household should not be indifferent to them.

"I do not know if it is possible to teach them some little of medicine and pharmacy, at least of that kind of medicine which is within the reach of a nurse. It would be well also if they knew a little part of the kitchen occcupied by medicinal herbs. I wish that a young girl, quitting Écouen to take her place at the head of a small household, should know how to cut out her dresses, mend her husband's clothes, make her baby-linen, and procure little comforts for her family by the means usually employed in a provincial household; nurse her husband and children when ill, and know on these points, because it has been early inculcated on her, all that nurses have learnt by habit. All this is so simple and trivial as scarcely to require reflection. As to dress, it ought to be uniform and of common material, but well made. I think that on that head the present female costume leaves nothing to be desired. The arms, however, must of course be covered, and other modifications adopted which modesty and the conditions of health require.

"As to the food, it cannot be too simple; soup, boiled beef, and a little *entrée;* there is no need for more.

"I do not dare, as at Fontainebleau, order the pupils to do their own cooking; I should have too many people against me; but they may be allowed to prepare their dessert, and what is given to them either for lunch or for holidays. I will dispense with their cooking, but not with their making their own bread. The advantage of all this is, that they will be exercised in all they may be called on to do, and find the natural employment of their time in practical and useful things.

"If I am told that the establishment will not be very fashionable, I reply that this is what I desire, because it is my opinion that of all educations the best is that of mothers; because my intention is principally to assist those young girls who have lost their mothers, and whose relations are poor. To sum up all, if the members of the Legion of Honor who are rich disdain to put their daughters at Écouen, if those who are poor desire that they shall be received, and if these young persons,

VII.—14

returning to their provinces, enjoy there the reputation of good women, I shall have completely attained my end, and I am certain that the establishment will acquire a high and genuine reputation.

"In this matter we must go to the verge of ridicule. I do not bring up either dressmakers, or waiting-women, or house-keepers, but women for modest and poor households. The mother, in a poor household, is the housekeeper of the family."

The spirit of the age and the fascinations of luxury in an agitated epoch were too strong for the determined and reasoned will of the legislator. The houses of the Legion of Honor were not destined to become the best schools for the mothers of families "in modest and poor households." Napoleon had well judged the superior influence of daily example when he said, "My opinion is, that the best education is that of mothers." The wisest and most far-seeing rules know not how to replace it. Religion cannot be taught by order, like sewing or cooking. The great lesson of daily virtue and devotion will ever remain the lot of mothers.

The delicate question of female education carried the mark of the Emperor Napoleon's genius for organization. He had also sought to reduce to rules the encouragement that power owed to genius. Since the year 1805, he had instituted prizes every ten years, intended to recompense the authors of the best works on the physical sciences, mathematics, history, the author of the best theatrical piece, the best opera, the best poem, the best painters and sculptors; "so that," according to the preamble of the decree, "France may not only preserve the superiority she has acquired in science, literature, and the arts, but that the age which commences may surpass those which have preceded it."

It would be an arrogant pretension for the nineteenth century to assert its superiority over its illustrious predecessors, the sixteenth, seventeenth, and eighteenth century, in all that concerns literature or art. However, we have had the good fortune and the honor to be witnesses of a wonderful display of creative genius in France in all branches of literature and art; we have seen orators, poets, artists who could take rank with the most illustrious chiefs of the ancient schools; all this splendor, all this national and peaceful glory, has only taken root in regular liberty and constitutional order. The troubles of the French Revolution, the violent and continual emotions of the war, above all the rule of an arbitrary will, which opened or shut at pleasure both lips and printing-presses, had not been propitious to the expansion of human thought under the reign of the Emperor Napoleon. Those who possessed a spark of the admirable gift of genius, preserved at the same time in their hearts that passion for liberty which necessarily ranked them among the enemies or suspected persons. At the height of his supreme power, Napoleon could never suffer independence either of thought or speech. He long persecuted Benjamin Constant after he had taken his place among the members of the Tribunate; and he manifested a persecuting aversion towards Madame de Staël, which betrayed that littleness of character often lying hid under a greatness of mind and views. When I turn over the table of contents of that immense correspondence of Napoleon which reveals the entire man in spite of the prudence of the editors, I find continually the name of Madame de Staël, joined to rigorous measures of spiteful epithets. " I write to the Minister of Police to finish with that mad Madame de Staël," he wrote on the 20th April, 1807, to the Count Regnault St. Jean d'Angely, who had apologized for his correspondence with the illustrious outlaw. " She is not to be suffered to leave Geneva, unless she wishes to go to a foreign country to write libels. Every day I obtain new proofs that no one can be worse than that women, enemy of the government and of France, without which she cannot live;" and several days previously he wrote to Fouché, " When I occupy myself with Madame de Staël, it is because I have the facts before me. That woman is a true bird of bad omen; she believes the tempest already arrived, and delights in intrigues and follies. Let her go to her Lake Leman. Have not the Genevans done us harm enough?"

Inspired from other sources than Madame de Staël was, but as ardent in his opposition to the sovereign master of the destinies of France, Chateaubriand supported, like her, the flag of an independent spirit and of genius against the arbitrary will of one man. He manifested this in a brilliant manner. Already famous by the publication of his *Genius of Christianity*, he was then writing in the *Mercure*. "Eighteen months before the publication of the *Martyrs*," says M. Guizot, in his memoirs, " in August, 1807, I stopped several days in Switzerland, when going to visit my mother at Nîmes, and in the eager confidence of youth, as curious to see celebrated persons as I was unknown myself, I wrote to Madame de Staël to ask for the honor of an interview. She invited me to dinner at

Ouchy, near Lausanne, where she then resided. I was seated by her side, and having come from Paris she questioned me on all passing there, what people were saying, what occupied the public and the salons. I spoke of an article by Chateaubriand in the *Mercure*, which attracted attention at the moment of my leaving. One sentence had particularly struck me, and I quoted it word for word, for it was fixed in my memory: ' When in the abject silence the only sound heard is the chain of the slave, and the voice of the informer, when all tremble before the tyrant, and it is as dangerous to incur his favor as to merit his displeasure, it seems to be the historian's duty to avenge the people. The prosperity of Nero is in vain, Tacitus is already born in the empire, he grows up unknown by the ashes of Germanicus, and already a just providence has delivered to an obscure child the glory of the master of the world.' My accent was doubtless impressive and full of emotion, for I was impressed and moved myself. Madame de Staël seized me quickly by the arm, saying, 'I am sure that you would act tragedy admirably; stop with us and take a part in *Andromaque.* That was her hobby and amusement of the moment. I resisted her kindly suggestion, and the conversation came back to Chateaubriand and his article, which was much admired, and caused some anxiety. There was reason to admire it, for the passage was truly eloquent; and also cause for anxiety, for the *Mercure* was suppressed precisely because of that passage. Thus the Emperor Napoleon, conqueror of Europe, and absolute master of France, thought that he could not suffer it to be said that his future historian would perhaps be born under his reign, and felt himself obliged to take the honor of Nero under his protection. It was scarcely worth while to be such a great man to have such fears to show, or such clients to protect."

If the emperor pursued with anger the spirit of opposition in the salons, which he endeavored ceaselessly to rally around him, and if, above all, he feared their glorious representatives, Madame de Staël and Chateaubriand, he watched still more harshly the newspapers and the journalists. His revolutionary origin, and the early habits of his mind had rendered him hostile to that liberty of the press which flourished under the Constituent Assembly, withered away under the Legislative Assembly, and expired during the Terror in a sea of blood. When Daunou wished to insert the liberty of the press in the constitution of the year VIII., he encountered great opposition on the part of former Jacobins. They and their friends had secured the right of saying always what they chose, and knew the means of preserving what they had acquired at the price of many massacres; the liberty their adversaries demanded appeared to them dangerous and unjust. Such has always been in the main the revolutionary idea, and the Emperor Napoleon had not forgotten this theory and this arbitrary practice. However, he also knew what might be the influence of the periodical press, and he endeavored to submit to the discipline of his will the small number of newspapers which existed under his reign. "Stir yourself up a little more to sustain public opinion," he wrote to Fouché, on the 28th April, 1805. "Print several articles, cleverly written, to deny the march of the Russians, the interview of the Emperor of Russia with the Emperor of Austria, and those ridiculous reports, phantoms born of the English fog and spleen. Say to the editors, that if they continue in their present tone I will pay them off; tell them that I do not judge them hardly for the bad things they have said, but for the little good they have said. When they represent France vacillating on the point of being attacked, I judge that they are neither Frenchmen nor worthy to write under my reign. It is all very well to say that they only give their bulletins; they have been told what these bulletins are; and since they must give false news, why not give them in favor of the public credit and tranquillity?"

The *Journal des Débats*, in the first rank of the periodical press, under the intelligent direction of the Bertins, had already been favored with a special inspector, whose duty was to superintend its editing, and to whom the proprietors of the paper were forced to pay 12,000 francs a year. Fouché had menaced the other papers with this measure of discipline, by ordering them to " put into quarantine all news disagreeable or disadvantageous to France." This patriotic prudence did not long suffice for the master. "Let Fiévée know that I am very dissatisfied with the manner in which he edits his paper," he wrote, on the 6th March, 1808. "It is ridiculous that, contrary to the rules of good sense, he still continues to believe all that the German papers say to frighten us about the Russians. It is ridiculous to say that they put 500,000 men in the field, when, for the coalition itself, Russia only furnished 100,000 men, while Austria furnished 300,000. It is my intention that he should only speak of the Russians to humiliate them, to enfeeble their forces, to prove how their trashy reputation in military matters, and the praises of their armies, are without foundation." And the same day to Talleyrand: "It is my intention that the political articles in the *Moniteur* should be guided by the foreign relations. And after seeing how they are done for a month, I shall prohibit the other papers talking politics, otherwise than by copying the articles of the *Moniteur*."

We have known the dangers and the formidable effects of an unlimited liberty of the press. Never was it more licentious than when just recovered from a system arbitrarily oppressive. The fire which appears to be extinct smoulders under the ashes, to shortly break out with new fury. The thirty-three years of constitutional régime which France had enjoyed, powerfully contributed to the moderation of men's acts, and even their words, at the time of the revolution of 1848. The outburst of invectives and anger which saluted the fall of the Emperor Napoleon, had been slowly accumulated during the long silence imposed under his reign.

Arbitrary and despotic will succeeds in creating silence, but not in breaking it at a given time, and in a specified direction. In vain did Napoleon institute prizes every ten years; in vain did he demand from the several classes of the Institute reports on the progress of human thought since 1789. Literary genius remained deaf to his voice, and the real talent of several poets of a secondary order, Delille, Esmenard, Millevoye, Chênédollé, was not sufficient to triumph over the intellectual apathy which seemed to envelope the people he governed. "When I entered the world, in 1807," said Guizot, "chaos had reigned for a long time; the excitement of 1789 had entirely disappeared; and society, being completely occupied in settling itself, thought no more of the character of its amusements; the spectacles of force had replaced for it the aspirations towards liberty. In the midst of the general reaction, the faithful heirs of the literary salons of the eighteenth century remained the only strangers in them. The mistakes and disasters of the Revolution had not made the survivors of that brilliant generation abjure their ideas and desires; they remained sincerely liberal, but without pressing demands, and with the reserve of those who have succeeded little and suffered much in their endeavors after reform and government. They held fast to the liberty of speech, but did not aspire to power; they detested, and sharply criticised, despotism, but without doing anything to repress or overturn it. It was an opposition made by enlightened and independent spectators, who had no chance and no desire to interfere as actors."

Thus it was that the lassitude of the superior classes, decimated and ruined by the French revolution and the Terror, inspired by the splendid and triumphant military despotism, contributed together to keep the public mind in a weak and supine state, which the sound of the cannon alone interrupted. I am wrong; the great men, naturalists or mathematicians, who had sprung up, either young or already ripe, in the era of the French revolution—Laplace, La Grange, Cuvier—upheld, in the order of their studies, that scientific superiority of France which has not always kept pace with literary genius, but which has never ceased to adorn our country. The personal tastes of the emperor served and encouraged the learned men, even when their opinions had remained more independent than suited him. He sometimes reproached Monge, his companion during the campaign of Egypt, that he had remained in his heart attached to the Republic. "Well, but!" said the great geometrician, gayly, "your Majesty turned so short!"

Napoleon had certainly *turned short*, and he expected France to follow him in the rapid evolution of his thought. Jealous of his right to march in the van and show the way to all, he indicated to dramatic authors the draft of their theatrical pieces, and to painters the subject of their paintings. "Why," he wrote to Fouché, "should you not engage M. Raynouard to make a tragedy on the transition from the first to the second race? Instead of being a tyrant, his successor would be the saviour of the nation. It is in pieces of that kind that the theatre is new, for under the old régime they would not have been permitted." On the other hand, and by an unconscious return to that fear of the house of Bourbon which he always instinctively felt, Napoleon opposed the representation of a tragedy of Henry IV. "That period is not so remote but that it may awake the passions. The scene should be more ancient."

The passions sometimes awake easily, at points where no threatening or danger appeared. Immediately after the consecration and the Concordat, what could be more natural or simple than a wish to draw up a catechism for the use of all the schools? The organic articles had declared that there would be only one liturgy and one catechism for all the

churches of France. At first the court of Rome made no difficulty. The Abbé Emery, Superior of St. Sulpice, gave an excellent piece of advice to Portalis, the Minister of Religion.
"If I were in the emperor's place," said he, "I should take
purely and simply the catechism of Bossuet, and thus avoid
an immense responsibility." Napoleon had a liking for Bossuet's genius and doctrine, and the idea pleased him. The
new catechism intended to form the minds and hearts of coming generations was placed under the patronage of Bossuet,
"that celebrated prelate, whose science, talents, and genius
have served the Church and honored the nation," said Portalis
in his report. "The justice which all the bishops of Christendom had rendered to the memory of this great man, is to us a
sufficient guarantee of his accuracy and authority. The work
of the compilers of the new catechism is in reality but a second
copy of Bossuet's work."

The great bishop would certainly have felt some difficulty in
recognizing certain pages of the work so prudently presented
under his ægis. Strictly faithful to the spirit of the Gospel as
to the supreme equality of all men in the presence of God,
whatever might occasionally have been his consideration for
the wishes of Louis XIV., Bossuet, when expounding the
fourth commandment, the respect and submission due by children to their parents, was satisfied with adding,—"What else
is commanded to us by the fourth commandment? To respect
all superiors, pastors, kings, magistrates, and others."

The submission of the subjects of Louis XIV. was known to
him, and therefore that exposition was enough in his time.
Portalis was of opinion that immediately after the French
Revolution the principles of respect and obedience ought to be
more exactly defined. "The point is," he wrote to Napoleon,
on the 13th February, 1806, "to attach the conscience of the
people to your Majesty's august person, by whose government
and victories the safety and happiness of France are secured.
To recommend subjects generally to submit to their sovereign
would not, in the present hypothesis, direct that submission
towards its proper end. I therefore thought it necessary to
make a clear explanation, and apply the precept in a precise
manner to your Majesty. That will prevent any ambiguity,
by fixing men's hearts and minds upon him who alone can and
really ought to fix their minds and hearts."

Napoleon readily coincided with the pious officiousness of
his Minister of Religion, and undertook to draw up himself the

question and answer in the new catechism. "Is submission to the government of France a dogma of the Church? Yes; Scripture teaches us that he who resists the powers resists the order of God; yes, the Church imposes upon us more special duties towards the government of France, the protector of religion and the Church; she commands us to love it, cherish it, and be ready for all sacrifices in its serivce." The theologians, whom Portalis said he always distrusted, pointed out that, the Church being universal, her dogmas could not inculcate respect for a particular government. It was therefore drawn up afresh, and was so extended that the commentary on the fourth commandment became longer than the exposition of the principle itself. I wish to give here the actual text as a curious document of the spirit of the time.

LESSON VII.—*Continuation of the Fourth Commandment.*

Question. What are the duties of Christians with reference to the princes by whom they are governed; and what are our special duties towards Napoleon I., our emperor?

Answer. Christians owe to the princes by whom they are governed, and we owe specially to Napoleon I., our emperor, love, respect, obedience, fidelity, military service, the tribute ordered for the preservation and defence of the empire and his throne; we also owe him fervent prayers for his health and for the temporal prosperity of the State.

Q. Why are we bound to perform all those duties towards our emperor?

A. First, because God, who creates empires, and distributes them according to His will, by loading our emperor with gifts, both in peace and in war, has established him as our sovereign. Secondly, because our Lord Jesus Christ, as well by His teaching as His example, has taught us Himself what we owe to our sovereign: at His birth His parents were obeying an edict of Cæsar Augustus; He paid the prescribed tribute-money; and just as He has ordered us to render to God the things that are God's, He has also ordered us to render unto Cæsar the things that are Cæsar's."

Q. Are there no special motives which strengthen our attachment to Napoloen I., our emperor?

A. Yes; for it is he whom God has stirred up, during difficult circumstances, to restore the public worship and holy religion of our fathers and be its protector. He has brought back and preserved public order by his profound and active wisdom; he defends the State by his powerful arm; he became the Lord's anointed by the consecration which he has received from the sovereign pontiff, head of the Church universal.

Q. What ought we to think of those who fail in their duty towards our emperor?

A. According to the apostle Paul they resist the order established by God Himself, and render themselves worthy of eternal damnation.

Q. Are those duties which we owe towards our emperor equally binding upon us with regard to his legitimate successors in the order established by the constitution of the Empire?

A. Yes, certainly: for we read in the Holy Scripture that God, Lord of heaven and earth, by a disposition of His supreme will, and by His providence, gives empires not only to one person individually, but also to his family.

Q. What are our obligations towards our magistrates?

A. We ought to honor them, respect them, and obey them, because they are the depositaries of our emperor's authority.

The catechism was revised and corrected by a theological commission, by Portalis, by the emperor, and by the cardinal legate himself, in spite of a formal prohibition which he had received from Rome. "It does not belong to the secular power to choose or prescribe to the bishops the catechism which it may prefer," wrote Cardinal Consalvi on the 18th August, 1805. "His Imperial Majesty has surely no intention of arrogating a faculty which God trusts exclusively to the Church and Vicar of Jesus Christ."

Caprara had kept the Secretary of State's despatch sealed, and when at last the text of the catechism appeared, in 1806, it had received his approbation. By an article in the *Journal de l'Empire* of the 5th May, 1806, the court of Rome learnt that a catechism was soon to be published, uniform and obligatory for all the dioceses of France, with the official approbation of the cardinal legate. A despatch of Cardinal Consalvi, expressing to Caprara the astonishment and displeasure of the sovereign pontiff, remained secret and without effect. The influence of the court of Rome upon their envoy failed before the seductive power, mixed with fear, which Napoleon had exercised upon Cardinal Caprara since his arrival. The

French bishops were not less troubled than the Pope. "Has the emperor the right to meddle in those matters?" wrote Aviau, Bishop of Bordeaux, to one of his friends; "who has given him the mission? To him the things of earth, to us the things of heaven. Soon, if we let him, he will lay hands on the censer, and perhaps afterwards wish to ascend the altar."

One modification only was granted, on the demands of the bishops supported by Cardinal Fesch. In contempt of Bossuet and his teaching, the standing doctrine of Catholicism, "Out of the Church there is no safety," had been omitted in the new catechism. That phrase being restored, the catechism, invested with the approbation of the legate, was published in the beginning of August, 1808. Placed in the alternative of contradicting or recalling Caprara, the court of Rome prudently remained silent. Differences of opinion were now accumulating between the Pope and the emperor—between the spiritual authority, which still preserved some pretensions to independence, and the arbitrary will of the conqueror, resolved to govern the world, Rome included. We at last reach the moment when the excess of arrogance was about to provoke the effect of contrary wills. We shall now see the Pope captive, the Spanish people in insurrection, the climate and deserts of Russia leagued together against the tyrannical master of Europe. England had never accepted the yoke; and she had everywhere seconded resistance. For the future, it was not alone by sea, nor by the assistance of subsidies, that she entered the lists; Sir Arthur Wellesley was now in his turn to join in the struggle.

A last act of the absolute will of the Emperor Napoleon signalized that period of the interior government of France which preceded the war in Spain and the campaigns in Germany and Russia. It was the suppression pure and simple, by a "sénatus-consulte," of the "Tribunate" formerly instituted with so much pomp, and which had gradually fallen into insignificance, owing to the successive changes it had undergone, and to the secrecy imposed on its deliberations. The absolute power could support neither contradiction nor even the appearance of discussion, however moderate it might be. The lively remembrance, however, of an eloquent and daring opposition was still associated with the name of the Tribunate. Some honored names had survived the great silence. "The abolition of the Tribunate will be less a change than an improvement in our institutions," said M. Boulay de

la Meurthe in his report, "because, since the constitution of
the empire the Tribunate only appears useless, out of place,
not in harmony with the times." The Legislative Body
formed a place of refuge to the members of the Tribunate who
were in exercise: they took their places as a right among its
ranks, where they were no more heard of, annihilated by the
servitude that reigned around them. Their admission into
the Legislative Body had, however, been graced by an appearance of liberality: the right of discussion was restored to
that assembly.

M. de Fontanes took care beforehand to indicate what spirit
was to preside at their discussions. "These precincts, which
have wondered at their silence, and whose silence is now at
an end, will not hear the noisy tempests of popular harangues.
May the tribune be without storms, and may the only ap-
plause be at the triumphs of reason. Above all, may truth
appear there with courage, but with wisdom, and may she
shine there with all her light! A great prince must love her
brightness. She alone is worthy of him, why should he be
afraid of her? The more he is looked at, the more he rises;
the more he is judged, the more is he admired." By the
mouth of Carrion-Nisas, the Tribunate thanked the emperor
for having discharged it from its functions. "We believe,"
said they, "that we have not so much arrived at the end of
our career, as attained the object of all our efforts, and the
recompense of our devotion." Being now certain of the docility of the great bodies of State, and no longer uneasy about
that of the magistracy, all the obnoxious members having
been weeded out by his orders, the Emperor Napoleon could
turn his thoughts abroad. The question was how to place
King Joseph on the throne of Spain.

CHAPTER XI.

GLORY AND ILLUSIONS. SPAIN AND AUSTRIA.

NAPOLEON did not keep his promise to the Bourbons of Spain.
He had not come to Madrid in order to heal their divisions,
and strengthen the tottering power. One after another, he
had drawn all the members of the royal family to Bayonne,

and there, on French soil, had easily consummated their ruin. It was also on French soil that he made preparations to raise his brother to the throne. King Joseph was late in arriving, entering Bayonne only on the 8th June; and already the imperious will and clever management of the emperor had brought into that town a certain number of great lords, favorable to the new power from interest or fear. Already Joseph was proclaimed King of Spain and the Indies; and scarcely had he had time to put foot to the ground when he was surrounded by Spanish deputations, which had been carefully prepared by Napoleon's orders. The king regretted much having to leave Naples. Without foreseeing the difficulties that awaited him, he loved the gentle, easy life of Italy, and had not yet forgot the annoyance of taking possession, or the obstacles to be met by a new régime. The emperor took care to dazzle him at the outset. The Junta formed at Bayonne prepared a constitution. Napoleon had collected much information as to the lamentable state of the administration in Spain. "These papers are necessary to me for the measures which I have to order," he had written to Murat, who was still in Madrid, ill and sad; "they are also necessary to me to show some day to posterity in what state I have found the Spanish monarchy." Useless precaution of a great mind, who thought to dispose of the future and of the judgment of posterity, as, till then, he had dazzled or overthrown all the witnesses of his marvellous career!

Eight days after the arrival of King Joseph at Bayonne, the new constitution was adopted by the improvised Junta. "It is all that we can offer you, sire," said imprudently the Duke de l'Infantado, formerly the most eager accomplice of the Prince of Asturias in his intrigues against his father; "we are waiting till the nation speaks, and authorizes us to give freer course to our sentiments." They stopped the duke from saying any more; the Spanish nation had not been consulted.

The Spanish constitution was prepared generally on the model of the French constitution. The first article paid homage to the strong religious feeling of Spain: "The religion of the State is the Catholic religion; no other is permitted." Several of the ministers chosen by the King Joseph had been members of the government of Charles IV. After taking the oath to their new monarch, the Junta first of all went to the Emperor Napoleon at Marac, to offer their thanks and congratulations.

At the same moment, and whilst summoning to Bayonne the reinforcement of troops which he intended to accompany and

support King Joseph on his entry into his new kingdom, Napoleon wrote to the Emperor Alexander:—

"My brother, I send your Majesty the constitution which
the Spanish Junta have just decided upon. The disorders of
that country had reached such a degree as can scarcely be conceived. Obliged to take part in its affairs, I have by the irresistible tendency of events been brought to a system which,
while securing the happiness of Spain, secures the tranquillity
of my states. I have cause to be satisfied with all the persons
of rank, fortune, and education. The monks alone, who occupy
half the territory, anticipating in the new order of things the
destruction of abuses, and the numerous agents of the Inquisition, who now see the end of their existence, are now agitating
the country. I am very sensible that this event opens a very
large field for discussion. People are not likely to appreciate
the circumstance and events, but will maintain that all had
been provoked and premeditated. Nevertheless, if I had only
considered the interest of France, I should have adopted a
simpler means, viz., extending my frontiers on this side, and
diminishing Spain. A province like Catalonia or Navarre,
would have affected her power more than the change which
has just taken place, which is really of use only to Spain."

Whilst the Emperor Napoleon thus announced in Europe the
interpretation which it suited him to put upon the events of
Spain, and whilst the new king, leaving Bayonne on the 9th
July, was planting his foot upon his new territory, the whole
of Spain, from north to south, from east to west, was in a blaze.

After the departure of the Bourbon princes for Bayonne, the
popular agitation and uneasiness in Madrid became extreme,
and gradually extended to the more remote provinces, and into
the depths of the old Spanish race, honorable and proud, still
preserving in their fields their ancestral qualities. "Trust
neither your honor nor your person to a Spanish Don," was
said to M. Guizot by a man who learned to form severe judgment upon them during several revolutions; "trust all that is
dearest to you to a Spanish peasant." In spite of the emperor's
assertions, all the great lords were not favorable to the King
Joseph. In the country, the peasants had risen in a body, and
the burgesses did the same in the towns.

Carthagena was the first town to give the example of revolt.
On the 22nd May, at the news of the abdication of the two
kings, published in the journals of Madrid on the 20th, the people shouted in the streets, "Long live Ferdinand VII.!" and

Admiral Salcedo, who was preparing to convey the Spanish fleet to Toulon, was arrested. The arms shut up in the arsenals were distributed among the populace. A Junta was immediately formed. Murcia and Valencia followed the example of Carthagena. The people, roused by the preaching of a monk, Canon Calvo, killed the Baron Albulat, a "lord of the province," who was in vain defended by another monk, called Rico. The French who lived in Valencia had taken refuge in the citadel, but being persuaded to come out, they were quickly massacred to the last man. This first ebullition of popular fury was followed by the horror of all respectable people. In spite of himself, Count Cerbellon was put at the head of the insurrection. Everybody took arms, and waited for the arrival and vengeance of the French soldiers.

All the provinces rose in insurrection one after another. The most apathetic waited for St. Ferdinand's Day; and on the 30th May, at daybreak, before the saint's flag was displayed in the streets, in Estremadura, at Granada, and Malaga, the shouts of the populace proclaimed King Ferdinand VII. Blood was shed everywhere, with an atrocious display of cruelty. The magistrates, or gentlemen, who attempted to stop a dangerous rising were massacred. The Asturias had shuddered at the first report of the abdication; the Junta of Oviedo proclaimed a renewal of peace with England, and sent delegates to London. The clergy succeeded in protecting the lives of two Spanish colonels who had opposed the insurrection of their troops. In Galicia the honorable efforts of Captain-General Filangieri cost him his life; after accepting, with regret, the presidency of the Junta, when he attempted to maintain order amongst the insurgents he was killed in the street. Valladolid obliged the Captain-General, Don Gregorio de la Cuesta, to take a part in the rising of the populace. At the first sign of resistance shown by the old soldier, they erected a gibbet under his windows. Burgos, occupied by Marshal Bessières, remained quiet, but Barcelona attempted an insurrection. The Catalans were armed to the teeth, and, on General Duhesme threatening to set fire to the town, the more violent of them escaped to places which were less threatened. Saragossa had placed at the head of its heroic population Don Joseph Palafox de Melzi, an amiable young man, well known in his own country. He summoned the Cortes of the province, and ordered a general rising of the population of Aragon. On the confines of Navarre, almost under the eyes of the French army, Santander and Logrono formed an insurrection. The Castilles, with their vast open plains, and their proximity to the French Government, showed only a silent agitation, without yet attempting an insurrection. Murat was ill—frequently delirious; but General Savary watched over Madrid: the capital awaited its new master.

Nowhere was the insurrection more spontaneous or more general than in Andalusia. Seville had conceived the hope of becoming the centre of the national movement, and grouping round it the patriotic efforts of the whole of Spain. The provisional government assumed a pompous name—"Supreme Junta of Spain and the Indies"—and sent messengers to stir up the towns of Badajoz, Cordova, and Jaen. At Cadiz they surrounded the hotel of the Captain-General Solano, Marquis of Socorro. All the troops throughout the south of Spain were under his orders. With difficulty he was persuaded to give a forced assent to the disorderly wishes of the populace, but persisted in opposing the bombardment of the French fleet, commanded by Admiral Rosily, which had been in the harbor for three months. He in vain pleaded the danger to the Spanish vessels mixed with the French. The crowd became mad, dragged the Marquis on to the ramparts, and massacred him.

Without any preliminary understanding, in a country everywhere intersected by rivers and mountains, and even under the fire of the French cannon, Spain thus rose spontaneously against an arrogant usurpation, preceded by base perfidy. In this first burst of her patriotic anger, she bore the courage, ardor, and passion which were to make certain her triumph; she at the same time displayed a savage cruelty and violence, of which our unhappy soldiers were too often the victims. The emperor was still at Bayonne, occupied in arranging the affairs of Spain from without Spain: he was informed slowly and imperfectly of the insurrection convulsing the whole country. Accustomed to give orders to his lieutenants from a distance and arbitrarily, he ordered all the movements of his troops from Bayonne, affecting to attach but small importance to the revolt, sending to Paris and Valençay false news of the success of his arms, and doing his best to conceal from King Joseph the extent and importance of the resistance which was being prepared against him. In many places the couriers were arrested or killed. The emperor ordered General Savary to set out again for Madrid.

Nevertheless, all the forces of the French army were on their march to crush the insurrection. General Verdier and General Frère quickly took satisfaction for the insurrection of Logrono and Segovia. General Lasalle, before Valladolid, defeated Don Gregorio de la Cuesta, who had been forced to leave the town, afraid of having his throat cut there. "You have only had what you deserve," said the old Spanish general, as he re-treated upon Leon; "we are only a handful of undisciplined peasants, yet you imagine you can conquer those who have conquered all Europe." General Lefebvre-Desnouettes met more resistance at Tudela, where the insurgents had broken down the bridge over the Ebro. On the 15th June he was before Saragossa, where Don Joseph Palafox had shut himself up; the whole population covered the roofs of the houses, where there was a constant hail-storm of musket balls. The French general at once concluded it was a question of regular siege, and sent to Barcelona for reinforcements and artillery. Marshal Moncey had not succeeded in taking Valencia. General Duhesme was shut up in Barcelona by the insurrection, which daily gained ground in Catalonia. Yet he was com-pelled to send away General Chabran, that he might join Marshal Moncey; and the insurgents took advantage of this division of our forces to throw themselves on General Schwartz's column, which had been ordered to search the con-vent of Montserrat. The tocsin was heard everywhere in the mountain villages; the bridges over the streams were broken down, and every little town had to be carried with the bayo-net. By a sudden sally, General Duhesme dislodged the enemy from their post on the River Llobregat, took posses-sion of their cannons, and brought them back to Barcelona. "Let the whole town of Barcelona be disarmed," wrote the emperor on 10th June to Marshal Berthier, "so that not a single musket is left, and let the castle of Montjouy be sup-plied with provisions taken from the inhabitants. They must be treated in thorough military fashion. War justifies any-thing. On the slightest occasion, you should take hostages and send them into the fortress."

General Dupont had been entrusted with the most difficult as well as most important undertaking. With from 12,000 to 13,000 men under his orders, he advanced into Andalusia, with the object of reducing that great province to submission, and protecting the French fleet in Cadiz. The emperor had ordered General Junot to support Dupont's advance by send-

VII.—15

ing him Kellermann's division, but Portugal was imitating the example of Spain, and had all risen in insurrection. On his first entrance into Andalusia, Dupont recognized the importance of the movement, and immediately asked for a reinforcement. "I shall then have nothing to do but a military promenade," he wrote to General Savary.

On the 7th June, after a pretty keen fight, the French troops took the bridge of Alcolea, on the Guadalquivir, and arrived the same evening before Cordova. After the gates were burst open with cannon-shot, the barricades and houses had to be carried with the bayonet; and the soldiers, losing their temper, cruelly abused the victory they gained. The hatred against the invaders increased; and in the van of our army, on this side of the Sierra Morena, on the road from Cordova to Andujar, the men who had not kept up in marching, the sick and wounded who were obliged to stay in the villages, were put to death with refinements of barbarity. General Dupont still waited for the divisions of Vedel and Frère, which he had sent to Madrid for; and at Cadiz, in the French fleet, they were counting the days, and soon the hours.

The leader in the insurrection, Thomas de Morla, at first seemed faithful to the alliance of the Spanish and French navy, recalling the memories of the battle of Trafalgar, the glorious ruins of which composed the French squadron in the Cadiz roads. Gradually, however, he took care to separate the two fleets, persuading Admiral Rosily to take his position within the roads, and placing the Spanish vessels at the entrance, in order, he said, to defend Cadiz against the English, who had been trying in vain to land 5,000 men. The admiral soon found himself cantoned in the midst of the lagoons which form and protect the Cadiz roads; while a contrary wind prevented the attack which, from desperation, he wished to make upon the Spanish, their gun-boats and sloops were already gathering round him, and on the 9th June the firing began, but it was weak and unavailing on the part of our ships, in spite of the heroic resolution of the crews. The fighting lasted two days, and on the Junta of Seville demanding a surrender pure and simple, Admiral Rosily, who knew that General Dupont had entered Cordova, asked for a delay, hoping to receive help. On the 14th June, after four days had elapsed, the French fleet, being deprived of every resource, and with certain ruin before them, surrendered at discretion. The officers were distributed in the fortresses, and the vessels disarmed. The mob, crowding round the harbor, shouted fiercely and cheered as the French prisoners passed before them and the English, who had just succeeded in effecting their landing.

General Dupont had not been reinforced. He did not know whether his couriers had arrived, many having been already intercepted by the robbers of the Sierra Morena; he knew of the rising of the St. Roque troops, and of the treachery of the Swiss regiments recently engaged in the insurrection; and finding himself threatened on the right by the insurgent army of Andalusia, and on the left by the army of Granada, he resolved to fall back upon the Guadalquivir, and on the 18th June took up his position in the small town of Andujar, to wait for the divisions which he had sent for. That of Vedel was already on its march.

Marshal Moncey had failed before Valencia, and could not commence the investment for want of siege guns; he had brought back his division in good condition, and effected his junction with General Frère at San Clemente. Marshal Bessières advanced at the same time against Don Gregorio de la Cuesta, and against General Blake, a descendant of English Catholic refugees. Their forces were considerable, and composed of old soldiers; they had, however, asked for time to prepare their troops and had been forced by the Junta of the Corogne to march to battle. On the evening of the 13th July, the Spaniards, badly informed as to the march of the French, were formed in two lines on the plateau of Medino de Rio-Seco, not far from Valladolid. Attacked one after the other by Marshal Bessières, the two lines were completely beaten and put to flight, not without some resistance at certain points. The slaughter was terrible. General Mouton, at the head of two regiments with fixed bayonets, entered the town of Medina, which was sacked. Marshal Bessières again took the road towards Leon, sweeping before him the disbanded remains of the Spanish army. King Joseph had just entered Madrid.

He took possession of his capital in the midst of the melancholy silence of the inhabitants, more irritated than cowed by the news of the victory of Rio-Seco, which reached them a few hours before the entry of their new monarch. Since his entrance into Spain the eyes of Joseph had been opened. "Up to this time no one has told the whole truth," he wrote to the Emperor Napoleon on the 12th July. "The fact is that not a single Spaniard is on my side, except the small number who were present at the Junta, and travel with me. The others, on arriving here, hid themselves, terrified by the unanimous opinion of their countrymen." And some days later: "Fear does not make me see double: since I have been in Spain I say to myself every day that my life is of small account, and that I give it up to you. I am not alarmed at my position, but it is unique in history; I have not a single partisan here." Every day he repeated the same demand; "I still want 50,000 men of old troops, and 50,000,000 of money; in a month I must have a 100,000 men, and a 100,-000,000." The French army in Spain numbered already 110,000 men, young, it is true, and for the most part without experience, but Europe almost entirely was occupied by our troops; Napoleon was irritated at the sensible remarks of Savary, still more gloomy than those of King Joseph. "The emperor finds that you are wrong to say that nothing has been done for six weeks," wrote Marshal Berthier. "All sensible men in Spain have changed their opinion, and are very sorry to see the insurrection. Affairs are in the most prosperous position since the battle of Rio-Seco." On the 19th July, when making his preparations to quit Bayonne to visit the towns of the south, Napoleon wrote to King Joseph:

"My brother, I received your letter of the 18th, at three o'clock in the morning. I see, with sorrow, that you trouble yourself. It is the only misfortune I fear. Troops are entering on all sides, and constantly. You have a great many partisans in Spain, but they are intimidated; they are all the respectable people. However, I acknowledge none the less that your task is great and glorious.

"The victory of Marshal Bessières, who has wholly beaten Cuesta and the army of Galicia, has greatly improved the position of affairs. It is worth more than a reinforcement of 30,-000 men. The divisions of Gobert and Vedel having joined General Dupont, offensive measures must be vigorously pushed on that side. It is the only point menaced, and there must soon be a success there; with 25,000 men, comprising infantry, cavalry, and artillery, there are more than necessary to obtain a great result. At the worst, with 21,000 men present on the field of battle, he can boldly take the offensive; he will not be beaten, and will have more than four-and-twenty chances in his favor.

"You ought not to find it so extraordinary to conquer your

kingdom. Philip V. and Henry IV. were obliged to conquer theirs. Keep your spirits up, and never doubt for an instant that everything will finish better and more quickly than you now imagine.

"Everything goes on very well at Saragossa."

The attack upon Saragossa, on the 1st July, was unsuccessful. General Verdier, who commanded the siege, had seized the convent of St. Joseph, without being able to penetrate into the town, all the streets being well fortified. He had asked for troops and a train of artillery. General Dupont was threatened, in a badly chosen position, by the insurgents of Grenada, commanded by General Reding, formerly colonel of one of the Swiss regiments; General Castaños brought up the troops of Andalusia. The orders of the emperor were precise; General Dupont was not to repass the Sierra Morena, he was not to retreat on Andalusia.

In the hitherto restricted sphere of his operations, General Dupont had shown himself constantly bold and successful under chiefs more skilful and more experienced than himself; but left to his own resources, he knew not how to profit by his advantages, nor choose his quarters advantageously. The food of the troops was bad and insufficient, and the sick were numerous; isolated in the midst of a country passionately hostile, without means of information as to the enemy's movements, without news of Madrid or the government, the French remained stationary, sad and depressed. General Vedel occupied Baylen, General Gobert La Carolina; thus they commanded the defiles of the mountain.

On the 14th July, General Castaños appeared before Andujar, while the corps of Reding threatened Baylen; the imprudent movement of our troops had uncovered this last position. General Dupont was informed of this.

He resolved to march himself upon Baylen, but he was encumbered with an immense train of baggage, and by numerous sick, whom he would not abandon to the cruelties of the enemy; the movement was deferred till the next day, the 18th July. At the approach of night the army began its march. The heat was still suffocating. A great number of soldiers, suffering from dysentery, had been unable to find a place in the wagons, and dragged themselves behind the train, scarcely able to bear the weight of their arms. The anxiety of General Dupont was entirely for his rearguard; he feared that General Castaños, informed of his movements by the hun-

dreds of voluntary spies who served the Spanish cause, would
throw himself on his rear. The vanguard was feeble, composed of young and undisciplined soldiers; when it deployed
at three in the morning, on the rocky banks of the Rumblar,
the Spanish posts occupied the passage. Before the combat,
the soldiers rushed towards the bed of the torrent. It was
dried up. " The Spaniards have taken away the river!" cried
the French, even then disposed to treat painful thoughts with
gayety. The Spanish battalions barred the route of Baylen,
which General Reding had occupied the previous day.

Worn out by the heat, by thirst, by the march, our soldiers
charged the enemy, and drove them back as far as the plain
of Baylen. There lay extended before us the Spanish army,
in front of the little town, in an amphitheatre of hills, covered
with olive-trees. The Spanish artillery was formidable: the
field-pieces brought up by the French were soon dismounted.
The centre of the Spanish army remained solid, and even the
charges of cavalry could not break it. When at last the front
ranks opened under the shock of the horses, or the steel of the
bayonets, the lines reformed at the end of the plain, always
pitilessly barring the road. The cannonade did not slacken for
a single instant.

The soldiers began to show signs of discouragement, and the
officers proposed to the general to abandon the sick and the
baggage, and to form into a compact mass, in order to open a
passage by force in the direction of La Carolina, occupied by
General Vedel. Dupont expected his lieutenant every moment. He refused to abandon his train, and vainly renewed
the attack on all the length of the Spanish lines. Up to this
time the Swiss regiments in the service of France, mixed with
our soldiers, and marching in our ranks, had remained faithful; the bad fortune of our arms, the view of their comrades
fighting among the Spaniards under a chief of their race, triumphed at last over their good resolutions—they deserted in a
body. At the same moment the sound of cannon was heard in
the distance, but it was not in the direction of La Carolina, it
was at the bridge of Rumblar: General Castaños arrived to
crush us.

This was too much, and the unfortunate General Dupont was
to show on this day that he was not one of those whose courage defies fortune. "Find General Reding," said he to one of
his officers, "and ask from him a suspension of arms." The
battle was already ceasing of its own accord, on account of the

extreme fatigue of the troops. The Spanish general gave the
order to cease firing, but said, however, to the officer who had
been sent, "The truce must be ratified by General Castaños."
General de la Peña, who commanded the vanguard, accepted
the same conditions. "The French army must surrender at
discretion," he said haughtily, "for the present let us rest ourselves." The aide-de-camp of General Dupont went forward to
General Castaños, in order to obtain his assent to the truce. A
melancholy sadness weighed upon both officers and men; the
general-in-chief, formerly brilliant, bold, even emphatically
eloquent, hid his despair inside his tent; scarcely would he listen to the voice of those who surrounded him. Broken down
by his misfortune, he had lost all energy and all presence of
mind.

The same fault of irresolution and despair seems to have
taken hold on General Vedel. He had resolved to return to
Baylen, of which he too late understood the importance. But
the troops were worn out, he was forced to allow them a day
of rest. Since three o'clock in the morning of the 19th, the
continual echo of the cannon announced to the least vigilant
the coming engagement. The division began its march at five
o'clock, at eleven it had only advanced half-way; the men
left their ranks at every moment to seek a drop of water in
the rocks. The cannon was heard more faintly; at noon it was
heard no more. It was five o'clock when, in the midst of silence, the corps which had been so impatiently expected debouched above Baylen. The Spaniards guarded all the passages;
an officer appeared announcing the truce. General Vedel refused to believe it. He sent off an aide-de-camp to ascertain
the truth from General Reding. "If you do not return in
half-an-hour," said he, "I shall commence firing." At the
given moment, having no news from their emissary, the French
sounded the charge, and already a battalion of Spanish infantry had been surrounded, while the cuirassiers advanced at full
gallop; at the same instant the officers of the enemy, accompanied by an aide-de-camp of General Dupont, came up to
Vedel. The orders of the general-in-chief were precise, they
must cease firing. The negotiations had commenced. General
Castaños marched on Baylen.

The enthusiasm and triumph of the Spaniards did not give
him time to arrive there. The general of engineers, Marescot,
had been charged with the sad duty of treating with the Spaniards. General de la Peña, still posted at the bridge of Rum-

blar, threatened to crush the unfortunate army caught between his corps and that of General Reding. " I must have an answer in two hours," said he, repeating at the same time his only condition, "the French army must surrender at discretion."

General Dupont appealed to his lieutenants, general officers, and colonels; all declared that the soldiers would not fight. The general-in-chief surveyed the ranks some moments; his courage failed him entirely. " Our honor is saved," repeated the members of the council of war, " we have done yesterday all that men could do." One resource remained to them, to die to the last man in endeavoring to rejoin General Vedel. They had the misfortune not to try this last and glorious chance. The capitulation was resolved on. Don Castaños entertained the French officers while hatred shone in the eyes of all his staff. Polite, and full of attention to the vanquished, the Spanish general remained wholly inflexible. All the divisions of the army of Andalusia, engaged or not in the battle of Baylen, were to be comprised in the capitulation.

The conditions were about to be signed, the French troops were authorized to retreat on Madrid; the Barbou division alone commanded by General Dupont, was to be disarmed. At the same instant a letter from General Savary to General Dupont was brought by the mountaineers, into whose hands it had fallen. The aide-de-camp of the emperor announced a general concentration of the troops of the south at Madrid, and General Dupont was ordered to take the road to La Mancha. The Spaniards could not allow their victory to serve the designs of the emperor. General Castaños immediately declared to the French negotiators that the conditions were changed, and communicated to them the letter of General Savary. Overwhelmed by this new blow, General Marescot and his companions saw themselves forced to give up the Barbou division prisoners of war; the two other corps were to be transported to France under the Spanish flag; the officers retained their baggage, but the knapsacks of the soldiers were to be submitted to examination. " All Spaniards believe the sacred vessels of Cordova are in the bags of your soldiers," said General Castaños.

While the wretched negotiators accepted a capitulation which delivered them to their enemies, Vedel had proposed to General Dupont to attempt a new attack; he sent at the same time one of his aides-de-camp to plead the cause of his division. At one time Dupont authorized Vedel to save, at any price, his troops, and those of General Dufour's, by taking in forced marches the road to Madrid.   Already Vedel had obeyed, and hastened across the defiles of the Sierra Morena, but the news of his departure was not long in coming to the camp of the Spaniards. They accused the French of breaking the truce, and threatened to immediately massacre the Barbou division, which found itself at that time completely surrounded.   The Spanish negotiators broke out into fury, overwhelming with insults the unhappy officers charged to treat with them.   Heroism had disappeared from their souls.   They hastened to the tent of the general-in-chief, still plunged in melancholy dejection.   He gave way at last, and to his eternal dishonor, and that of the men who tore from him this cowardly concession, he sent to General Vedel the order to retrace his steps, and to submit with his soldiers to the lot the capitulation reserved for him.

Like General Dupont, Vedel consulted his lieutenants.   At first all refused a submission which would lead to their destruction.   A new messenger came, throwing on them all the responsibility of the inevitable massacre of their comrades.   They gave way, and with despair in their souls they slowly retraced their steps; as the sole solace to their sufferings they still retained their arms, while they saw their unhappy comrades defile before the Spanish army laying down their muskets at the feet of the victors.   During three days the troops had not received any food; the Spaniards had counted on hunger as well as defeat to lead the French to capitulate.   At last they got some food, and soon the columns began their march.   The ports of embarkation had been fixed upon.

They advanced slowly, for from all the towns, villages, and scattered houses, flocked multitudes in fury, who insulted the frightful misfortune of our soldiers.   General Castaños, moderate in his triumph, had said to the French negotiators, "De la Cuesta, Blake, and myself, were not of the same opinion as the insurgents.   We yielded to the national movement; but this movement is becoming so unanimous that it has a chance of success.   Let Napoleon not insist upon an impossible conquest, let him not force us to throw ourselves into the arms of the English.   Let him give us back our king, and the two nations will be forever reconciled."

It was in fact the same thought, clothed in offensive language that Thomas de Morla, the chief of the insurrection at Cadiz, flung at General Dumont when he complained of the bad treatment undergone by his soldiers.   "Your excellency forces me to express truths which must be bitter to you. What right have you to insist on the execution of a treaty concluded in favor of an army which entered Spain under the mask of alliance and friendship, which has imprisoned our king and his family, sacked his palaces, assassinated and robbed his subjects, ravaged his country, usurped his crown? How it would rouse the populace to know that a single one of your soldiers was the possessor of 2180 livres. !"

The pillage of Cordova had been exaggerated by the public imagination, and served the chiefs of the insurrection to justify their want of faith. The entire army of Andalusia was detained under various pretexts. The Junta of Seville refused to ratify the capitulation. The divisions of Dufour and Vedel saw their army taken away, and 20,000 men of those French troops, who up to the present time had been accustomed to victory, remained during long years prisoners of war, subjected to the worst treatment, slowly decimated by sickness and sorrow. Spain first gave to the world the spectacle of a successful resistance to the oppression the Emperor Napoleon had made to weigh upon all nations.

We understand by sad experience the astonishment and anger which seized upon our armies everywhere when they heard of the capitulation of Baylen. This name has remained fixed as an indelible stain on the memory of the men who concluded it in a moment of despair, after numerous faults, of which the most unpardonable cannot be imputed to them. Perhaps in his secret thought, Napoleon began to foresee the difficulties of the enterprise he had undertaken against Spain; perhaps he comprehended his error, but his indignation was excessive, and broke out in his words as well as letters. There was also a shade of discouragement when he wrote to King Joseph, on the 3rd August, "My brother, the knowledge I have that you are struggling, my friend, with events foreign to your habits as well as to your natural character, pains me. Dupont has dishonored our flag. What stupidity! What baseness! Those men will be taken by the English. Events of such a nature require my presence at Paris. Germany, Poland, Italy, all join together. My sorrow is really great when I think that I cannot be at this moment with you, and in the midst of my soldiers. I have given orders to Ney to go there. He is a man of honor, zeal, and thorough courage. If you get accustomed to Ney, he might command the army. You will have 100,000 men, and Spain will be conquered in the autumn. A suspension of arms, made by Savary, might perhaps lead to commanding and directing the insurgents; we shall hear what they say. I think that, so far as your personal likings go, you care little for reigning over the Spaniards."

At the moment when Napoleon was writing these lines, King Joseph retreated before the enemy, and abandoned his capital. Deprived of the succor that General Dupont was to have brought, the defenders of Madrid did not consider the concentration of troops sufficiently considerable to protect the Castiles against the ever-rising flood of the national insurrection. "The emperor could hold his own here," said Savary, "but what is possible to him is not so to the others." It was resolved to make a stand on the line of the Ebro; King Joseph quitted Madrid, abandoned by the intimate servants of his household, as well as by a certain number of his ministers. 2000 domestics of the palace had fled for fear of being forced to follow the royal retreat. Burgos not appearing to be a retreat sufficiently sure, the monarch and his little court soon established themselves at Vittoria. After a second assault, as sanguinary and without result as the first, General Verdier, recalled to the Ebro, found himself obliged to abandon the siege of Saragossa. Already the position of the French in Spain became defensive, and the fears of King Joseph increased. "I can only repeat, once for all, that nearly all the grand army is marching, and that between this and autumn Spain will be inundated with troops," wrote the emperor, on the 9th of August. "You must try to preserve the line of the Douro to maintain a communication with Portugal. The English are not much, they never have more than a quarter of the troops they announce. Lord Wellesley has not 4000 men. Besides, they are intended, I believe, for Portugal."

It was in truth on Portugal that the efforts of England were directed at this moment, as she discerned clearly that there lay the true road to Spain. In Galicia, as well as Andalusia, the Spanish insurgents had refused the active intervention of the English. Sir Arthur Wellesley, who at first appeared before Corunna, contented himself by furnishing the suspicious Spaniards with ammunition and money, and on the 1st August he appeared at the mouth of the Mondego, in Portugal. His fleet carried 10,000 English troops. A reinforcement of 4000 men was shortly expected.

For two months General Junot had been isolated in Portugal,

separated from Spain by the insurrection of the frontier provinces, menaced by a similar rising of the Portuguese nation, already chafing under the foreign yoke, and sure of soon seeing England hasten to the succor of her faithful ally. He understood his danger, and, assembling around him his troops, recalled General Kellermann from Elvas and General Loison from Almeida. The insurrection already commenced around them, when Sir Arthur Wellesley set foot on the Portuguese soil. The French did not hold more than four or five towns. The entire people was in insurrection. But General Junot still occupied Lisbon; his forces were unfortunately diminished by the garrisons left in the forts, and by a corps of observation that had been detached under the orders of General Delaborde. After a courageous resistance, this vanguard of the French army had been already beaten when the English advanced on Vimeiro. Junot marched against them with an army of twelve or thirteen thousand men. The English numbered about 18,000. The arrival of Sir John Moore with his brigade was announced.

An unfortunate respect for the rights of seniority had placed Sir Arthur Wellesley under the orders of Sir Henry Burrard, and the latter under the command of Sir Hew Dalrymple, who had already left Gibraltar to place himself at the head of the army. The instructions of Wellesley obliged him to wait at Vimeiro for the arrival of Sir John Moore. General Junot wished to anticipate the reinforcements, and attacked the English on the 31st August, in the morning.

Sir Arthur Wellesley occupied the heights of Vimeiro; behind him were precipices, and all retreat was impossible. The access to the rocks was difficult; a strong artillery protected all the positions. When the French advanced to the assault of this natural fortress, they could not at first reach the English lines. General Kellermann alone succeeded in scaling the steep slopes which led to the enemy, and was received by a deadly fire, which forced him to retire. Our cavalry superior to that of the English, was useless in this difficult attack; its only duty was constantly to protect the corps of infantry, repulsed one after another. The English army had not moved. At noon, General Junot ordered the retreat. Sir Arthur Wellesley, always on watch on the heights, was already on the move to follow and crush those who had been unable to make him lose an inch of ground; but Sir Henry Burrard had arrived, and the command passed into his hands. He was opposed to all thought of pursuit. Junot took the road to Torres Vedras. Sir Arthur Wellesley listened with mingled respect and impatience to the arguments of his chief, and, turning towards his staff, "After this, gentlemen," said he, "we have only to go and shoot the red partridges."

General Junot had comprehended better than his adversary the danger which threatened him; he felt the impossibility of maintaining himself in a country suddenly become hostile, in face of an English army already superior to his own, and soon to be reinforced by excellent troops. General Kellermann was charged to treat, at first for an armistice, then for the convention bearing the name of Cintra, which provided honorably for the evacuation of Portugal by the French generals. The conditions accorded were so favorable that public opinion in England accused the negotiators of it as a crime, of which the obloquy weighed some time on Sir Arthur Wellesley. He had not, however, been too favorable to it. "Ten days after the battle of the 21st," he wrote to Lord Castlereagh, "we are less advanced than we might and ought to have been on the evening of the battle." The Emperor Napoleon had, for his part, manifested some discontent at the convention, which brought back to France all his troops free from engagement, and possessing their arms. "I was going to send Junot before a council of war," said he; "but, happily, the English have been before me in sending their generals, and have thus spared me the mortification of punishing an old friend." The confidence of Napoleon remained, however, shaken with respect to his officer. "Everything which was not a triumph he looked upon as a defeat," said the Duchess of Abrantes in her memoirs.

It often happened to Napoleon to judge unjustly of men and things, because he appreciated them exclusively from a personal and selfish point of view. Thus, he accused of treason the Marquis de la Romana and his brave companions. After the battle of Friedland, the Spanish battalions wrung in 1807 from the shameful terror of the Prince de la Paix, were sent by Napoleon to regions which would appear the most fatal to the temperament and habits of southern people. They had been confided to the King of Denmark, and charged to protect from the English his little kingdom, hitherto so cruelly oppressed by them. The health of the troops was, however, excellent when the news came to them of the general rising which had taken place in Spain, and the unforeseen success of the national resistance. They immediately conceived the thought of returning to their country, to join their efforts to those of their countrymen. An English squadron, under the orders of Admiral Keith, appeared suddenly on the coasts of Jutland, at the entrance to Niborg, in the island of Funen. Immediately the Marquis de la Romana, with difficulty warned by secret advices, seized the fishing-boats, which were numerous on the coast; then, making himself master of the citadel and port of Niborg, and crossing two arms of the sea, he assembled around him all those of his companions-in-arms who were within reach. He arrived at the English fleet, and sailed towards Gothenburg, from which place he put to sea for Spain. Several regiments far in the interior of the land could not be warned in time, and remained prisoners of war. One of them, having by chance heard of the enterprise of their comrades, succeeded in rejoining them at the exact moment of their embarkation, after a march long even for Spaniards. In the middle of September, they at last landed in Galicia amidst the joyous acclamations of the people.

At Vittoria the unhappy King of Spain continually received one after another news which damped his courage and convinced his reason of the futility of all attempts to support his throne. On the 9th of August he wrote to the Emperor Napoleon: "I do not think it possible to treat with the insurgent chiefs; all their heads are turned; no one has sufficient direction of affairs or influence enough upon the masses to lead them in a determinate manner. On the supposition that France will gratuitously spend her blood and treasure to place and maintain me on the throne of Spain, I cannot hide from your Majesty that I cannot endure the thought of any other than your Majesty commanding the French armies in Spain. If I become the conqueror of this country by the horrors of a war in which every individual Spaniard takes part, I shall be long an object of terror and execration. I am too old to have time for repairing so many evils, and I shall have sown too much hatred during the war to be able to gather in my last years the fruit of the good that I may be able to do during peace. Your Majesty sees, then, that even by this hypothesis—that of the conquest and establishment of the monarchy—that I should not desire to reign in Spain. . . . . This nation is more concentrated in its sentiments than any other people of Europe; it has something of the character of the peoples of Africa, which is peculiar to itself. Your Majesty cannot form an idea, because certainly no one has ever told you, in what degree the name of your Majesty is execrated. This, then, is what I desire: to keep the command of the army sufficiently long to beat the enemy, return to Madrid with the army, because it left with me, and from this capital put forth a decree to the effect that I renounce reigning over a people I should be obliged to reduce by force of arms; and I return to Naples with wishes for the happiness of Spain, and the desire to effect the welfare of the Two Sicilies. In resigning to your Majesty the rights I hold from you, you will make of them whatever use your wisdom will indicate. I beg, then, your Majesty to suspend all operations relative to the kingdom of Naples. The means will not be wanting to your Majesty for compensating the prince you wished to place on the throne of Naples; for the rest, exact justice and affection plead in my favor in your Majesty's heart." And two days later he wrote: "It would take 200,000 Frenchmen to conquer Spain, and a hundred thousand scaffolds to maintain the prince who should be condemned to reign over them. No, sire, you do not know this people; each house will be a fortress, and every man of the same mind as the majority. I repeat but one thing, which will suffice as an example; not a Spaniard will be on my side if we are conquerors; we cannot find a guide or a spy. Four hours before the battle of Rio-Seco, Marshal Bessières did not know where the enemy was. Every one who speaks or writes differently either lies or is blind."

On the 15th of July the kingdom of Naples had been solemnly conferred on "Prince Joachim Murat, Grand Duke of Cleves and Berg." The haughty obstinacy of Napoleon, his habit of conquering, and the growing want of the prestige of victory, did not permit him to admit for a single instant the modest pretensions of King Joseph. He was already preparing to pass into Spain, counting upon success as soon as his presence should inspire his generals with foresight and boldness. Other cares had till this time detained him from this expedition, which became more necessary every day. Already, for a long time, Napoleon had nourished suspicions of the loyalty of Austria. On several occasions he had, not without reason, accused her of making armaments and hostile preparations. The occupation of Rome and the events of Spain had, on the other side, increased the distrust and irritation of Vienna. The Archduke Charles, usually favorably inclined towards France, exclaimed, "Well, if we must, we will die with arms in our hands; but they shall not dispose of the crown of Austria as easily as they have disposed of the crown of Spain!"

Napoleon had scarcely arrived at Paris, returning from a long journey in France, when a great fête had assembled around him all the diplomatic body (15th August, 1808). His anger broke out against Austria, as it had previously broken out against England in his celebrated interview with Lord Whitworth. The frequent menaces of Champagny had not intimidated Metternich, at that time Austrian ambassador in Paris. The emperor advanced suddenly towards him: "Austria wishes, then, to make war against us? She wishes to frighten me? . . ." And without listening to the pacific protestations of the prince, "Why, then, these immense preparations? They are defensive, you say. But who attacks you, to make you think so much of defence? Is not all peaceful around you? Since the peace of Presburg, has there been the slightest disagreement between you and me? Have not all our relations together been extremely amicable? And yet you have suddenly raised a cry of alarm; you have put in motion all your population; your princes have overrun your provinces; your proclamations have summoned the people to the defence of the country; your proclamations and measures are those which you used when I was at Leoben.

"You are well aware that I ask nothing from you, and make no claim upon you, and that I even regard the preservation of your power in the present state of affairs as useful to the European system, and to the interests of France. I have encamped my troops to keep them fit for marching. They do not camp in France, because that costs too much; they camp abroad, where it is less expensive. My camps have been distributed; none of them threatens you. In the excess of my security I dismantled all the places of Silesia. I am ready to remove my camps, if that is necessary to your security.

"In the meantime what will happen? You have raised 400,000 men; I am about to raise 200,000. Germany, who was beginning to breathe after so many ruinous wars, is about to see again all her wounds reopened. I shall reconstruct the places of Silesia, instead of evacuating that province and the Prussian States, as I wished to do. Europe will be all up in arms. Soon the very women must become soldiers.

Those are the evils you have produced, and, as I believe. without intending it. In such a state of things, when the strain everywhere is so great, war will soon become desirable, in order

to hasten the end. A sharp pain, if short, is better than prolonged suffering.

"But if you are as disposed for peace as you allege, it is necessary that you speak out, that you countermand the measures
which have excited so dangerous a fermentation, and that all
Europe be convinced that you wish for peace. It is necessary
that all should proclaim your good intentions, justified by your
acts as well as your language."

Definitively, and as a proof of Austria's submission, Napoleon
asked for a recognition of King Joseph. On this special demand—which no doubt was made less harsh in form by the
report of Champagny, which has been preserved—Austria did
not give way, nor did she refuse; she delayed, still constantly
and unobtrusively engaged in warlike preparations, which
were actively pushed forward by the Archduke Charles and
Stadion, the prime minister.

Napoleon wished to intimidate Austria, his bold foresight assuring him of her hostility. He required several months for
his Spanish expedition. Finding it necessary to send new
troops into the Peninsula, he was obliged to quit the countries
which were occupied, and at last put an end to the long suspense imposed upon Prussia, and aggravated by intolerable
war-contributions. Prince William, appointed by his brother
to the painful mission, had in vain tried to obtain favorable
conditions. Napoleon feeling the necessity of recalling his
forces, fixed at 140,000,000 the sum still left of what had been
demanded from Prussia; but before signing the treaty the conqueror exacted more than one sacrifice. The French continued
to occupy Stettin, Custrin, Glogau on the Oder, and Magdeburg on the Elbe: a secret article forbade Prussia to raise an
army for ten years of more than 42,000 men. No militia was
allowed; and in case war should break out in Germany, King
Frederick William undertook to supply the Emperor Napoleon
with an auxiliary force of 16,000 men.

To those painful conditions Napoleon added another, which
was entirely personal and political. "I have asked for Stein's
dismissal from the cabinet," wrote the emperor to Marshal
Soult on the 10th September; "without that the King of
Prussia will not recover his states. I have sequestrated his
property in Westphalia."

Baron Stein resigned, but continued working ardently in re-
viving and fostering the national spirit in Germany against
the Emperor Napoleon, as he had been preparing for more than

VII.—16

a year. He began an able and prudent scheme of reform, which was continued by his colleagues after his fall. The convention of the 8th September, 1808, being signed between France and Prussia, King Frederick William took possession of his diminished states, and the Emperor Alexander was freed from the importunities of the unfortunate sufferers, who blamed him for their lot. Napoleon feeling the need of drawing closer the alliance with Russia, an interview was agreed upon between the two emperors, and Erfurt was chosen for the scene of the illustrious interview.

The Emperor Alexander had looked with secret satisfaction upon the events in Spain. Constantly influenced by the hopes by which Napoleon had dazzled him at Tilsit, and haunted by that passion for obtaining Constantinople which had so long been common to all the Russian sovereigns, he had accepted without any difficulty the spoliation of the Spanish Bourbons, in order to justify beforehand the spoliations in which he was interested. The national rising of the Spanish people served his design: the all-powerful conqueror had met with a serious resistance, undergone checks, and had need of the moral support of his allies; their material assistance might be needed. Alexander reckoned upon gaining at Erfurt the cession of that "cat's tongue which was the key of the Bosphorus, 'and which he coveted so eagerly. He set out from St. Petersburg on the 7th of September, somewhat against the will of his mother and the "Russian party," and with but few attendants.

The Emperor Napoleon, on the contrary, had assembled at Erfurt all the resources of French elegance, joined to the brilliance which is inseparable from a powerful and victorious court. All the small princes of Germany were present, and the great sovereigns sent their most able representatives. The celebrated actors of the Théâtre Français, with Talma at their head, were appointed to amuse the two emperors in the intervals of business. The representation of *Cinna* was the first of a series of master-pieces of the French stage. The emperor forbade comedies, saying that the Germans did not understand Molière.

A fortnight was thus spent in the midst of the most magnificent fêtes combined with serious negotiations. Napoleon decided to at once abandon the Danubian provinces to his ally, though resolved never to grant Constantinople. After long conferences between Champagny and Romanzoff, as to the suitable form to give to this division of other people's property which was to render the Franco-Russian alliance indissoluble, the convention was signed on the 12th October. Both emperors agreed to address to England a formal demand for immediate peace, the base of the negotiations to be the *uti possidetis*, that is to say, the acknowledgment of conquests and occupations which were already accomplished. France was only to agree to a peace which should secure Finland, Wallachia, and Moldavia to Russia; and Russia only to one which should secure to France all her possessions, including the crown of Spain for King Joseph.

Supposing the negotiations or acts of the two powers for the execution of the treaty should bring on war with Austria, France and Russia made promises of mutual support: their hostilities were to be in common. At the urgent request of Alexander, the Emperor Napoleon granted a reduction of 20,000,000 on the war-contribution of Prussia. At the same time, and by the clever mediation of Talleyrand, he threw out a hint to the young Czar that he wished to be united to him by family alliance. "The emperor had resolved to have recourse to a divorce," said the prince, "and his thoughts turned naturally towards the sisters of his ally and his dearest friend." Alexander blushed, being by no means all-powerful in the bosom of his family, and the empress-mother having a strong dislike to Napoleon. Complimentary and friendly attentions, therefore, could not remove reserve on this delicate point. The two emperors separated on the 14th October, after hunting together on the plain of Jena, and supping and chatting familiarly with Goethe and Wieland, at Weimar. Germany showed every attention to her conqueror, while silently preparing to take revenge.

The Emperor Napoleon on returning to Paris finished his preparations for the Spanish campaign. He had told King Joseph, when in Erfurt, that he should march as soon as the Corps Législatif was opened. On the 1st October he had put in the mouth of Champagny suitable arguments to prepare the way for a new levy of soldiers. In his report to the emperor, the Foreign Minister thus publicly denounced the ingratitude of the Spanish people:—

"Your Majesty hoped to prevent the return of the troubles in Spain, by means of persuasion and by measures of a wise and humane policy. Intervening as a mediator in the midst of the divided Spanish, your Majesty indicated to them the safety of a wise and prudent constitution, suitable for providing every want, and in which liberal ideas are reconciled with those ancient institutions which Spain wished to preserve.

"Your Majesty's expectation was deceived. Private interests, the intrigues of the foreigner, and his corrupting gold, have prevailed over the influence which you had a right to exercise. The Spanish people having shaken off the yoke of authority, aspired to govern. The intrigues of the agents of the Inquisition, the influence of the monks, who are so numerous in Spain, and who dreaded reform, have at this critical moment occasioned the insurrection of several Spanish provinces, in which the voice of wise men has been disavowed or smothered, and several of them made the victims of their courageous opposition to the disorderly populace. We have seen a frightful anarchy spreading over the greater part of Spain. Will your Majesty allow England to be able to say that Spain is one of her provinces, and that her flag, driven from the Baltic, the northern seas, the Levant, and even the Persian coasts, rules over the gates of France? Never, sire.

"To avoid so great disgrace and misfortune, there are two millions of brave men ready, if need be, to cross the Pyrenees; and the English will be driven out of the Peninsula."

In expectation of the supreme effort thus boldly proclaimed, the Senate ordered a levy of 160,000 men, anticipating by sixteen months the regular call. The recruits were intended to replace in Germany the trained soldiers of the Grande Armée, who had already started to go to Spain, and were everywhere fêted in the towns they passed through. Skilled in all the plans by which great success is procured, the emperor, on the 3rd of September, had written to Cretet, Minister of the Interior: "Give order, so that the town of Metz may fête the troops as they pass through; and as the town is not rich enough, I shall give three francs a man, but all must be done in the name of the town. The municipal body will make a speech to them, treat them, give the officers dinners, get triumphal arches raised at the gates through which they pass, and put inscriptions on them. Give the same order for the town of Nancy, which is the place where the central column will pass. As for the column of the right, it will be fêted at Rheims. I wish you to see that the prefects of departments on their route pay special attention to the troops, and in every way keep up the enthusiasm which animates them and their love of glory. Speeches, verses, shows gratis, dinners,—that is what I expect from the citizens for the soldiers returning victorious." On the 17th, with the list of towns which had responded to his call as well as those from which he expected the same display: "Get songs written in Paris, and send them to the different towns. These songs will tell of the glory gained by the army and that it is still to gain, of the liberty of the seas which will result from its victories. These songs will be sung at the dinners which will be given. Get three kinds of songs made, so that the soldier may not hear the same sung twice."

It was not without secret emotion and an inquietude which showed itself by numerous heroical declamations, that the Emperor Napoleon himself passed into Spain with his old troops, which had gained for him the sovereign rule in Europe. For the first time in his military career, he felt himself face to face with the spontaneous resistance of a people. "Soldiers," said he to the regiments which were to march before him on the Spanish soil, "after triumphing on the banks of the Danube and Vistula, you have crossed Germany by forced marches; and now I make you cross France without allowing you a moment's rest. Soldiers, I have need of you. The hateful presence of the leopard contaminates the continents of Spain and Portugal; let him fly in terror at the sight of us. Let us carry our eagles in triumph as far as the columns of Hercules; there also we have outrages to avenge. Soldiers, you have surpassed the renown of modern armies, but have you equalled the glories of the armies of Rome, which in one campaign triumphed on the Rhine and the Euphrates, in Illyria and on the Tagus? A long peace and lasting prosperity will be the fruit of your labors. A true Frenchman neither can nor ought to rest till the seas are open and freed. Soldiers, all that you have done, all that you will yet do for the happiness of the French people, for my glory, will remain eternally in my heart."

According to the custom of constitutional monarchies, the English cabinet replied to the personal letter addressed to King George III. by the two emperors. Without formally rejecting the overtures of peace, Canning urged that all the allies of England ought to have been admitted to the negotiation; and he included in the list of allies the Kings of Naples, Portugal, Sweden, and even the Spanish insurgents, although no formal treaty had yet been concluded with them. Soon after, to put an end to the pretence of negotiation, an official declaration of the British Government announced to the world that England could not treat with two courts, one of which dethroned legitimate kings and kept them prisoners, while the other assisted from interested motives. Resolved "to attack by every means a usurpation to which there was nothing comparable in the history of the world, Great Britain will never abandon the generous Spanish nation, nor any of the people who, though at present hesitating, may soon shake off the yoke which oppresses them." For the future all pretences disappeared, and the struggle began afresh between the Emperor Napoleon and England. The latter had long been looking for a ground of attack against the conqueror; now at last it was supplied by the Spanish soil and people.

It is extremely painful to have to prove the injustice of a course which is naturally dear to us. That is bitterly felt at every step during the long years of the war of Spain, in presence of the generous efforts of a people who, with arms in their hands, vindicated their national liberty and independence. The first outbursts of the Spanish insurrection showed this with a brilliancy that soon partially disappeared. The efforts of the English their courage and feats of arms, were soon to eclipse to some extent the obstinate animosity of the Spanish. The long series of checks which began on Napoleon's arrival was sufficient to prove with what a decisive weight the alliance which they were soon to conclude with Great Britain weighed in the balance of their destinies.

Setting out from Paris on the 29th October, the emperor, on arriving at Bayonne, showed great anger at the delay in the preparations, the bad state of the roads and the shortness of supplies. "You will see how disgracefully I am served," he wrote to General Dejean, in charge of the war administration. "I have only 7000 cloaks instead of 50,000; 15,000 pairs of shoes instead of 129,000. I am in want of everything; my army is naked, and yet we are entering on a campaign. Yet I have spent a great deal of money, which is so much thrown into the sea."

Napoleon's displeasure was not diminished when he reached Vittoria. He had beforehand forbidden the attempt upon Madrid which King Joseph proposed to him, mistrusting his brother's military skill. "The military art is an art the principles of which must never be violated," he wrote, in some observations of great sense and force. "To change one's line of operation is an operation of genius; to lose it, is an operation so serious that it constitutes a crime in the general who is guilty of it. If, before taking Madrid, organizing the army there, with military stores for eight or ten days, and providing sufficient supplies, one had just been defeated, what would become of that army? where could they rally? where transport their wounded? whence draw their war supplies, having nothing but provisions for a short time? We need say no more; those who have the courage to advise such a measure would be the first to lose their head so soon as the result proved the madness of their procedure. With an army entirely composed of men like those of the guard and commanded by the most able general—Alexander or Cæsar, if they could act with such folly —one could answer for nothing; much more therefore in the circumstances in which the army of Spain is placed. In war everything depends on opinion—opinion as to the enemy, opinion as to one's own soldiers. When a battle is lost, the difference between the conquered and the conqueror is but trifling; yet opinion makes it immeasurable, because two or three squadrons are then sufficient to produce a great effect. Nothing has been done to give confidence to the French; there is not a soldier but sees that timidity pervades everything, and therefore forms from that his opinion of the enemy. He has no other data for knowing what is opposed to him except what is told him, and the bearing which he is expected to assume."

By a chance which prudent minds might have anticipated, but which astonished and confounded the inexperience of the insurgent leaders, the national rising, which lately was universal, irresistible, and triumphant, lost all its power and energy immediately after the victory of Baylen. The hesitation and inaction of King Joseph, his government, and his army, had met with an unexpected counterpart in their adversaries.

It is often a difficult undertaking, even when desired and concerted beforehand, to stir up an entire nation and animate them for war; and when their rising is spontaneous, brought on by the same patriotic and revolutionary idea, it is a still more difficult undertaking to organize their efforts and direct aright their impassioned impulses. After the first shock, which had agitated Spain from one extremity to the other, after the formation of provincial or municipal Juntas, after the success of some of the insurgent generals, the trial of government suddenly presented itself to the leaders of the national movement. It was necessary to command all those proud and independent men, intoxicated with a new liberty and an ancient self-respect; it was necessary at any cost to get from them obedience, for Napoleon was at hand—he, the master of so many armies waiting for his bidding, and who at his will had made princes and kings bend down. The Spanish alone had resisted him successfully; how were they to keep up and continue the resistance?

With considerable difficulty, a central Junta was formed at Aranjuez, composed of delegates from the local Juntas, too numerous to be a council of government, and too restricted to possess, or even claim, the rights of a representative assembly. The new Junta wished to exercise absolute authority. The Council of Castile had proposed that the Cortes be assembled, but most of the generals were opposed to a measure which necessarily tended to diminish their power. The Cortes were not assembled, and the Junta called all the Spaniards to arms.

Though the patriotic ardor in Spain was undoubtedly great, and the patriotic uneasiness profound, the results of the general rising were insufficient, and came greatly short of the hopes of the insurrectional government. About 100,000 men were mustered when the military organization was decided upon by the Junta. Three main armies—that of the left, under the orders of General Blake; that of the centre, under General Castanos; that of the right, under Palafox—were to combine their operations in order to surround the French army. A fourth army, called the reserve, was to be afterwards formed; and the troops scattered over Catalonia were ordered to defend that province against General Duhesme. In spite of the repugnance inspired by foreign assistance to Spanish pride, the Junta had accepted the assistance of an English army, which had already collected at Lisbon, under the orders of Sir John Moore. He had marched across Portugal, and his lieutenant, Sir David Baird, was bringing him reinforcements from England, which afterwards joined him at Corunna. These forces and resources were sufficient to harass the French army, and make an easy occupation of Spain impossible; but not sufficent to keep up a regular war against the first troops in the world. The Spanish, as well as the English, soon found the truth of this.

Before Napoleon arrived at Vittoria, several battles had already taken place, generally favorable to the French army, though it was badly led, and had its forces scattered, instead of concentrated, as the emperor wished them to be, for his ready use. He bitterly blamed Marshals Lefebvre and Victor, and already the presence of the general who had been everywhere victorious was being promptly felt in the management of the army and the vigor of the operations. Marshal Soult had been sent to attack Burgos, then protected by 12,000 men of the Estremadura army; and on the 10th November, on the charge of Mouton's division alone, the Spanish wavered and took to flight, delivering up Burgos and its castle to the French army. The cavalry eagerly pursued the retreating enemy, who quickly formed again, and were as quickly scattered: many of the prisoners were killed. Napoleon at once set out for Burgos. "I start at one in the morning," he wrote to Joseph, "in order to reach Burgos incognito before daybreak, and shall make my arrangements for the day, because to win is nothing if no advantage is taken of the success. I think you ought to go to-morrow to Briviesca. The less ceremony I wish made on my own account, the more I wish made on yours. As for me, it does not suit well with the business of war; besides, I have no wish for it. On arriving, I shall give the necessary orders for disarming, and for burning the standard used for Ferdinand's proclamation. Use every endeavor that it may be felt to be no idle form."

Burgos already felt all the weight of the conqueror's anger. The town was pitilessly sacked. "A sad sight," say the memoirs of Count Miot de Melito, who accompanied King Joseph as he entered the town; "the houses nearly all deserted and pillaged; the furniture, smashed in pieces, scattered in the mud of the streets; one quarter, on the other side of the Arlanzen, on fire; the soldiers madly forcing in doors and windows, breaking everything that came in their way, using little and destroying much; the churches stripped; the streets crowded with the dead and dying—in a word, all the horrors of an assault, although the town had offered no defence!" The emperor ordered all the wool to be seized which was found in the town: it belonged to the great Spanish nobles, and he had resolved to confiscate their property everywhere. "The Duke of Infantado and Spanish great lords," he wrote a few days afterwards to Cretet, the Minister of the Interior (on the 19th November), "are sole proprietors of half the kingdom of Naples, and in this kingdom they are worth not less than 200,-000,000. They have, besides, possessions in Belgium, Piedmont, and Italy, which I intend to sequestrate. That is only the first rough draft of my plans." A decree of proscription had already been published, and a capital condemnation pronounced (12th November) against ten of the principal Spanish nobles. At that price, pardon was promised to all who made haste to make submission.

Marshal Soult, the conqueror of Burgos, had already been despatched by the emperor in the direction of Reinosa, in order to complete the destruction of General Blake's army, already partially defeated, on the 11th and 12th by General Victor, near the small town of Espinosa, at the spot where the road from the Biscayan mountains crosses the road of the plain. Soult was late in arriving; but, after a vigorous resistance, the overthrow of Blake's army was so complete that there was no fear that the army of the left could soon rally. Napoleon ordered Lannes and Ney to crush the armies of the right and the centre, commanded by Palafox and Castanos. Ney failing to keep his appointment at Tudela on the 23rd November, owing to a mistake on the march, Lannes made the attack alone, taking by surprise the Spanish generals, who were undecided as to their course of action, disagreeing as to the place for meeting the enemy, and yet urged on to the engagement by the popular cries, already accusing them of treason. The battle was a serious one; and for a short time Lannes, reduced to his own troops, found himself in a difficult position. He was, moreover, ill from a fall from his horse, but succeeded in winning the battle, and drove before him, one after another, all the divisions of the enemy's army. With the cruel and heedless fickleness of revolutionary governments, the Junta of Aranjuez hurriedly cashiered Generals Blake and Castanos. The Marquis of Romana's soldiers having distinguished themselves at Espinosa, he was appointed general of the united armies. Already, in spite of the consternation which reigned in the national party in Spain, small bodies of troops collected in various parts. Napoleon soon understood that the masterly strokes of his usual tactics were not sufficient to conquer men who were as prompt in again taking up arms as in throwing them down on the roads in order to run away. He hurried in pursuit everywhere, and multiplied his modes of attack. Junot, scarcely returned to France, received orders to go into Spain. Napoleon resolved to march upon Madrid.

The resources left at the disposition of the Junta for the defence of the capital were obviously insufficient. A body of 10,000 to 12,000 men, under the command of Benito San Juan, occupied the height Somo-Sierra, and on the 30th November Napoleon in person appeared before the small Spanish army. The passage being quickly forced by a charge of General Montbrun, the French cavalry rode to the gates of Madrid, causing indignation and alarm. The Junta had already left Aranjuez to meet in Badajoz, and the capital, entrusted to a small detachment of troops of the line under the Marquis of Castellar, at one time supported, at another hindered by the populace, corregidor of Madrid, the Marquis of Perales, was massacred by a handful of madmen, on the charge of having mixed sand with the powder of their cartridges. Thomas de Morla, the tribune of Cadiz, commanded the defence. Barricades were raised at every point, and ramparts improvised, Madrid never having been surrounded with fortifications.

On the morning of the 2nd December the emperor arrived at the gates of the capital, and at once had a summons sent to those in command of the place. His messenger had great difficulty in obtaining admission to the town; and the Spanish general appointed to convey the refusal of surrender was accompanied and watched by a band of insurgents, who dictated to him his reply. A second summons producing no result, the firing at the walls and the town began; and in a few hours the palace Buen Retiro and all the northern and eastern gates were in the power of the French. At several points the resistance was most obstinate. The emperor again summoning the Junta of Defence to spare the capital the horrors of a general assault, Thomas de Morla soon presented himself before him, in the name of the insurrectional government.

The emperor's features clearly expressed his anger at the sight of the governor of Andalusia, who had recently retained the troops taken prisoners, in defiance of the capitulation of Baylen. Napoleon had more than once violated treaties: he attached always an extreme importance to military conventions. On this occasion, his natural sense of wrong and offended vanity alone had the mastery in his soul. Thomas de Morla, generally arrogant and bold, seemed troubled and confused. "The people," said he, "are ungovernable in their patriotic passion; the Junta ask for one day to bring them back to reason."

"It is in vain for you to use the name of the people," exclaimed Napoleon. "If you cannot succeed in calming them, it is because you yourselves have excited them, and have led them astray by your falsehoods. Bring together the curés, the heads of convents, the principal proprietors, and let the town surrender between this and six o'clock in the morning, or else it will have ceased to exist. I have no desire to withdraw my troops, nor ought I. You massacred the unhappy French prisoners who fell into your hands. A short time ago you allowed to be dragged in the streets and put to death two servants of the Russian ambassador because they were Frenchmen. The want of skill and the cowardice of a general placed in your hands some troops which had capitulated on the battlefield, and the capitulation was violated. What kind of letter, M. Morla, did you write to that general? It became you well to speak of pillaging, you who entered Roussillon and carried off all the women, to divide them among your soldiers like booty. What right had you, on other grounds, to use such language? You were prevented by the capitulation. Consider the conduct of the English, who certainly do not boast of being rigid observers of the rights of nations. They have complained of the convention of Portugal, but they executed it. To violate military treaties is to renounce all civilization; it is to place one's self on a level with the Bedouins of the desert. How dare you ask a capitulation, you who violated that of Baylen? I had a fleet at Cadiz, the ally of Spain, and you turned against it the mortars of the town under your command. Go back to Madrid. I give you till six o'clock in the morning. Return then, if you have nothing to say of the people except that they have submitted: otherwise, you and your troops will all be put to the sword."

The situation left to the insurgents no alternative but that of submission. During the night, the Marquis of Castellar went out with his troops by the gates which the French had not yet seized. At six in the morning, on the 4th December, Madrid surrendered. All the citizens were disarmed. Napoleon took possession of a small country-house at Chamartin, and King Joseph held his court at the Pardo, some distance from Madrid; the rebel town being thus held unworthy to be honored by the presence of its masters. Several great lords were arrested: the Marquis of St. Simon was even condemned to death, as a French emigrant in the Spanish service; but the sentence was badly received by the soldiers, and left unexecuted. A series of decrees abolished the feudal rights, the Inquisition, and the custom duties in passing from one province to another. The number of convents was reduced by a third. The conquests of liberty and civilization thus imposed on the Spanish by their oppressors naturally became hateful to them. Thus one of the results of Napoleon's Spanish campaign was to prepare a reaction in favor of the Inquisition.

While the emperor took possession of Madrid, and endeavored to reduce the undisciplined spirit of the capital, General

Gouvion St. Cyr had been appointed to bring Catalonia to submission. A man of skill and prudence, though obstinately attached to his own opinions, St. Cyr was never a favorite with
Napoleon, though he knew his merit. He had entrusted him
with the duty of reducing an isolated province, where his command ran no risk of being interfered with by contradictory
wishes or orders. The general delayed some time at the siege
of Rosas, which he was anxious not to leave in his rear, and
when he at last advanced towards Barcelona, General Duhesme and his garrison were short of provisions. On his approach the blockade was raised, and, on the 15th December,
General Vives offered battle to St. Cyr at Cardeden, before
Barcelona. The French having left their artillery behind, so
as to advance more quickly, the order was given to open a road
through the enemy's ranks with the bayonet. The soldiers
obeyed, keeping their heads down as they advanced under the
fire of the Spanish; the latter were unable to resist the impetuosity of such an attack, and the columns of our troops passed
through the enemy's lines, which were soon broken and scattered. The Spanish artillery fell entirely into our hands, and
next day the French entered Barcelona. On the 21st the entrenched camp on the Llobregat was taken, and complete dis-
persion of the Spanish troops in Catalonia soon followed, only
a few places still holding out, which General Gouvion St. Cyr
prepared to besiege.

The English, however, henceforward united to the cause of
the Spanish insurrection by a solemn declaration, published on
the 15th December, and everywhere the objects of Napoleon's
most persistent hatred, had not yet undergone the shock of his
arms. Having only imperfect information as to Sir John
Moore's operations, the emperor had reckoned with certainty
upon the retreat which that general began at the moment of
the attack upon Madrid, when he found that it was absolutely
impossible to concentrate his forces in time for resistance.
Moore was not hopeful as to the results of the campaign, and
had little satisfaction in his Spanish auxiliaries, who always
distrusted foreigners, even when allies; when urged by the
Junta, however, and after receiving instructions from England,
he advanced towards Valladolid, relinquishing his line of retreat upon Portugal, and directing his march to Corunna.
From some intercepted despatches he believed he might surprise
Marshal Soult in the kingdom of Leon, with inferior forces to
his own; and, at the same time, ask Sir David Baird to join

him with his troops, and sent to ask the Marquis Romana for reinforcements. On the 21st December, the English army, more than 25,000 men strong, had reached Sahagun, near to Marshal Soult's position.

The emperor was not deceived by the first report, that the English had changed their line of march. He at once penetrated Sir John Moore's object, and resolved to at once fall upon his rear, and crush him by a superiority of forces. In a letter to Paris he says, "The English have at last showed signs of life. They seem now to have abandoned Portugal, and taken another line of operations. They are marching upon Valladolid, and for three days our troops have made operations to manœuvre them, and advance on their rear. If the English don't make for the sea, and beat us in speed, they will find it hard to escape us, and will pay dear for their daring attempt upon the continent."

On the 22nd, the emperor, uniting the divisions of his army with that rapidity which all his lieutenants had learned from him, set out himself on march with 40,000 men, in the hope of intercepting the advance of the English to the coast. The weather had become wet and cold, and when the French army reached the foot of Guadarrama the snow was falling in thick masses. The chasseurs of the guard, dismounting, led their horses by hand, and opened a road to their comrades through the snow. Napoleon himself was on foot. The snow-storm being followed by rain, their progress was slow. On receiving a message from Soult that he was at Carrion, and that he believed the English were one day's journey distant, Napoleon said, "If they stay one day longer in that position they are lost, for I shall presently be on their flank."

Sir John Moore was a prudent and skilful soldier, and on receiving information sufficient to indicate the emperor's intention, he at once began his retreat towards Corunna. When Marshal Ney, entering Medina from Rio-Seco, was preparing to march upon Benaventa, the English had already reached that post, and, after crossing the Ezla, blew up the bridges. When the French advance-guard, commanded by General Lefebvre-Desnouettes, arrived before the town the last wagons of the English army were disappearing in the distance. The cavalry officer too eagerly made his squadrons ford the river, and Lord Paget, who protected the retreat, repulsed the attack of the French, and took their general prisoner. The first detachments of Napoleon's army entered Astorga a short time after the

English had evacuated the place, the Marquis de la Romana withdrawing as well as his allies, having followed by the same way. The roads were much cut up by the wheels and foot-steps, besides being encumbered by the dead bodies of many horses, which the English had killed when too tired to go on. There were also traces left everywhere by the English army of a troublesome want of discipline; soldiers left drunk because they could not keep up in the rapid march which their leader had ordered, houses pillaged, and the Spanish peasants, op-pressed both by their defenders and their enemies, became every day more distrustful and gloomy. Sir John Moore com-plained that he could obtain neither food nor information from the frightened and discontented population.

On the 2nd January, the Emperor Napoleon changed his plans. Feeling that the danger of a war with Austria became daily more imminent, and finding that the English would reach the sea in spite of any efforts of his to intercept them, and that the brilliant stroke which he intended was daily be-coming more impossible of execution, he entrusted the pur-suit of the enemy to Marshal Soult, who was then nearer him than Ney, and marched with the imperial guard towards Valladolid. Before arriving there he wrote from Benaventa to King Joseph, on the 6th January, 1809,—

"My brother, I thank you for what you say regarding the New Year. I have no hope of Europe being at peace in 1809. On the contrary, I yesterday signed a decree for a levy of 100,000 men. The hatred of England, the events at Constanti-nople, everything forewarns that the hour of rest and tran-quillity has not yet sounded. As to you, your kingdom ap-pears to me to be almost at peace. The kingdoms of Leon, the Asturias, and New Castile, only want rest. I hope Galicia will soon be pacified, and that the English will leave the coun-try. Saragossa must soon fall; and General St. Cyr, with 30,000 men, will soon attain his object in Catalonia."

The English were in fact preparing to leave Spain; and though the determination was quite recent, it was with a sense of depression, which, in the case of the general, was increased by the sad plight of his army and its want of discipline. Their disorder was at its worst when at last they reached the small town of Lugo (6th January, 1809), exhausted by the bad weather, want of food, and excess of brandy and other strong liquors.

Sir John Moore had resolved to offer battle to the French,

and the hope of fighting had restored courage and obedience to the soldiers. He waited three days for Marshal Soult, but the French general's forces were diminished by the rapidity of the pursuit, and he did not accept the offer of fighting. Moore resumed his march towards Corunna, reckoning to find, on his arrival at the coast, the transport vessels which were necessary for his army. When at last, on the 11th January, he came in sight of the sea, not a single sail appeared over its vast extent. The contest becoming inevitable, Sir John ordered the bridges over the Mero to be blown up, and took up his position on the heights which command Corunna.

Marshal Soult had been delayed, by the necessity of repairing the bridges and rallying a division of his army which had fallen behind; and when at last, on the morning of the 16th, he attacked the English positions, the long-expected transports were crowding into the harbor, and a way of escape was open to the English army. A keenly-contested struggle took place, however, around the small village, Elvina, occupied by the troops of Sir David Baird, who was severely wounded. Sir John went to the assistance of his lieutenant, and when leading his men within range to the front, had his arm and collarbone shattered by a ball. He was carried back to the town by his soldiers, in a dying condition. The English still retaining their positions at nightfall, their embarkment was now certain, and General Hope, who had taken the command, pushed forward the preparations for departure.

Sir John Moore had just expired. "You know well," said he to his friend Colonel Anderson, "that this is how I always wished to die." After a short pause, he added, "I hope the English people will be satisfied; I hope that my country will do me justice." Without losing time in procuring a coffin, his soldiers dug a grave with their swords, and committed to earth the body of their general, still wrapped in his military cloak. The English army, which he had saved by his prudence and resolution, then hurriedly embarked, "and left him alone in his glory," as the poet has finely put it. Several weeks afterwards, when Marshal Ney took possession of Corunna, he had a stone placed on the tomb of his heroic enemy.

From Valladolid, where he was still staying, the Emperor Napoleon directed the movements of his armies; fortifying the defences of Italy, and commanding the movements of the troops intended for Germany, he at the same time wrote to all the princes of the Rheinish Confederation, reminding them peremptorily of their engagements, and referring to the lengthened war preparations of Austria as equivalent to a declaration of war. "Russia, as well as myself, is indignant at the extravagant conduct of Austria," he wrote to the King of Wurtemberg, on the 15th January; "we cannot conceive what madness has taken possession of the court of Vienna. When your Majesty reads this letter I shall be in Paris. One part of my army of Spain is now returning, to form an army of reserve; but, independently of that, without touching a single man of my army of Spain, I can send into Germany 150,000 men, and be there myself to advance with them upon the Inn at the end of February, without counting the troops of the Confederation. I suppose that your Majesty's troops are ready to march on the slightest movement: you are sensible of the great importance, if war is absolutely necessary, of carrying it on in our enemy's territory, rather than leaving it to settle on that of the Confederation. I beg of your Majesty to let me know in Paris your opinion on all those points. Can the waters of the Danube have acquired the property of the river Lethe?"

At the same time, to instruct King Joseph in the government of Spain, at the moment when that prince was about to visit his capital again, he thus wrote to him, at Prado:—
"General Belliard's movement is excellent; a score of worthless fellows ought to be hanged. To-morrow I am to have seven hanged here, known to have had a share in all the excesses, and a nuisance to the respectable people, who secretly denounced them, and who now regain courage on finding themselves rid of them. You must do the same at Madrid. Five-sixths of the town are good, but honest folks should be encouraged, and they cannot be so except by keeping in check the riff-raff. Unless a hundred or so of rioters and ruffians are got rid of, nothing is done. Of that hundred, get twelve or fourteen shot or hanged, and send the rest into France to the galleys. I think it necessary, especially at the first start, that your government should show a little vigor against the riff-raff. They only like and respect those whom they fear, and their fear alone may procure you the love and esteem of the rest of the nation.

"The state of Europe compels me to go to spend three weeks in Paris, and if nothing prevent I shall return here about the end of February. I believe I wrote you to make your entry into Madrid on the 14th. Denon wishes to take some paint-
VII.—17

ings. I should prefer you to take all that are'in the confiscated houses and suppressed convents, and make me a present of about fifty of its master-pieces, for the Paris museum. At the proper time and place I shall give you others. Send for Denon, and give him a hint of this. You understand that they must be really good; and it is said you are immensely rich in that kind."

King Joseph retook possession of his capital with a great display of magnificence, the brilliant success of the French arms having rallied round him the timid, and the discontented keeping silence. Before setting out for Paris, where he arrived on the 24th, the emperor said, "The attack upon Valentia must not be thought of until Saragossa is taken, which must be during the month of February:" and Marshal Lannes, who had charge of the siege operations for a month, justified the hopes of his master. On the 21st February, 1809, Saragossa at last surrendered, having been the object of several French attacks since June, 1808.

After the battle of Tudela the whole of the army in Aragon had fallen back upon Saragossa. Joseph Palafox had shut himself up in it with his two brothers, and the country population having followed in great numbers, 100,000 human beings were crowded together behind the ramparts of the town, in its old convents, within the dull walls of its embattled houses—almost everywhere without outside windows, and already threatening the enemy with their gloomy aspect. Throughout the province, at the call of the defenders of Saragossa the insurgent peasants intercepted the convoys of provisions intended for the French army, and the besiegers no less than the besieged suffered from want of food.

Napoleon had undervalued the resistance of the inhabitants of Saragossa. Always ordering the movements of his troops himself, and from a distance, he had sent Marshal Moncey with insufficient forces; and soon after, Junot was entrusted with the attack. The sallies of the Spanish were easily repulsed, but each assault cost a large number of men. The Aragonian riflemen, posted on the ramparts or the roofs of the houses, brought down, without exposing themselves, the bravest of our grenadiers. Everywhere the women brought the artillery-men food and ammunition; and one of them, finding a piece abandoned, applied the match to it herself, and continued firing it for several days. The whole of the population fought on the walls until they should have to fight in the streets and houses.

From redoubt to redoubt, from convent to convent, General Junot had slowly advanced, till the middle of January, 1809. When at last Marshal Lannes appeared before Saragossa, he had called to his assistance large reinforcements; and the troops posted in the suburbs, and who had not yet shared in the action, dispersed the hostile crowd there. The attack commenced with a vigor which quite equalled the energy of the resistance; and on the 27th January, after a general assault, which was deadly and long-continued, the entire circuit of the walls was carried by the French troops. It is a maxim of war that every town deprived of the protection of its walls capitulates, or surrenders at discretion; but in Saragossa the real struggle—the struggle of the populace—was only beginning. On the 28th, Lannes wrote to the emperor: "Never, sire, have I seen such keen determination as in putting our enemies here on their defence. I have seen women come to be killed at a breach. Every house has to be taken by storm; and without great precaution we should lose many soldiers, there being in the town 30,000 or 40,000 men, besides the inhabitants. We now hold Santa-Engracia as far as the Capucine convent, and have captured fifteen guns. In spite of all the orders I have given to prevent soldiers from rushing forward, their ardor getting the better of them has given us 200 wounded more than we ought to have."

And a few days afterwards: "The seige of Saragossa resembles in nothing any war we have hitherto had. It is a business requiring great prudence and great energy. We are obliged to take every house by mining or assault. These wretches defend themselves with a keen determination which is inconceivable. In a word, sire, it is a horrible war. At this moment three or four parts of the town are on fire, and it is crushed with shells, yet our enemies are not intimidated. We are laboring might and main to get to the faubourg; and once we are masters of it, I hope the town will not long hold out."

During the first siege of Saragossa, Marshal Lefebvre, on getting possession of one of the principal convents, sent to Joseph Palafox the short despatch: "Head-quarters, Santa-Engracia. Capitulation." And the defender of the place replied: "Head-quarters, Saragossa. War to the knife." It was war to the knife, to the musket, to the mine, which was pursued from house to house, from story to story. To go along the streets, the French soldiers were obliged to slip past close to the walls, the enemy being so keen and eager that a

shako or coat held up on the point of a sword to deceive them
was instantly riddled with balls.   More than one detachment
after taking a building were suddenly blown up, by being
secretly undermined.   Our soldiers in their turn replied by
some important underground works, which were ably organized by Lacoste, colonel of the engineers.   From the 29th
January to the 18th February the same struggle was pursued,
with the same keen determination.   A day was chosen for the
assault of the faubourg, which General Gazan had long invested.   The troops were impatient to make this last effort,
being both irritated and depressed.   They both suffered and
saw others suffer.   The misery in the town, however, was
greater than the besiegers could suspect.   A terrible epidemic
was decimating those who were left of the defenders of Saragossa.   Joseph Palafox himself was dying.

After the breach was opened in the ramparts of the faubourg,
a frightful explosion announced the destruction of the immense
University buildings, laying open to our soldiers the Coso, or
Holy Street, which passed through the whole town.   The
ground was everywhere mined, and the very heart of Saragossa was at its last extremity, when the Junta of Defence at
last yielded to the necessity which was bearing them down,
and a messenger presented himself before Marshal Lannes in
the name of Don Joseph Palafox.   We have seen the painful
illusions created by the isolation of a besieged town: the defenders of Saragossa believed that the Spanish had been victorious everywhere, and it was only on the word of honor of
Marshal Lannes that they accepted the sad truth.   The 12,000
men of the garrison who had resisted all the horrors of the
siege, surrendered as prisoners of war.   Of 100,000 inhabitants
who had crowded Saragossa, 54,000 had perished.   There were
heaps of dead bodies round the old church, Our Lady del
Pilar, object of the passionate devotion of the whole population.
In their real heart, and at the first moment of victory, the
French soldiers felt for the defenders of Saragossa an admiration mixed with anger and alarm.   Rage alone animated the
heart of their most illustrious leader.   Napoleon had sometimes
honored the resistance of his enemies, as at Mantua: now, on
his attaining the height of power and glory, he no longer
admitted that the Spanish should defend their independence
against a usurpation stained with perfidy.   "My Brother," he
wrote to King Joseph on the 11th March, "I have read an
article in the *Madrid Gazette*, giving an account of the taking

LANNES.

DUC DE MONTEBELLO.

of Saragossa, in which they eulogize those who defended that town—no doubt to encourage those of Valencia and Seville. That is certainly a strange policy. I am sure there is not a Frenchman who has not the greatest scorn for those who defended Saragossa. Those who allow such vagaries are more dangerous for us than the insurgents. In a proclamation, mention is already made of Saguntum: that, in my opinion, is most imprudent."

Many things at this juncture chafed the mind of the imperious master of the world. He had left Spain immediately after a series of successes, without deceiving himself as to their importance and decisive value with reference to the permanent establishment of the French monarchy in Madrid. He foresaw the difficulties and perpetually recurring embarrassments of a command being divided, when the nominal authority of King Joseph was unable to govern lieutenants who were powerful, distinguished, and jealous. To obviate this inconvenience, and maintain that unity of action which he considered an indispensable element of success, he had kept to himself the supreme direction of the military operations, and attempted to govern the war in Spain from a distance, at the moment when he was organizing and recruiting his armies to support in Germany a determined struggle against all the forces of the Austrian empire. Italy, Holland, the Rhenish Confederation, all the states which he had founded or subdued, claimed his support or vigilance. Russia remained quiet because she was powerless and disarmed, but a serious check would have speedily thrown her with ardor on the side of his enemies. Russia, compelled by recent treaties and pressing interests, concealed under friendly phrases a secret indifference, and the beginning of her enmity: being, moreover, occupied by her own conquests, by the uncompleted subjugation of Finland, and a renewal of her struggle with Turkey. England, irritated and humiliated by the check undergone by her attempts at intervention in Spain, was energetically preparing new and more successful efforts. In presence of so many enemies, concealed or declared—compelled to regulate so many affairs, the government, oppression, and conquest of so many races—Napoleon, on returning to Paris after his Spanish campaign, had found men's dispositions changed, and precursory signs of an open discontent which he was not acctstomed to meet or to suffer.

Even in Spain the rumor of this modification of the national thought had already reached Napoleon's ears: he had read it

in the letters of his most intimate correspondents, and
imagined it even in the eyes of his soldiers. The rage of the
despot burst forth one day in Valladolid: when passing along
the ranks of the troops he was leaving behind, on hearing
some of them muttering he is said to have snatched from the
hand of a grenadier a musket, which seemed awkwardly held,
exclaiming, "You wretch! you deserve to be shot, and I have
a good mind to have it done! You are all longing to go back
to Paris, to resume your habits and pleasures:—well, I shall
keep you under arms till you are eighty."

On reaching France, and especially Paris, Napoleon thought
the atmosphere felt charged with resistance and disobedience.
There was more freedom of speech, and men's thoughts were
more daring than their words. Those whom he distrusted
now came nearer, and others had taken the liberty to criticise
his intentions and his acts. Even in the Legislative Body, the
arrangements of the code of criminal justice, recently submitted
to the vote, had undergone a rather lively discussion. Fouché
had the courage to raise the question of the succession to the
throne, when speaking to the Empress Josephine herself about
the necessity of a divorce. The most daring had ventured to
anticipate the possibility of a fatal accident in the chances of
war, some affirming that Murat aimed at the crown. The
Arch-chancellor Cambacérès, who always showed prudence
and ability in his relations with his former colleague, now
his master, attempted in vain to calm the increasing irritation
of his mind. His anger burst forth against Talleyrand during
a sitting of the Ministerial Council. For several months previously a coldness and distrust had reigned between the emperor
and this confidant of several of the gravest acts of his life—
who was always self-possessed even when he seemed devoted,
too clever ever to give himself up entirely, and invariably impassible in manner and feature. Napoleon poured forth his
displeasure in a long speech, reminding Talleyrand of advice
he had formerly given him, being carried away both by his
passion and the desire to compromise and humiliate a man
whose intrigues he was afrai of. At the conclusion of this
noisy scene, still more humiliating for the emperor than for the
minister, Talleyrand quietly withdrew, limping through the
galleries, among the officers and courtiers, astonished at the
noise which had reached even them, and looking at him with
curiosity or spite. It was the starting-point of that seeret animosity to which Talleyrand was afterwards to give cold and

biting expression, when, in 1813, after a similar scene, he said, "You have a great man there, but badly brought up!" Napoleon's anger did not last long, although his distrust remained fixed. Talleyrand's pride underwent numerous eclipses. Commencing, however, from that day, the separation between them became irreparable; and when the emperor's decadence began, Talleyrand was already gained over to other hopes, and ready to serve another cause.

It was during the first moments of a growing discontent, already unmistakable in Paris and the large towns, that Napoleon found himself compelled to ask from France new efforts and cruel sacrifices. To make the old contingents equal to the new, he has already, they said, raised 80,000 men by the past conscriptions; the same expedient if soon applied to more remote years will bring to his standards grown-up men able to undergo long fatigue. The contingent of 1810 was at the same time raised to 110,000 men. In order to furnish officers to this enormous mass of conscripts, the emperor wrote on the 8th March, to General Clarke, minister of war: "I have formed sixteen cohorts of 10,000 conscripts of my guard. Present to me sixteen lists of four pupils in the St. Cyr Military College, to be appointed as sub lieutenants in those cohorts; that will supply employment to sixty-four scholars. These youths will be under the orders of the officers of my guard, and will assist them in forming the conscripts, and fulfilling the duties of adjutant. They can also be of use in marching with detachments to the regiments where they will have their definitive appointment. Thus, with the 104 scholars necessary for the fifth battalions, the school must supply 168 pupils this year. Present to me 168 young people to replace those at St. Cyr.

"Let me know what can be supplied by La Flèche School, and the lycées. I have forty lycées; if each of them can furnish ten pupils of eighteen years old, that makes 400 quartermasters. I shall have to send 200 to the different regiments, and 200 to the army of the Rhine. Find also whether the Polytechnic School cannot supply fifty officers; and whether the Compiègne School cannot supply fifty youths of over seventeen, to be incorporated with the companies of artillery workmen."

As if to supply the troublesome gaps thus made in the schools by the unexpected removal of so many boys, Napoleon had written beforehand to Fouché from Benaventa (31st December, 1809):

"I am informed that some families of the emigrants are removing their children to avoid conscription, and keeping them in troublesome and culpable idleness. It is clear that the old and rich families who are not for our system are against it. I wish you to get a list drawn up of ten of those principal families in each department, and fifty for Paris, showing the age, fortune, and quality of each member. My intention is to pass a decree to send to the Military School of St. Cyr the young men belonging to those families whose ages are between sixteen and eighteen. If any objection is made, the only answer to make is, that it is my good pleasure. The future generation should not suffer from the hatred and petty spite of the present generation. If you have to ask the prefects for information, do so in similar terms."

With her will or against it, by the impulse of enthusiasm still left or under the law of good pleasure, France followed her insatiable master upon the ever open battle-fields. Napoleon was not deceived as to his arbitrary measures. "I wish to call out 30,000 men by the conscription of 1810," he wrote on the 21st March to General Lacuée, director-general of the reviews and conscription; "I am obliged to delay the publication of the 'Senatus-consulte,' which can only be done when all the documents are published. Let the good departments be preferred in choosing. The levy for France generally will only be one fourth of this year's conscription. The prefects might manage it without letting the public know, since there is no occasion for their assembling or drawing lots."

Financial difficulties also began to be felt. For a long time, by war contributions and exactions of every kind imposed upon the conquered countries, Napoleon had formed a military treasury, which he alone managed, and without any check. This resource allowed him to do without increasing taxes or imposing additional burdens. The funds, however, became exhausted, and war alone could renew them. "Reply to Sieur Otto," he wrote on the 1st April, 1809, to Champagny, "that I will have nothing said about subsidies. It is not at all the principle of France. It was well enough under the ancient government, because they had few troops, but at the present day the power of France, and the energy impressed upon my peoples, will produce as many soldiers as I wish, and my money is employed in equipping them and putting them on the field."

Negotiations were still being carried on. The fifth coalition was secretly formed, and diplomatic plots were everywhere joining their threads. Napoleon strove to engage Russia in a common declaration against Austria; England enrolled against France the new government just established at Constantinople by revolution. On both sides the preparations for war became more patent and hurried. Metternich complained at Paris of the hostile attitude of France, and announced the reciprocity imposed upon his master. On the 1st April, Napoleon wrote, "Get articles put in all the journals upon all that is provoking or offensive for the French nation in everything done at Vienna. You can go as far back as the first arming. There must be an article of this tendency every day in the *Journal de l'Empire*, or the *Publiciste*, or the *Gazette de France*. The aim of these articles is to prove that they wish us to make war."

In France the decided, if not expressed, wish of the Emperor Napoleon, and in Austria the patriotic indignation and warlike excitement of the court and army, must necessarily have brought on a rupture; and the most trifling pretext was enough to cause the explosion. The arrest of a French courier by the Austrians at Braunau, the violation of the imperial territory by the troops of Marshal Davout then posted at Wurzburg, provoked hostilities several days sooner than Napoleon expected; and Metternich had already asked for his passports when, on the 10th April, the Archduke Charles crossed the Inn with his army. The Tyrol at the same time rose in insurrection under the orders of a mountain innkeeper, Andrew Hofer; and the Bavarian garrisons were everywhere attacked by hunters and peasants. Like the Spanish, the Tyrolese claimed the independence of their country.

The troops of the Emperor Napoleon already covered Germany; Davout being at Ratisbon, Lannes at Augsburg, and Masséna at Ulm. Marshal Lefebvre commanded the Bavarians, Augereau was appointed to lead the Wurtembergers, the men of Baden and Hesse; the Saxons were placed under the orders of Bernadotte. On the evening of the 9th April, the Archduke Charles wrote to the King of Bavaria that his orders were to advance, and treat as enemies all the forces which opposed him; that he fondly trusted that no German would resist the liberating army on its march to deliver Germany. The Emperor Napoleon had already offered to the Kings of Saxony and Bavaria one of his palaces in France as an asylum, should they find themselves compelled to temporarily abandon their capitals. The King of Bavaria set out for Augsburg.

The unexpected movement of his enemies modified Napoleon's plan of attack. A delay in the arrival of the despatches sent to Major-General Berthier caused some difficulty in the first operations of the French army. When the emperor arrived at Donauwerth, on the morning of the 17th, his army was spread over an extent of twenty-five leagues, and was in danger of being cut in two by the Archduke Charles. It was Napoleon's care and study on beginning the campaign to avoid this danger, which soon afterwards he subjected his adversary to. The Austrians, after passing the Isar at two places, and driving back the Bavarians who had been appointed to defend the passage, advanced towards the Danube.

Already, before touching Donauwerth, Napoleon's orders had begun the concentration of his forces. Masséna was at Augsburg, and received the order to march upon Neustadt, and similarly Davout left Ratisbon to advance to the same place. The Archduke Charles was also striving to reach it, hoping to gain upon the French by speed, and pass between the divisions posted at Ratisbon and Augsburg. This manœuvre was baffled by Napoleon's prompt decision. "Never was there need for more rapidity and activity of movement than now," he wrote on the 18th to Masséna. "Activity, activity, speed! Let me have your assistance."

The emperor's lieutenants did not fail him in this brilliant and scientific movement, everywhere executed with an ability and precision worthy of the great general who had conceived it. The Archduke Charles was a consummate tactician, but often his prudence degenerated into hesitation—a dangerous fault in presence of the most overpowering military genius whom the world had yet beheld. Napoleon himself said of Marshal Turenne that he was the only general whom experience had made more daring. A long military experience had not exercised that happy effect on the archduke; he still felt his way, and neglecting to take advantage of the concentration of his forces, dispersed the different parts of his army. The chastisement was not slow in following the fault. On the 19th, Marshal Davout, ascending the Danube from Ratisbon to Abensberg, met and defeated the Austrian troops at Fangen, thus being able to effect his junction with the Bavarians. On the 20th, the emperor attacked the enemy's lines at several points, and forced his way through them towards Rohr after several active engagements, thus securing the point of Abensberg, and separating the Archduke Charles from General

Hiller and the Archduke Louis. On the 21st, this last part of the enemy's army precipitated itself in a body upon the important position of Landshut, where all the Austrian war material was collected, with a large number of wounded; but at the same moment the emperor himself came up, eagerly followed by Lannes and Bessières, commanding their regiments. Masséna also made haste to join them. The bridges on the Isar were all attacked at once, and bravely defended by the Austrians: when carried they were already in flames. The Archduke Charles, however, attacking Ratisbon, which Davout was obliged to leave protected only by one regiment, easily took possession of that important place, commanding both banks of the Danube. He was thus, on the 22nd, before Eckmühl opposite Davout. Informed of this movement, which he had partly guessed from the noise of the cannon on the 21st, the emperor directed the main body of his army towards Eckmühl. His troops had already been fighting for three days, and Napoleon asked a fresh effort from them. "It is four o'clock," he wrote to Davout, "I have resolved to march, and shall be upon Eckmühl about midday, and ready to attack the enemy vigorously at three o'clock. I shall have with me 40,000 men. I shall be at Ergoltsbach before midday. If the cannon are heard I shall know I am to attack. If I don't hear it, and you are ready for the attack, fire a salvo of ten guns at twelve, another at one, and another at two. I am determined to exterminate the army of the Archduke Charles to-day, or at the latest to-morrow."

The day was not finished, and the cuirassiers were still fighting by moonlight to carry and defend the Ratisbon highway, yet the victory was decisive. The Archduke Charles was beaten, and falling back upon Ratisbon, he, during the night, took the wise step of evacuating the town and withdrawing into Bohemia, where General Bellegarde and his troops awaited him. Henceforth the Austrian army formed two distinct bodies. On the 23rd, Napoleon marched upon Ratisbon, which bravely defended itself. Slightly wounded in the foot by a ball, the emperor remained the whole day on horseback, Marshal Lannes directing the assault. At one moment the soldiers hesitating because the Austrians shot down one after another of those who carried the ladders, Lannes seized one, and shouted, "I shall show you that your marshal has not ceased to be a grenadier." His aides-de-camp went before him, and they themselves led the troops to the escalade. At last the gates were opened, and Napoleon entered Ratisbon.

He spent three days there, preparing his movement of attack against Vienna, which was slightly and badly defended, fortifying his positions, and taking precautions against an unexpected return of the Archduke Charles. At the same time, by his proclamations to the army, as well as by his letters to the princes of the Rhenish Confederation, he spread throughout all Europe his inebriation with success, and the declaration of his projects.

"Soldiers!

"You have justified my expectations; you have made up for numbers by bravery. You have gloriously proved the difference which exists between the soldiers of Cæsar and the armed hordes of Xerxes.

"In a few days we have triumphed in the three pitched battles of Thann, Abensberg, and Eckmühl, and in the engagements of Peising, Landshut, and Ratisbon. A hundred cannon, forty flags, 50,000 prisoners, three sets of bridge-apparatus, all the enemy's artillery, with 600 harnessed wagons, 3000 harnessed carriages with baggage, all the regimental chests,—that is the result of your rapid marches and your courage.

"The enemy, intoxicated by a perjured cabinet, seemed to have retained no recollection of you; his awakening has been speedy, you have appeared to him more terrible than ever. Recently he crossed the Inn, and invaded the territory of our allies. Recently he was in full hopes of carrying the war into the bosom of our country; to-day defeated, terrified, he flies in disorder. My advance-guard has already passed the Inn. Within a month we shall be at Vienna."

It was at Ratisbon that the emperor at last received the news of the army of Italy which he was impatiently demanding. When attacked, on the 10th April, by the Archduke John, as the generals separated by Napoleon had been in Germany by the Archduke Charles, Prince Eugène, who was in command for the first time, had not been able, as Napoleon was, to retrieve, by a sudden stroke and powerful effort, an engagement badly begun. Being unable to hold head against the Austrian forces, he resolved to retire, in order to rejoin the main body of his army. This retrograde movement he performed with regret; hesitating, and feeling annoyed by the grumbling of the soldiers, because they wished to march to the enemy, and by the hesitation of the generals who dared not offer him advice, he halted on the 15th before the town of Sacile, and on the 16th made an unexpected attack on the Archduke John, who on the previous evening had surprised and beaten the French rear-guard at Pordenone, though, as it now appeared, not any better guarded himself. Confused at the first moment by an un-looked-for attack, the Austrians defended themselves with great bravery. Their superior forces threatened to cut off our communications, and the prince, afraid of being isolated, ordered retreat when the issue of the battle was still uncertain. He had just left the battle-field—which the soldiers would scarcely leave, furious at not having gained the day—when the Viceroy of Italy, modest and brave, but evidently not equal to the task which the emperor had imposed upon him, wrote thus to the latter:—" My father, I have need of your indulgence. Fearing your blame if I withdrew, I accepted battle, and I have lost it." He accompanied this sad news with no message nor any details, and the want of information annoyed Napoleon still more than the check undergone by his troops. " Whatever evil may have taken place," he wrote, " if I had full knowledge of the state of things I should decide what to do; but I think it an absurd and frightful thing that a battle taking place on the 16th, it is now the 26th, without my knowing anything about it. That upsets my plans for the campaign, and I cannot understand what can have suggested to you that singular procedure. I hope to be soon at Salzburg, and make short work in the Tyrol; but for God's sake! let me know what is going on, and what is the situation of my affairs in Italy." And on the 30th April: "War is a serious game, in which one can compromise his reputation and his country. A man of sense must soon feel and know if he is made for that profession or not. I know that in Italy you affect some contempt for Masséna; if I had sent him, that which has happened would not have taken place. Masséna has military qualities before which one must humble himself. His faults must be forgot, for all men have their faults. In giving you the command of the army I made a mistake, and ought to have sent you Masséna, and given you the command of the cavalry under his orders. The Prince Royal of Bavaria commands a division under the Duke of Dantzic. Kings of France, emperors, even when reigning, have often commanded a regiment or division under the orders of an old marshal. I think that if matters become pressing you ought to write to the King of Naples to come to the army: he will leave the government to the queen. You will hand over the command to him, and serve under his orders. The case simply is, that you have less experience of war than a man who has served since he was sixteen. I am not displeased at the mistakes you have made, but because you don't write to me, and put me in a position to give you advice, and even direct operations from this place."

Fortunately for Prince Eugène, as well as the army of Italy, General Macdonald had just arrived at head-quarters, then moved beyond the Pena. Able, honorable, and brave as he had shown himself in the wars of the revolution, Macdonald underwent the weight of imperial disgrace on account of his intimacy with General Moreau. The young officers of the empire used to turn to ridicule his grave disposition and simple habits; but the soldiers loved him, and had confidence in him, and Prince Eugène had the good sense to let himself be guided by his advice. The retreat being continued to the Adige, the army rested there, waiting for the enemy, who were slow in coming in. When at last the Archduke John appeared, he durst not attack the line of the river, and waited for news from Germany. Prince Eugène was still ignorant of the emperor's success. On the 1st of May, Macdonald, who was taking observations, believed he saw a retreating movement of the enemy towards the Frioul. "Victory in Germany!" he shouted, running towards the viceroy; "now is the moment to march forward!" True enough, the Archduke John, being informed of Napoleon's movement upon Vienna, made haste to return to Germany, in the hope of joining his brother, the Archduke Charles. Prince Eugène immediately started in pursuit, passed the Piave hurriedly, and driving the archduke through the Carnatic and Julian Alps, marched himself, with a part of his army, towards the victorious emperor. On the 14th May, after dividing his forces, he sent General Macdonald with one part to meet General Marmont, who was advancing towards Trieste. The army of Italy was soon after reunited at Wagram.

The first reverses of Prince Eugène were not the only thing to disturb the emperor's joy at Ratisbon. In Tyrol a rising of the peasants, prepared and encouraged by Austrian agents, had suddenly engaged the whole population, men, women, and children, in a determined struggle against the French conquest and the Bavarian domination. A proclamation of the Emperor

Francis was spread through the mountains, and General Chasteler was sent from Vienna to put himself at the head of the insurrection. The Bavarian garrisons were few, and the French detachments which came to their assistance being composed of recruits, the patriotic passion of the mountaineers easily triumphed over an enemy of inferior numbers. From Linz to Brunecken all the posts were carried by the Tyrolese; Halle, Innspruck, and Trente quickly fell into the power of the insurgents. A French column arriving beneath Innspruck when General Chasteler and Hofer had just taken possession of the place, was surrounded, and compelled to capitulate. General Baraguey d'Hilliers, who occupied Trente, had to fall back upon Roveredo, and then upon Rivoli. The Italian as well as the German Tyrolese had reconquered their independence; from one end of the mountains to the other re-echoed the name of the Emperor Francis and that of the Archduke John, whom the peasants were impatiently awaiting since the news of his first successes in Italy. The insurrection had been entirely patriotic, religious, and popular: the first leader, Andrew Hofer, was a grave and pious man, who rejoiced and triumphed with simplicity, asking God's pardon in the churches for the crime and violence which he had been unable to prevent, and which were only acts of reprisal for the Bavarian oppression. The modest glory of the honest innkeeper reached the Emperor Napoleon with the news of the loss of the Tyrol.

The whole of Germany seemed moved by the same breath of independence in the subject or conquered countries. In Swabia, Saxony, Hesse, a silent emotion thrilled all hearts; at certain points bands of insurgents collected together. In Prussia, the instinct of patriotic vengeance was still more powerful; the commandant of Berlin gave to the garrison as watchword "Charles and Ratisbon;" one of the officers at the head of the cavalry here, Major Schill, formerly known as leader of the partisans in 1806 and 1807, had just resumed his old task, drawing with him the body which he commanded; and several companies of infantry deserted to join him. The protestations of the Prussian ministers were not enough to convince Napoleon of the ignorance of government with regard to these hostile manifestations. The Archduke Ferdinand at the head of an army of 35,000 men, had just entered Poland, taking by surprise Prince Poniatowski and the Polish army, still badly organized. After a keenly-contested battle in the environs of Raszyn, near Warsaw, Prince Poniatowski was obliged to surren-

der his capital, and fall back upon the right bank of the
Vistula.

Napoleon alone had conquered, and his lieutenants acting for
him in more distant parts, by being surprised or incapable, had
only caused him embarrassment.   This was a natural and inevitable consequence of a too extensive power, and a territory
too vast to be at all points usefully occupied and skilfully defended.   All these events confirmed the emperor in the resolution which he had already taken to march upon Vienna.
Neglecting the Archduke Charles's army, the Marshals Lannes
and Bessières crossed Bavaria, Napoleon himself setting out
for Landshut in order to take the management of his forces.
Thus the whole army advanced towards the Inn.   Masséna
took possession of Passau, and by the 1st May all the troops
had crossed the river.   Masséna was ordered to make himself
master of Linz, and secure the bridge over the Danube at
Monthausen.   There the archdukes and General Hiller might
effect their junction, and there, therefore, must the road to
Vienna be opened or closed.

Masséna never hesitated before a difficulty, and never drew
back before the most fatal necessities.   The Austrians were
superior to him in number, and occupied excellent positions.
Linz was carried and passed through in a few hours.   When
Napoleon arrived before the small town of Ebersberg which
defended the bridge, the place, the castle and even the bridge
were in our power, at the cost of a horrible carnage which
caused some emotion to the emperor himself.   He refused to
occupy Ebersberg, everywhere swimming in blood and
strewed with dead bodies.   There was still a rallying-point
left to the archdukes at the bridge of Krems, but they did not
think they could defend it.   The Archduke Louis and General
Hiller passed to the right bank of the Danube, and the road to
Vienna lay open.

Generally slow in his operations, the Archduke Charles was
too far from the capital to assist it.   The place had made no
preparations for defence, but the population was animated by
great patriotic zeal, and the sight of the French troops before
the gates at once caused a rising.   The new town, which was
was open and without ramparts, was quickly in our
power.   Preparations were made to defend the walls of the
old town, behind which the Archduke Maximilian was entrenched, with from 15,000 to 18,000 regular troops.

Napoleon took up his abode at Shönbrunn, in the palace

abandoned by the Emperor Francis; and after appointing as governor of Vienna, General Andréossy, recently his ambassador in Austria, waited calmly for the result of the bombardment. The archduke had imprudently exposed the town to an irresistible attack: on the morning of the 12th May he left Vienna with the greater part of his troops, leaving to General O'Reilly the sad duty of concluding the capitulation. The French took possession of the place on the 13th. The population were still excited when Napoleon issued a proclamation denouncing the princes of the house of Lorraine for having deserted, "not as soldiers of honor yielding to the circumstances and reverses of war, but as perjurers pursued by their remorse. On running away from Vienna their farewells to its inhabitants were fire and bloodshed; like Medea, they have cut the throats of their children with their own hands. Soldiers! the people of Vienna, to use the expression of the deputation from its faubourgs, are forsaken, abandoned, and widowed; they will be the object of your regards. I take the good citizens under my special protection. As to turbulent and bad men, I shall make examples of them in the ends of justice. Soldiers! Let us treat kindly the poor peasants, and this good population who have so many claims upon our esteem. Let us not be made haughty by our success; but let us see in it a proof of that divine justice which punishes the ungrateful and the perjured."

That boundless vanity which always pervaded Napoleon's soul, in spite of his protestations of thankfulness towards divine justice, did not prevent him from clearly seeing beforehand the difficulties which surrounded him, and the obstacles still to be overcome, even after reaching Vienna, and gaining the victory in every battle. Success had again attended on all his combinations, and the extreme extension of his forces. Prince Eugène after recovering the advantage over Archduke John, was now coming nearer the emperor as he pursued the enemy. Marshal Lefebvre at the head of the Bavarians and French divisions, had commenced offensive operations against General Chasteler and Jellachich, come to the assistance of Tyrol, and after beating their forces and those of the mountaineers combined at Worgel, on the 13th May, advanced to Innspruck and took possession of it. The peasants had retired to the mountains, and the Austrian forces fell back upon Hungary. Prince Poniatowski defended victoriously the right bank of the Vistula, and threatened Cracow, while

Galicia was rising in favor of Polish independence. The Archduke Charles's army, however, still existed—large, powerful,
and eager to avenge its defeats. The Archduke Louis had
brought him the remainder of the troops, and the Archduke
John was advancing to the assistance of his brothers. In order
to prevent this junction, and conquer his enemy before he had
been reinforced by the army of Italy, Napoleon decided upon
crossing the Danube in the very suburbs of the capital, by
making use of the numerous islets there. At the island of
Lobau, which was the point chosen for the passage, the bed of
the Danube was broad and deep; and the island not being in the
middle of the stream, the branch separating it from the bank
was comparatively narrow. The emperor gave orders to construct bridges.

The attempt was a bold one at any time; it was rash, at the
moment when the waters of the Danube, swollen by the melt-
ing of the snow, threatened to sweep away the bridges, prepared with difficulty, on which depended the success of the
operation. On the 20th May, Marshal Masséna's troops crossed
the river entirely, and took up position in the villages of
Aspern, and Essling; a ditch full of water joined the two villages, and its banks were immediately covered with troops.
The archduke's advance-guard had alone appeared, till at
three o'clock in the afternoon of the 21st May, the Austrian
army, 70,000 to 80,000 men strong, at last poured on the plain
of Marchfeld. The large bridge thrown from the right bank
to the island of Lobau had been broken for the second time
during the night, and therefore only 35,000 or 40,000 Frenchmen were there to meet the enemy. The emperor, however,
was there, the bridge was about to be repaired, and the generals were opposed to every thought of retreat. Marshal
Lannes had gone forward to occupy Essling, while General
Molitor had fortified himself in Aspern. The struggle began
with the passionate ardor of men playing the great game in
which their glory or their country's liberty is at stake. The
position at Aspern, covering the bridge to the island of Lobau,
was several times taken and retaken, till at last Molitor barri-
caded the houses of the village, and drove back the Austrian
attack with the bayonet. No assault, however fierce, was
able to dislodge Masséna from the burying-ground, nor Lannes
from the village of Essling. At one time the Prince of Hohenzollern's division was very nearly cutting off our communication
between the two villages, at sight of which Lannes, turning

towards Marshal Bessières, ordered him, in a voice of thunder,
and without regard for his rank or age, to put himself at the
head of the cuirassiers for a "thorough" charge. Deeply hurt
by this order, and the tone in which it was given, Bessières
deferred demanding an explanation, and made a dash upon the
Austrian lines. He had to meet in succession the artillery,
the infantry, and the cavalry; General Espagne, who was in
charge of the heavy horse, was killed by his side; then General Lasalle made a charge in his turn, bringing to the
marshal assistance of which he stood in great need, and Prince
Hohenzollern's division was stopped. In the evening, when
bivouacking, the emperor was obliged to interpose to prevent
Lannes and Bessières from using against each other the swords
which they had so gallantly used during the fighting against
the enemy.

The archduke having ordered retreat after nightfall, both
armies camped in their positions. Large forces had already
crossed the Danube, including the whole corps of General
Lannes. The guard also arrived, which had not yet shared in
any engagement during the campaign. Seventy or seventy-
five thousand men having reached the left bank, they only
waited for Marshal Davout's corps, which had received orders
to hasten its march, when the large bridge broke for the third
time. Part of the artillery and most of the ammunition-
wagons were still on the right bank. When communication
was again effected, the fighting was everywhere carried on
with fresh fury.

Another attack was made on the villages of Aspern and
Essling, which had already been reduced to ruins. One after
another, Masséna recovered the positions which Molitor was
forced on the previous evening to abandon; he also carried the
church occupied by the Austrian general, Vacquant. Lannes
had received orders, while protecting Essling, to march into
the plain, and by a circular movement pierce the enemy's line
and cut them in two. This operation was about to be accomplished, and the marshal sent an aide-de-camp to the emperor
to ask him to have his rear protected by the guard on his
leaving Essling unprotected, when frightful news was brought
to Napoleon. The trunks of trees, stones, and rubbish of every
kind, brought down by the rapid current of the river, had
again broken the cables which held together the boats composing the great bridge, and both parts were carried down the
stream, taking with them a squadron of cuirassiers, who were

then defiling over. The passage of the troops being stopped, and the ammunition running short, Napoleon ordered Lannes to fall back on the line of the villages and abandon the pursuit of the Austrians, who were just before that hardly pressed everywhere. Whilst the marshal, bitterly disappointed, was effecting this backward movement, the archduke ordered all his artillery to be directed upon him: General St. Hilaire was killed at the head of his division, and whole files of General Oudinot's regiments were shot down—unfortunate lads, so recently enrolled that their officers durst not deploy them before the enemy. It was now midday; Major-General Berthier had just written to Marshal Davout, retained on the opposite bank of the Danube: "The interruption of the bridge has prevented provision-supplies: at ten o'clock we were short of ammunition, and the enemy, perceiving it, marched back upon us. Two hundred guns, to which we cannot reply, have done us much harm. In these circumstances, it is extremely important to repair the bridges and send ammunition and food. Write to the Prince of Ponte Corvo (Bernadotte) not to open a campaign in Bohemia, and to General Lauriston to be ready to join us. See that Daru sends us ambulance-stores and provisions of every kind. As soon as the bridge is ready, or during the night, come and have a consultation with the emperor."

At the same moment the Austrians began a movement similar to that which Lannes so recently was on the point of effecting. The Archduke Charles combined his best troops, to overpower our centre and finally break our lines. Marshal Lannes was immediately on the spot, bringing up in close succession the already decimated divisions—the cuirassiers, the old guard; and these were soon supported by the charges of the light cavalry. The conflict was now frightful. The French artillery, placed on the bank of the ditch connecting Aspern and Essling, fired slowly, with the precaution and prudence due to their shortness of ammunition, while the Austrian cannons thundered unceasingly. Lannes galloped in front of his regiments, which were immovable before the enemy, whose advance had been stopped; and when encouraging his soldiers by gesture and voice, one of his aides-de-camp conjured him to dismount. When in the act of obeying, a cannon-ball struck him, shattering both his knees. Marshal Bessières assisted his terrified officers in wrapping round him a cuirassier's cloak and getting him carried to an ambulance; but, recollecting his irritation of the evening before, he turned away his head as he grasped the hand of his dying friend, lest the sight of him should cause any sorrow or vexation.

Ominous news were now coming from all parts to Napoleon, who had not quitted the angle formed by the line between Aspern and Essling. Marshal Masséna still kept in the midst of the smoking ruins which marked the spot where stood so recently the pretty village of Aspern. The Austrians were advancing in dense masses against the village of Essling. Marshal Bessières defended that post, indispensable to the safety of the army. The emperor sent for the fusileers of the guard and placed them under General Mouton's orders. "I give them to you," said he; "make another effort to save the army; but let us put an end to this! After these, I have only the grenadiers and chasseurs of the old guard; they must be reserved for a disaster." General Mouton advanced, and his first effort was rewarded by freeing General Baudet, who was hemmed in in a barn, which he defended like a fortress. Five times did the enemy return to the charge, and now they prepared for a new attack, when General Rapp, shouting, "The emperor says we must put an end to this!" combined his forces with Mouton's, and both rushed forward, followed by their soldiers, with their bayonets in front and their heads held low. The Austrians at last recoiled, and Essling remained in our hands. The battery which had been raised on the island of Lobau had fired with effect upon the masses of the enemy when, for a short time, they were near the river. The bridge was free, the only way left us to effect our retreat, when night at last permitted us to withdraw without disgrace or danger. The long summer's day was at its close.

Having for a long time understood the necessity of this backward movement, the emperor longed only for its execution, and wished to inspect himself the resources of defence afforded by the island of Lobau. He would not hear of leaving the battlefield without being certain of the position of Aspern, and sent to ask Masséna if he could undertake to hold the village, as he had constantly done for the two previous days. The old soldier was sitting on a heap of ruins, in the midst of the smoking remains of the place, and, rising at the first words of the aide-de-camp, he stretched out his arm towards the Danube, as if to hasten the messenger's return: "Go and tell the emperor that I shall keep here two hours, six, twenty-four, if need be— so long as the safety of the army requires it."

The Archduke Charles, however, was himself tired of a struggle that led to no decision—cruel and bloody beyond all that he had seen in his long military career. He had brought together all his forces, and placed all his artillery in a line, in order to crush once more with his cannon-shot the invincible battalions which separated him from the river and still forbade his passage. General Mouton brought to this threatened point the fusileers of the guard who had just freed Essling; our dismounted guns replied at rare intervals to the continued fire of the enemy; the bodies of infantry, slightly protected by the inequalities of the ground, were massed behind useless cannon, and supported by the cavalry, which covered at one part the road from Essling to Aspern, and at another the unprotected space between Essling and the Danube. Parallel to them were arranged the guard in order. All these glorious remnants of a two days' unexampled struggle, motionless under the cannon-balls, looked in silence upon their officers moving about in front of the lines between the cannon of the enemy and the men whom they commanded. "Only one word escaped our lips," said General Mouton, afterwards Count Lobau, when telling the story of that day; "we had only one thing to say, 'close up the ranks!' whenever the soldiers fell under the fire of the archduke's 200 guns."

On crossing to the entrance of the bridge on the river's bank, where there were confused heaps of wounded men, transport carts, empty artillery-wagons, and dismounted guns, Napoleon went to see Marshal Lannes, who had just undergone amputation, and showed more emotion than he usually showed at the tragical end of his lieutenants. The dying farewell of the illustrious officer to his chief, still unsated with glory and conquest, has been told in various ways. The emperor himself reported the words as he wished them to be known, full of kindness and sadness on the part of Lannes. Some of those who stood by reported that the instinct of the dying soldier awoke with the bluntness frequently characterizing it, and that Lannes cursed the cruel ambition which strewed Napoleon's brilliant route with the corpses of his friends. He only survived that scene two days, and was praised as he deserved by Napoleon. On again mounting his horse, the emperor inspected the island of Lobau in detail, and satisfied himself that the position could be easily defended by a large body of troops well equipped and well commanded. He resolved to leave Masséna there—the natural leader in all cases of supreme resistance—while he made preparations at Vienna and on the right bank of the Danube for definitively crossing the river and bringing the campaign to a close. His project thus conceived, and combinations decided on in his mind, the emperor repassed the small arm of the river, and, stopping at the head of the bridge, called his generals around him. It was nightfall; the battle had finished; on both sides they were still occupied in removing the wounded; the dead everywhere strewed the plain, the border of the ditch, and the ruins of the villages. Napoleon held a council of war on the field, on that bank of the Danube defended during two days with so much obstinacy.

The emperor was not accustomed to consult his generals; his thought was spontaneous as his will was imperious. On the evening of the 22nd of May, he listened patiently to the ideas, the objections, even the complaints of the generals who surrounded him. Nearly all were discouraged, and conceived the necessity of a complete and long retreat; they weighed, however, all the inconveniences of this, and felt beforehand all the humiliation; their perplexity was extreme. Napoleon at last spoke; his plan was decided. By abandoning the island of Lobau, and repassing the great arm of the Danube with the entire army, it would be necessary to leave behind 10,000 wounded, the whole of the artillery, to be covered with disgrace, and consequently to bring about at once a rising in Germany, which was ready to fall eagerly upon an enemy she believed vanquished. It was not the retreat on Vienna, which would be thus prepared; it was the retreat upon Strasburg. What they must do was to occupy the island of Lobau with 40,000 men, under the orders of Masséna; to appoint Davout to protect Vienna and the right bank of the Danube against the attacks of the Archduke Charles, and prevent him from effecting his junction with the Archduke John; while all the personal efforts of Napoleon would be directed to repairing the great bridge, preparing provisions and transports, concentrating his troops until the day when, rejoined by Prince Eugéne, and sure of traversing the Danube victoriously, he would again unite the entire army to crush his enemies by a decisive blow, thus terminating the campaign gloriously on a field of battle already chosen in the conqueror's mind.

As he spoke, developing his plan with that powerful and spontaneous eloquence which he drew from the abundance and clearness of his thoughts, his generals listened, and felt their trouble disappear, and the heroic ardor of the combat take possession of their hearts. Masséna rose, carried away by his admiration, forgetful of his habitual ill-humor and the discontent he so constantly manifested. He took several steps towards the emperor. "Sire, you are a great man," cried he, "and worthy to command men like myself. Leave me here, and I promise you to fling into the Danube all the Austrian forces who may try to dislodge me." Marshal Davout undertook, in the same way, to defend Vienna. Tranquillity had reappeared on every face. Within the limits of that plain covered with dead, by the side of the wagons ceaselessly defiling with wounded and dying, a great work remained to be done, a great enterprise to be achieved, whatever obstacles might present themselves. Hope had reappeared, together with the end to be pursued. Napoleon crossed the island and embarked with Berthier and Savary in a small boat, which brought him back safely to the right bank of the river. Masséna returned to Aspern, momentarily invested with the chief command. The retreat commenced.

The cannonade was still heard in the plain, but faint, and separated by long intervals: the artillerymen, worn out, stood to their guns with great difficulty. The Austrians were overcome with fatigue; already several corps had passed into the island under cover of the darkness, when the Archduke Charles at length perceived that we were escaping from him. He at once began to follow, but slowly, without spirit or eagerness. The troops defiled in order over the little bridge which Marshal Masséna protected in person. He remained almost alone upon the bank, his entire army having effected its retreat; and after collecting the arms and horses abandoned by the soldiers, he at last resolved to follow his men and destroy the bridge behind him, intrepid to the last moment in his retrograde movement, as the captain of a shipwrecked vessel is the last to quit the remains of his ship. Day was now dawning; the balls from the enemy's batteries recommenced to rain around him, when the marshal at length gained the centre of the island, beyond their range.

More than 40,000 French or Austrians, dead or wounded, had fallen in the struggle of these two terrible days. In spite of the emphatic bulletins of the Emperor Napoleon, Europe looked upon the battle of Essling as a striking check to our arms. The warlike excitement of Germany increased; the Tyroleans were again rising, and General Deroy found himself forced to evacuate Innspruck; a corps of German refuges, under the orders of the Duke of Brunswick-Œls, took the road to Dresden, the court immediately taking refuge in Leipzic; a second detachment threatened King Jerome in Westphalia. He was afraid for his crown, and the emperor wrote to him on the 9th June: "The English are not to be feared; all their forces are in Spain and Portugal. They will do nothing—they can do nothing, in Germany; besides, time enough when they do. As to Schill, he is of little moment, and has already put himself out of the question by retreating towards Stralsund. General Gratien and the Danes will probably give an account of him. The Duke of Brunswick has not 8000 men; the former Elector of Cassel has not 600. Before making a movement it is well to see clearly. Experience will show you the difference there is between the reports spread by the enemy and the reality. Never, during sixteen years that I have commanded, have I countermanded a regiment, because I always wait for an affair to be ripe, and have thorough knowledge before commencing operations. There is no need for anxiety; you have nothing to fear, all this is nothing but rumor."

At Paris, where the most confident had become anxious, Napoleon severely reprimanded the timid. He wrote, on the 19th May, to General Clarke, the minister of war: "Sir, you have alarmed Paris too much about the affairs of Prussia, even if it were true that she had attacked us. Prussia is of very small importance, and I shall never want for means to enforce her submission—all the more so when these reports are contradicted. You have not used sufficient prudence on this occasion; it produces a bad effect for any power to imagine that I am without resource. The minister of police has taken his text from this to make a lot of foolish talk, which is very much out of place."

Austria had in fact sent to Prussia an ambassador with instructions to engage King Frederick William to break his chains, and take at last his part in the resistance; but that monarch had refused. "Not yet," said he; "it is too soon I am not ready: when I come, I will not come alone. Only strike one other blow." The efforts of Major Schill had not been supported, and that courageous partisan had failed under the walls of Stralsund. The secret diplomacy of Austria appeared to have met with more favor at St. Petersburg; the declaration of war by Russia against Austria remained absolutely without result; the Russian troops which were in Poland seemed more disposed to suppress the insurrection of Galicia than to second the efforts of Prince Poniatowski.

It was one of the great characteristics of the genius of the Emperor Napoleon to place no importance upon reports or appearances, although he was not ignorant of their action on the public. In his public proclamations he made an effort to disguise the check he had received at Essling; but in practice, in his military operations, he comprehended all the gravity of it, without allowing himself to be troubled an instant by bad fortune; he even derived original and powerful combinations from the embarrassments of his situation. Prince Eugène had already joined him near Vienna (26th May, 1809), driving back the Archduke John upon Hungary, and over-throwing the corps of the Jellachich Ban, which had in vain tried to stop his progress at Mount Saint-Michel, near Leoben. The army of Italy was not to rest long, the emperor having immediately sent his adopted son to follow the traces of the archduke. "To do the utmost harm to the archduke; to drive him back to the Danube; to intercept his communications with Chastelar and Giulay, who apparently intend to join him; to reduce the fortress of Graetz by isolating it, and to maintain your communications on the left with the duke of Auerstaedt, to construct the bridges on the Raab—these should be your aims," wrote the emperor to Prince Eugène, on the 13th June, and on the 15th: "It is probable that Raab has not sufficient fortifications for the enemy to dare to place a considerable garrison there of his best troops. If he only puts in bad ones the town will surrender on being invested, which will give us the advantage of taking his men, and of having a good post. If the archduke flies before you, you will pursue him, so that he may not be able to pass the Danube at Komorn, where there is, I think, no bridge, but he may be obliged to take refuge at Bude: do not go farther from me. The line behind the Raab is, I think, suitable for you, because my bridges over the Danube will be completed, and I can recall you in four days, taking at least two from the enemy, which will permit you to be present at the battle, while the enemy will be unable to be there. Your aim, then, is to hinder him from passing to Komorn, and then to oblige him to throw himself upon Bude, which will take him away from Vienna."

On the 14th June, even before Napoleon had written these last lines, Prince Eugène, after an obstinate combat, had taken from the Archduke John, and his brother the Archduke Palatine, the important line of the Raab. Generals Broussier and Marmont had effected their junction in the environs of Graetz, repulsing the attacks of the Giulay Ban; General Macdonald, whom the Viceroy of Italy had left behind at Papa, for the purpose of facilitating this concentration of forces, arrived on the field of battle when the day was gained; the archdukes were driven behind the Danube, and the troops furnished by the Hungarian nobility, were dispersed. " I compliment you on the battle of Raab," wrote the emperor to Prince Eugène; "it is the grand-daughter of Marengo and Friedland." General Lauriston immediately laid siege to the place, which capitulated on the 23rd June. Marshal Davout had bombarded Presburg without effect for several days, in the hope of succeeding in destroying the bridge; the garrison defended itself heroically. Every means had been adopted to rapidly concentrate the whole of the French forces upon Vienna, and to frustrate everywhere the progress of the enemy. Large reinforcements had arrived from France. The emperor himself directed the preparations on the Danube, displaying in this work all the resources of his most inventive genius, and that faculty of usefully employing the talent of others which constitutes one of the most necessary elements of government. At the commencement of July all was at length ready—men, provisions, ammunition, and bridges. " With God's help," wrote Napoleon to King Jerome, on the 4th July, " in spite of his redoubts and his entrenched camps, I hope to crush the army of the Archduke Charles."

During the forty days which had elapsed since the battle of Essling, the Archduke Charles had limited his efforts to fortifying his positions on the left bank of the Danube, without attempting any offensive operations against Napoleon, and had in vain waited for the reinforcements that his brothers, and the generals dispersed over the Austrian territory, were to bring him. The skilful generals of Napoleon had everywhere intercepted their communications. However, 130,000 or 140,000 of the enemy prepared to dispute with us the passage of the Danube. One hundred and fifty thousand French were assembled around Vienna; Masséna had not quitted the island of Lobau; Napoleon established himself there with his staff on the 1st July.

Skilful and learned in the theory of war, the Archduke Charles felt his inferiority in face of the unexpected genius of the Emperor Napoleon. He had carefully fortified Aspern,

Essling, Ensdorf, but he had not foreseen that the place of disembarkation, and the point of attack, would be changed. The heights which ranged from Neusiedel to Wagram, well occupied by excellent troops, were not furnished with redoubts; it was, however, these same heights the conqueror was about to attack.

The bridges which united the right bank to the island of Lobau were at present out of danger from all inundations and accidents. New and ingenious inventions had utilized all the resources drawn from the magazines of Vienna and the vast forests of Austria. A stockade protected the roadway, and flying bridges of an extraordinary size and solidity could be thrown in several hours over the small arm of the stream which separated the island of Lobau from the left bank. Two days previously the archduke had quitted the heights to approach the banks of the Danube, waiting uselessly for the attack of the enemy; on the 3rd July he drew back his forces towards the hills. The columns of the French continued to defile over the great bridge, and massed themselves little by little on the island. The cannon-balls of the enemy began to rain on the shores of Lobau, but the space was too vast to permit the Austrian batteries to sweep the interior. During the night of the 4th the first bridges were thrown over the small arm of the Danube between the island and the mainland; flat-bottomed boats brought over soldiers without interruption, and these moored the boats and fixed the plankings. The enemy's fire had become incessant and deadly. The engineers continued their work without appearing to perceive the danger which threatened them, any more than the thunder which rolled over their heads, the lightning which flashed through the darkness, or the rain, which did not cease to fall in torrents. The batteries of the island of Lobau were at length unmasked, everywhere furnished with guns of the largest calibre, and the fire was directed towards the little town of Enzensdorf; after that the Archduke Charles could not deceive himself as to the menaced point. The troops of the Austrian General Nordmann, which had occupied the plain, had fallen back under the fire of the guns. The day rose brilliant and pure, the last clouds massed by the storm were dispersed by the rays of the sun. The long files of our troops advanced without precipitation and without disorder; at the first break of day, the emperor himself had crossed the river.

The Archduke Charles contemplated this scene from the

heights of Wagram. His advanced posts had already been
forced to give up to their enemies the ground they had occupied
the day before. The Austrian general had not yet counted on
the irresistible impetuosity of the torrent of men, horses, and
artillery, which the island of Lobau continued to vomit on the
shores of the Danube. "It is true that they have conquered
the river," said the Archduke Charles to his brother the Emperor Francis, standing by his side. "I allow them to pass,
that I may drive them presently into its waves." "All right,"
said the emperor, dryly; "but do not let too many pass."
Seventy thousand French already deployed in the plain. As
they defiled past, the soldiers cried, "Long live the emperor!"

The town of Enzensdorf was merely a mass of ruins when
Marshal Masséna commanded the attack upon it, and the little
corps of Austrians defending it were soon put to the sword;
while on the right, General Oudinot had taken possession of
the chateau of Sachsengang. The entire army advanced,
without obstacle, against the heights of Wagram; Essling and
Aspern were occupied by our troops. The dispositions of the
troops of the Archduke Charles were not made; he was obliged
to order detached bodies to retreat, abandoning positions which
were badly defended: the great battle was deferred till the
morrow. A rash attack against the plateau of Wagram was
repulsed, and for a moment several corps were in disorder;
the retreat sounded, and the troops bivouacked at their posts.
The last instructions had been given. Marshal Davout alone
still remained with the emperor. The Archduke Charles did
not sleep—the supreme effort of the Austrian monarchy was
to be tried at the break of day.

The extent of the field of battle, and the distance between
the positions, presented serious difficulties for both armies.
The genius of organization possessed by the Emperor Napoleon
had in some measure obviated this by the care he had taken of
his centre; the Archduke Charles felt it from the commencement of the combat. Obliged to send his orders great dis-
tances, he saw them badly obeyed; the left wing of his army
attacked us first, whereas the right wing had been intended to
take the offensive. Contrary to his custom, the Emperor Napoleon had ordered his troops to wait for the enemy.

It was four o'clock in the morning when the fire commenced.
Marshal Bernadotte, who had remained in advance on the field
of battle after his attack of the previous night against the plateau of Wagram, found himself menaced by the Austrians,

and fell back on Marshal Masséna, still ill from a fall from his horse, and commanding his corps from an open carriage. The two marshals had brought back their troops against the little village of Aderklaa; but the archduke occupied it; the French were repulsed, and pushed by the enemy beyond Essling, which had again fallen into the hands of the Austrians.

Meantime, Marshal Davout, on the extreme right, had vigorously resisted the first attack of the columns of Rosenberg, and obliged the Austrians to repass the rivulet of Russbach, and fall back upon Neusiedel. The marshal threw all his forces immediately against them. It was to him that was confided the honor of taking the plateau of Wagram.

The emperor had joined Marshal Masséna, talking a few minutes with him under a storm of balls which fell round the carriage: Napoleon walked his horse across the plain, impatiently waiting the great movement that he had ordered on the centre. At the head advanced a division of the army of Italy, commanded by Macdonald, little known to the young soldiers because of his long disgrace; he marched proudly, attired in his old uniform of the armies of the republic. Napoleon saw him unmoved under the fire, attentive to the least incidents of the battle: "Ah, the fine fellow! the fine fellow!" he repeated in a low voice.

The artillery of the guard arrived at a gallop, supporting by its hundred guns the impetuous attack of the centre: the Austrians recoiled from this enormous mass, the irresistible impulse of which nothing could stay. Macdonald had already reached Sussenbrunn, where the archduke and his generals had concentrated their last effort; and the French columns were stopped by their desperate resistance. For a moment they seemed destined to retreat in their turn; but Davout had succeeded in his attack against the heights of Neusiedel. The plateau of Wagram was in our hands; General Oudinot had effected his junction, after taking the position of Baumersdorf; and the Prince of Hohenzollern retreated before them. In vain the Archduke Charles had hoped to see his brother, the Archduke John, arrive in time to restore their chance; the struggle lasted for more than ten hours—all the positions had fallen into our power; the retreat of the Austrian army commenced, regular and well ordered, without precipitation or rout. Disorder, on the contrary, showed itself in the ranks of the conquerors, when, at the last moments of the struggle, some soldiers of the vanguard of the Archduke John appeared in the environs of Leopoldsdorf. The young troops, already disbanded in the joy of the victory—the servants of the army, the sutlers, the carriers of the wounded, were seized with a panic terror, and fell back with loud cries on the main body of the army, announcing that the enemy were returning to crush us. It was too late; the Archduke John had slowly executed the orders tardily received. His arrival could not change the issue of the battle: he fell back upon Hungary. The Archduke Charles had taken the road to Bohemia before the Emperor Napoleon was well informed of his march. The pursuit was, therefore, divided between Bohemia and Moravia. The forces of the enemy were dispersed during their retreat. The archduke had with him about 60,000 men, when General Marmont, with a corps of only 10,000, rejoined him at Znaïm, on the road to Prague.

It was there that Napoleon arrived on the 11th; Masséna was in advance, and a battle took place on the banks of the Taya, and after a sharp combat the bridge was forced. But already Prince John of Lichtenstein had come to ask a suspension of hostilities, announcing openly the intention of the Austrian government to begin negotiations for peace. The deliberations were carried on at the head-quarters, while the army ranged itself in the plain of Znaïm. The emperor recapitulated rapidly in his mind the dangers and chances of a prolonged war. The opinion of several of his generals was to follow up Austria, and crush the coalition finally. Napoleon felt the enormous burden weighing on his shoulders: he saw a difficult and lingering war in Spain, Prussia agitated, Russia cold and secretly ill-disposed, the difficulties of Rome, England for the future taking her part in the continental struggle: he cried, "Enough blood has been shed; let us make peace!" It was necessary to repeat his words several times to the hostile parties at Znaïm, to induce them to cease fighting. The officers whose duty it was to carry the intelligence to the field of battle were wounded before they were able to stop the combat.

The armistice was signed in the night of the 11th July, and Napoleon immediately returned to Schœnbrunn. Negotiations had commenced, but their success was by no means sure. The Austrian armies had been brilliantly vanquished, but they were neither dispersed nor destroyed, and the efforts their resistance had cost sufficiently proved the military qualities of the chief and his soldiers. The Emperor Napoleon, encamped in the centre of the Austrian monarchy—of which he occupied the capital; he could not, and durst not in any way, relax his warlike watchfulness. New bodies of men were summoned from France. The Tyrol not being comprised in the armistice, the Bavarians and Prince Eugène were ordered to reduce its two portions, German and Italian. The posts were everywhere fortified, and works of defence pursued with vigor. The greater part of the army occupied vast barracks in the suburbs of Vienna. Napoleon distributed rewards to the officers and soldiers; he even showed his displeasure to Marshal Bernadotte, who had presumed to address a personal order of the day to the corps of the army under his direction at Wagram.

" His Majesty commands his army in person," he sent word to the Prince of Pontecorvo by Major-General Berthier; "it belongs to him alone to distribute the degree of glory with each merits." Napoleon added, in a letter to the minister of war, "I am glad also that you are aware that the Prince of Pontecorvo has not always conducted himself well in this campaign. The truth is, that this column of bronze has been constantly in disorder." By thus wounding his vanity, unexpected political difficulties afterwards arose, by leaving in the heart of Bernadotte implacable resentment against the emperor.

I wished to pursue without interruption the history of the campaign of Germany during these three months, so fertile in obstinate combats, in works as vast as they were novel, in pitched battles, more sanguinary and important from the number of troops engaged than any which had preceded them. Germany was not, however, the only theatre of the struggle; and the attention of Europe, always attracted to the places where Napoleon commanded in person and carried out his own plans, was occasionally diverted towards the Spanish and Portuguese peninsula. There several of the most skilful generals of the emperor fought against populations eagerly struggling for their independence; there gradually rose to greatness the name of Sir Arthur Wellesley, and that reputation for stability and heroic perseverance which at a later date constituted his power and splendor.

Fighting was carried on in Spain, not without glory or success; the insurgents having more than once had the honor of annoying the all-powerful conqueror in the midst of his triumphs. There was no fighting at Rome, and oppression reigned there without material resistance; yet for more than a year a struggle continued between the Emperor Napoleon and the Pope, Pius VII., without all the advantages remaining on the side of force, or the conqueror feeling certain that he held the prey he had confided to the care of General Miollis. On the 6th July, 1809, the same day as the battle of Wagram, the Pope was suddenly taken away from Rome, and condncted as a prisoner out of that palace and that town which he had never previously quitted, except to visit Paris for the purpose of consecrating the very man who was to-day stripping him of his throne. Since the month of February, 1808, the thoughts and hearts of many had still found time to seek the aged pontiff at the Quirinal, and they now followed him with sympathy into exile and captivity.

After the occupation of Rome by General Miollis, when the foreign cardinals had received orders to return to their respective countries, and the Pope had recalled his legate from Paris, the Emperor Napoleon, on stepping into his carriage to visit Bayonne, had ordered Champagny to transmit to Cardinal Caprara the following note:—

"The *sine quâ non* of the emperor is, that all Italy, Rome, Naples, and Milan make a league offensive and defensive, so as to remove disorder and war from the peninsula. If the holy father consents to this proposition, all is terminated; if he refuses, by that he declares war against the emperor. The first result of war is conquest, and the first result of conquest is change of government. This will not occasion any loss to the spiritual rights of the Pope; he will be Bisho pof Rome, as have been all his predecessors in the eight first centuries, and under Charlemagne. It will, however, be a subject of regret, which the emperor will be the first to feel, to see foolish vanity, obstinacy and ignorance destroy the work of genius, policy and enlightenment.

"The recall of your Eminence is notified contrary to custom, against the formalities in usage, and on the eve of the Passion week—three circumstances which sufficiently explain the charitable and entirely evangelical spirit of the holy father. No matter, his Majesty recognizes your Eminence no more as legate. From this moment the Gallican Church resumes all the integrity of its doctrine. More learned, more truly religious, than the Church of Rome, she has no want of the latter. I send to your eminence the passports you have demanded. We are thus at war, and his Majesty has given orders in consequence. His Holiness will be satisfied—he will have the happiness of declaring war in the holy week. The thunders of the Vatican will be all the more formidable. His Majesty fears them less than those of the castle of St. Angelo. He who curses kings, is cursed by God."

At the same time, and by order of Napoleon, a decree was prepared enumerating all the grievances of which he accused the court of Rome, and enacting that "the provinces of Urbino, Ancona, Macerata, and Camerino, should be irrevocably and forever united to the kingdom of Italy, to form three new departments." The Code Napoleon was to be proclaimed there.

The violent and arbitrary measures employed by the emperor towards the Pope naturally bore their fruits. In removing from Pius VII. the cardinals who were not natives of the Roman states, he had deprived the pontiff of the most enlightened and moderate counsels which could reach his ears, and had delivered him, in his weakness and just indignation, to all the influences against which Cardinal Consalvi had constantly struggled. From this time every despotic act of Napoleon, every rude word of the soldiers charged to execute his orders, increased the irritation of the Pope, and urged him to advance on a course of blind resistance. A prohibition to swear allegiance to the new government was addressed to the bishops and all the priests of the territories taken away from the pontifical states; this prohibition was founded upon principles of dogma and religion. Henceforth the personal will of the Pope, his dignity as a sovereign, and his conscience as a priest, were all engaged in the struggle against the Emperor Napoleon. "Those who have succeeded in alarming the conscience of the holy father are still the strongest," Lefebvre, the chargé-d'affaires of France, who had not yet quitted Rome, wrote to Champagny. "The tenor of the reply to the ultimatum that I have been instructed to remit to him has been changed twice this morning—so much did they still hesitate upon the decision to take. The theologians themselves were divided even in the Sacred College, and I doubt not that the refusal of his Holiness to agree with the emperor will throw into consternation a number of his warmest partisans."

The rupture was from this time official, and the relations of the Pope with the French authorities who occupied the pontifical city became every day more bitter. Pius VII. had chosen for his secretary of state, Cardinal Pacca, witty, amiable, devoted to the holy father, but strongly attached to the most narrow ideas as to the government of the Roman Church in the world; in other respects, prudent in his conduct towards

General Miollis, and often excited to action by the Pope, who complained of his timidity. "They pretend in Rome that we are asleep," said Pius VII. to his minister; "we must prove that we are awake, and address a vigorous note to the French general." The protest was posted everywhere in Rome, on the morning of the 24th August, 1808; eight days later, and under the pretext that the secretary of state interfered with the recruiting for the civic guard, Cardinal Pacca received the order to quit Rome in twenty-four hours. "Your Eminence will find at the gate of St. John an escort of dragoons, whose duty is to accompany you to Benevento, your native town." In the meantime a French officer was appointed to watch over the cardinal. The latter was still talking with his jailer, when Pius VII. suddenly entered the cabinet of his minister.

"I was then witness of a phenomenon which I had often heard spoken of," relates Cardinal Pacca in his memoirs. "In an access of violent anger, the hair of the holy father bristled up, and his sight was confused. Although I was dressed as a cardinal, he did not know me. 'Who is there?' he demanded, in a loud voice. 'I am the cardinal,' I replied, kissing his hand. 'Where is the officer?' demanded the holy father; and I pointed him out near me, in a respectful attitude. Then the Pope, turning towards him, 'Go and tell your general that I am weary of suffering so many insults and outrages from a man who dares still to call himself a Catholic. I command my minister not to obey the injunctions of an illegitimate authority. Let your general know, that if force is employed to tear him from me it shall only be after having broken all the doors; and I declare him beforehand responsible for the consequences of such an enormous crime.' And making a sign to the cardinal to follow him, 'Let us go,' said the Pope. The officer had gone out to carry to the general the message of the holy father. The secretary of state was installed in an apartment which opened into the Pope's bedroom. The gates of the Quirinal remained closed to all the French officers, and General Miollis did not claim his prisoner."

Months had meanwhile passed away. The emperor had quitted Spain to make preparations for the campaign of Germany. Without ever ceasing to load the Pope with unfriendly words and treatment, Napoleon had been engaged in affairs more important than his troubles with the pontifical court. Public order was maintained in Rome, thanks to the Italian prudence of the secretary of state, and the strict discipline which General Miollis knew how to maintain among his troops, and even among the auxiliaries he had recruited from the revolutionary middle-class. The time arrived, however, when this situation, more violent in fact than in form, was suddenly to assume its real character. Napoleon was at Schœnbrunn, already victor in the five days' battle which had rendered him master of Vienna, and more certain than he was immediately after Essling of the promptitude and extent of his success. It was then that he drew up, and sent by Champagny, two decrees relating to the taking possession, pure and simple, of the States of the Pope. He explained the reasons of this to his minister in a long letter, which was to serve as a basis for Champagny's report, and which, by its singular mixture of thoughts and principles, showed the historical heredity connecting the power of Napoleon with that of Charlemagne, united to the sovereign power which disposed in the name of conquest of territories and states, were confused in the imagination of the emperor, and made him look upon the independent attitude of the Pope as an act of criminal opposition.

"When Charlemagne made the popes temporal sovereigns, he wished them to remain vassals of the empire; now, far from thinking themselves vassals of the empire, they are not even willing to form a part of it. The aim of Charlemagne in his generosity towards the popes was the welfare of Christianity; and now they claim to ally themselves with Protestants and the enemies of Christianity. The least impropriety that results from these arrangements is to see the head of the Catholic religion negotiating with Protestants; whilst according to the laws of the Church he ought to shun them, and excommunicate them. (There is a prayer to this effect recited at Rome.)

"The interest of religion, and the interest of the peoples of France, Germany and Italy, require that an end should be made of this ridiculous temporal power—the feeble remnant of the exaggerated pretensions of the Gregories, who claimed to reign over kings, to give away crowns, and to have the direction of the affairs of earth as well as of heaven. In the absence of councils, let the popes have the direction of the affairs of the Church so far as they do not infringe on the liberties of the Gallican Church—that is all right; but they ought not to mix themselves up with armies or state policy. If they are the successors of Jesus Christ, they ought not to exercise any other dominion than that which He Himself exercised, and His 'kingdom is not of this world.'

"If your Majesty does not do that which you alone can do, you will leave in Europe the seeds of dissension and discord. Posterity, whilst praising you for having re-established religion and re-erected her altars, will blame you for having left the empire (which is in fact the major portion of Christendom) exposed to the influence of this fantastic medley, inimical to religion and the tranquillity of the empire. This obstacle can only be surmounted by separating the temporal from the spiritual authority, and by declaring that the states of the Pope form a portion of the French Empire."

It is too often an error of men, even of the first rank, to believe in the universal power and duration of their wishes and decisions. The Emperor Napoleon though he had solved forever this question of the temporal power of the popes—a question which we have so many times heard discussed by the most eloquent voices; we have seen armies upholding on fields of battle contradictory principles on this subject, and diplomacy painfully accomplishing imperfect settlements.

He displayed towards Pope Pius VII. the most arrogant contempt of the rights and independence of others, and a passionate self-will as regards all resistance. Under shelter of ancient authority, of which he retrospectively took possession, he boldly invoked the highest reasons and the most venerated names, in order to justify an arbitrary resolution, and the grasping selfishness which swayed his mind. It was the practice of the French Revolution to prop up its violent and desspotic proceedings by the loftiest principles; the Emperor Napoleon had not forgotten this tradition.

In all the manifestly criminal acts of his powerful career—in the fatal resolves of his mistaken and culpable caprices, whether it was a question of the assassination of the Duc d'Enghien or the brutal removal of the Pope from Rome—Napoleon always chose his part in the complete isolation of his soul, and by the spontaneous act of a personal decision; he made sure of the execution of his will with minute precautions: he did not the less subsequently seek to throw back the responsibility of the acts themselves upon the instruments too ready to obey him. When Europe suddenly learnt that the Pope had been removed from the states henceforth united to the French Empire, Napoleon wrote to Fouché, "I am vexed that the Pope has been arrested; it is a great folly. It was necessary to arrest Cardinal

Pacca, and leave the Pope in tranquillity at Rome;" and to Cambacérès, the 28th July: "It is without my orders, and against my will, that the Pope has been made to leave Rome."

Measures had, however, been taken with that provident exactitude which characterized the personal orders of the Emperor Napoleon. Immediately he had resolved upon the confiscation of the Roman States he had divined the consequence and importance of this act; the new government was organized, Murat had been charged with the command of the troops, and to hold himself ready for any event. "Since your Majesty has made me aware of your intentions as to Rome, I shall not withdraw from Naples," wrote Murat to the emperor. "Word has been sent me that the Pope wished to send forth an excommunication, but that the majority of the Consistory were opposed to it. All your orders will be fulfilled, and I hope without trouble."

This was hoping for much from the patience of the holy father, and maintaining great illusions as to the decision long since taken by the Court of Rome. The project of the spoliation of the pontifical states had not been kept so secret that the Pope and his minister had not been apprised of it; and several times Pius VII. had let it be understood that he was prepared for resistance. "We see plainly that the French wish to force us to speak Latin," he had said quite recently; "ah, well! we will do it."

General Miollis, supported and directed by the King of Naples, did not take much account of the Latin of the court of Rome when it was a question of obeying the orders of the Emperor Napoleon. The military preparations completed (the 10th June, 1809), the tricolor flag was mounted upon the castle of St. Angelo in place of the pontifical arms, and the imperial decrees were everywhere read before the population of Rome and the assembled troops. The report of these things soon reached the Quirinal. "I rushed suddenly into the apartment of the holy father," writes Cardinal Pacca, "and on meeting we both pronounced the words of the Redeemer, *Consummatum est!* I was in a condition difficult to describe, but the sight of the holy father, who maintained an unalterable tranquillity, much edified me, and reanimated my courage. A few minutes afterwards my nephew brought me a copy of the imperial decree. Observing the Pope attentively at the first words, I saw emotion on his countenance, and the signs of indignation only too natural. Little by little he recovered himself, and he heard the reading with much tranquillity and resignation." Cardinal Pacca was even obliged to urge the pope to promulgate the bull of excommunication, which had been prepared already since 1806. Pius VII. still hesitated. "Raise your eyes towards heaven, Thrice Holy Father," said the secretary of state, "and then give me your order, and be sure that that which proceeds from your mouth will be the will of God." "Ah, well! let the bull go forth," cried the Pope; "but let those who shall execute your orders take great care, for if they are discovered they will be shot, and for that I should be inconsolable."

The bull of excommunication against the Emperor Napoleon was everywhere placarded in Rome, without the agents of Cardinal Pacca undergoing the vengeance dreaded by the Pope. Anger and fear were wrestling in a higher sphere. The instructions of the emperor had been precise: "I have confided to you the care of maintaining tranquillity in my Roman states," he wrote to General Miollis. "You are to have arrested, even in the house of the Pope himself, those who plot against public tranquillity, and against the safety of my soldiers. A priest abuses his character, and merits less indulgence than another man, when he preaches war and disobedience to temporal power, and when he sacrifices spiritual things for the interest of this world, which the Scripture declares not to be his." And to the King of Naples, in two different letters, of the 17th and 19th of June: "If the Pope wishes to form a reunion of caballers like Cardinal Pacca, it will be necessary to permit nothing of the kind. and to act at Rome as I should act towards the cardinal archbishop of Paris. . . . I have given you to understand that my intention was that the affairs of Rome should be quickly settled, and that no species of opposition should take place. No asylum ought to be respected, if my decrees are not submitted to; and under no pretext whatever ought any resistance to be allowed. If the Pope, in opposition to the spirit of his office and of the Gospel, preaches revolt, and wishes to make use of the immunity of his house for the printing of circulars, he ought to be arrested. The time for this sort of thing is past. Philippe le Bel caused Boniface to be arrested; and Charles V. kept Clement VII. in prison for a long time, for far less cause. The priest who to the temporal powers preaches discord and war, instead of peace, abuses his character."

The orders were precise, and admitted of no hesitation. The confiscation of the papal states had been responded to by the papal bull; open war had broken out between Pius VII., and the Emperor Napoleon. The latter was desirous of insuring the execution of his will by sending to Rome General Radet, less honorably scrupulous than General Miollis; an instrument docile and daring, as regards the details of the general scheme. Radet has himself given an account of the removal of the Pope in a report to the minister of war, dated July 13th, 1809. In 1814, he had forgotten the existence of this letter, and vainly sought to minimize the importance of the part which he played on the 6th of July. History must preserve for General Radet his place in her annals. The man to carry out the projects of Napoleon had been well chosen.

Already for several months the Pope had been carefully guarding himself in the Quirinal; the precautions had been redoubled since the decrees, and the publication of the bull. Pius VII. and his counsellors foresaw the removal. General Radet took all possible measures to turn aside suspicion. "On the 5th, at the break of day," he himself wrote, " I made the necessary arrangements, which I succeeded in screening from the eyes of the Romans by double patrols and measures of police. I kept the troops in the barracks all day, in order to lull the public and the inhabitants of the Quirinal into a feeling of security. From that spot the Pope governed with his finger more than we did with our bayonets. At nine o'clock, I caused the military chiefs to come to me, one after another, and gave them my orders. At ten o'clock, we were collected in the place of the Holy Apostles, and at the barracks of La Pilota, which was the centre of my operations. At eleven o'clock I myself placed my patrols, my guards, my posts, and my detachments for carrying out the operations, whilst the governor-general caused the bridges of the Tiber and the castle of St. Angelo to be occupied by a Neapolitan battalion."

General Radet had received a written order from General Miollis, for the arrest of Cardinal Pacca. The order to arrest the Pope was not written down. Nobody had dared to put his signature to it; verbal instructions only were given.

Three detachments of soldiers, furnished with scaling-ladders, ropes and grappling-irons, surrounded the Quirinal. At half-past ten, the sentinel who kept guard on the tower of the Quirinal disappeared. The signal was immediately given. With varying success the small battalions introduced themselves into the palace. The Swiss guard was disarmed; it had for a long time previously received orders to make no resist-

ance. The chief anxiety of the Pope had always been that he
might be up and about when they should come to arrest him.
He had gone to bed late, and was roused up by the noise in the
middle of his first sleep. Cardinal Pacca, however, found him
completely dressed, when the former rushed precipitately into
his chamber. The gate was already yielding to the efforts of
the assailants. Pius VII. seated himself under a canopy;
making a sign to the secretary of state, and to Cardinal Desp-
ing, to place themselves near him. "Open the gate," said
he.

General Radet had never seen the Pope; he recognized him
by the attitude of his guides; and immediately sending back
the soldiers, he caused the officers to enter with drawn swords:
a few gendarmes, with muskets in their hands, also glided
into the chamber. The priest was waiting in silence; the
soldier was hesitating. At length the latter, hat in hand,
spoke: "I have a sorrowful mission to accomplish," said
General Radet; "I am compelled by my oaths to fulfil it."
Pius VII. stood up. "Who are you," said he, "and what is
it you require of me, that you come at such an hour to trouble
my repose and invade my dwelling-place?" "Most Holy
Father," replied the General, "I come in the name of my
government to reiterate to your Holiness the proposal to
officially renounce your temporal power. If your holiness
consents to it, I do not doubt but that affairs may be arranged,
and that the emperor will treat your holiness with the greatest respect." The Pope was resting one hand upon the table
placed before him "If you have believed yourself bound to
execute such orders of the emperor by reason of your oath of
fidelity and obedience, think to what an extent we feel compelled to sustain the rights of the holy see, to which we are
bound by so many oaths? We can neither yield nor abandon
that which belongs to it. The temporal power belongs to
the Church, and we are only the administrator. The emperor
may tear us in pieces, but he will not obtain from us what he
demands. After all that we have done for him, ought we to
expect such treatment?"

"I know that the emperor is under many obligations to
your holiness!" replied Radet, more and more troubled.
"Yes, more than you are aware of; but, finally, what are
your orders?"—"Most Holy Father, I regret the commission
with which I am charged, but I must inform you that I am
ordered to take you away with me." The pontiff bent slightly

towards the speaker, and said in tones of sweet compassion, "Ah! my son, your mission is one that will not draw down upon you the divine blessing." Then, turning again towards the cardinals, and appearing to speak to himself, "This, then, is the recognition which is accorded to me of all that which I have done for the emperor! This, then, is the reward for my great condescension towards him and towards the Church of France! But perhaps in this respect I have been culpable towards God. He wishes to punish me; I submit with humility."

General Radet had sent for the final orders of General Miollis. The brigadier of gendarmerie charged with this commission re-entered the chamber of the Pope. "The order of his excellency," said he, "is, that it is necessary for the holy father and Cardinal Pacca to set out at once with General Radet: the other persons in his suite will follow after." The Pope rose up; he walked with difficulty. Moved in spite of himself, Radet offered his arm to support him, proposing to retire, in order to leave the holy father free to give his orders and dispose of any valuable objects that he might have a fancy for. "When one has no hold upon life, one has no hold upon the things of this world," replied Pius VII., taking from a table at the side of his bed his breviary and his crucifix. "I am ready," said he.

The carriage was already at the palace gate, the postillions ready to start. The Pope stood still, giving his benediction to the city of Rome, and to the French troops ranged in order of battle on the place. It was four o'clock in the morning; the streets were deserted. The Pope got into the carriage beside Cardinal Pacca; the doors were locked by a gendarme. General Radet and a marshal of the household got on to the box-seat; the horses set off at a quick trot along the road to Florence.

General Radet offered a purse of Gold to the Pope, which the latter refused. "Have you any money?" asked the holy father of his companion. "I have not been permitted to enter my apartment," said the cardinal; "and I did not think of bringing my purse." The Pope had a papetto, value twenty sous. "This is all that remains to me of my principality," said he, smiling. "We are travelling in apostolic fashion," responded Pacca. "We have done well in publishing the bull of the 10th of June," replied Pius VII.; "now it would be too late."

For nineteen hours the coach rattled along; the stores were getting low. Everywhere, and in spite of a few accidents, the passage of the Pope forestalled the news of his capture. The suite of the holy father joined him on the morrow; the Pope was suffering, he was in a fever. The populace began to be stirred up with the rumors which were circulating: they crowded round the carriages. "I disembarrassed myself of them," writes Radet, "by calling out to them to place themselves on their knees on the right and left of the road, in order that the holy father might give him his benediction; then all of a sudden I ordered the postillions to dash forward. By this means the people were still on their kness whilst we were already far away at a gallop. This plan succeeded everywhere."

Arrived on the 8th of July at the chartreuse of Florence, Pius VII. expected to rest there a few days: but the Princess Baciocchi had not received instructions from the emperor: she hurried the departure. "I see well that they want to cause my death by their bad treatment," said the exhausted old man; "and if there is but a little more of it I feel that the end will not be far off." Cardinal Pacca was no longer with him. At Genoa the Prince Borghese, who was commanding there, was seized with the same panic as the Princess Baciocchi. After a few moments of repose at Alexandria, Pius VII. was carried, by way of Mondovi and Rivoli, towards Grenoble. In the last stages, in the little Italian villages, the bells pealed forth, and the crowd who besought the benediction of the prisoner everywhere retarded the advance. It was the same in all the districts of Savoy and Dauphiny. When the Pope made his entry into Grenoble, on the 21st of July, the ardor of the population had not diminished, but the bells rang no longer; the clergy had been forbidden to present themselves before the pontiff. The prefect was absent, Fouché having been designedly detained at Paris. The orders of the emperor had at length arrived from Schœnbrunn. "I received at the same time the two letters of General Miollis and that of the Grand Duchess," he wrote, on the 18th of July, to Fouché. "I am vexed that the Pope has been arrested; it is a great folly. It was needful to arrest Cardinal Pacca, and to leave the Pope quietly at Rome. But there is no remedy for it now: what is done is done. I know not what the Prince Borghese will have done, but my intention is that the Pope should not enter France. If he is still in the Riviere of Genoa, the best place at which he could be placed would be Savona. There is a house there large enough, where he would be suitably lodged until we know what course he decides upon. If his madness terminates, I have no objection to his being taken back to Rome. If he has entered France, have him taken back towards Savona and San Remo. Cause his correspondence to be examined. As to Cardinal Pacca, have him shut up at Fenestrella; and let him understand that if a single Frenchman is assassinated through his instigation, he will be the first to pay for it with his head."

Fifteen days later (August 6th, 1809), in the midst of his prudent and foreseeing preparations for the possible resumption of hostilities, enlightened by reflection, or by the report of the popular emotion in the provinces traversed by Pius VII., Napoleon modified his orders as to the residence of the Pope. "Monsieur Fouché, I should have preferred that only Cardinal Pacca had been arrested at Rome, and that the Pope had been left there. I should have preferred, since the Pope has not been left at Genoa, that he had been taken to Savona; but since he is at Grenoble, I should be vexed that you should make him set out to be re-conducted to Savona; it would be better to guard him at Grenoble, since he is there; the former course would have the appearance of making sport of the old man. I have not authorized Cardinal Fesch to send any one to his holiness; I have only had the minister of religion informed that I should desire Cardinal Maury and the other prelates to write to the Pope, to know what he wishes, and to make him understand that if he renounces the Concordat I shall regard it on my side as null and void. As to Cardinal Pacca, I suppose that you have sent him to Fenestrella, and that you have forbidden his communication with any one. I make a great difference between the Pope and him, principally on account of his rank and his moral virtues. The Pope is a good man, but ignorant and fanatical. Cardinal Pacca is a man of education and a scoundrel, an enemy of France, and deserving of no regard. Immediately I know where the Pope is located I shall see about taking definitive measures; of course if you have already caused him to set out for Savona, it is not necessary to bring him back."

The Pope was at Savona, where he was long to remain. Already the difficulties of religious administration were commencing, and the emperor's mind was engrossed with the institution of bishops to the vacant sees. He had ordered all the prelates to chant a public *Te Deum* with reference to the victory of Wagram. The bishops of Dalmatia alone had frankly and spiritedly replied to the statement of reasons which preceded the circular. In France the silence was still profound. The emperor had beforehand forbidden the journals to give any news from Rome. "It is a bad plan to let articles be written," he wrote to Fouché; "there is to be no speaking, either for or against, and it is not to be a matter for discussion in the journals. Well-informed men know perfectly that I have not attacked Rome. The mistaken bigots you cannot alter. Act on this principle." The *Moniteur* held its tongue. All the journals followed its example. No one talked of the bull of excommunication. The circuits of the missionary priests were forbidden, as well as the ecclesiastical conferences of St. Sulpice. "The missionaries are for whoever pays them," declared the emperor, "for the English, if they are willing to employ them. I do not wish to have any missions whatever; get me ready a draft of a decree on that subject; I wish to complete it. I only know bishops, priests, and curates. I am satisfied with keeping up religion in my own country; I do not care about propagating it abroad." All the cardinals still remaining at Rome were expelled. In the depths of his soul, and in spite of the chimerical impulses of his irritated thoughts, Napoleon was already feeling the embarrassments which he had himself sown along his path. The Pope a prisoner at Savona, indomitable in his conscientious resistance, might become more dangerous than the Pope at Rome, powerless and unarmed. The struggle was not terminated; a breath of revolt had passed over Europe. Henceforth Napoleon was at war with that Catholic religion, the splendor of whose altars he had deemed it a point of honor to restore; he struggled at the same time violently against that national independence of the peoples which he had everywhere in his words invoked in opposition to the arbitrary jealousy of the monarchs. The Spanish sovereigns had succumbed to his yoke; the Spanish people, henceforth sustained by the might of England, courageously defended its liberties. At the moment when the supreme effort of the victory of Wagram was about to snatch humiliating concessions from the Emperor Francis, the captive Pope and the Spanish insurgents were presenting to Europe a salutary and striking contrast, the teachings of which she was beginning to comprehend.

Not the least significant of the lessons on the frailty of the

human colossi raised by conquerors is the impossibility of
tracing their history on the same canvas. For a long time
Napoleon alone had filled the scene, and his brilliant track
was easily kept in view. In proportion as he accumulated on
his shoulders a burden too heavy, and as he extended his empire without consolidating it, the insufficiency of human will
and human power made itself more painfully felt. Napoleon
was no longer everywhere present, acting and controlling, in
order to repair the faults he had committed, or to dazzle the
spectators with new successes. In vain the prodigious activity
of his spirit sought to make up for the radical defect of his universal dominion. The Emperor Napoleon was conquered by
the very nature of things, before the fruits of his unmeasured
ambition had had time to ripen, and before all Europe, indignant and wearied out, was at length roused up against
him.

There was already, in 1809, a confused but profound instinctive feeling throughout the world that the moment for resistance and for supreme efforts had arrived. The Archduke
Charles had proved it in Austria by the fury of his courage;
the English cabinet were bearing witness to it by the great
preparations they were displaying on their coast and in their
arsenals, as well as by the ready aid lent by them to the insurgents of the Peninsula. The Emperor Napoleon on quitting
Spain, in the month of January, had left behind him the certain germs of growing disorder. Obliged of necessity to commit the chief command to King Joseph, he had been desirous
of remedying the weakness and military incapacity of the
monarch whom he had himself put on the throne by confer-
ring upon the marshals charged with continuing the war an
almost absolute authority over their *corps d'armée.* Each of
them was to correspond directly with the minister of war, su-
premely directed by Napoleon himself. Deprived thus of all
serious control over the direction of the war, King Joseph saw
himself equally thwarted in civil and financial affairs. Spanish
interests were naturally found to conflict with French interests.
King Joseph defended the former; an army of imperial functionaries were charged with the protection of the second. In
this mission they proceeded at times even to insult. King
Joseph threatened to place in a carriage M. de Fréville, administrator for the treasury of confiscated goods, and to send
him directly to France. The complaints of the unfortunate
monarch to his brother were frequent and well founded.

"Your Majesty has not entire confidence in me," he wrote on the 17th of February to Napoleon, "and meanwhile, without that, the position is not tenable. I shall not again repeat what I have already written ten times as to the situation of the finances; I give all my faculties to business from eight o'clock in the morning to eleven o'clock in the evening; I go out once a week; I have not a sou to give to any one; I am in the fourth year of my reign, and I still see my guard with the first frock-coat which I gave it, three years ago; I am the goal of all complaints; I have all pretensions to overcome; my power does not extend beyond Madrid, and at Madrid itself I am daily thwarted. Your Majesty has ordered the sequestration of the goods of ten families, it has been extended to more than double. All the habitable houses are sealed up; 6000 domestics of the sequestrated families are in the streets. All demand charity; the boldest of them take to robbery and assassination. My officers—all those who sacrificed with me the kingdom of Naples—are still lodged by billets. Without capital, without income, without money, what can I do? All this picture, bad as it is, is not exaggerated, and, bad as it is, it will not exhaust my courage; I shall arrive at the end of all that. Heaven has given me everything needful to overcome the hindrances from circumstances or from my enemies; but that which Heaven has denied me is an organization capable of supporting the insults and contradictions of those who ought to serve me, and, above all, of contending with the dissatisfaction of a man whom I have loved too well to be ever willing to dislike him. Thus, sire, if my whole life has not given you the fullest confidence in me; if you judge it necessary to surround me with petty souls, who cause me myself to redden with shame; if I am to be insulted even in my capital; if I have not the right to appoint the governors and commandants who are always under my eyes,—I have not two choices to make. I am only King of Spain by the force of your arms. I might become so by the love of the Spaniards; but for that it would be necessary to govern in my own manner. I have often heard you say, 'Every animal has its instinct, and each one ought to follow it.' I will be such a king as the brother and friend of your Majesty ought to be, or I will return to Mortefontaine, where I shall ask for nothing but the happiness of living without humiliation, and of dying with a tranquil conscience."

Joseph Bonaparte had presumed too much on his forces and the remains of his independence. Constantly hard and severe with regard to his brothers, the emperor replied with scorn to King Joseph: "It is not ill-temper and small passions that you need, but views cool and conformable to your position. You talk to me of the constitution. Let me know if the constitution forbids the King of Spain to be at the head of 300,000 Frenchmen? if the constitution prohibits the garrison from being French, and the governor of Madrid a Frenchman? if the constitution says that in Saragossa the houses are to be blown up one after another? You will not succeed in Spain, except by vigor and energy. This parade of goodness and clemency ends in nothing. You will be applauded so long as my armies are victorious; you will be abandoned if they are vanquished. You ought to have become acquainted with the Spanish nation in the time you have been in Spain, and after the events that you have seen. Accustom yourself to think your royal authority as a very small matter."

The emperor had correctly judged the precarious condition of the French power in Spain; he had reckoned, and he still reckoned, on the success of his arms. The military counsellor whom he had left near his brother possessed neither his esteem nor his confidence. Marshal Jourdan was a cold and prudent spirit, always imbued with the military habits of the French Revolution, and had never courted the favor of Napoleon; King Joseph was attached to him, and had brought him with him to Naples. The lieutenants of the emperor showed him no deference; it was, however, by his agency that the orders of the minister of war passed to the staff-officers at Madrid. Already, and by the express instructions of the emperor, Marshal Soult was on march for Portugal. His rapid triumphs did not appear doubtful; and the operations of Marshal Victor in the south of Spain were to be dependent on the succors that were to reach him when Lisbon was conquered. The difficulties everywhere opposed to Marshal Soult by the passionate insurrection of the Portuguese population, however, retarded his march. He only arrived on the banks of the Minho on the 15th of February; the peasants had taken away the boats. An attempted passage near the mouth of the river having failed, the *corps d'armée* was compelled to reascend its course, after a series of partial combats against the forces of the Marquis of Romana, who had given his support to the Portuguese insurrection. When he had at length succeeded in crossing the Minho at Orense, Soult seized successively the towns of Chaves and Braga, which were scarcely defended. The chiefs of the insurgents had been constrained by their soldiers to this useless show of resistance, General Frère having been massacred by the militia whom he ordered to evacuate Braga. At Oporto the disorder was extreme; the population fought under the orders of the bishop. The attack had been cleverly arranged. At the moment when the bewildered crowd was pressing tumultuously over the bridge of boats across the Douro, the cables broke; men, women, and children were engulfed in the waves. In spite of the efforts of the general, the city was sacked. The long wars, the rude life of the camps, the daily habit of subsisting by pillage, had little by little relaxed the bonds of discipline. Marshal Soult established himself at Oporto, incapable of advancing even to Lisbon with his forces reduced by garrisoning towns, in presence of the English troops, who had not ceased to occupy the capital. He could not, or he would not make known at Madrid the position in which he found himself. Behind him the insurrection had closed every passage. He found himself isolated in Portugal, and conceived the thought of submitting the environs of Oporto to a regular and pacific government, re-establishing order all round, and constantly attentive to gain the favor of important persons. Perhaps the marshal raised his hopes even to the foundation of an independent and personal power, more durable than imperial conquests. It was with his consent that the draft of a popular pronunciamento was circulated in the provinces of Minho and Oporto, praying " his Excellency the Duke of Dalmatia to take the reins of government, to represent the sovereign, and to invest himself with all the attributes of supreme authority, until the emperor might designate a prince of his house or of his choice to reign over Portugal."

The sentiments of the army were divided, and an opposition was preparing to the schemes of the marshal, when the latter learned that an enemy more redoubtable than the Portuguese insurrection was threatening him in this province, where he had dreamed of founding a kingdom. Sir Arthur Wellesley had arrived at Lisbon on the 22nd of April, with reinforcements which swelled the English *corps d'armée* to £5,000 men; fifteen or twenty thousand Portuguese soldiers marched under his orders; a crowd of insurgents impeded rather than aided his operations. He advanced immediately against Marshal Soult, now for five weeks immovable at Oporto. On the 2nd of May he was at Coimbra. Well informed of the plots which were preparing at Oporto, to which a French officer named Argen-

tan had been engaged to lend a hand, he resolved upon attacking as speedily as possible the positions of the marshal. When
the latter was informed of the projects of the English general,
retreat was already cut off in the valley of the Tamega by a
strong assemblage of the insurgents, and in the valley of the
Douro by the English general Beresford. Only one route remained still open to Marshal Soult—by Braga and the provinces
of the north. Retreat was resolved upon, the powder saturated,
the field artillery horsed; the departure was ordered for twelve
at noon, and a part of the army was already defiling on the
road to Amarante.

In the night between the 11th and 12th two English battalions
had crossed the Douro at Avinto, three leagues above Oporto,
collecting all the vessels which were to be found on the river, and
descending the course of the stream under cover of the darkness.
The army of Sir Arthur Wellesley had meanwhile occupied the
suburbs of the left bank, concealing his movements behind the
heights of La Sarca. Marshal Soult was ignorant of that
operation. At daybreak a small body of picked men, boldly
crossing the river within sight of our soldiers, took possession of
an enclosure called the Seminary. Entrenching themselves
there, and constantly receiving new reinforcements, the English made a desperate defence against the attempts of General
Delaborde. The main body of the enemy's army beginning to
fill all the streets of Oporto, the marshal at once sounded retreat, and the wounded and sick were left to the care of the
English. When, on the evening of the 12th, the army reached
the town of Baltar, Soult learned that the roads by Braga had
been intercepted, as well as by the valley of the Douro. General Loison, unable to force the passage of the Tamega, had
evacuated Amarante. The roads from the north would bring
the army back to the suburbs of Oporto. The marshal, not
wishing to risk a fresh encounter with the enemy, at once
made up his mind to sacrifice without hesitation his baggage,
ammunition, artillery, and even the greater part of the treasure of the army, to enter the mountain passes, and join at
Guimaraens the divisions which had preceded him. When at
last the army reached Orense, after seven days' marching,
varied by small skirmishes, the soldiers were exhausted and
depressed Portugal was for the second time lost to us. Marshal Soult immediately marched towards Galicia, which had
for two months been the theatre of Ney's operations, and freed
Lugo, while that marshal was making a brilliant expedition

in the Asturias along with General Kellermann. The two
chiefs made an arrangement as to the measures to be taken
against the insurgents who had assembled at St. Jago under
the orders of the Marquis Romana; after which Soult was to
march upon Old Castile as far as Zamora, to be near the English, who were said to be threatening the south of Portugal.
Ney proposed to attack Vigo, where General Noriena had fortified himself, supported by the crews of several English vessels.   From the very first, since the junction of the two
armies, both officers and soldiers had exchanged keen and
bitter recrimination.   A better feeling, however, had reappeared, and the mutual good-will of the chiefs for each other
silenced the ill-disposed.   After their separation, Ney freed
St. Jago; but after advancing to the suburbs of Vigo, and seeing its strong position, he waited for the result of Soult's
movement against Romana.

Several days having elapsed, he learned that, after driving
Romana back to Orense without fighting, and staying several
days at Montforte, the marshal had taken the road to Zamora,
without replying to the letters of his companion-in-arms. From
information received from Lugo, Ney was persuaded that
Soult's project had long been premeditated, and that he had
of deliberate purpose broken the bargain stipulated between
them.   His anger burst forth with a violence proportioned to
the frankness he had shown when treating with Soult, and
this anger was shared by the officers and soldiers of his army.
He at once determined to evacuate Galicia, which was threatened both by the English and the Spanish insurgents.   Leaving a strong garrison at Ferrol, Ney slowly advanced towards
Lugo, where he collected the sick and wounded left by Soult,
and then returned to Astorga, in the beginning of July.   He
wrote to King Joseph: "If I had wished to resolve to leave
Galicia without artillery, I could have remained there longer, at
the risk of being hemmed in; but, avoiding such a mode of departure, I have retreated, bringing with me my sick and
wounded, as well as those of Marshal Soult, left in my charge.
I inform your Majesty that I have decided not to serve again
in company with Marshal Soult."

King Joseph now had a most troublesome complication, and
a position that daily became more serious.   At one time, in
April, he was in hopes of seeing his affairs right themselves
again, in spite of the absence of all news of Soult's operations
in Portugal.   Marshal Victor, urged by the King of Spain and

by his staff to obey the emperor's instructions and invade Andalusia, had crossed the Tagus in three columns, and, re-forming again on the Guadiana, had, after passing that river, joined near Medellin Don Gregorio de la Cuesta, who retreated for several days before him. A severe battle having dispersed those large forces of the Spanish insurgents, on the 28th March, the marshal took up his position on the banks of the Guadiana, at the very time when General Sebastiani, at the head of two divisions, was defeating the army of Estremadura at Ciudad Real, and driving it back to the entrance of the Sierra Morena. There they awaited the movement ordered in the instructions given to Soult, the pivot of the whole campaign, projected by Napoleon before his departure for Paris. It was in Germany, just after the battle of Essling, that the emperor learned of the check caused to all his combinations by Soult's immobility at Oporto. Obstinate in directing himself the operations of armies at a distance, without the power of taking into account the state of public opinion, and without any knowledge of all that had occurred between the departure of the couriers and the arrival of peremptory orders no longer suitable to the sit-uation, the emperor conceived the idea of concentrating three armies under one man. Making all personal considerations bend to the order of seniority, he entrusted the command to Marshal Soult, thus investing him with supreme authority over Marshals Mortier and Ney. The order reached Madrid at the moment when the leaders of the armies were most keenly antagonistic. "You will send a staff-officer to Spain," Napo-leon had written to the minister of war, " with the orders that the forces of the Duke of Elchingen, the Duke of Trevisa, and the Duke of Dalmatia will form only one army, under the com-mand of the Duke of Dalmatia. These forces must only move together, to march against the English, pursue them inces-santly, defeat them, and throw them into the sea. Putting all considerations aside, I give the command to the Duke of Dal-matia, as being senior in rank. These forces ought to form from 50,000 to 60,000 men, and if the junction is promptly effected, the English will be destroyed, and the affairs of Spain arranged finally. But they must keep together, and not march in small parties. That principle applies to every country, but especially to a country where there can be no communication. I cannot appoint a place for the armies to meet, because I do not know what events have taken place. Forward this order to the king, to the Duke of Dalmatia, and to the two other marshals, by four different roads."

Whilst thus writing, constantly and justly apprehensive of the danger caused by the English army, Napoleon was still ignorant of the evacuation of Portugal. "Let your instructions to them be, to attack the enemy wherever they meet him," he said three days previously to General Clarke, "to renew their communications with the Duke of Dalmatia, and support him on the Minho. The English alone are to be feared; alone, if the army is not directed differently, they will in a few months lead it to a catastrophe."

The order sent by the emperor necessarily assisted in bringing about the catastrophe of which he was afraid. Marshal Soult, being deceived as to the plan of the English, and meditating an attack upon Portugal by Ciudad Rodrigo, wished to concentrate large forces for this purpose. He sent for Marshal Mortier, who was posted at Villacastin, where he covered Madrid, and demanded reinforcements from Aragon and Catalonia. The latter troops were refused him, and Generals Suchet and St. Cyr had great difficulty in keeping those two provinces in respect. Marshal Jourdan had foreseen the attack of the English on the Tagus, and was anxious about the position of Marshal Victor, isolated in Andalusia. Like the other leaders, the marshal acted independently, without attending to the orders from Madrid: he found himself compelled to fall back upon Talavera.

He was not to hold that post long. In spite of the extreme difficulty experienced by Sir Arthur Wellesley in maintaining a good understanding with his Spanish allies, he had marched to attack Marshal Victor, to whom King Joseph was sending reinforcements as quickly as he could. About 22,000 English soldiers were now on the field, reduced to such scarcity of provisions and money as to cause pillage and disorder, in spite of their commander's anger. Don Cuesta, with about 40,000 men under his orders, had been appointed, much against his will, to occupy the mountain passes. A Spanish army of 30,000 men, collected by General Venegas, was expected to join the two principal armies. On leaving Madrid, with the forces at his disposal, King Joseph had impressed upon Soult the necessity of attacking the enemy's rear, so that the Anglo-Spanish army might be crushed between superior forces. The marshal announced his departure.

Victor had had time to fall back upon Vargas, behind the Guadarama. Sir Arthur Wellesley crossed the Alberche, a tributary of the Tagus, and as soon as he found himself in presence of the enemy, wished to offer battle, urging Cuesta to join him in attacking Victor before the arrival of the enemy's reinforcements. The Spanish general declared that his honor was at stake in holding his positions, and absolutely refused to fight. The English alone, had not men enough at their disposal to contend with the French troops. Scarcely had the latter commenced their retreat when the Spanish, suddenly seized with the ardor of battle, rushed in pursuit, complaining that the " rascals withdrew so fast," wrote Cuesta to Wellesley, " that one cannot follow them in their flight." " If you run like that, you will get beaten," replied the English general, scornfully, annoyed at seeing himself perpetually thwarted in his able plans.

In fact when the Spaniards, a few days afterwards, at last engaged with the French, Marshal Victor's advance-guard were sufficient to drive Cuesta back as far as the English battalions, which had been prudently told off to support him. The fighting was gallant on the part of our troops, and helped to excite their ardor. King Joseph was urged to join battle: he feared an attack on Madrid, which he had been compelled to leave undefended, and reckoned upon the rapid movements of Soult, who had received orders to advance with all haste from Salamanca to Placentia. He had no experience of war, and neglected to take into account the chances of delay and the loss of troops during the march. Marshal Victor was daring, full of contempt for the Spanish troops, and ignorant of the qualities of the English army, which had not for a long time been seen on the continent. The French army advanced upon Talavera, which was strongly held by Sir Arthur. Hampered by the obstinacy and want of discipline of his Spanish allies, the English general had relinquished all attempts at daring, entrenching himself on the defensive. Marshal Soult had not arrived, being unable, he wrote, to effect his operation on the enemy's rear before the beginning of August. On the 27th of July, however, on occupying the ground before the English positions at Talavera, Victor gave orders to attack a height which was badly defended, and was driven back with heavy loss. Marshal Jourdan insisted on a delay of a few days, to allow Soult time to arrive; but the anxiety of King Joseph, and Victor's impatience, gained the day, and on the 28th, at daybreak, they attacked the mamelon, already threatened on the 27th.

Our troops gained the top under the English fire, but Sir Arthur had doubled the ranks of those in defence, and a terrible charge under General Hill compelled the French again to abandon the position.

The check was serious, and the soldiers began to be discouraged. By common consent, and without orders given by the leaders, the fight ceased. The English and French crowded on the two banks of a small brook which separated the two armies, and all quenched their thirst, without suspicion of treason or perfidy, and without a single shot being fired on either side. The French generals again discussed the question of resuming hostilities. "If this mamelon is not taken," exclaimed Victor, impetuously, "we should not take any part in a campaign." King Joseph, deficient in authority both of position and character, gave way. Sir Arthur Wellesley, seated on the grass at the top of a hill, surveyed the enemy's lines, and the defences, which he had just strengthened by a division, and a battery of artillery obtained with great difficulty from Cuesta. Till then the English had borne the brunt of the fighting; on General Donkin coming to tell Sir Arthur that the Spanish were betraying him, the general-in-chief quietly said, "Go back to your division." The attack was again begun, and this time directed against the whole line of the English positions, while Villate's brigade turned the mamelon to assail them in flank.

At this moment a charge of the enemy's cavalry poured upon our columns. A German regiment followed Seymour's dragoons, but were stopped by a watercourse, and pulled up: the English horsemen alone, boldly crossing the obstacle, made a furious attack on the French ranks, which opened to let them pass. In their daring impetuosity the dragoons went as far as our rear-guard, where they were stopped by new forces, and finally brought back with great loss to the foot of the mamelon. They stopped the flank movement however; and the centre of the English army, shaken for a moment, formed again round Colonel Donellan after a brilliant charge, and our soldiers were again driven back towards their position. The losses were great on both sides. The English did not attempt to pursue their advantages, and when the fight had ceased were satisfied with encamping on the heights of Talavera. Next day the French army withdrew beyond the

Alberche without being disturbed by the enemy, and waited finally for Marshal Soult's arrival.

He appeared on the 2nd of August at Placentia, too late for his glory as well as for the success of the French arms, though in time to modify Wellesley's plans. The latter had commenced to advance towards him, thinking he should meet forces inferior to his own; but Mortier had already followed Soult, Ney's troops were advancing by Salamanca, and King Joseph was preparing to put under him all his regiments, except those accompanying General Sebastiani in his march towards Madrid. Sir Arthur Wellesley understood the dangers of his position: his troops were tired, and badly fed; and not wishing to risk again the lot of arms, he hurriedly recrossed the Tagus, taking care to blow the bridges up, and fell back upon Truxillo, by the rugged mountain passes. The want of a proper understanding, and the mutual distrust which during the whole campaign had reigned between the English and Spanish, had borne their fruits. Wellesley's soldiers, deprived of the resources to which they had been accustomed, and which they had a right to expect from their allies, died in great numbers in their encampments on the bank of the Guadiana: their wounded had been abandoned at Talavera, when Cuesta evacuated that position. Sir Arthur gave vent to his bitter complaints in writing to Frère, the English *chargé d'affaires* at the insurgents' head-quarters: "I wish the members of the Junta, before blaming me for not doing more, and charging me beforehand with the probable results of the faults and imprudence of others, would be good enough to come here, or send somebody to supply the wants of our army dying of hunger, and actually after fighting two days, and defeating in the service of Spain an enemy of twice their number, without bread to eat. It is a positive fact that for the last seven days the English army has not received a third of its provisions, that at this moment there are 4000 wounded soldiers dying for want of the care and necessaries which any other country in the world would have supplied, even to its enemies, and that I can derive assistance of no kind from the country. I cannot even get leave to bury the dead bodies in the neighborhood. We are told that the Spanish troops sometimes behave well: I confess that I have never seen them behave otherwise than badly."

The emperor's anger was extreme on learning the check our troops had received at Talavera. He wrote to Marshal Jourdan, indignantly recapitulating all the blunders made during the campaign, without at all considering the difficulties everywhere caused by orders sent from a distance, in ignorance of the actual facts of the situation. "When at last they decided to give battle," Napoleon summed up, "it was done without energy, since my arms were disgraced. Battle should not be given, unless seventy chances in one's favor can be counted upon beforehand: even then, one should not offer battle unless there are no more chances to be hoped for, since the lot of battle is from its nature always doubtful: but once the resolution is taken, one must conquer or perish, and the French eagles must not withdraw till all have equally put forth every effort. There must have been a combination of all these faults before an army like my army of Spain could have been beaten by 30,000 English: but so long as they will attack good troops, like the English ones, in good positions, without reconnoitring these positions, without being certain of carrying them, they will lead my men to death, and for nothing at all."

The Spanish armies were, after the battle scattered everywhere, according to their custom, to appear again in a short time like swarms of wasps to harass our soldiers. Sir Arthur Wellesley entrenched himself at Badajoz, ready to fall back upon Portugal. No definitive result had crowned the bloody campaign just completed, but it had an influence upon the negotiations then being carried on in Spain. An attempt, long prepared by the English, and to which they attached a great importance, now occupied the Emperor Napoleon's mind still more than the affairs of Spain.

For several weeks it was believed that the great maritime expedition organized on the coasts of England was for the purpose of carrying overwhelming reinforcements to Spain. A first attempt, of less importance, was directed against our fleets collected at the island of Aix, near Rochefort. Admiral Willaumez, in charge of an expedition to the Antilles, had to rally the squadrons of Lorient and Rochefort, and being unavoidably delayed at the latter place, it was there that Admiral Gambier came to attack our vessels. Vice-Admiral Allemand carefully fortified the isle of Aix against an attack, the nature of which he had foreseen, though not the extent. During the night of the 11th and 12th April, conducted by several divisions, composed of frigates and brigs, thirty large fire-ships were suddenly launched against our vessels, exploding in all directions, breaking the wooden bars by the weight of their

burning masses, adhering to the sides of the ships and compelling even those which they did not set on fire to go aside to
avoid dangers which were more to be dreaded.   Thanks to the
skill and bravery of our sailors, none of the vessels perished by
fire; but four of them ran aground at the mouth of the Cha-
rente, and were attacked by the English.   The *Calcutta* surrendered after several hours' fighting—her commander, Captain Lafon, having to pay with his life for the weak resistance he
is said to have made.   The English blew up the *Aquilon* and
Varsovie, and Captain Roncière himself set fire to the *Ton-
nerre*, after landing all his crew.   Napoleon's continued efforts
to form a rival navy in France constituted a standing menace
to England.   After the cruel expedition of the isle of Aix, the
principal effort was to be directed against Antwerp, always an
object of English jealousy and dissatisfaction, as a commercial
port, or as a place of war.   The works which the emperor had
been carrying on there increased their anxiety, and on the 29th
July forty vessels of the line and thirty frigates appeared in
sight of the island of Walcheren.   From 700 to 800 transport-
ships brought an army to be landed, under the orders of Lord
Chatham,   Pitt's elder brother, and containing about 40,000
men, with much artillery.   The emperor was at once informed,
and M. Decrès, minister of the marine, proposed to station at
Flushing the fleet of Admiral Missiessy.   The latter refused,
saying that he would not let himself be taken, and did not
wish to see his crews decimated by the Walcheren fever.   That
was the auxiliary upon which Napoleon reckoned against the
English expedition; and rightly, too.

Walcheren was slightly and badly fortified; the emperor
considering Flushing to be quite impregnable.   "You say that
the bombardment of Flushing makes you apprehensive of its
surrender," he wrote on the 22nd August.   "You are wrong
to have any such fear.   Flushing is impregnable so long as
there is bread in it, and they have enough for six months.
Flushing is impregnable, because there is a moat full of water,
which must be crossed; and finally, because by cutting the
dykes they can inundate the whole island.   Write and tell
everywhere that Flushing cannot be taken, unless by the
cowardice of the commandants; and also that I am certain of
it, and that the English will go off without having it.   The
bombs are nothing—absolutely nothing; they will destroy a
few houses, but that has no effect upon the surrender of a
place."

General Monnet, who commanded at Flushing, was an old officer of the revolution wars, brave and daring and he did his best in opposing the landing of the English, with a part of his forces, and in gallantly defending the place; but the inundation did not succeed, on account of the elevation of the ground and the wind being contrary. Therefore when Napoleon wrote to Fouché, Flushing had already capitulated, under the efforts of the most formidable siege artillery. The Dutch commandant surrendered the forts Denhaak and Terweere at the same time as Middelburg. The feeling of the Dutch nation, formerly favorable to republican France, had been modified since the imperial decrees ruined all the transit trade, the source of Holland's wealth. King Louis alone hastened to the assistance of the French army, advancing with his little army between Santvliet and Antwerp. Four Dutch regiments were fighting in Germany, and a small corps had been sent into Spain. Thus, while extending his enterprises in remote parts, the unbounded ambition of Napoleon left unprotected the very centre of his empire.

General Rousseau, however, succeeded in protecting the island of Cadsand, and Admiral Strachan and Lord Chatham recalled to the eastern Scheldt the forces which had been intended for the attack on that island. The English forces began to land upon the islands of North and South Beveland, in order to attack Fort Batz at the junction of the two Scheldts, and thus outflank the French fleet lying in the western Scheldt. Fortunately, Admiral Missiessy had the advantage over the English commanders in speed, and sailing up into the higher Scheldt, formed by the two branches of the river, he arranged his vessels under forts Lillo and Liefkenshoek which by their cross-fires protected the river from bank to bank. Antwerp was thus safe from attack by sea; at Paris there was great anxiety as to attacks by land.

A few provisional demi-brigades, the gendarmes, and picked national guards, about 30,000 men altogether—such were the forces at the disposal of the war minister. He durst not—nobody durst, change the destination of the troops already marching to Germany. The minister of marine and Fouché at once proposed a general levy of the national guard, under the orders of Bernadotte—one being daring and dissatisfied, the other fostering discontent of every kind openly or secretly, and still remembering the revolutionary procedure. The Council, presided over by the Arch-chancellor Cambacérès, refused to authorize the calling out of the national guards without the emperor's express order; but Fouché, without waiting for orders, wrote on his own authority to all the prefects, and stirred up everywhere a patriotic zeal. At first Napoleon approved of the ardor of his minister of police, and severely rated the arch-chancellor and minister of war for their prudence. "I cannot conceive what you are about in Paris," he wrote to General Clarke on the 10th August; "you must be waiting for the English to come and take you in your beds. When 25,000 English are attacking our dockyards and threatening our provinces, is the ministry doing nothing? What trouble is there in raising 60,000 of the national guard? What trouble is there in sending the Prince of Pontecorvo to take the command there, where there is nobody? What trouble is there in putting my strongholds, Antwerp, Ostend, and Lille, in a state of siege? It is inconceivable. There is none but Fouché who appears to me to have done what he could, and to have felt the inconvenience of remaining in a dangerous and dishonorable position:—dangerous, because the English, seeing that France is not in movement, and that no impulse is given to public opinion, will have nothing to fear, and will not hurry to leave our territory; dishonorable, because it shows fear of opinion, and allows 25,000 English to burn our dockyards without defending them. The slur thus cast upon France is a perpetual disgrace. Circumstances vary from moment to moment. It is impossible for me to give orders to arrive within a fortnight. The ministers have the same power as I, since they can hold a council and pass decisions. Make use of the Prince of Pontecorvo—make use of General Moncey. I send you besides Marshal Bessières, to remain in Paris in reserve. I have ordered a levy of 30,000 men of the national guard. If the English make progress, make a second levy of 30,000 in the same or other departments. It is evident that the enemy, feeling the difficulty of taking Flushing, intend marching straight to Antwerp, to make a sudden attempt upon the squadron."

Flushing had succumbed, but the operations of the English were delayed by their indecisive generalship. Hope's division easily took possession of Fort Batz, but the main body of the army remained behind. The fortifications of Antwerp were daily increased and strengthened. The engineers, under Decaux, who checked the warlike ardor of King Louis, rendered the forts impregnable to sudden assault, inundated the country all round, and erected the old dams on the Scheldt; and troops

also began to arrive, rapidly concentrating upon the threatened spot. According to the emperor's order the Prince of
Pontecorvo had set out for Antwerp, and took the command
there. While the army was being formed round the town, the
English with great difficulty got their fleet into the Scheldt as
far as Fort Batz. Their forces being already considerably reduced by the fever, and the preparations made at Antwerp to
receive them causing Lord Chatham some uneasiness, he held
a council of war on the 26th, and sent their decision to London, where it was approved by the ministry. It was too late
now to attack Antwerp, the opportunity having been lost; and
the huge army, collected with so much display, fell back upon
the island of Walcheren, and a large number of the vessels
sailed for the Downs. Every day 800 casks of fresh water
were brought from the Downs to the garrison still occupying
Flushing, Middelburg, and the forts. The English were completely checked; and there were already signs that they might
evacuate the island of Walcheren altogether.

The emperor triumphed at Shœnbrunn. Advising his generals not to attack the English, but to leave them to be killed
by ague, he congratulated himself on the unexpected reinforcement thus gained by his army. "It is a continuation of the
good fortune attending our present circumstances," he wrote,
"that this expedition, which has reduced to nothing England's
greatest effort, gives us an army of 24,000 men, which otherwise we should have been unable to get." He at once made
use of it to organize the new army of the north, suddenly
called out by the country's danger. At the same time, by a
strong instinct of government, he severely blamed the revolutionary movement which Fouché had excited in the depart
ments. On the 26th September he wrote to him: "I have your
letter informing me that the ' cadres ' of the regiment for the
national guard are formed everywhere. I know it, but am
not pleased at it. Such a measure cannot be taken without
my order. There has been too great haste; all that has been
done will not hasten by a single hour the arming of the national guard, if they are needed. That causes fermentation,
whereas it would have been sufficient to put in movement the
national guards of the military divisions which I have indicated. Then you call out the national guards of Flanders to assist on the frontiers by which the enemy intend invading
Flanders; the reason is obvious. But when there is a levy in
Languedoc, Piedmont, Burgundy, people think there is an

agitation, though there is none.   My intentions are not fulfilled, and I am put to unnecessary expense."

The command, accordingly, was withdrawing from the Prince of Pontecorvo, who, though always called to serve at the moment of danger, was considered fickle and suspicious by the emperor.   "You will let him know," wrote Napoleon to his minister of war, "that I am displeased with his 'order of the day;' that it is not true that he had only 15,000 men, when, with the soldiers of the Duke of Conegliano and Istria, I have on the Scheldt more than 60,000 men; but that even if he only had 15,000, his duty was to give the enemy no hint of it.   It is the first time that a general, from excess of vanity, has been seen to betray the secret of his position.   He at the same time eulogized the national guards, who know very well themselves that they have had no opportunity of doing anything.   You will also express to him my dissatisfaction with his Paris correspondence, and insist upon his ceasing to receive mischievous letters from the wretches whom he encourages by such conduct.   The third point as to which you will indicate to him my intentions is, that he should go to the army or to the waters."

The useless attempt of the English at Walcheren, and their prudent retreat from Antwerp, was made use of by the French diplomatists who were still discussing the terms of peace at Altenburg.   The Emperor Napoleon, however, was tired of the delays of their negotiations.   Being now certain that Austria could have no more support, he received Bubna and Prince John of Lichtenstein, who had been sent to him directly by the Emperor Francis.   Napoleon haughtily dwelt upon the value of the concessions which he had already granted.   "What!" said he to the envoys, "I had not yet relinquished the principle of the *uti possidetis*, and now I relinquish it at your emperor's request!   I claimed 400,000 souls of the population of Bohemia, now I cease to demand them!   I wished 800,000 souls in Upper Austria, and I am satisfied with 400,000!   I asked for 1,400,000 souls in Carinthia and Carniola, and I give up Klagenfurth, which is a further sacrifice of 200,000 souls.   I therefore restore to your master a population of a million of subjects, and he says I have made no concession!   I have only kept what is necessary to keep the enemy away from Passau and the Inn—what is necessary to connect the territories of Italy and Dalmatia; yet they persuade him that I have not modified any of my demands!   It is thus that they have led on the Emperor Francis to war; it is thus that they will finally bring him to ruin!" He refrained, however, from replying to the Emperor Francis's letter. "It were undignified for me to say to a prince, 'You don't know what you say;' but that is what I find myself compelled to say, since his letter is founded upon an error." "Leave vain repetitions and silliness to the Austrians," he wrote to Champagny. At the same time he reviewed his troops, and hurried the movements of the reinforcements which were arriving. The Emperor Alexander had received Austria's promise to make a speedy settlement, refusing to take part in the negotiations, and trusting that Napoleon would look after his interests. The only point which he reserved was the Polish question: he was afraid of the increase of the grand duchy of Warsaw. "Your Majesty can give me a certain pledge of your friendship towards me," he wrote to Napoleon on the 31st August, "by recalling what I frequently said at Tilsit and Erfurt, as to the interests of Russia with reference to the affairs of Poland (lately so-called), and what I have since instructed your ambassador to repeat to you."

It was precisely upon Galicia that the ambitious views of Napoleon were at that moment directed. Being repeatedly pressed by the Austrian envoys to explain his definitive intentions, he at last declared that he wished Carniola, the circle of Wilbach, and the right bank of the Save as far as Bosnia; ceding Linz, and keeping Salzburg. He thus became master of 1,500,000 souls in Austria. In Galicia he claimed all the territory which Austria had obtained at the second partition of Poland, as well as the circles of Solkiew and Zeloczow, which he intended to cede to Russia, in order to restrain her displeasure. The population of these territories amounted to 2,000,000 souls. To these conditions Napoleon added a war contribution of 100,000,000, and the obligation of Austria reducing her army to 150,000 men. The Austrian diplomatists succeeded in getting off 15,000,000 from the military contribution. That was the only favor granted. "I have given Austria the most advantageous peace she could expect," wrote Napoleon to the Emperor Alexander, on the 10th October, 1809. "She only cedes Salzburg and a small district on the Inn; she cedes nothing in Bohemia; and on the Italian side she only cedes what is indispensable to me for communication with Dalmatia. The monarchy therefore remains entire. It is a second experiment which I wished to make, and I have shown towards her a moderation which she had no right to expect. In doing so I trust to have pleased your Majesty. You will see that, in accordance with your desires, the greater part of Galicia does not change masters, and that I have been as careful of your interests as you could have been yourself, by reconciling everything with what honor demands from me. For the prosperity and well-being of the duchy of Warsaw, it is necessary that it should be in your Majesty's good graces; and the subjects of your Majesty may be assured that in no case, on no contingency, ought they to expect any protection from me."

So many protestations and flattering assurances could not destroy the effect of the development of the grand duchy of Warsaw, and the constant menace created for Russia by that partial resuscitation of a Poland submitted to French influence. The Emperor Alexander made Caulaincourt sensible of this by a few sharp words. The secret discord was now increasing between the two allies, in proportion as the divergence of their interests made itself felt. The unreasonable passions of Napoleon were soon to open between them the gulf into which he was to drag France.

The Tyrol was not included in the negotiations of peace, any more than in the armistice. When at last the treaty was signed at Vienna, on the 20th October, a few days after the discovery of a plot to assassinate Napoleon, the fighting was still continued in the mountains with the keen determination of despair. In vain did Prince Eugène offer the insurgents a general pardon, confirming the subservience of their country; the peasants proudly rejected the conditions offered them. Crushed by the combined French and Bavarian forces, the Tyrolese succumbed with glory: their popular leader, Andrew Hofer, was taken in a remote mountain retreat where he had taken refuge, brought to Mantua on the 19th January, 1810, and there shot on the 25th February, by Napoleon's express order. "I gave you instructions to have Hofer brought to Paris," wrote Napoleon to the Viceroy of Italy; "but since he is at Mantua, send an order to have him tried at once by court-martial, and shot on the spot. Let it be an affair of twenty-four hours." Hofer underwent his fate with an heroic and pious simplicity. It was only in 1824 that Austria paid to this humble patriot the honors due to his memory, his body being then transported to Innsbruck, and buried there with pomp in the cathedral. A statue was placed on his tomb.

CHAPTER XII.

THE DIVORCE (1809—1810).

On his return to France, after the peace of Vienna, the Emperor Napoleon, though triumphant and all-powerful to those who looked only on the surface, felt secretly conscious that his supreme prestige had been shaken. He experienced the necessity of strengthening and consolidating his conquests by some startling act, and of finally founding upon immovable bases that empire which he had raised by his victorious hands without ever believing it really permanent. The advances made at Erfurt towards a family alliance with the Emperor of Russia remained without any result, in spite of the friendly protestations of the Emperor Alexander; and since Napoleon's return to Paris those admitted to his closest intimacy detected a perceptible change in his manner. "He seemed to be walking in the midst of his glory," wrote the Arch-chancellor Cambacérès. It was to him that Napoleon first broached the project of divorce, which was soon to become a settled determination. The loving tone in which he wrote to her as his wife might well deceive the Empress Josephine; for Napoleon still retained some love for her, though it was powerless in hindering his ambitious resolutions. The rumor of the great event was already spreading in Paris and Europe, though Josephine was still unaware of it. She was uneasy, however, and numerous indications daily increased her anxiety: her children shared her apprehension. The whole of the imperial family were assembled about their renowned head, divided as they were in their inclinations and interests; and Napoleon had himself summoned Prince Eugène to Paris.

Under the emperor's order, Champagny had already written to Caulaincourt: "You will wait upon the Emperor Alexander, and speak to him in these terms: 'Sire, I have reason to believe that the emperor, at the request of the whole of France, is making arrangements for a divorce. May I write to say that they can reckon on your sister? Let your Majesty take two days to consider it, and give me frankly your reply, not as

French ambassador, but as a man warmly devoted to both families. It is not a formal request that I now make; it is a confidential expression of your intentions that I beg from you. I am too much accustomed to tell your Majesty all my thoughts to be afraid of ever being compromised by you.' "

Caulaincourt was greatly perplexed. The peace of Vienna had been badly received at St. Petersburg, and had caused so many complaints and recriminations that the French ambassador found himself compelled to appease the irritation which threatened to break the alliance, by translating Napoleon's promises into official engagements. The terms of the convention were agreed upon by the diplomatists, and it was about to be signed. Napoleon engaged never to re-establish the kingdom of Poland; the names Poland and Polish were to disappear in all the acts; the grand duchy could not for the future be increased by annexing any part of the old Polish monarchy: the conditions of the convention were binding upon the King of Saxony, Grand Duke of Warsaw. At the same time that he was begged to accept this unsuitable engagement, Napoleon had harshly reminded his ally of the inaction of his forces during the war. " I wish," said he, " that in the discussions which take place, the Duke of Vicentia should make the following remarks to Romanzoff: ' You are sensible that there is nothing of the past that the emperor has laid hold of: in the affairs of Austria you made no sign. How has the emperor acted? He has given you a province which more than repays all the expense you have incurred for the war; and openly declares that you have joined to your empire Finland, Moldavia, and Wallachia.' "

However delicate the circumstances and question were which Caulaincourt had to propose, he obeyed. The Emperor Alexander was not disinclined to listen to the proposals, but would have preferred first to make sure of the signature to the convention relative to Poland as the price of his acceptance. The empress mother, dissatisfied and spiteful, suggested religious objections. The kind considerations of Napoleon seemed boundless. The Emperor Alexander and his advisers asked time to consider.

Meantime the projected divorce had become known in Paris, even in the bosom of the imperial family. Napoleon could not longer keep his secret. In presence of the vague uneasiness of the empress his mind was burdened with some feeling of remorse for the act which he was secretly meditating, and he at last gave her some hint of his intention, as well as of the reasons for his decision, and the pain it had caused him. The unhappy Josephine screamed, and fell fainting. When she recovered consciousness, she was supported by her daughter the Queen of Holland, who was also in tears, and proudly offended at the harshness which Napoleon had shown her in the first moment of his anger at the sight of Josephine's sufferings. Soon moved by the return of better and truer sentiments which still exercised a certain influence upon him, the emperor shared the sorrows of the mother and daughter, without for a moment relaxing by word or thought the determination which he had formed. Prince Eugène, as well as Queen Hortense, had declared their intentions of following their mother in her retirement; Napoleon opposed it, and overwhelmed with presents and favors the wife whom he was forsaking for reasons of state. Two days after solemnly breaking the tie by which they were united, he wrote to her at Malmaison, with much genuine affection in spite of his strange and imperious style:—"My dear, you seem to me to-day weaker than you ought to be. You showed courage, and you will do so again in order to support yourself. You must not let yourself sink into a fatal melancholy. You must be happy, and, before everything, take care of your health, which is so precious to me. If you are fond of me and love me, you ought to show some energy, and make yourself happy. You understand my sentiments towards you very imperfectly, if you imagine that I can be happy when you are not so, and satisfied when you are still anxious. Good-bye, darling; pleasant dreams! Be assured that I am sincere."

The Empress Josephine had often shown a fickle character and frivolous mind; but being kind, obliging, and gifted with a grace that had gained her many friends before her greatness had surrounded her with courtiers and flatterers, she was popular; and the public, who were not in favor of the divorce, sympathized with her sorrow. On the 15th December, 1809, in a formally summoned meeting of the imperial family, with the arch-chancellor and Count Regnault d'Angely also present, Napoleon himself openly announced the resolution which he had taken. "The policy of my monarchy, the interest and wants of my peoples which have invariably guided all my actions, require," said he, "that I should leave this throne on which Providence has placed me, to children inheriting my love for my peoples. For several years, however, I have lost hopes of having children by my marriage with my well-beloved spouse the Empress Josephine, which urges me to sacrifice the dearest affections of my heart, to consider only the well-being of the State, and to will the dissolution of our marriage. God knows how much such a resolution has cost my heart; but there is no sacrifice which is beyond my courage, if proved to be useful to the well-being of France."

The Empress Josephine wished to speak, but her voice was choked by her tears; she handed to Count Regnault the paper evidencing her assent to the emperor's wishes. A few words spoken by Prince Eugène, as he took his place in the Senate, confirmed the sacrifice; and by a "senatus-consulte" the civil marriage was formally dissolved. The religious marriage gave rise to greater difficulty. The absence of the proper curé and of the witnesses required by the rules of the Church served as a pretext, in spite of the protestations of Cardinal Fesch, who had celebrated the marriage, and declared that the Pope had granted him full dispensation. There was no intention of consulting the pontiff on this occasion. The emperor sent an address to the magistracy of Paris, like the meanest of his subjects, declaring that his consent had not been complete; he had only agreed to a useless formality with the object of tranquillizing the conscience of the empress and that of the holy father, feeling certain since then that he must have recourse to a divorce. The scruples of the ecclesiastics were overcome; and the religious marriage declared null by the diocesan and metropolitan authorities. The news was inserted in the *Moniteur*, together with the decree settling upon the repudiated empress a magnificent dowry.

The reply from St. Petersburg, however, was still forthcoming, and the emperor began to feel very angry. The King of Saxony had already made overtures, offering the hand of his daughter to his illustrious ally; and soon still more flattering hopes were aroused. The peace party ruled in Vienna, Metternich having replaced Stadion in power; and some words of Swartzenburg, the new ambassador at Paris, seemed to imply matrimonial advances. The Archduchess Marie-Louise was eighteen years of age, amiable and gentle in disposition: the alliance was a brilliant one, and would permanently establish a good understanding between Austria and France. Many intrigues were now started: those of the politicians or courtiers who held to the old régime by tradition or taste were in favor of the Austrian marriage; they were supported by Prince Eugène, Queen Hortense, and even by the Empress Josephine herself, though not avowedly. The imperial family and councillors, sprung from the French Revolution, had a repugnance to alliance with the house of Austria, as a return towards the past, which was still present to the minds of all: they dwelt upon the dangers of a rupture with Russia, who would be indignant at seeing herself scorned after being sought for. There were fewer objections on the side of Austria, already beaten and humiliated. The emperor hesitated, and twice consulted his most intimate council. At the second sitting his mind was made up. The delay of Russia had stirred up his anger, and, according to his custom, he listened only to his haughty and implacable will. Orders were given to Caulaincourt to overthrow the negotiations respecting the Grand Duchess Catherine. Marriage with the Archduchess Marie-Louise was resolved upon.

The Emperor Francis showed none of the repugnance or hesitation which irritated Napoleon against the Russians. No gloomy forecast seems to have passed through the minds of that august family, which had formerly seen Marie-Antoinette leave Vienna to sit at Paris upon a fatal throne. Yet all the efforts of both the emperors tended to suggest constant analogies. Napoleon's contract was copied from the act which united the destinies of Louis XVI. and Marie-Antoinette. The marriage ceremonial was throughout the same, with the redoubled splendor of an unprecedented magnificence. The new empress had willingly accepted the throne which was offered her. The Archduke Charles agreed to represent the Emperor Napoleon at the celebration of the official marriage. Marshal Berthier, major-general of the Imperial army, was appointed to go and fetch the princess. Her first lady of honor was the Duchess of Montebello, widow of Marshal Lannes, who was killed at Wagram. The tragical remembrances of by-gone alliances between France and the reigning house of Austria, the bitter and bloodstained recollections of recent struggles, seemed to serve only to enhance the brilliancy of the new ties uniting the two countries. The Emperor Napoleon took possession of the imperial family, as he had recently conquered their capital and occupied their palaces. The people of Paris thought they saw in this alliance a final and permanent triumph: and the magnificence of the *fêtes* given in honor of the young empress's arrival increased their intoxication. "She brings news to the world of peaceful days," was the inscription on all the triumphal arches.

In fact the world was hopeful, but men of foresight and

wisdom were not deceived. There were germs of discord everywhere, in spite of the appearance of peace. Fighting was still going on in Spain, and the obstinacy of the Spanish insurgents equalled the perseverance of Sir Arthur Wellesley. The Emperor Alexander had courteously congratulated Caulaincourt upon the assurance of peace between Austria and France, resulting from the projected union; at the same time not failing to point out the contradictory negotiations simultaneously carried on by Napoleon at St. Petersburg and Vienna. The substitution, which the emperor had just proposed, of a new convention for the articles decided upon in the Polish question, deeply excited the Czar's displeasure. "It is not I who shall disturb the peace of Europe or attack any one," said he, with a keen and determined irony; "but if they come to look for me, I shall defend myself."

Another protestation, startling in its silence, annoyed the imperious ruler of Europe. Most of the cardinals had been brought to Paris, not without some threats of physical com pulsion, several of them weakly hoping to obtain important concessions. Cardinal Consalvi energetically supported the courage of a large number, who were determined to take no part in the emperor's religious marriage, as being illegal. They told Cardinal Fesch of their intention, adding, that they would afterwards wait upon the empress to be presented, but that they were bound to defend the rights of the holy seat, injured on that occasion by the appeal pure and simple to the magistracy of Paris. "That," said Cardinal Consalvi, "was wounding the emperor in the apple of the eye." "They will never dare!" answered Napoleon, angrily, when his uncle told him of the resolution of the cardinals.

Thirteen of them dared, notwithstanding. When, on the 2nd April, 1810, the Emperor Napoleon entered the great saloon of the Louvre, changed for that day into a chapel, after casting his eyes over the crowd who thronged the benches and galleries, he turned towards his chaplain, Abbé Pradt, and said, "Where are the cardinals? I don't see any." There were, however, fourteen there, though not enough to conceal the number of absentees. "There are many here," replied the abbé, "and several are old and infirm." "Ah! the idiots! the idiots!" exclaimed the emperor. He again repeated those words when the ceremony began.

Napoleon's anger was especially directed against Cardinal Consalvi. "The rest have their theological prejudices," said he, "but he has offended me on political grounds; he is my enemy; he has dared to lay a trap for me by holding out against my dynasty a pretext of illegitimacy. They will not fail to make use of it after my death, when I am no longer there to keep them in awe!" On the day after the marriage the whole court were to defile before the new empress, and the cardinals were in attendance with the utmost punctuality, as they had announced. After the distinguished assemblage had waited three hours, an aide-de-camp came to announce the order that the prelates who had not been present on the previous evening in the chapel of the Louvre were to withdraw, because the emperor would not receive them. On the same day, Napoleon wrote to M. Bigot de Préameneu: "Several cardinals did not come yesterday, although invited, to the ceremony of my marriage. They have, therefore, failed in an essential duty towards me. I wish to know the names of those cardinals, and which of them are bishops in France, in my kingdom of Italy, or in the kingdom of Naples. My intention is to discharge them from their office, and suspend the payment of their salaries by no longer regarding them as cardinals."

In the first impulse of his anger, Napoleon thought of summoning the rebel prelates before a special court. "Since there is no ecclesiastical jurisdiction in France," said he to the minister of public worship, "nothing prevents them from being condemned." He was contented, however, with making use only of his own supreme authority. Despoiled of the insignia of their ecclesiastical dignity—which procured them the nickname of the "black cardinals"—and deprived of their private fortunes as well as of the revenues of their dioceses, which had been sequestered by the treasury, Consalvi and his colleagues were interned, two and two. in towns assigned to them for the purpose, put under police supervision, and reduced to the most precarious means of living. "Without the Pope they are nothing," said Napoleon. The Pope was still kept at Savona, meekly inflexible, like the cardinals.

A few men thus resolutely opposed their wills to the formidable power of the Emperor Napoleon. Just after the peace of Vienna, his hands filled with new conquests, he modified the frontiers of several of the states which he had recently formed or increased; some territories he yielded up, others he took back; to some he was prodigal of his favors, to others he denied them. He showed at this time special severity towards King Louis, a prince who was naturally of a serious, honorable, and

upright character, and had tried sincerely to fulfil his duties as
king towards the Dutch. He thought it his duty to protect
against Napoleon himself the subjects which the latter had
given him, and whom he saw ruined by the arbitrary acts of
the imperial power. When, at the end of 1809, the emperor's
family all met in Paris, King Louis had great difficulty in persuading himself to obey the order by which he was summoned.
Napoleon had already threatened Holland in his speech at the
opening of the Legislative Body. "Placed between England
and France, the principal arteries of my empire meet there,"
said the emperor. "Changes will be necessary; the safety of
my frontiers, and naturally the interests of both countries, imperiously demand it." Zealand and Brabant had not been
evacuated by our troops, who advanced there when the English
took possession of the island of Walcheren.

It was the union of Holland and France which Napoleon
then intended, and he did not conceal it from his brother.
Recriminations and reproaches were only followed by an
obstinate determination. "Holland is really only a part of
France," said the minister of the interior, officially, "and it is
time she held her natural position." This determination was
announced to Louis on his arrival in Paris. "That is the
most deadly blow I can inflict upon England," said Napoleon.

The King of Holland had long and frequently cursed the
imperious will which had called him to the throne. He had
extolled the charms of private life; when abdication was, as it
were, forced upon him, he drew back and defended himself.
Napoleon insisted upon having a disguised national bankruptcy, an increase of their navy for French service alone, the
strict application of the "continental blockade," which till
then had been frequently evaded by the Dutch merchants, the
rejection of the honorary titles accepted or created by his
brother for the benefit of his subjects. King Louis struggled
against such hateful conditions, implying the ruin of his
adopted country as well as of his personal authority in Holland. The intimate relationship of the imperial family was
disturbed by the discussions carried on between the two
brothers; Champagny naturally had some share in them, and
Fouché also. Napoleon seemed to become more reasonable.
Nevertheless, he wished to take advantage of the alarm he
had caused, and make its influence extend even to England.
A trustworthy agent was appointed to inform the English
ministry of the impending union between France and Holland.

and the consequent danger for England; vast armaments were said to be prepared in our harbors. Peace was the only means of avoiding so many dangers; Holland would do herself honor by assisting to guarantee Europe of a rest now become possible by Napoleon's union with Marie-Louise.

Labouchère, descended from a family of French refugees, was appointed by the emperor, in the name of King Louis, to carry these overtures to the English cabinet. On account of the unfortunate campaign in Walcheren, which caused universal indignation in England, Canning and Castlereagh had been replaced in power by Perceval and the Marquis Wellesley, elder brother of Sir Arthur, formerly governor-general of India and the intimate friend of Pitt. He courteously received Labouchère, who was introduced by his brother-in-law, Mr. Baring, one of the principal bankers in London. It was not the first time that overtures of peace had reached the ministry. On his own account, and from the incessant passion for intrigue which seemed to haunt him everywhere, Fouché had instructed one of his agents to make to Lord Wellesley advances which had no real aim or earnestness. To these, as well as those, the English cabinet replied that they were firmly resolved never to abandon Spain or the kingdom of Naples to Bonaparte. Holland in King Louis' hands was unreservedly under French influence, and its union to the empire conveyed no threat of danger to England, which was, besides, well accustomed to the evils of the war, and determined to suffer the consequences to the last. Some new overtures with reference to modifying the continental blockade had been entrusted to Labouchère, but they were hampered and complicated by Fouché's intrigues. The minister of police had recently authorized Ouvrard to leave Vincennes, and employed him in those mysterious negotiations which was soon afterwards to cost him the confidence and favor of his master. At this time, however, it was against the King of Holland that the anger of the latter was let loose.

The emperor had agreed to delay his projected union, thus a second time granting his brother the honor of obedience. In accordance with his strict demands, he resolved to rectify the frontier separating Holland from Belgium, and by taking the Waal as the future limit to form two new French departments on this side the river, called Bouches-du-Rhin and Bouches-de-l'Escaut. Zealand and its islands, North Brabant, part of Guelder, and the towns Bergen-op-Zoom, Breda, Bois-le-Duc, and Nimeguen were thus taken away from Holland, with a population of 400,000 souls. Heavy conditions were imposed on the commerce; and the guard of all the river mouths was entrusted to Franco-Dutch troops under the orders of a French general.

Against this the conscience and reason of the King of Holland revolted equally. He gave secret instructions to his ministers to fortify Amsterdam, and forbid our troops to enter any stronghold. General Maison found the gates of Bergen-op-Zoom shut before him.

The action was as imprudent as the resolution was honorable. At the news of it Napoleon's violence exceeded all bounds. In accordance with the custom which he had followed for several weeks in his communications with his brother, with whom he was not on visiting terms, he wrote to Fouché, at the same time sending him a letter from Rochefoucault, the French minister in Holland:—

"I beg of you to read this letter, and call upon the King of Holland and let him know of it. Is that prince become quite mad? You will tell him that he has done his best to lose his kingdom, and that I shall never make arrangements which may make such people think they have imposed upon me. You will ask him if it is by his order that his ministers have acted, or if it is of their own authority: and let him know that if it is by their authority I shall have them arrested and their heads cut off, every one of them. If they have acted by the king's order, what must I think of that prince? And how, after that, can he think of commanding my troops, since he has perjured his oaths?"

Any personal resistance was impossible to the unhappy king of Holland, melancholy and obstinate, but without energy. He became afraid, and yielded every point; his ministers were dismissed, and the strongholds opened to the French generals. "Hitherto there has been no western empire," wrote Louis to his terrible brother; "there is soon to be one, apparently. Then, sire, your Majesty will be certain that I can no longer be deceived or cause you trouble. Kindly consider that I was without experience, in a difficult country, living from day to day. Allow me to conjure you to forget everything. I promise you to follow faithfully all the engagements which you may impose upon me."

King Louis set out again for Holland, after signing the conventions which were to disgrace him in the eyes of his subjects. Only one bitter item was spared him; he was not compelled to plead bankruptcy. Henceforth the valuation of things taken was to take place in Paris, and the French troops were already seizing in the annexed provinces the prohibited goods which were stored in the warehouses; and Marshal Oudinot fixed his head-quarters at Utrecht. On the 13th March, 1810, the emperor wrote to his brother: "All political reasons are in favor of my joining Holland to France. The misconduct of the men belonging to the administration made it a law to me; but I see that it is so painful to you, that for the first time I make my policy bend to the desire of pleasing you. At the same time, be well assured that the principles of your administration must be altered, and that, on the first occasion which you offer for complaint I shall do what I am not doing now. These complaints are of two kinds, and have as their object either the continuation of the relations of Holland with England, or reactionary speeches and edicts which are contrary to what I ought to expect from you. For the future your whole conduct must tend to inculcate in the minds of the Dutch friendship for France. I should not have taken Brabant, and I should even have increased Holland by several millions of inhabitants, if you had acted as I had a right to expect from my brother and a French prince. There is no remedy, however, for the past. Let what has happened serve you for the future."

Scarcely had the King of Holland returned to his kingdom, bringing back to his subjects the solitary consolation that their national independence was precariously preserved, when the emperor, who was then travelling through Belgium, came in great pomp to visit the new departments which he had just taken from his weak neighbor. The Empress Marie-Louise, who accompanied him, was everywhere surprised at the unprecedented display of forces and the activity of the empire. Napoleon inspected Flushing, which had been recently evacuated by the English; and at Breda received deputations from all the constituted authorities, the presence of a vicar-apostolic supplying an occasion for a violent attack upon the papacy. "Who nominated you?" asked he. "The Pope? He has no such right in my empire. I appoint the bishops charged with administering the Church. Render to Cæsar the things that are Cæsar's; it is not the Pope who is Cæsar, it is I. It is not to the Pope that God has committed the sceptre and the sword, it is to me. I have in hand proofs that

you will not obey the civil authority, that you will not pray
for me.   Why?   Is it because a Roman priest has excommuni-
cated me?   But who has given him the right to do so?   Who
can, here below, relieve subjects from their oath of obedience
to the sovereign instituted by the laws?   Nobody.   You ought
to know it, if you understand your religion.   Are you ignorant of the fact that it is your culpable pretensions which
drove Luther and Calvin to separate from Rome half the
Catholic world?   I also might have freed France from the
Roman authority, and forty millions of men would have fol
lowed me.   I did not wish to do so, because I believed the true
principles of the Catholic religion reconcilable with the principles of civil authority.   But renounce the idea of putting me
in a convent or of shaving my head, like Louis le Debonnaire,
and submit yourselves, for I am Cæsar; if not, I will banish
you from my empire, and I will disperse you, like the Jews,
over the face of the earth."

These irregular outbursts of arbitrary will loudly proclaim-
ing its omnipotence were excited by the very appearance of resistance.   The King of Holland had sought to defend the interests of his subjects; the captive chief of the Catholic Church
sometimes allowed the remains of his broken authority to appear; the most intimate counsellors of the emperor could not
always hide their disapprobation and uneasiness.   Fouché had
gone further still.   The emperor had in his hands proof of the
intrigues in which he had been engaged in Holland and England.   When Napoleon returned to Paris, Fouché did not present himself at the Council.   "What would you think," said
the emperor, "of a minister who, abusing his position,
should, without the knowledge of his sovereign, have opened
communications with the foreigner on bases of his own inven-
tion, and thus have compromised the policy of the State?
What punishment can be inflicted on him?"   Fouché had few
friends; no one, however, dared to pronounce his doom.   "M.
Fouché has committed a great fault," said Talleyrand.   "I
should give him a successor, but one only—M. Fouché himself."
Napoleon, dissatisfied, shrugged his shoulders, and sent away
his ministers.   His decision was taken.   "Your remarkable
views with regard to the duties of the minister of police do not
agree with the welfare of the State," he wrote to Fouché.
"Although I do not mistrust your attachment and your
fidelity, I am, however, compelled to maintain a perpetual surveillance, which fatigues me, and to which I ought not to be

condemned. You have never been able to understand that one may do a great deal of harm whilst intending to do a great deal of good."

Fouché was despoiled of his dignities, and relegated to the senatorship of Aix. General Savary, now become Duke of Rovigo, was chosen as minister of police. Napoleon was sure of his boundless and unscrupulous devotion, as well as of his executive ability. The decision of the emperor was ill received by the public. "I inspired every one with terror," says the Duke of Rovigo, in his "Memoirs;" "every one was packing up; nothing was talked about but banishments and imprisonments, and still worse; in fact, I believe that the news of a pestilence at some point on the coast would not have produced more fright than my appointment to the ministry of police." Savary succeeded to the ministry without any other resources than his personal sagacity and the activity of the police. Fouché had destroyed all traces of his administration. "I had not a great deal to burn, but all that I had I have burnt," said the disgraced minister, when the emperor sent to demand his papers. Many people breathed more freely when they heard this news. The Duke of Otranto became popular.

Nearly at the same moment the public interest was fastened on another rebelling personage, more worthy than Fouché of general esteem, and who had just dealt the emperor a more perceptible stroke. New difficulties had arisen between Napoleon and Louis Bonaparte, the vexations of the surveillance everywhere instituted in his States, the sufferings and the hindrances which resulted from it as regards the affairs of his subjects; the humiliation which he himself experienced from it every moment, exasperated the heart of King Louis. He wrote affectionately to the ministers whom he had been forced to dismiss. To this powerless manifestation of a natural feeling, strongly encouraged by the state of public opinion in Holland, was added the resolution to interdict the complete occupation of the territory by the French troops. The gates of Haarlem were closed to the imperial eagles. The populace of the Hague ill-treated in the street a servant of the minister of France. The emperor was only waiting for a pretext for a long time foreseen. Marshal Oudinot received orders to enter Haarlem and Amsterdam, with flags displayed. At the same time, the division of General Molitor entered Holland by the north and the south; everywhere the Netherlands found themselves occupied. The minister of Holland at Paris, Admiral Verhuell, received his passports.

Resistance was impossible; the councillors of King Louis felt it as bitterly as he did himself. The king was resolved upon not accepting the personal yoke that his brother wished to impose upon him; he signed an act of abdication in favor of his eldest son, until then favorably treated by the Emperor Napoleon. He committed to his ministers a touching farewell message for the Corps Législatif, and secretly entering a carriage, on the night of the 1st of July, 1810, he quitted Haarlem, in order to take refuge at the baths of Töplitz. The fugitive carefully concealed his journey and his presence; he was weary of the power which he sorrowfully exercised; he remained esteemed and regretted in the country which he sadly abandoned without having ever been able to defend it.

This flight from the throne, and this mute protest against the tyranny which rendered it insupportable, caused some ill-humor in Napoleon, and constrained him to act openly, and without the soothing forms with which he had reckoned upon enveloping his taking possession of Holland. An imperial decree of the 9th of July, 1810, announced to the world that Holland was reunited to France. The abdication of King Louis in favor of his son was treated as null and void. Rome had been declared the second city of the empire after the confiscation of the Papal States. Amsterdam was promoted to the third rank. Seven new departments were formed from the territory of the Netherlands. Holland was to send six members to the Senate of the Empire, six deputies to the Council of State, twenty-five to the Corps Législatif, two Councillors to the Court of Cassation. The emperor often vaunted the rare capacity of the Dutch whom he had thus drawn into his service. The first use which he now made of his supreme authority was to reduce the public debt from 80,000,000 to 20,000,000. This act of bankruptcy introduced into the charges of the budget an economy which it was thought ought to satisfy all those who had not personally to suffer the consequences. "The Corps Législatif will be another object of economy," wrote Napoleon, on the 23rd of July, to Lebrun, his arch-treasurer, whom he had charged to represent him in Holland; "the external relations will be an object of economy; the Council of State will be an object of economy; the civil list will be still another object of economy." The emperor had not reckoned on two sentiments, more powerful than all others in this little country, which had conquered its liberty at the price of so many sufferings.   Its union to France cost Holland its national independence; the bankruptcy tainted its honor and its credit; whilst submitting to an imperious necessity, the Dutch nation never forgot it.

The condition of Europe thus underwent, under the hand of the Emperor Napoleon, fundamental modifications, of which he scarcely took the trouble to inform his allies.   The Emperor Alexander alone received some explanations on the subject of the union of Holland and France.   "The Netherlands have not in reality had a change of master," Caulaincourt was instructed to say; "it is a country of lagoons, ports, and dockyards.   They are not much known on the continent, and have no importance except for England; the naval forces of France will be augmented by it, and the general peace will become more easy and more certain."   A few months only were to pass away before Napoleon would complete his maritime lines of defence, by taking possession of the coasts as far as the Weser and the Elbe. In the month of December, 1810, a simple decree formed three French departments* from the territory of the Hanseatic towns, the States of the Prince of Oldenburg and a small portion of Hanover.   In his quality of uncle to the Emperor Alexander, the Prince of Oldenburg received the town of Erfurt by way of indemnity.   At the same time the territory of the Valais became French, under the name of the department of the Simplon.   The former masters of the annexed countries received purely and simply a notification of the sovereign will. Irritation was everywhere increasing; no one resented these things more keenly than the Emperor Alexander, still a nominal ally of France.   Meanwhile he silently waited.

Quite close to Russia, in a country recently dismembered by the Emperor Alexander with the consent of Napoleon, there was preparing at this time an event which was soon to assure to the fifth European coalition one of its most useful supports. The King of Sweden, Gustavus IV., unstable, violent, and eccentric enough to warrant doubts as to the soundness of his reason, had been deposed on the 10th of May, 1809, by the assembled States, as the result of a military conspiracy.   His uncle, the Duke of Sudermania, elevated to the throne under the title of Charles XIII., had no children; the Diet designated as his successor the Duke of Augustenburg.   This prince expired suddenly, in the midst of a review.   The claimants were

---

* L'Ems Supérieur, les Bouches-du-Weser, and les Bouches-de-l'Elbe.

numerous, and the King of Sweden desired to know the wish of Napoleon. The latter secretly favored the King of Denmark, but the States were not well disposed in his favor: the emperor refused to give a decision. "A word from his Majesty would suffice to decide everything," said Désaugiers, the chargé-d'affaires at Stockholm. Some proposed to choose a stranger, and Marshal Bernadotte was thought of. During our occupation of Pomerania he had known how to render himself agreeable to the population over whom he ruled, and to persons of consideration who had known how to appreciate the vivacity and capacity of his mind. He was a kinsman of the Bonapartes, and conspicuous amongst the lieutenants of Napoleon. An obscure member of the Diet repaired to Paris, and knitted the first threads of an intrigue, destined to succeed by the very fact of the ignorance and illusions of its authors. By placing Bernadotte upon the steps of the throne, the States of Sweden thought to assure themselves of the good-will of the Emperor Napoleon; his name was popular amongst the lower classes. He was proclaimed Prince Royal of Sweden 17th August, 1810.

Napoleon had delayed too long to express his mind. A messenger arrived at Stockholm bearing despatches which emphatically disavowed the declarations of the partisans of Bernadotte. "I cannot think," said Napoleon, "that these individuals could have had the impudence to assert themselves to be charged with any mission whatever." The official announcement of the elevation of the Prince of Pontecorvo was already on its way to Paris. "I was little prepared for this news," replied Napoleon to the letter of King Charles XIII. He wished to wrest from Bernadotte a pledge never to bear arms against France. The marshal formally refused. For a long time in secret hostility to the emperor, he severely judged the errors of his ambition, and the consequences that would result for the peace of Europe. "Go then," said Napoleon, "and let destiny be accomplished!" On the evening of the 18th Brumaire, Bernadotte wrote to General Bonaparte: "My idea of liberty differs from yours, and your plan kills it. Three weeks ago I retired; but if I receive orders from those who have still the right to give me them, I shall resist all illegal attempts against the established powers."

The struggle was not to be long in breaking forth between the new heir to the throne of Sweden and the exacting master who claimed to subject all European powers to his laws. Everywhere the questions that grew out of the continental blockade in right as well as in practice, brought about difficulties, and gave rise to sufferings by which all the governments were injured. In annexing Holland to France, Napoleon had authorized, under a duty of 50 per cent., the sale of goods of English production which the contraband had kept stored up in their warehouses. He conceived the idea of applying the same duty to all sales of colonial products which until then had only been able to enter France by virtue of a special license. All the merchandise of this kind found in store, either in the countries dependent on the French Empire, or in foreign territories within four hours' journey of the frontier, were suddenly affected by this tax, and placed under the obligation of a certificate of origin (5th August, 1810). In default of this justification, the goods were seized as of English production, and in consequence contraband. The colonial produce was to be sold; the manufactured articles were to be everywhere burnt. In Spain, in the Canton of Tessin, at Frankfort, in the Hanseatic towns, at Stettin, at Custrin, at Dantzig, the troops were ordered to carry out the searches and seizures. A few dependent or vanquished sovereigns—Saxony or Prussia, for example— themselves consented to make the required requisitions. The sums produced by sales made in Prussia were generously credited by the Emperor Napoleon as deductions from the Prussian debt to France. A director of the French Customs superintended the Swiss troops in their inquisitions. At all points of the immense territory subjugated by Napoleon, the merchants crowded to the markets opened for confiscated goods, whilst every article proved to be of English manufacture was delivered to the flames in public. " For confiscation, for expulsion from the country, they came to substitute the punishment of burning," writes Mollien in his Memoirs; "and the reading of the correspondence of commerce might have convinced Napoleon what complaint the bankers and maritime speculators were making against a policy which, in the most industrious century, was destroying by fire the creations of industry. Until then, however, French manufacturers had flattered themselves with being able to supply the consumers whom English commerce was to lose by so severe a system of prohibition; but this illusion vanished when Napoleon, seduced by the hope of assuring to France a part in the enterprises of the commercial monopoly of England, was seen to be putting in some sort up to auction the right of introducing into Europe the productions of America and India, loading several raw ma-

terials—such as cotton and wool—with enormous duties, and,
by an inexplicable contradiction, rendering to the productions
of English industry, by these very taxes, more advantages than
prohibition caused them to lose.   Then this fictitious system,
which was to free the continent from the domination of English
commerce, became patent to all eyes as nothing else but the
most disastrous and false of fiscal inventions; for it was creating two monopolies in place of one—aggravating at once the
condition of the French manufacturers and that of the speculators of all countries, and giving up the privilege of commercial speculation to a few interested adventurers."

Hitherto the United States of America alone had protested
equally against the Emperor Napoleon's system of continental
blockade and the English ordinances.   Already, for several
months past, an embargo had been placed in their ports on
French and English vessels, unless driven to take refuge in
consequence of a tempest.   Mistress, the one of the seas, the
other of the land, it was on the United States that both England and France lavished their caresses, eager to enrol them
in the service of their hostile passions.   For a long time the
Emperor Napoleon had required the seizure of American
vessels sailing under a neutral flag, in spite of the interdiction
of their government, and this rigor had been one of the causes
of the dissensions between him and the King of Holland.   In
the month of July, 1810, he made known to Congress, that on
and after the 1st of November the Americans should not be
subject to the decrees of Berlin and Milan, and that they might
enter into the ports of France, provided that they could obtain
from England a revocation of the ordinances of the Council.
"In continuing to submit to them," Napoleon had formerly
said, "the peoples who are menaced by the pretensions of
England would do better to recognize her sovereignty, and
America ought to press forward to return under the yoke
from which she has so gloriously delivered herself."

On its part, the English cabinet revoked the ordinances of
the Council with regard to the Americans, and relieved them
of the toll by way of harbor dues imposed on all other vessels;
but it persisted in forbidding to neutral vessels the entry into
French ports, thus confirming its system of a paper blockade.
The measure was insufficient for the satisfaction of the United
States; it did little harm to that commerce and industry of
Great Britain which Napoleon strove so madly to injure by
land as well as by sea.

A sign of the discontent of the Emperor Alexander was his clearly manifested resolution not to impose upon his subjects new and exorbitant pecuniary sacrifices. Nearly all the European powers had accepted or submitted to the decree of the 1st of August. "There are no true neutrals," maintained Napoleon; "they are all English, masked under divers flags, and bearers of false papers. They must be confiscated, and England is lost." Russia constantly refused to yield to these entreaties. Faithful to the law of the blockade as regards the capture of English vessels, the Emperor Alexander authorized navigation under a neutral flag. No seizure was effected in his States.

Sweden protested in vain. Denmark had been authorized to effect the sale of prohibited merchandise by means of the fifty per cent. tariff; the new Prince of Sweden begged a similar indulgence in favor of his adopted country. The emperor, dissatisfied, was angered. "Choose," said he, "between the cannon-balls for the English or war with France." Bernadotte consented to commence hostilities against the English; he was without resources, and without defences. "We offer you our arms and our iron," wrote he to the emperor; "give us in return the means that nature has refused to us." Other allies were soon to accept the offers of the illustrious marshal of the empire.

Meanwhile the months rolled past, and Napoleon did not quit Paris. He had just contracted new ties; he was occupied with the cares necessitated by the internal administration of the empire—with the legal creation of the extraordinary Domain, the fruit of conquests and confiscations, and which had already served to supply without control the divers needs of the emperor. The very appearance of authority was thus little by little escaping from the Corps Législatif, the retiring deputies of which had their commissions arbitrarily prolonged. The representatives of the new departments had been directly chosen by the Senate. The censorship had been re-established, and its favorable decrees did not always suffice to save works and their authors. The "Germany" of Madame de Staël had received the authorziation of the censors, when the edition was seized and placed in the pillory. Madame de Staël was compelled to quit France in twenty-four hours. The rigors of Savary with regard to the press surpassed the traditions left by Fouché; the greater number of the journals were subjected to permanent fines, under the form of pensions to literary men.

The erection of eight state prisons seemed to presage times
still more harsh; however, the emperor demanded from the
Council of State, in order to explain the motive for these erec-
tions, a couple of pages of clauses "containing liberal ideas."
He had for a long time exercised towards France the power of
words; he knew their influence and weight. More than once,
in deeds of warfare his acts had gone beyond his promises;
the day had come when he was about to promise more than he
could perform. Liberal phrases no longer concealed from the
nation the yoke which crushed it. The pompous declarations
against the English leopard, hurled forth at the opening of the
session of the Corps Législatif, in December, 1809, did not
hasten the end of the war in Spain. The emperor did not set
out as he had solemnly announced. He called Marshal Masséna, scarcely recovered from his fatigue and his wounds
during the war in Germany, and confided to him the task of
vanquishing the English in Portugal. Sir Arther Wellesley
continued to occupy his positions between Badajoz and Alcantara. Since the battle of Talavera and the combats which then
accompained his last movements of troops, the English general
had not actively taken part in hostilities.

The war had not, however, ceased in Spain, and the insurgents had not diminished their efforts. General Kellermann
had depicted in its true light the particular character of the
struggle, when he wrote to Marshal Berthier: "The war in
Spain is not at all an ordinary affair. Doubtless one has not
to fear reverses and disastrous checks; but this stubborn nation wears away the army with its detailed resistance. Independently of the regular corps, which must be faced, it is also
necessary to guard against the numerous swarms of brigands
and strong organized bands, which infest the country, and
which by their mobility, and above all by the favor of the inhabitants, escape from all pursuit, and come up behind you a
quarter of an hour after your return. It is in vain that we
beat down on one side the heads of the hydra; they reappear
on the other, and without a revolution in the minds of men
you will not succeed for a long time in subduing this vast
peninsula. It will absorb the population and the treasures of
France. They wish to gain time, and to weary us by persistency. We shall only obtain their submission by their exhaustion, and the annihilation of half the population. Such is
the spirit which animates this nation, that one cannot even
create in it a few partisans. It is in vain to treat it with mode

ration and justice; in a difficult moment, no governor or
leader whatever would find ten men who would dare to arm
for his defence. We must, then, have more men. The emperor perhaps grows weary of sending them, but it is necessary
to make an end of the business, or to be contented with establishing ourselves in one half of Spain in order afterwards to
conquer the other. Meanwhile, resources diminish, the means
perish, money is exhausted or disappears; one knows not
where to direct one's energies to provide for the pay, for the
maintenance of the troops, for the needs of the hospitals, for
the infinite details necessary for an army in need of everything. Misery and privations increase sickness, and enfeeble
the army continually; whilst, on the other side, the bands
that swarm on all sides seize every day upon small parties or
isolated men, who venture into the open country with extreme
imprudence, notwithstanding the most positive, reiterated pro-
hibitions."

It was the effort of all the generals commanding in Spain to
destroy the bands of guerillas, who harassed their soldiers and
slowly decimated their armies. General Suchet had, more
than any other, succeeded in Aragon; General Gouvion St. Cyr
had been absorbed by the siege of Girone, which had at length
just submitted to him when Marshal Augereau was sent into
Catalonia, in order to take from him at once his command and
the glory of his conquest. The end of the campaign of 1809
had been signalized by a victory, gained on the 19th of November, at Ocaña, by Marshal Mortier and General Sebastiani over
the insurgent army of the centre. The central Junta had confided its powers to a commission, at the head of which was
the Marquis de la Romana, always more active than effective.
The insurrectional government retired into the Ile de Leon,
boldly convoking the Cortes at Madrid for the 1st of March,
1810.

Marshal Soult had become major-general of the army of
Spain, since Marshal Jourdan had been recalled after the battle of Talavera; he was meditating a great campaign against
Andalusia. Napoleon hesitated to consent to it; the English
alone appeared to him to be formidable, and he had been wishing to concentrate all his forces against them: Marshal Masséna was not, however, ready to enter on the campaign. King
Joseph received the authorization to advance upon Andalusia;
he ordered, at the same time, Marshals Ney and Suchet to lay
siege to Ciudad Rodrigo and Valencia. Both attempted opera-

tions with insufficient forces, and were to fail in an enterprise
which drew upon them the bitter reproaches of the emperor.
The army of the King of Spain advanced towards Seville; the
defiles of the Sierra Morena had been occupied without resistance by Marshal Victor.   The intestine dissensions which
divided the capital of Andalusia had deprived it of its means
of defence; a great part of the population took to flight.   A
few cannon, pointed from the ramparts, did not arrest for a
moment the march of the French.   Marshal Soult summoned
the place to surrender, and the Junta of the province consented
to capitulate.   All the military chiefs recently assembled in
Seville had succeeded in escaping.   King Joseph made his entry on the 1st of February, 1810.   Malaga and Granada were
not long in surrendering.

All the leaders of the insurrection were found henceforth at
Cadiz; the central Junta and its executive commission had
abdicated in favor of a royal regency.   The preparations for
resistance in this place, fortified on the side of the land by man,
as on the side of the sea by nature, disquieted King Joseph,
who had long been desirous of detaching a *corps d'armée*
against Cadiz.   "Assure me of Seville, and I will assure you
of Cadiz," said Marshal Soult.   Now it was found necessary to
guard Seville, Granada, and Malaga; a corps of observation
was being maintained before Badajoz; the forces which were
laying siege to Cadiz were necessarily restrained; everywhere
the Spanish armies were forming again.

Napoleon had been for a long time weary of the war in
Spain, which he had at first regarded as an easy enterprise;
he had conceived ill-feeling towards his brother, whom he
rightly judged incapable of accomplishing [the work which he
himself had been wrong in committing to his charge.   The
continual demands for men and money which came to him
from the peninsula hindered his operations and his schemes;
he resolved upon modifying the organization of the government in Spain.   On the 28th of January, 1810, he wrote to the
Duke of Cadore (Champagny): "Write by the express, and
several times, to the Sieur Laforest, at Madrid, in order that
he may present notes as to the impossibility of my continuing
to sustain the enormous expenses of Spain; that I have already
sent there more than 300,000,000; that such considerable ex-
portations of money exhaust France; that it is, then, indispensable that the engineers, the artillery, the administrations,
and the soldiers' pay should be henceforth supplied from the

Spanish treasury; that all which I can do is to give a supplemental grant of two millions per month for the soldiers' pay; that if this proposition is not agreed to, it will only remain for me to administer the provinces of Spain on my own account—in that case they will abundantly supply the maintenance and pay of the army. To see the resources of this country lost by false measures and a feeble administration, and to send thither my best blood, is impossible. The provinces have plenty of money, when the soldier is not paid he will pillage, and I know not what to do with him."

It was in the midst of his joy and his easy triumph in Andalusia that the severe protests of Napoleon arrived to surprise King Joseph. A few liberalities he had permitted himself with regard to his servants had succeeded in exasperating the emperor. He decreed the state of siege in all the provinces* to the left of the Ebro, confiding the military command to four generals—Augereau, Suchet, Reille, and Thouvenot. All the administrative powers were at the same time, committed to these generals, who were to correspond directly with the emperor. The idea of Napoleon, with which he acquainted his lieutenants, was to unite to France the territories which he thus isolated from the rest of the empire, as an indemnity for the sacrifices which the war had imposed upon him. General Suchet was charged with completing the conquest of the towns in Catalonia and Aragon which were still held by the insurgents. He achieved brilliantly the siege of Lerida.

At the same time, and in order to take away from King Joseph an authority which he knew not how to use, the armies in the country were divided into three corps. The army of the south was confided to Marshal Soult; the army of Portugal was waiting for the arrival of Marshal Masséna; the army of the centre—the least important of all—was alone left under the personal direction of King Joseph, who was appointed its general-in-chief. The embassies of King Joseph, the complaint of his wife, who was still in Paris, remained without result. In place of a central, powerless, and insufficient power, Napoleon was desirous of esablishing delegates of his supreme authority. He had sanctioned anarchy; the rights of the hierarchy had disappeared before the lieutenants of a chief arbitrary, but until now constantly attended by victory. Far from the presence of Napoleon, [in a country given over for

---

* Catalonia, Aragon, Navarre, and Biscay.

two years to the disorder of civil war, obedience had given place to mistrust, and regularity to disorder. Scarcely had Marshal Masséna joined the army of Portugal, of which he had accepted the command with regret, than he had immediately a perception of the difficulties which awaited it. The emperor had given orders to commence by the siege of Ciudad Rodrigo and of Almeida. Marshal Ney and General Junot, whose corps were placed under the command of Masséna, made such clamorous protests that the old marshal was obliged to display all his authority. "They say that Masséna has grown old," cried he with just anger; "they will see that my will has lost nothing of its force." Already Sir Arthur Wellesley, become Lord Wellington, was preparing not far from Lisbon, between the Tagus and the sea, that invulnerable position which history has designated "the lines of Torres Vedras." It was thither that he counted on drawing the French army, slowly exhausting its forces before an enemy patiently unassailable. The orders of Napoleon, and the deference of Masséna to these instructions, had spared us the danger of being attacked in the rear; when the French army advanced to encounter Lord Wellington, it had taken possession of Ciudad Rodrigo and Almeida, but the two sieges had been long and painful, having cost the lives of many soldiers; important garrisons occupied the places. In accordance with a mental habit which grew upon him through default of contradiction, the Emperor Napoleon did not admit the enfeeblement of his forces, whilst depreciating beforehand those of his enemy. "My cousin," wrote he on the 10th of September, 1810, to Marshal Berthier, "let a French officer set out immediately as bearer of a letter for the Prince of Essling, in which you will make him understand that my intention is that he should attack and rout the English; that Lord Wellington has no more than 18,000 men, of which only 15,000 are infantry, and the remainder cavalry and artillery; that General Hill has no more than 6000 men, infantry and cavalry; that it would be ridiculous for 25,000 English to hold in suspense 60,000 Frenchmen; that, by not groping about, but by attacking them openly, after having reconnoitred them, they will be made to experience severe repulses. The Prince of Essling has four times as many cavalry as he needs for defeating the enemy's army. I am too far off, and the position of the enemy changes too often, for me to be able to counsel you as to the manner of leading the attack, but it is certain that the enemy is not in a state to resist."

Marshal Masséna was wrong in accepting a mission of which he foresaw the immense dangers, and in refraining from personally impressing the emperor, by the weight of his old experience, as regards the illusions that were prevalent in Paris on the subject of the respective situations of the two armies. Counting upon victory on the day when he should succeed in meeting the enemy, he became involved, with 50,000 men, in the impracticable roads of Portugal in the vicinity of Lord Wellington, already his equal in forces, and seconded by the whole Portuguese nation in insurrection against the French. The lieutenants of Masséna, as bold and more youthful, estimated as he did the disastrous chances of the campaign. "Do not stand haggling with the English," replied Napoleon. He was obeyed.

Lord Wellington remained in his retreat upon the heights of Busaco, above the valley of Mondego, in front of Coimbra; he barred the passage to Marshal Masséna, who resolved to give battle. After a furious and sanguinary combat (27th of September, 1810), the attack of the French was decisively repulsed. For the first time the Portuguese, mixed with the English troops, had courageously sustained their allies. They have shown themselves worthy of fighting beside English soldiers," says Lord Wellington in his report. The road remained closed, and the English, masters of their position, saw already Marshal Masséna constrained to retreat. He had recovered on the field of battle all his indomitable ardor. "We ought to be able to turn the hills," said he to his lieutenants, and he detached immediately General Montbrun upon the right, to traverse an unknown country, hostile, and already enveloped in the darkness of night. The perspicacity and perseverance of the marshal had not been deceived; his scouts discovered a passage which the English had not occupied. On the 29th, at sunset, Lord Wellington learnt all of a sudden that the French army had defiled by the little village of Bazalva upon the back of the mountain; it was already debouching upon the plain of Coimbra, when the English saw themselves compelled to evacuate the town in all haste: the French passed through behind them, only leaving their sick and wounded. The Portuguese militia immediately resumed possession of the town. Masséna advanced upon Lisbon by forced marches; on the 11th of October he arrived before the lines of Torres Vedras, by this time completely finished, and furnished with 600 pieces of ordnance. Behind three successive series of

formidable entrenchments, supplied with resources of every
kind, and supported on one side by the Tagus and on the other
by the ocean, Lord Wellington had resolved to shut up his
army, until then victorious, and to wait until hunger, sickness,
and exhaustion should at length deliver him from his enemies,
whatever might be the difficulties of the undertaking, and the
clamors that might be raised against him.

"I am convinced," wrote the English general to his government, "that the honor and the interest of the country require
us to remain here to the latest possible moment, and, with the
aid of Heaven, I will hold on here as long as I can. I shall not
seek to relieve myself of the burden of responsibility by causing the burden of a defeat to rest upon the shoulders of ministers; I will not ask from them resources which they cannot
spare, and which will not contribute perhaps in an effective
manner to the success of our enterprise; I will not again give
to the weakness of the ministry an excuse for withdrawing
the army from a situation which the honor and interest of the
country compel us to guard. If the Portuguese do their duty,
I can maintain myself here; if they do not do their duty, no
effort in the power of Great Britain to make will suffice to
save Portugal; and if I am obliged to retire, I shall be in a
situation to bring away the English army with me."

It was with this firm and modest confidence in a situation
that he had prudently chosen, and of which all the resources
had been multiplied by his foresight, that Lord Wellington
awaited the attack of Masséna, and the seasoned troops who
were deploying before his lines. The soldiers were exasperated
at this unforeseen obstacle raised by the hand of man, and of
which no one had penetrated the secret. "We shall succeed,
as we should have succeeded at Busaco, if we had been allowed
to," said the troops. Masséna judged otherwise.

On the 16th of October the marshal with his staff-officers
examined with care the enemy's lines; one discharge of a cannon, one only, resounded in their ears, and the wall upon
which the telescope rested was overthrown. Masséna looked
at his lieutenants. "The only thing to do is to occupy both
shores of the Tagus, and keep them and Lisbon blockaded,"
said he: "we will wait for reinforcements, and when the army
of Andalusia shall have arrived we will see if, behind those
cannons there, there are other cannons and other walls, as the
peasants say."

In their rigid simplicity, the conceptions of Lord Wellington had taken little account of the sufferings of the Portuguese nation. Resolved upon defending Portugal to the last extremity, he had left Lisbon exposed to cannon-balls, and the country a prey to the systematic depredations of the French. Masséna decided upon constituting a military establishment in face of the enemy's lines. Everywhere the resources of the surrounding country were stored in the magazines; an hospital was prepared; General Eblé, old and fatigued, but always inexhaustible in resources, was preparing boats in order to form a bridge. Effecting a movement in rear, Masséna and his lieutenants occupied all the positions from Santarem to Thomar, eager to instal themselves upon the two shores of the Tagus, to seize upon Abrantes, and to invest the English each day more closely in their lines. Already discontent was great in Lisbon, where provisions arrived with difficulty. Wellington urged upon the regency of Portugal the devastation of the country districts, and especially that of Alemtejo, the natural resource of the French army; the Portuguese authorities resisted. "Deliver Portugal, instead of famishing it," said they.

This was repeated in England, where the Prince of Wales had just assumed the regency, in consequence of a decided relapse into madness of King George III. The opposition thought itself returning to power; it had long sustained against the ministers of his father the policy of the heir to the throne; it now pleaded the cause of peace. The dangers to which the army of Portugal was exposed, the evils it might have to undergo, formed the subject of the debates in Parliament. The Prince Regent did not hasten to change his cabinet, but the violence of the recriminations in the ranks of the opposition affected the Marquis of Wellesley; he pressed his brother to make an effort to relieve England from the enormous weight that was crushing her. "I know it will cost me the little reputation I have been able to obtain, and the good will of the population that surrounds me," said Wellington; "but I shall not accomplish my duty towards England and this country, if I do not persevere in the prudence which can alone assure us success." Marshal Masséna had sent the eloquent and adroit General Foy to Paris, charged with representing to the Emperor the difficulties of the situation of the army, and the absolute need of a supreme effort in its favor.

The general arrived at Paris at the moment when new complications were preparing. The harshness of the proceedings of Napoleon, the violence which he had displayed towards the small independent princes whose territories he had confiscated, the yoke of iron under which he claimed to place all the commercial interests of Europe, had, little by little, effaced the remains of the youthful admiration and confidence with which his brilliant genius had inspired the Emperor Alexander. Personally wounded by the sudden abandonment of the matrimonial negotiations, the Czar experienced serious uneasiness at the insatiable ambition which threatened to invade the most distant regions. He had made some preparations for defence, of little importance in themselves, and simply manifesting his fears. Napoleon took umbrage at it; the mad passion for conquests was again roused in his mind; he already meditated a new enterprise, bolder and less justifiable than all those which he had hitherto accomplished, necessitating efforts which became every day more difficult. No resource would be neglected; no reinforcement could be detached for Portugal and Spain from the armies which were being prepared in France and Germany. The intelligent ardor of General Foy, his loyal pleadings on behalf of Marshal Masséna, did not completely succeed in enlightening Napoleon as to the situation of affairs in the peninsula; he understood enough of it, however, to order new dispositions of his troops. The corps of General Drouet, in Old Castile, and the fifth corps of the army of Andalusia, commanded by Marshal Mortier, were to proceed to the aid of Marshal Masséna. The emperor recommended the latter to occupy without delay the two shores of the Tagus—to throw a couple of bridges across, as formerly over the Danube at Essling, in order to assure his communications whilst waiting for the reinforcements, which would permit him to attack the English lines with 80,000 men, perhaps to seize them, and in any case to inflict such sufferings upon the Portuguese population and upon the English that the latter should be obliged to retire. "The policy of the English Government inclines to change," added Napoleon; "my grand and final efforts will at last bring us the general peace." He commenced at the same moment his preparations for the Russian campaign.

"Everything depends of the Tagus!" Such was the watchword sent back to Spain by General Foy, and the tenor of the correspondence between Major-General Berthier and the leaders of the armies in the Peninsula. General Drouet began the march with his army reduced to 15,000 men, which Napo-

leon reckoned as 30,000. In consequence of the delay of the
operations, only one division of 7000 men was effectively at the
disposal of the general when he took the road from Santarem.
General Gardanne, sent forward in advance, had become
alarmed through the report of a movement of the English,
and had promptly fallen back upon Almeida, leaving to the
soldiers of Masséna, and to the general-in-chief himself, the
wretchedness of a hope deceived. The instructions sent to
General Drouet still gave evidence of the obstinate illusions of
the Emperor Napoleon as regards the respective situation of
the two armies in Portugal. "Repeat to General Drouet the
order to go to Almeida," wrote Napoleon to Marshal Berthier,
"and to collect considerable forces, in order to be of use to the
Prince of Essling, and to aid in keeping open his communications. It will be necessary that he should give to General Gardanne, or any other general, a force of 6000 men, with six
pieces of cannon, in order to reopen the communication, and
that a corps of the same force should be placed at Almeida, to
correspond with him. In short, it is important that the communications of the army of Portugal should be re-established,
in order that during all the time that the English remain in
the country the rear of the Prince of Essling may be securely
guarded. Immediately the English have re-embarked he will
make his headquarters at Ciudad Rodrigo, my intention being
that only the ninth corps should be engaged in Portugal, unless
the English still hold it; and even the ninth corps ought never
to let itself be separated from Almeida; but it ought to manœuvre between Almeida and Coimbra."

When General Drouet, collecting all his forces, arrived at
length with 8000 or 9000 men at Thomar (January, 1811),
Marshal Masséna had been struggling for five months in complete isolation against a situation which became every day
more critical. He had successively seized Punhete and Leyria,
constantly occupied in preparing for that passage of the Tagus
which Napoleon was recommending to him without fathoming
the enormous difficulties of the task. The soldiers had been
organized into companies of foragers, from day to day obliged
to go out further from the encampments in order to be sure of
some resources, exposing themselves in consequence to attacks
from a population everywhere hostile. Marauders often detached themselves from their regiments, living for several
weeks by veritable pillage before returning under their flags.
The officers suffered still more than the soldiers, for they did

not pillage. Money and rations failed them; their clothes were worn to rags; courage alone remained inexhaustible; discipline grew feeble in every rank of the military hierarchy. The lieutenants of Marshal Masséna did not experience the same confidence in him which sustained the soldiers. The bridges at length reached completion, thanks to prodigies of perseverance and cleverness; bitter discussions arose every day as to the most favorable point for the passage, when the approach of General Drouet infused joy and hope into the entire army. General Gardanne, who commanded the vanguard, announced the arrival of all the straggling divisions of the ninth corps, and the orders sent to Marshal Soult for the movement of Marshal Mortier. Money as well as reinforcements was about to rain upon the army. The instructions of the emperor were precise. The English were to be speedily dislodged from their famous lines; and, if it was necessary still to blockade them for some time, the Tagus once crossed, the troops would no longer want for resources. The plain of Alemtejo would be open to them; the fine season was approaching; all efforts would become easy. Confidence and cheerfulness spread through all the encampments.

Marshal Masséna alone remained sad and uneasy. He had read the despatches which General Drouet brought him; he had smiled bitterly at the hopes and counsels of the Emperor Napoleon; he comprehended that the reinforcements were insufficient, and that the attempt at resistance was in advance condemned to failure. General Drouet had the order to maintain communications between Santarem and Almeida; already the insurrection had closed up all the roads behind him, and new skirmishes were necessary to open a passage. Only the corps of General Gardanne was destined to remain in the encampments, and that corps did not amount to 1500 men. Masséna resolved upon keeping General Drouet near himself; not without pain did he arrive at this conclusion. Discouragement was already penetrating the army, with a true knowledge of the situation and of the notorious insufficiency of the succors. General Foy had just arrived, accompanied by a small corps of recruits or convalescents, which he had formed at Ciudad Rodrigo. Before quitting that post, he had written to Marshal Soult, continually occupied in Andalusia: "I beseech you, Monsieur le Maréchal, in the name of a sentiment sacred to all French hearts—of the sentiment which inflames us all for the interests and glory of our august master—to present at the

soonest possible moment a corps of troops upon the left bank
of the Tagus, opposite to the mouth of the Zezere.   It is scarcely
four days' journey from Badajoz to Breto, a village situated
opposite Punhete.   The English are not numerous on the left
bank of the Tagus; they cannot dare anything in this part
without compromising the safety of their formidable entrenchments before Lisbon, which are only eight leagues from the
bridge of Rio Mazac.   According to the decision that your Excellency may arrive at, the army of the Prince of Essling will
pass the Tagus, hold in check the English on both banks of the
river, will fatigue them, will prey upon them, will keep them
in painful and ruinous inaction, will form between them and
your sieges a barrier likely to accelerate the surrender of the
towns; or, on the other hand, this army, failing to effect the
passage that has become necessary, will be forced to withdraw
from the Tagus and from the English in order to find sufficient
to eat, and by the same movement will give the day to our
eternal enemies, in a struggle in which till now the chances
have been in our favor.   The country between the Mondego
and the Tagus being eaten up and entirely devastated, there
can be no question as to the army of Portugal having to make
a retrograde step of about five or six leagues.   Hunger will
follow it even into the provinces of the north.   The consequences of such a retreat are incalculable.   It appertains to
you, Monsieur le Maréchal, to be at once the saviour of a great
army and the powerful instrument in carrying out the ideas of
our glorious sovereign.   On the day when the troops under
your orders shall have appeared on the ba ks of the Tagus, and
facilitated the passage of this great river, you will be the true
conqueror of Portugal."

When Marshal Soult received this eloquent and truthful
summing up from General Foy, already forestalled by the
formal orders of the emperor, he was personally in a grave embarrassment.   Like Masséna in Portugal, he was disposing in
Andalusia of forces less considerable than Napoleon estimated
them in France.   General Suchet, after having brilliantly accomplished his enterprise against Tortosa, which was reduced
on the 2nd of January, had immediately commenced the difficult siege of Tarragona, which occupied almost all his forces.
General Sebastiani with difficulty sufficed for guarding Granada; Marshal Victor was detained before Cadiz, where the
Cortes had solemnly assembled on the 4th of September.   The
resistance was to be long, the place being manned by good

troops, and constantly revictualled by the English vessels. Generals Blake and Castaños had collected their forces, and ceaselessly harassed the corps occupied by the sieges, as well as the armies which kept the country.   Marshal Soult had just asked for important reinforcements from Paris, when he received the order to attempt the difficult enterprise of an expedition into Portugal.   He thought he had the right to comment on the instructions sent to him, and whilst urging the obstacles which were opposed to his prompt obedience, he announced his intention of proceeding to the aid of Marshal Masséna, by reducing the hostile towns found upon the road to Portugal.   The sieges accomplished, nothing more would hinder the march upon Santarem.   He advanced then, with Marshal Mortier and the fifth corps, to the attack of Olivença, which did not oppose a long resistance.   On the 27th of January he invested Badajoz.

The place was strong, protected by the Guadiana and by solid ramparts; it communicated by a stone bridge with Fort St. Cristoval, built upon the right bank, and defending the entrenched camp of Santa Engracia.   At the moment when Marshal Soult approached Badajoz, the corps of the Marquis de la Romana, formerly occupied in Portugal in the service of the English, and recently recalled by the Spanish insurrection, took possession of these entrenchments; its indefatigable chief had just died at Lisbon.   It was in presence of these hostile forces that the fifth corps commenced the work of a siege destined to detain them for several weeks.   A successful attack on a little detached fort permitted the marshals to attempt the passage of the Guadiana, then much swollen by the rains, and to give battle to the Spanish army.   On the 19th of February, in the morning, upon the banks of the Gevara, the corps of the insurgents were completely defeated, without having been able to succeed in establishing themselves in the entrenched camp of Santa Engracia.   Marshal Soult was now in a situation to hasten the taking of Badajoz, and to push forward into Portugal before the Spanish army could be re-formed.   He does not appear to have conceived this idea, and resumed with perseverance the work of the trenches.   "I hope that Badajoz will have been taken in the course of January, and that the junction with the Prince of Essling will have taken place before the 20th of January," wrote the emperor, meanwhile.   "If it is necessary, the Duke of Dalmatia can withdraw troops from the fourth corps.   I repeat to you, everything depends upon the Tagus."

The cannon of Badajoz were heard at Santarem and at Torres Vedras, and the hearts of the two armies beat with uneasiness and hope. Upon the arrival of General Foy, in presence of the insufficiency of the disposable forces, the question lay between a retreat upon Mondego and an attempt at the passage of the Tagus. The wish of the emperor strongly expressed to Foy himself, the patriotic honor which animated all the generals, even the most dissatisfied, had made the balance incline in favor of a prolonged occupation. It was necessary, then, to attempt to cross the river; the distress which reigned in certain divisions, absolutely reduced by famine, did not permit of hesitation; the shores of the stream were reconnoitred with care. For a moment the idea was entertained of making use, as a guiding mark, of the isle of Alviela, situated in the midst of the river, as the isle of Lobau was found placed in the midst of the Danube. The materials of the bridge were collected at Punhete, but horses were wanting. General Eblé opposed an attempt, the advantages of which were to be too tardily recognized. The passage from Santarem to Abrantes offered the inconvenience of an immediate attack from the enemy in possession of that town, recently fortified by General Hill. It was resolved to wait for the arrival of Marshal Soult, or for the reinforcements which he had been ordered to send into Portugal. Masséna had never believed, and did not believe, in the promises which had been made him on this side; he consented, however, upon the advice of all, to retard for a few days a retrograde movement which became necessary, the impossibility of attempting alone the passage of the Tagus being recognized. The enemy had occupied the isle of Alviela; all the local resources were exhausted; the reserve of biscuit assured still fifteen days' provisions to the army. The weeks passed without news: the wind no longer brought the sound of the cannonade; the soldiers felt themselves abandoned at the end of the world; the anger of the generals no longer permitted them to reanimate the failing courage of an army famished and without hope. Masséna commenced the skilful preparations for his retreat upon Mondego. Under pretext of effecting a concentration of the corps necessary for the passage of the Tagus, he detached Marshal Ney towards Leyria, with a view of cutting off from the enemy the roads to the sea, in order to form afterwards a rear-guard. The wounded and the sick had been taken on before. On the 5th of March, at the end of the day, the whole French army was on the march, sad

VII.—23

and gloomy in spite of their joy at quitting the places where they had suffered without compensation and without glory. The materials of the bridges, prepared with so much care by General Eblé, were burnt. General Junot pressed forward, in order to occupy Coïmbra and the Mondego—a rallying-point indicated beforehand to all the corps.

Lord Wellington issued forth from his entrenchments on learning the movements which announced to him our retreat. His accustomed prudence kept him from precipitating the pursuit by an effort that might become dangerous; the well-known character of Marshal Ney protected the rear-guard no less than the valor of his troops. He ranged his forces in order of battle before Pombal, which obliged Wellington to recall the troops which he had detached for the succor of Badajoz. But the hurry of the retreat had resumed possession of the mind of General Drouet, ever haunted by compunctions for his disobedience to the formal orders of Napoleon. Ney was not in a position seriously to defend his positions against the English; after a brilliant skirmish, he fell back upon Redinha. His division of infantry had constantly fought under his orders in all the campaigns of the six previous years; it disputed the land, foot to foot, with the 25,000 English, who followed the French army, without letting itself, for a single moment, be troubled or pressed by the superiority of the enemy. The least offensive movement of the English columns was responded to by a charge from our troops, which soon re-established the distance between the two armies. Masséna, who was present at the manœuvres of Marshal Ney, admired them without reserve, beseeching his clever and courageous lieutenant not to abandon the heights, in order to give the other corps the time and space necessary for the continuance of their march. A last engagement, which took place upon the banks of the Soure, in front of the position of Redinha, permitted Ney at last to cross the river, and gain the town of Condeixa.

The position was strong, and Masséna counted on the energetic resistance of his rear-guard, in order to hinder the English, and leave time for the different corps to reassemble at Coïmbra. Marshal Ney on this occasion failed to realize the just hopes of his chief; after a slight skirmish, he abandoned Condeixa, and overtaking in his haste the corps that his movement had exposed, he fell back upon the main body of the army. A position at Coïmbra became impossible, as Lord

Wellington was following closely on our divided forces. Masséna gained the Alva by a series of clever manœuvres, constantly thwarted by the want of discipine in his lieutenants. Marshal Ney had let himself be surprised at Foz d'Arunce by the English; General Regnier extended his camp to a distance, without care for the safety of other corps; the position of the Alva was no longer tenable. Masséna, exasperated and grieved, continued his march towards the frontier of Spain; re-entered it without glory, after having displayed, during six months, all the resources of his courage, and the energy of his will in a situation which had been imprudently imposed upon him by peremptory orders. He led back an army inured to fatigue and privations, but disorganized by an existence at once idle and irregular, directed by chiefs soured and discontented. The consequences of this state of things were not long in bursting forth; scarcely had the troops taken a few days' rest in Spain, when Marshal Masséna conceived the idea of assuming the offensive by descending upon the Tagus by Alcantara, in order to re-enter Portugal and recommence the campaign. Marshal Ney frankly refused to follow him without the communication of the formal orders of the emperor. In consideration of this act of revolt, twice repeated, Masséna took from Ney the command of the sixth corps, which was confided to General Loyson. Ney obeyed, not without some regret for his conduct; the ill-humor of all the chiefs of the corps rendered the resumption of the campaign in Portugal utterly impossible: the army was cantoned between Almeida, Ciudad Rodrigo, and Salamanca. The emperor had just confided the general command of all the provinces of the north to Marshal Bessières; the latter had promised much to Marshal Masséna, who still nursed the hope of a great battle. Lord Wellington, following the French, had entered Spain.

The situation of affairs became critical, in spite of the *éclat* of the taking of Badajoz, which had been at length reduced to capitulate, on the 11th of March, on the eve of a general assault. Marshal Soult now found himself pressed to fly to the assistance of Cadiz. Marshal Victor was threatened in his positions of siege by the Spanish general Blake, and by an English corps recently embarked at Gibraltar. But already the energetic defence of Victor had triumphed over the enemy in the battle of Barossa. The assailants had retired, but remained in a threatening attitude. The army of Wellington, formerly kept immovable by Masséna at Torres Vedras, became every day a danger for those who had not been able, or who had not been willing, to go to the aid of the expedition in Portugal. Our forces, everywhere dispersed, were everywhere insufficient. Marshal Soult, justly uneasy, demanded reinforcements from all sides. General Foy had returned to Paris, in order to explain to the emperor the retreat of Masséna.

Great was the wrath of Napoleon. He had not yet opened his eyes to the profound causes of so many repeated checks. He did not comprehend the lessons which events were pointing out to his conquering ambition. He imputed to his lieutenants faults sometimes inevitable, or easily to be foreseen, in the circumstances in which they were placed. The inexhaustible resources of his military genius were not, however, at a loss on the occasion of this first outburst of embarrassments, destined daily to increase. He recalled Marshal Ney, incapable of serving under any other than himself, and replaced him by Marshal Marmont, more docile, more skilled in questions of military organization, and very earnest in the service of Marshal Masséna. The latter was charged with watching Lord Wellington, and with closely following the English army. Marshal Soult received the reinforcements which had become necessary to him in order to defend the frontiers of Estramadura. The garrison of Badajoz was insufficient; that of Almeida had been furnishing provisions for several weeks to the troops of Masséna cantoned in the environs of the place; resources began to be exhausted. Wellington was triumphing in Portugal, in Spain, and even in England. His detractors had been constrained to admire the wisdom of his contrivances, and to admit their success; the opposition loudly proclaimed it in Parliament; the war party prevailed in the councils, and nobody any longer haggled over the succors to the victorious general. Past clamor did not trouble Lord Wellington; the flatteries of public favor did not intoxicate him. He decided on laying siege to the places recently conquered by the French. He himself proceeded to the environs of Badajoz, in order to settle his plan for the campaign. The bulk of his army were menacing Almeida.

Masséna was informed of the departure of Wellington; he conceived the hope of profiting by his absence to inflict upon the English a startling defeat. Hastily collecting a convoy of provisions destined to revictual Almeida, he pressed Marshal Bessières to join with him in order to attack the army of the

NEY.

PRINCE DE LA MOSKOWA.

enemy. Bessières lingered; the lieutenants of Masséna did not give evidence of the ardor which still inflamed the heroic defender of Genoa. Using on this occasion all his rights as general-in-chief, Masséna ordered at length the concentration of the forces. He was getting ready to set out, "without bread, without cannons, without horses," wrote he to Marshal Bessières, resolved upon no longer deferring his attack. The Duke of Istria (Bessières) arrived at last, on the 1st of May, with a reinforcement of 1500 horses and a convoy of grain. When the troops quitted Ciudad Rodrigo, on the 2nd of May, they had appeased their hunger. About 36,000 men were under arms. Wellington had had time to rejoin his army.

The English occupied the village of Fuentes d'Onoro, between the two streams of the Dos Casas and the Furones; they covered thus their principal communications with Portugal by the bridge of Castelbon over the Coa, and defended against us the road of Almeida. The combat began (3rd May, 1811) upon the two shores of the Dos Casas. Extremely furious on both sides, it left the English in possession of the village. Our columns of attack found themselves insufficient, and dispersed over too wide an extent of country. They occupied, however, both shores of the stream, when, night falling, caused the combat to cease. On the morrow Marshal Masséna, changing the point of his principal effort, marched with the main body of his forces upon Pozo-Velho. He attacked on May 5th, at daybreak. Some brilliant charges of cavalry threw the English into disorder, but the guard refused to act without the orders of Marshal Bessières, who was not found in time on the field of battle. The division of General Loyson went astray in the woods, while General Reynier limited himself to keeping back the English brigade which was directly opposed to him. The ammunition failed; Marshal Bessières, alleging the fatigue of the teams, refused to despatch immediately the wagons to Ciudad Rodrigo, where there was a store of cartridges. Discussion and want of discipline had borne their fruits. The first glorious outburst at the beginning of the day remained without result. Messéna slept upon the field of battle, within range of the guns of the English; but the latter had not recoiled, and everywhere maintained their position. When the marshal, provided with ammunition, wished to recommence hostilities, the most devoted amongst his lieutenants dissuaded him from the enterprise. Discouragement spread among the soldiers, as ill-humor among the officers. With despair in his heart, Massséna remained in face of the English whilst he gave orders to blow up the ramparts of Almeida. The movement of retreat had scarcely commenced, on the 10th of May, when the explosion was heard which announced the execution of the orders given. The town of Almeida existed no longer. The garrison had succeeded in escaping the watchfulness of the English, rejoining the corps of General Heudelet, who had been sent to meet it. "That act is as good as a victory!" cried Lord Wellington in anger. Messséna, however, did not allow himself to be deceived.

A few days later (16th May, 1811), Marshal Soult failed in his turn to overcome the resistance of the English posted before Badajoz, on the shores of the Albuera. A corps of the Anglo-Spanish army had laid siege to the place. The efforts of the French general to seize the village of Albuera were not successful. The marshal was constrained to place his cantonments at some distance, without, however, withdrawing from Badajoz. Massséna had just been recalled to France, and replaced in his command by Marshal Marmont. He had the misfortune to be constantly sacrificed to an ambition bolder and cleverer than his own, and to bear more than once the punishment for faults which he had not committed. His soul remained indomitable, even in his bitter sorrow; but his military career was terminated. Henceforth he was to fight no more: none of the last efforts of Napoleon were confided to the warlike genius of an ancient rival, who had become a loyal and useful lieutenant, without ever sinking to the *rôle* of the courtier or the servant.

For three years past, the stubborn antipathy of the Spaniards to the foreign yoke had been struggling foot to foot against the power of Napoleon. For two years the most brilliant efforts of our courage had been vainly employed against the boldly-planned resistance of the English. The enormous sacrifices necessitated by the conquest of Spain were not compensated for, either by repose or glory. The armies were exhausted, and the generals grew weary of struggling with enemies impossible to destroy, whilst they fled only to form again immediately, like the Spaniards; or whilst they defended intrepidly positions cleverly chosen, like the English. The power and the reputation of Wellington went on increasing in proportion to our defeats. King Joseph, feeble and honorable, unjustly imposed by a perfidious contrivance on a people who repelled him, carried to France the recital of his griefs and sorrows.

Such was the situation in Spain in the month of May, 1811, after the hopes and long illusions of the campaigns of Andalusia and Portugal. The emperor had just experienced a great joy; he possessed at last a son. The King of Rome was born at Paris on the 20th of March. But day by day the situation was becoming more grave. The rupture with Russia was imminent. We had lost one after the other our most important colonies. In 1809 the English had seized upon our factories in the Senegal, and had succeeded in destroying our power in St. Domingo; in the months of July and December, 1810, the Isle of Bourbon and the Isle of France were in their turn snatched away. Our courageous efforts on the seas were powerless to defend the ancient possessions of France, as our brilliant valor failed in Spain to assure us an unjust conquest. In the interim, the industrial and commercial crisis was developing, though the superabundance of production in face of a European market more and more restricted. At the same time the Emperor Napoleon found himself battling with the heedlessly contracted difficulties of the spiritual government of the Catholic Church. The new prelates were still waiting for their bulls of institution, and the Pope still continued a prisoner.

Napoleon took his decision. He gave orders to the appointed bishops of Orleans, St. Flour, Asti, and Liège to repair to their sees without any other ecclesiastical formalities. He had elevated his uncle, Cardinal Fesch, to the archbishopric of Paris, after the death of Cardinal de Belloy. Fesch provisionally accepted, whilst continuing to hold his archbishopric of Lyons, the titles of which were canonically regular. The emperor flew into a passion. He had been to pay a visit to Notre Dame without being received by Cardinal Fesch. "I expect," said he, "to find the Archbishop of Paris at the door of his cathedral." He ordered the newly-elected prelate to take possession of his see. "No," said the cardinal; "I shall wait for the institution of the holy father." "But the chapter has given you powers." "It is true, but I should not know how to use them in this case." "Ah!" cried the emperor, "you condemn those who have obeyed me. I shall certainly know how to force you to it." "*Potius mori,*" replied the cardinal. "Ah! *mori, mori,*" repeated the emperor. "You choose Maury; you shall have him!"

Cardinal Maury, formerly the fiery defender of the rights and liberties of the Catholic Church before the Constituent Assembly, was appointed Archbishop of Paris on the 14th of October, 1810. On the 22nd, Osmond, the Bishop of Nancy, was called to the vacant archbishopric of Florence. Command was given to the two prelates to take possession of their sees. From Savona, Pius VII. had often succeeded in causing some canonical dispensations and some indications of his spiritual authority to reach the French and Italian clergy. Several associations were formed in order to supply him with the means for doing so. The Pope profited by them to send to Cardinal Maury, as Archbishop of Florence, a prohibition against ascending episcopal chairs without his institution. The brief addressed to Florence was promptly circulated in the city. A canon and two priests were on this account thrown into prison. At Paris the brief was secretly committed to the Abbé d'Astros, grand capitular vicar, cousin of Portalis, the councillor of state, and the son of the former minister of religion. The canon was moderate in his opinions as in his conduct; he conformed, however, to the instructions of the holy father. When Cardinal Maury wished to have the episcopal cross borne before him, the chapter abandoned him *en masse*, in order to retire to the sacristy. A second brief from the Pope fell into the hands of the police, "removing from the appointed archbishop all power and all jurisdiction, declaring null and without effect all that might be done to the contrary, knowingly or through ignorance." The emperor flew into a rage, attributing the resistance to the Abbé d'Astros, whom he violently apostrophized in public in a reception at the Tuileries. "I avow that I had kept myself a little on one side," Astros himself says; "but I did not wish to have myself sought for, and I always presented myself when the emperor asked for me." "Before all, monsieur, it is necessary to be a Frenchman," cried Napoleon; "it is the way to be, at the same time, a good Christian. The doctrine of Bossuet is the sole guide one ought to follow. With him one is sure of not losing one's way. I expect every one to acknowledge the liberties of the Gallican Church. The religion of Bossuet is as far from that of Gregory VII. as heaven is from hell. I know, monsieur, that you are in opposition to the measures that my policy prescribes. I have the sword on my side; take care of yourself!" The Abbé d'Astros was put in prison at Vincennes, and was to remain there until the fall of the empire. It was

not long before the Cardinals de Pietro and Gabrielli were
brought there also. Portalis had secretly learnt of the papal
interdiction from his relative. He limited himself to informing Pasquier, recently charged with the direction of the police.
He was expelled in full sitting of the Council of State by the
emperor, with the most harsh reproaches on his perfidy. "Go,
monsieur," said he to him, "and let me never again see you
before my eyes!" At the same time, and in accordance with
formal orders received from Paris, Pius VII. was surrounded
with the most paltry vexations; henceforth he was deprived in
his captivity of all his old servants. The papers and portfolios
of the Pope were all seized. " Never mind my purse," said the
holy father; "but what will they do with my breviary and
the office of the Virgin?" He did not consent to deliver to
Prince Borghese the ring of the Fisherman, which he wore
habitually on his finger, until he had himself broken it. About
the same time, on several occasions, Italian priests who had
refused to swear allegiance to the new state of things were
transported to Corsica. Napoleon had himself given his instructions to the minister of religion. The boundaries of the
dioceses and parishes in the Pontifical States underwent a complete alteration. Their number was much restricted. All the
archives of the court of Rome were transported to Paris.

The emperor had not lost the remembrance of the concessions he had formerly obtained from Pius VII. when strong
and free: he had reckoned upon a complete submission from
the aged prisoner. Already the refusal of the holy father to
the insinuations of the Cardinals Spina and Caselli had disquieted Napoleon: he had formerly flattered himself that he
could make the Pope accept the suppression of his temporal
power and the confiscation of his states by offering him palaces
at Paris and Avignon, a rich income, and the noble grandeur
of his spiritual authority over the whole Catholic Church. The
extent of this authority, such as the emperor conceived it, was
beginning to reveal itself. Napoleon wished to be the master
in the Church as in the State. The authority of the Czar over
the Russian Church, or of the Sultan over the Mussulmans,
could alone satisfy his ideas. " Render to Cæsar the things
that are Cæsar's," limiting within the narrowest boundaries
that portion which he still ostentatiously reserved for God.
He thought for a moment of regulating by a law the question
of episcopal institution. Diverted from this project by the
wise counsels of Cambacérès and of Bigot de Préameneu, he

resolved upon consulting a commission of ecclesiastics upon the convocation of a national Council. Already a first Council had been gathered, at the time of the debates on the investiture of the bishops. The illustrious Superior of St. Sulpice, the Abbé Emery, had sat in it, strongly against his will. "The emperor has appointed a commission of bishops and cardinals to examine certain questions," wrote the Abbé Emery, to his disciple, the Abbé Nageot, Superior of the Seminary of Baltimore. "He has desired that I should be added to it. All that I can say to you is, that I have come forth from it without having anything to reproach myself with; that I think God has given me the spirit of counsel in this affair. I am sure that He has given me the spirit of power through His holy mercy."

The Emperor Napoleon judged soundly of that spirit of power and counsel for which the Abbé Emery piously ascribed to God all the praise. "M. Emery is the only man who makes me afraid," said he; "he makes me do all that he wishes, and perhaps more than I ought. For the first time, I meet a man gifted with a veritable power over men, and from whom I ask no account of the use to which he will put it. On the contrary, I wish to be able to confide to him all our youth; I should die more reassured as to the future."

Notwithstanding the ascendancy which his holy character and the firm moderation of his spirit exercised over the emperor, the Abbé Emery was not deceived as to his personal action in the ecclesiastical commission. "Permit me," he wrote to the minister of religion, "out of respect for the bishops, to abstain from taking any deliberative part, and only to have a consulting voice; that is to say, that I may simply furnish upon the matters which may be discussed the lights and documents which my studies and experience may enable me to give." The Superior of St. Sulpice was once more to give his opinion freely before the impatient and haughty master, who claimed to subdue all wills and all consciences to his empire. "I do not call in question the spiritual power of the Pope," said Napoleon one day, when he had called the Ecclesiastical Commission to the Tuileries: "he has received it from Jesus Christ; but Jesus Christ has not given him the temporal power. It was Charlemagne who gave it to him, and I, as the successor of Charlemagne, wish to take it away from him, because he does not know how to use it, and because it hinders him from exercising his spiritual functions. What inconvenience will there be in the Pope being subject to me, now that

Europe knows no other master?" "Sire," replied Emery, "your Majesty is better acquainted than I am with the history of revolutions. The present state of things may not always exist. It is not, then, necessary to change the order wisely established. The holy father will not agree to the concessions which your Majesty demands from him, because he cannot do it." Napoleon did not answer. The Abbé Emery had refused to sign the propositions accepted by the Ecclesiastical Commission; he dreaded the Council. "How is it that our bishops do not see," wrote he, "that the means of conciliation which the emperor demands from them are only a trick on his part to impose upon the simple, and a mask to cover his tyranny? Let him leave the Church tranquil; let him restore their functions to the Pope, the cardinals, and the bishops; let him renounce extravagant pretensions, and all will soon be arranged." The emperor , meanwhile, let it be known amongst the delegates that he intended to send to Savona to have an understanding with the Pope. "This is a good time to die," said Emery. God granted him this favor. He had suffered long, and on the 28th of April, 1811, he breathed his last.

It was at this very moment that the Archbishop of Tours and the Bishops of Nantes and Treves set out for Savona, charged to obtain from the Pope the concessions necessary for the reestablishment of ecclesiastical order. Already the Council had been ostentatiously convoked without the circular letters making mention of the name of Pius VII. "One of the contracting parties has disowned the Concordat," said the summons to attend; "the conduct that has been persevered in, in Germany for ten years past, has almost destroyed the episcopate in that part of Christendom; the Chapters have been disturbed in their rights, dark manœuvres have been contrived, tending to excite discord and sedition among our subjects." It was in order to prevent a state of things contrary to the welfare of religion, to the principles of the Gallican Church, and to the interests of the state, that the emperor had resolved upon collecting, on the 9th of July following, in the church of Notre Dame at Paris, all the bishops of France and Italy in national council.

The prelates delegated to Savona had for their mission to announce to Pius VII. the convocation of the Council and the repeal of the Concordat. "We intend," said their instructions, "that the bishops should be instituted according to the Concordat of Francis I., which we have renewed, and in such a manner as shall be established by the Council, and shall have received our approbation.　However, it would be possible to revert to the Concordat on the following conditions: 1st. That the Pope should institute all the bishops that we have appointed; 2nd. That in future our appointment shall be communicated to the Pope in the ordinary form; that if three months after the court of Rome has not instituted, the institution shall be performed by the Metropolitan."　A letter, almost threatening, written by nineteen bishops assembled at the house of Cardinal Fesch, accompanied the officious propositions of the emperor.　The anger of Napoleon had weighed heavily on the Council.　On the 9th of May the three prelates arrived secretly at Savona.

Chabrol, the Prefect of Montenotte, announced their visit to the Pope.　"They can come in when they wish," replied Pius VII.　For four months the old man had been living alone, without external communication, deprived of his friends and his servants, without pen and ink, gently accepting his sufferings, but visibly enfeebled in mind and body.　Disturbed at first, he soon recovered himself, talked familiarly with the bishops, and limited himself to asking that he might be granted the support of a few of his counsellors on this grave occasion. The request was denied in the most respectful manner; the prelates delegated by the Emperor Napoleon offered their assistance to the holy Father.　The letter of the nineteen bishops dwelt upon the hope that the Pope would engage himself to do nothing contrary to the declarations of the Gallican Church in 1682; Pius VII. protested that he had never had any intention of doing so, but that it was impossible for him to enter into any written engagement on the subject, the declaration having been condemned by Pope Alexander VIII.　He discussed, without bitterness, the question of canonical institution, whilst altogether repelling the propositions put forth by the bishops.　"All alone by himself, a poor man could not take upon himself such a great change in the Church," said he, smiling.

The discussion was prolonged, not only on the part of the prelates, but also on the part of the Prefect of Montenotte, who had frequent interviews with the Pope, using by turns menaces and caresses, seeking to act on the mind of Pius VII. by the interposition of his physician, Dr. Porta, completely devoted to the imperial service.　The Pope was complaining of his health; his intellect appeared at times affected by his long anguish. "The chief of the Church is in prison, and alone," said he, "nothing can be decided by him."

The virtues of Pius VII., like his natural weaknesses, contributed to the trouble of his conscience and his mind. Gentle and good, easily tormented by scruples, he was tossed about between the conviction of the duties which he owed to the holy see, and the fear of prolonging in the Church a grave disorder, which might bring about grievous consequences. In his interviews with the bishops he yielded everything, whilst thinking he was resisting, and finished by accepting a note, drawn up under his own eyes, containing in principle all the required concessions. He had not signed it, but the negotiators were contented with what they had obtained. "This morning we have drawn up the whole clearly and in French," wrote the Archbishop of Tours. "We have presented it to the Pope, he has desired a few changes in expression, some addition of phrases, some trifling erasures, and there has resulted from it an *ensemble* quite as good, and indeed much better than we flattered ourselves on obtaining a few days ago." Next day, May 20th, in the morning, the negotiators took the road to Paris.

They had scarcely got a few leagues from Savona, and already the Pope was seized with remorse. Ill for several days past, deprived of sleep by the agitations of his mind and conscience, he reproached himself for all the articles of the note he had agreed to, and fell into a state of suffering which gravely disquieted his jailers. "I cannot conceive how I could accept these articles." repeated Pius VII.; "some of them are tainted with heresy; it is an act of folly on my part, I have been half mad." "Absorbed in a complete silence, he closed his eyes in the attitude of a man who pondered deeply," wrote Chabrol, on May 23rd; "he only roused himself to cry out, 'Happily, I have signed nothing.' I told him to put full confidence in that which he had adopted in his conscience, which had no need of signatures, nor of conventions made by civil laws. He answered me that from that moment he had lost all peace of mind, and he has again fallen into the same absorbed reverie."

Thus the courage, and even the reason, of the unfortunate pontiff momentarily gave way under the pressure of a moral suffering beyond his forces. In order to calm him, Chabrol was obliged to despatch a courier in pursuit of the bishops, withdrawing the concessions implied in the first article of the note; then, at last, the scruples of the Pope were concentrated.

"This suppression is absolutely necessary," said he, "without which I shall raise a disturbance in order to make my intentions known." In advance, and by the very fact of the violent pressure exercised over a captive, old, sick, and alone, the emperor found himself in reality disarmed in face of the Council which he had just convoked; the concession which he had snatched from Pius VII. became null, for the pope was protesting from the depth of his prison.

Napoleon judged thus; he did not avail himself of the articles immediately denied in the note drawn up by his negotiators, and painfully accepted by the Pope. In fact, the undertaking at Savona had failed; it began again at Paris, where the Council at length assembled on June 17th. The emperor had beforehand sought to intimidate a few of the priests called to take part in it. During his recent journey in Normandy he had Bois Chollet, the Bishop of Séez, called before him, accused of rigor towards the priests who had lately accepted the constitution. "You wish for civil war; you have already engaged in it," cried Napoleon, "you have embrued your hands in French blood. I have pardoned you, and you will not pardon others, miserable wretch; you are a bad subject, give me your resignation immediately." One of the canons of Séez, the Abbé Le Gallois, learned and virtuous, and who was looked upon as exercising a great influence over his bishop, was conducted to Paris, and put in prison in La Force. "The canon is too clever," said the emperor, "let him be brought to Vincennes." Le Gallois was to pass nine months there, and only the fall of the Empire was to put an end to his detention.

"Your conscience is a fool!" said Napoleon to De Broglie, Bishop of Ghent, whom he had made a chevalier of the legion of honor, when the latter protested against a clause in the oath. He had said as much to other prelates whom he had just convoked to the Council. It is a serious case for absolute power when it enters into a struggle with the most noble sentiments of human nature. The Emperor Napoleon had come to that point when he regarded as his enemies freedom of thought and freedom of conscience amongst his subjects still suspected of independence, *littérateurs* or bishops.

Ninety-five prelates assembled, on the 17th of June, in the morning, in the church of Notre Dame. They were joined by nine bishops appointed by Napoleon, although they had not yet received canonical institution. At the second séance, when the affairs of the Council began to be seriously considered, the

Ministers of Religion of France and Italy took their places in the assembly. In opening, on the 16th, the session of the Corps Législatif, the emperor had haughtily proclaimed his suprem-. acy. "The affairs of religion," he said, "have been too often mixed up with, and sacrificed to, the interests of a state of the third order. I have put an end to this scandal forever. I have united Rome to the Empire. I have accorded palaces to the popes at Rome and in Paris. If they have at heart the interests of religion, they will often desire to sojourn at the centre of the affairs of Christendom. It was thus that St. Peter preferred Rome to a sojourn in the Holy Land."

On taking his seat at the Council, Bigot de Préameneu, then Minister of Religion, pronounced in his turn a discourse which history ought to assign to its true origin. The emperor enumerated, by the mouth of his minister, his numerous grievances with regard to the court of Rome, dioceses without bishops, the prelates deprived of canonical institution. "By this means the Pope has tried to create troubles in the Church and in the state. The sinister projects of the Pope have been rendered null by the firmness of the chapters in maintaining their rights, and by the good feeling of the people, accustomed to respect only the legitimate authorities. His Majesty declares that he will never suffer in France as in Germany, that the court of Rome should exercise on vacancies in the sees any influence by vicars apostolic, because the Christian religion being necessary to the faithful, and to the state, its existence would be compromised in countries where vicars, whom the government might not recognize should be charged with the direction of the faithful. His Majesty wishes to protect the religion of his fathers; he wishes to preserve it; and yet it would be no longer the same religion if it ceased to have bishops, and if one claimed to concentrate in himself the power of all. His Majesty expects, as emperor and king, as protector of the Church, as the father of his people, that the bishops should be instituted according to the forms anterior to the Concordat, and without a see ever remaining vacant over three months, a time more than sufficient for its being filled up."

The declaration fell like a thunderbolt in the midst of the Council. With the exception of a very small number of prelates acquainted with the negotiations of Savona, or in the confidence of the emperor, the mass of the bishops, come from a distance, ignorant or deceived, thought to find peace accomplished, or on the way of being accomplished, in the Church between the civil power and the holy see. On the previous evening all had applauded the words of Boulogne, Bishop of Troyes, then the most celebrated amongst the religious orators, when he cried, "Whatever vicissitudes the see of Peter may experience, whatever may be the state and condition of his august successor, we shall always be linked to him by the bonds of respect and filial reverence. This see may be removed, it can never be destroyed. They may deprive it of its splendor, they can never deprive it of its force. Wheresoever the see may be, there all others will meet. Wheresoever this see may be transported, all Catholics will follow it, because wheresoever it may be settled there will be the stem of the succession, the centre of government, and the sacred depository of the apostolic traditions." When the prelates were successively called upon to give their consent to the opening of the Council, Mgr. d'Aviau, Archbishop of Bordeaux, replied, "Yes, I wish it; excepting, nevertheless, the obedience due to the sovereign pontiff, an obedience to which I pledge myself on oath." All the members of the Council, its president, Cardinal Fesch, at the head of it, took the oath of allegiance to the Catholic Church, apostolic and Roman, and at the same time a "faithful obedience to the Roman pontiff, successor of St. Peter, the prince of the apostles, and successor of Jesus Christ."

Such was not the end which the emperor had proposed to himself in convoking the Council, and his wrath towards Cardinal Fesch was violent, as well as towards Boulogne. "I have ever in my heart the oath taken to the Pope, which seemed to me very ill-timed," wrote he to Bigot de Préamenu; "make researches to discover what is meant by this oath, and how the parliaments regarded it. Let the sittings of the Council be secret, and let it not have, either in session or in committee, any motion of order. The report that you make to the Council ought not to be printed." The commissions were to be appointed by ballot: the first elected was charged with drawing up the address to the emperor. The task was confided to the Bishop of Nantes, Mgr. Duvoisin, clever and wise, well advanced in the good graces of Napoleon, and who had been one of the delegates to Savona. To the first objections that his colleagues presented to him, the prelate responded that his draft of the address had received the approval of the emperor.

It was much to presume on the docility of an assembly, incomplete in truth, for a very small part of the Italian and German bishops had been convoked, independent, however, by character and station. Whilst Mgr. Duvoisin submitted his draft with regret to a revision which allowed nothing to remain of the complaisance but lately evinced for the imperial policy, an obscure prelate demanded that the entire Council should entreat from the emperor the liberty of the Pope. "It is our right; it is also our duty," cried Dessolles, Bishop of Chambery; "we owe it not only to ourselves, but we owe it also to the faithful of our dioceses—what do I say, to all the Catholics of Europe, and of the whole world? Let us not hesitate; let us go, we must, let us go to throw ourselves in a body at the feet of the emperor, in order to obtain this indispensable deliverance." And as timid objections began to manifest themselves in the assembly, "What, messieurs?" resumed the bishop, "the Chapter of Paris has been able to ask for mercy to M. d'Astros, one of its members, and we will not have the courage to ask for the freedom of the Pope. And why should the emperor be provoked at it? Messeigneurs, the Divinity himself consents to be solicited, persecuted, importuned with our prayers; sovereigns are the image of God upon earth; by what right ought they to complain if we act towards them as towards the Master of Heaven?"

Emotion overcame all the members of the Council; the moderates and the waverers were drawn along by the ardor of the prelates personally attached to the Pope, or nobly resolved upon sustaining their convictions even to the end. The old Archbishop of Bordeaux, the Bishops of Ghent and of Troyes, claimed at once the liberty of the pontiff, and his canonical right to use the ecclesiastical thunderbolts. "Judge the Pope, if you dare, and condemn the Church if you can," cried Mgr. d'Aviau. The prelates pledged to the imperial power wished to adjourn the discussion; when they came to the vote on the draft of the address, now without color or life, Cardinal Maury proposed that it should only be signed by the president and the secretaries. This overture suited all the timid characters; the address was voted by sitting and standing. The emperor did not show himself satisfied. "The bishops are much mistaken if they think to have the last word with me," said he. The Bishop of Chambery alone found favor in his eyes. "One is never to be blamed for asking for the freedom of his chief," said Napoleon. He had an order sent to the Council to answer his message on the subject of canonical institution within eight days, without losing time in useless discussions. A few of the more moderate bishops happened to be going out of the Tuiler-

VII.—24

ies from the imperial mass; the emperor approached them. "I have desired to act by you as princes of the Church," said he; "It is for you to say if you will henceforth be only beadles, The Pope refuses to execute the Concordat; ah, well! I no longer wish for the Concordat." "Sire," said Osmond, "your Majesty will not tear with your own hands the finest page in your history. "The bishops have acted like cowards!" cried Napoleon, with violence. "No, sire," again replied the prelate, who had so lately accepted the Archbishopric of Florence without waiting for canonical institution, "they are not cowards, for they have taken the side of the most feeble." The emperor turned his back on him.

"The only and exclusive object of the council of 1811," the Abbé de Pradt has said in his "Histoire des quatre Concordats," "was to regulate the order of Canonical Institution, and to provide that it should not henceforth be hindered by any other cause than the objections urged against the appointments by the Pope. In this lay the whole dispute between the holy see and the princes. It was not only his own affairs that Napoleon was attending to in this settlement, it was also those of other sovereigns, whom he spared by his example the embarrassments which awaited them." The Council felt the extreme importance of the question. After a lively discussion, and in spite of the persistency of the prelates favorable to the court, the commission appointed for this purpose would not pronounce upon the message of his Majesty before sending a deputation to the holy Father, who might set forth to him the deplorable state of the churches in the empire of France and in the kingdom of Italy, and who might confer with him on the means of remedying these evils. "The emperor requires a decree of the Council before consenting to the sending of the deputation," repeated Cardinal Fesch and his friends. "That would be a sure method to make everything fail," cried the Bishop of Tournay, "for it would be exactly like saying to the Pope: Your purse or your life; give us the bulls and we shall be satisfied with you." Cardinal Fesch was constrained to carry to Napoleon the vote of the commission.

The emperor did not think highly either of the skill or the character of his uncle, and was not particular how he treated him. "He will not reject you," said the cardinal to a lady with a petition, "I have been turned out of doors, yes I, twice in a single day." He essayed vainly to explain to Napoleon the canonical reasons which had determined the commission.

"Still more theology," replied the emperor; "hold your tongue; you are an ignoramus. In six months I should get to know more than you. Ah! the commission votes thus! I shall not get the worst of it. I shall dissolve the Council and all will be finished. It is of small consequence what the Council wishes or doesn't wish, I shall declare myself competent, following the advice of the philosophers and lawyers. The prefects will appoint the curés, the chapters, and the bishops. If the metropolitan does not choose to institute them, I will shut up the seminaries, and religion will have no more ministers." The violence of the insult and the grandeur of the situation elevated the soul of Cardinal Fesch. "If you wish to make martyrs, commence in your own family, sire," said he. "I am ready to give my life to seal my faith. Be perfectly assured that unless the Pope shall have approved this measure, I, the metropolitan, will never institute any of my suffragans. I go even further: if one of them should bethink himself, in my default, of instituting a bishop in my province, I would excommunicate him immediately."

It was then that Napoleon recognized the advantages of the abortive attempt at Savona. "You are all noodles," said he to his ecclesiastical counsellors, "you do not understand your position. It will then be for me to extricate you from the affair; I am about to arrange everything." He dictated upon the spot the draft of a decree based upon the concessions at first accepted by the Pope. "The deputation of bishops to the holy Father has removed all difficulties," said he; "the Pope has condescended to enter into the difficulties of the Church; the sole difference is to be found in the length of the delay; the emperor wished for three months, the Pope asked for six. This difference not being of a nature to break up the arrangement already concluded, it became henceforth the duty of the Council to enact it. The deputation to the holy Father should convey to him the thanks of the prelates and the faithful."

At first the commission of the Council almost entirely fell into the trap. Could it be doubted that the authorization given by the Pope appeared to cut the question whilst reserving the rights of the holy see. The Archbishop of Bordeaux alone protested in the first place; he soon rallied to his side Broglie, Boulogne, and the Bishop of Tournay. In spite of the most ardent efforts of the bishops favorable to the court the majority of the commission ended by rejecting the decree. "You will answer for all the future evils of the Church," said

the Archbishop of Tours to the Bishop of Ghent, "and I cite
you before the tribunal of God." "I await you there yourself," replied Broglie.

The emperor appeared to acquiesce without anger in the
decision of the commission. "What is it in the decree that
most displeases the bishops?" he asked of Cardinal Fesch.
"It is the demand for it to be converted into a law of the
state," replied the Archbishop of Lyons. "If that hinders
them, they have only to take it out," replied Napoleon; "I can
just as well make it a law of the state when I please." Cardinal Fesch gave a report of his mission; he promptly broke
up the sitting (July 10th). On the following morning the
Council was dissolved. In the night the bishop of Ghent,
Troyes, and Tournay were arrested in their beds, taken to
Vincennes, and kept in secrecy. The Duc de Rovigo was
opposed to the arrest of the Archbishop of Bordeaux. "We
must not touch M. d'Aviau," said he; "he is a saint, and we
shall have everybody against us."

The Marshal Gouvion St. Cyr had but recently given a
peremptory reason against select companies. "There are not
many brave men in the world," said he; "when you collect
them all in the same corps, there is not enough leaven elsewhere to make the dough rise." Deprived of the most resolute
of its members, the Council found itself in the hands of Napoleon like dough, soft and unresisting. The grand reasons, the
elevated and powerful arguments which the captive prelates
had made so important, lost all influence over the mass of
their colleagues. "One is afraid of Vincennes and one has no
desire to loose one's revenues," replied Cardinal Fesch to the
entreaties of the persons who solicited the fathers of the
Council to use their efforts in favor of the prisoners. By fear
or persuasion the bishops, when personally urged and worked
upon, bent one after another under the imperial will. The
news from Savona were that the Pope's health was improved
and that he was inclined to go back to the original concessions.
The Council, dissolved on the 11th of July, quietly assembled
again on the 5th August. The signature of about eighty
bishops was considered certain. The public discussion was
not renewed; the Archbishop of Bordeaux alone protested
against sanctioning all the imperial claims by a decree, thirteen
or fourteen prelates joining their mute protest to Aviau's
declaration; and the votes were decided by sitting and rising.
Subject to a power which they durst not discuss, the Fathers of

the Council disliked to proclaim openly their personal subservience. The decree drawn up by the Emperor Napoleon came back to his hands confirmed by the approbation of the Council. " Our wine was not considered good in the wood," said Cardinal Maury cynically, "you will find it better in bottles." A deputation of bishops set out for Savona.

A few months afterwards, under the pressure of the same arbitrary and sovereign will, Pius VII., now alone at Fontainebleau as he had been in his prison at Savona, had in his turn to yield in a certain measure to Napoleon's demands. As it had recently been at Savona, he was destined to see his concessions deformed and exaggerated in order to serve as a basis for a convention which he never ratified. On the day after the Council he showed no displeasure to the bishops who had come as delegates, but promised the investiture of the twenty-seven prelates who were nominated, and even gave to the deliberations of the Council a sort of sanction in a brief which he reserved to himself the right of drawing up. The form of it did not please the emperor, who sent it back to the Council of State for examination. The bishops who still remained in Paris waiting for the decisions of the holy Father were sent to their dioceses. " I don't wish to have a meeting of saints always here," said the emperor to Rovigo. In summoning the Council he had made the blunder of reckoning upon the easy docility of an assembly. " To ask men questions is to acknowledge their right to be deceived," said the Parisians on the day after the refractory bishops were arrested; "why does he summon a Council to imprison afterwards those who are not of his opinion?" The triumph obtained by Napoleon over the terrified prelates did not add to his glory, though it assisted in lessening for the moment his ecclesiastical difficulties. All the dioceses were now provided with bishops, and order was restored to the chapters. That was all the emperor then wished; his outrages upon the independence of consciences and on personal liberty weighing nothing in his balance. He was accustomed to set little value on rights which prevented the accomplishment of his designs. He had brought the bishops to submission, imposed upon the captive Pope a partial acceptance of his will, loftily vindicated the heritage of Charlemagne, and proclaimed his moral and religious supremacy: and now, leaving Pius VII. still at Savona and the refractory prelates at Vencennes, there was nothing more to keep him in Paris. The Russian campaign was already preparing.

CHAPTER XIII.

GLORY AND MADNESS—THE RUSSIAN CAMPAIGN (1811—1812).

IT is painful to love one's country and see it advancing to
defeat; it is sad to see a great mind, whose good sense recently
equalled his power, dragged to ruin by his own faults and
dragging after him a wearied nation.   In 1812, France began to
judge the Emperor Napoleon: and long previously Europe had
denounced him as an insatiable conqueror who laid her waste
incessantly.   She was about to learn once more that neither
distance, nor the rigors of climate, nor threatening armies,
afforded sufficient protection against the emperor's schemes.
Whilst his armies were struggling hard in Spain and Portugal against the insurgent population assisted by England,
and whilst still holding in Germany the pledges of his conquests, Napoleon made preparations to attack the Emperor
Alexander, who was still officially honored with the name
of "ally," and to whom he thus wrote on the 6th April, 1811,
when his armaments were already everywhere being prepared:
"Has your Majesty ever had reason to repent of the confidence
which you have shown me?"

Several reasons urged Napoleon to begin hostilities against
the Emperor Alexander—reasons which, though bad and insufficient, weighed in his eyes, and, under the influence of his
personal passions, with a decisive weight in the balance.   He
wished to pursue, everywhere and by every means, his struggle against England and her influence in Europe.   Alexander
had refused to increase the rigors of the continental blockade.
To this infraction of the spirit of the treaties uniting the
emperors, Alexander had added, during the Austrian war, an
attitude of indifference and reserve which inspired confidence
in the Emperor Francis and his advisers.   He had shown no
eagerness for the family alliance which Napoleon twice offered,
while, at the same time, the latter was not deceived as to the
annoyance caused at St. Petersburg by the negotiations for the
hand of the grand-duchess being suddenly broken off.   In
short, Napoleon was convinced that the Emperor Alexander

was preparing for war, eager to recover his liberty, and be freed from the conditions of the treaty of Tilsit. He, at the same time, believed that the renewal of hostilities would be signalized by important advantages for whichever of the two belligerents could first enter on the campaign. His main efforts, therefore, in 1811, were to hasten his warlike preparations, while using diplomatic artifices to make his adversary sleep, and, at the same time, proving to Europe that the rupture of the treaties was on the part of Alexander, and that the Russians were the first to arm. On sending him Count Lauriston, who was appointed to the replace Caulaincourt, Napoleon wrote the Czar: "The man I send you has no consummate skill in business, but he is true and upright, as are the sentiments I bear towards you. Nevertheless I daily receive from Russia news which are not pacific. Yesterday I learned from Stockholm that the Russian divisions in Finland had left to go towards the frontiers of the Grand Duchy. A few days ago I had instructions from Bucharest that five divisions had left the Moldavian and Wallachian provinces for Poland, and that only four divisions of your Majesty's troops remain on the Danube. What is now taking place is a new proof that repetition is a powerful figure of rhetoric. Your Majesty has so often been told that I have a grudge against you, that your confidence has been shaken. The Russians quit a frontier where they are necessary, to go to a point where your Majesty has only friends. Nevertheless I had to think also of my affairs, and consider my own position. The recoil of my preparations will lead your Majesty to increase yours; and what you do, re-echoing here, will make me raise new levies, and all that for mere phantoms! It is a repetition of what I did in 1807 in Prussia, and in 1809 in Austria. As for me, I shall remain your Majesty's friend even when that fatality which rules Europe will one day compel our two nations to take sword in hand. I shall regulate my conduct by your Majesty's; I shall never make the attack: my troops will advance only when your Majesty has torn up the treaty of Tilsit. I shall be the first to disarm, and restore everything to the condition in which things were a year ago, if your Majesty will go back to the same confidence."

The emperor spoke the truth, and his treatment of Russia was nothing new. It had long been a clumsy artifice of his insatiable greed for war and conquest to charge his enemies with taking the sword in hand on account of their fears or expec-

tations, the fear and expectations being usually caused by his
attitude and the projects with which he was credited. Military
reasons assisted at this time in encouraging him to dissimulate
and talk of peace. He had conceived the idea of occupying
successively the vast territories by which he was separated
from Russia, and gaining first the Oder and then the Vistula
before the Russians were in motion to cross the Niemen. The
first links of this combination were already begun to be forged;
crowds of runaway conscripts were everywhere being dragged
from the woods and rocks where they hid themselves; and, by
sending columns of militia to scour the provinces, garrison the
villages, and freely pillage the houses of the young deserters,
there were 50,000 or 60,000 men thus compelled to give themselves up, whose hiding-places had not been discovered. The
emperor sent them in troops to the islands of Elba, Corsica, Ré,
Belle-Isle, and Walcheren, appointing the sea to keep his deserters. Scarcely had they acquired the most rudimentary
notions of military discipline, when they were despatched in a
body to Marshal Davout, who was still stationed on the Elbe,
with instructions to drill and form them. They often arrived
still clad in their peasant's dress, their bodies ill, and their
minds revolting against the existence thus forced upon them
far from their home and country. About one sixth of these
wretches escaped during the march, braving all the dangers
and suffering of flight across an unknown country rather than
be soldiers. Recruits from all the conquered nations filled up
the gaps in the regiments of the ever-increasing army. War
supplies as well as soldiers were also constantly accumulating
in Germany. Napoleon resolved to collect at Dantzig the resources necessary to support an army of 400,000 men for a
year. The marvellous fertility of his mind was entirely occupied in facilitating and rendering certain the movements of
that enormous mass of men and horses during a long campaign
and across vast spaces. The transport arrangements were in
charge of skilled lieutenants, who had been with him in all his
battles; and General Eblé was at the head of the engineer division for bridge-construction. ' With the means at our disposal, we shall eat up all obstacles," said Napoleon, confidently.

Alliances would have been difficult and few in Napoleon's
case, if he had insisted on having genuine sympathy and
hearty assistance; but he did not ask so much from Prussia,
nor even from the Emperor Francis, whose daughter he had
just married. Fear was enough for the accomplishment of his

wishes, and in that he reckoned rightly. King Frederick William asked for Napoleon's alliance, because he dreaded seeing himself suddenly hemmed in by the attack against Russia. After leaving him for a long time unanswered, and at last bringing his preparations as far forward as he had beforehand determined, the emperor accepted the offers of the King of Prussia and his minister Hardenberg. In their anxiety to close the bargain, the Prussian diplomatist had gone so far as to say that their sovereign could place 100,000 men at the service of France. By a skilful system of rotation in their military service, the King of Prussia had been able to exercise all his subjects who were of age to bear arms without appearing to exceed the narrow limits allowed to his army by Napoleon. Thus, under the weight of unjust restriction, were sown the seeds of that military organization which afterwards proved several times so fatal to us. In 1812, Napoleon let the King of Prussia know that he had observed the state of his military resources. By the treaty of alliance, concluded in February, 1812, the Prussian contingent in the war then preparing amounted only to 20,000 soldiers. Large supplies of provisions were to be received in part payment of the war contributions which Prussia still owed France; and on this condition the emperor guaranteed the security of the territory of his new ally—recently his mangled victim. Some hopes were also allowed him of several ulterior advantages; but Napoleon refused to restore Glogau, in spite of the entreaties of King Frederick William.

Austria would have wished to avoid the necessity of joining in the war and allying herself to Napoleon; but the situation of the daughter of the Emperor Francis upon the throne of France, and the eagerness which the Austrian court had shown for the union, prevented any refusal. In his negotiations Metternich insisted that the treaty should be kept secret: " There are only two of us in Austria who wish for a French alliance," said he; " the emperor is the first, and I am the second; but Russia must not know of our feeling towards you." Some regiments were being secretly prepared in Galicia.

In a famous conversation which Napoleon had, on 15th August, 1811, with Prince Kourakin, the Russian ambassador at Paris, he said, " Is it on Austria that you reckon? You made war upon her in 1809, and deprived her of a province during peace. Is it Sweden, from whom you took Finland? Is it Prussia, whose spoils you accepted at Tilsit after being

her ally?"   The same reproaches could with more justice have
been applied to France—or rather, to her ruler.   He was soon
to understand that truth, and weigh the value of the alliances
which he had imposed.   On the eve of the Russian campaign
he was, and seemed, more formidable than the Czar; and fear
made the weak cling to his side, while they still concealed their
secret hatred and long-cherished rancor.

Russia, nevertheless, was also negotiating, relying upon her
rival's natural and declared enemies.   The treaties were not
new when they were published, on the 20th July, 1812, between
the Czar and the Spanish insurgents, the 1st August with England, and on the 5th April with Sweden.

The powers hostile to France were astonished to hear of the
advances made by the new Prince Royal of Sweden.   From
recollection of the republican enthusiasm of his youth, as well
as personal antipathy, Bernadotte had never liked General
Bonaparte when they were comrades and rivals for military
fame.   The fortune of Napoleon had dug a gulf between them.
Raised to the throne by a curious freak of destiny, Bernadotte
had brought to his new country no attachment for Napoleon,
nor the enthusiastic recollections of France with which he was
generally credited.   He had asked the emperor to grant him
Norway; but Napoleon did not wish to rob Denmark, and a
contemptuous silence was the reply to the court of Sweden.
Bernadotte pursued in another direction the same views of
ambition and aggrandizement; and in allying himself to Russia
he asked for Norway, urging the importance of the personal
and national assistance which he could contribute to the coalition.   England was not a stranger to this arrangement.   Two
months afterwards, disregarding his engagements with Russia,
and alarmed at the huge display of Napoleon's power, the
Prince Royal of Sweden proceeded to make fresh overtures to
France.   Norway was to remain as the price of his alliance,
together with a subsidy of 20,000,000.   Napoleon was extremely
angry.   Bernadotte had never possessed his good graces; and
he, not unnaturally, felt indignant at the manœuvres of a
Frenchman who had so soon forgot his country.   "The
wretch!" exclaimed he; "he is true neither to his reputation,
to Sweden, or his native land, but is preparing bitter remorse
for himself.   When Russia wants the Sound, her soldiers have
only to cross the ice from Aland to Stockholm.   The present
opportunity of humbling Russia is unique, and he will never
have such another.   Never again will a man like me be seen

marching against the North with 600,000 men! He is not worth thinking about; let nobody mention him again to me; I forbid sending any communication to him, formal or informal." Thus repulsed, Bernadotte remained faithful to his engage. ments with Russia, and was soon after to make others, which were still more disastrous to his native country.

Soon after the official publication of the treaty uniting Sweden to the enemies of France, the Emperor Alexander concluded a war which had long occupied the greater part of his forces. The hostilities so long waged between Russia and Turkey had not contributed to the glory of Alexander's generals. "Your soldiers are very brave," said Napoleon once to the Czar's ambassador, "but your generals are not worthy of them. It is impossible not to see that they have managed their movements very badly, and acted against all the rules." The fear inspired by the Emperor Napoleon had been of still greater use to the Turks than the bad generalship of the Russians, Alexander being eager to conclude the peace, in order to concentrate his forces against an enemy more formidable than the Sultan. Admiral Tchitchakoff, at the head of the army of the Danube, was empowered to finish the war or negotiate peace. The Czar renounced part of his former claims, contenting himself with Bessarabia, and proposing the Pruth as the boundary for both empires, on condition that Turkey became an active ally. The influence of the English diplomatists turned the balance, and Mahmoud, yielding to the desire for peace, the Treaty of Bucharest was signed on the 28th May, 1812.

Napoleon was afraid of this peace, and had tried to prevent it. Perpetually trying to gain time, he succeeded in throwing off the scent Nesselrode, who had been sent with instructions to put the question of peace or war simply. Lauriston was directed to dwell constantly upon the emperor's friendly feeling towards the Czar. Napoleon was at the trouble of conversing for a long time with a Russian of position who was visiting Paris. Czernicheff was sent to gather information as to the importance of our armament, and had learned much, when the emperor sent for him to come to the Elysée, to unfold his intentions with regard to Poland. He had formerly said to Prince Kourakin, "I shall give you nothing in Poland— nothing! nothing!" Now he declared his resolution never to restore to Poland its national independence. "I had no wish to engage in the convention which was proposed to me," said he, "because that engagement was not compatible with my dignity; but I am well resolved on that point. I have no other reason for arming except the notoriously unkind disposition of the Russian court towards me. She is deceived as to my intentions; she serves England, whose commerce extends to all parts of her territory. I only ask her to come closer; by ourselves we two shall crush all our enemies." Napoleon gave Czernicheff a letter for the Emperor Alexander, which made him a sort of accredited agent at the Russian court. "My brother, after the arrival of the courier sent by Count Lauriston on the 6th instant, I laid down my views of the troublesome events of the last fifteen months in a conversation with Colonel Czernicheff. It only depends on your Majesty to finish it all."

At the same time a despatch of the Duke of Bassano (Maret), who had succeeded the Duke of Cadore (Champagny) as minister of foreign affairs, informed Lauriston of the importance of the mission. "The emperor is anxious," said he, "that the troops should gradually advance upon the Vistula, rest there, settle there, strengthen their position, fortify their bridges; in short, make use of every advantage, and be certain of taking the initiative in military movements. The emperor has shown great kindness to Colonel Czernicheff, but I must tell you that officer has used his time in Paris intriguing and disseminating corruption. The emperor knew it without interfering. The preparations of his Majesty are really enormous, and the more they are known it will only be the better for him. The Emperor Alexander will, no doubt, show you the letter sent him by his Majesty; it is very simple. . . . . The emperor has no wish for an interview, or even a negotiation which should take place out of Paris. He has no confidence in a negotiation of any sort, unless the 450,000 men whom his Majesty has put in movement, and their enormous mass of war apparatus, should have caused the cabinet of St. Petersburg to reflect seriously, and, by loyally restoring the system established at Tilsit, place Russia again in the state of inferiority in which she then was. Your single aim must be to gain time. The head of the army of Italy is already at Munich, and the general movement is being everywhere declared. Maintain on all occasions that, should war take place, it is Russia who wished for it."

It was no longer from Paris that the emperor dictated his diplomatic orders and directed the movements of his armies. Since March he had lived at St. Cloud, to avoid an opposition which vexed him to the bottom of his heart, and which he had in vain attempted to disarm. The Parisians, long enthusiastic in favor of his glory, were showing discontent, aversion, and complaint. After the long drought of the summer of 1811, bread was dear; and the financial measures which had been tried to reduce the prices in the capital were extremely onerous for the Treasury without acting successfully upon trade. Corn was scarce, and the threat of an arbitrary tariff kept back the supply of provisions. The strain upon all the commercial relations caused by the continental blockade reacted unfavorably on the necessary resources during a dearth. The Food Council appointed by the emperor tried in vain to supply by artificial means the beneficent action of commercial freedom and confidence.

Other causes contributed to the agitation and ill-temper of the Parisians; and the discontent, as well as the suffering caused by the dearness of corn, was not confined to the capital. Too clear-sighted, in spite of the mad impulses of his ambition, not to feel what risks he was running, and making France run, Napoleon wished to provide some protection. Though long inexhaustible in men and devotion, the country was becoming tired, and about to be deprived of its means of defence at the very moment when a new European conflagration was bursting forth. The emperor had therefore ordered the formation of a certain number of cohorts of the national guard, under the name of "First Ban" (Body of Defence). Thus 120,000 men, borrowed from the "sedentary contingents" of 1809 to 1812, had been formed into regiments, on the assurance that they should not have to leave their departments. Their families, however, were deprived of them, and the present hardships combining with their fear of the future, there was great dissatisfaction in the country. The number of deserters having increased, the columns of militia recommenced their hateful work: and in the conquered countries, Holland and the territory of the Hanse towns, the conscription was violently resisted. Insurrections took place, followed by executions. Several of the regiments raised in the ancient free towns had mutinied, and kept themselves for several days in the isle of Heligoland. These troops were incorporated with Marshal Davout's army, and put under the most rigid guard. In Italy itself, and even in the army of Prince Eugène, the discontent and fatigue were unmistakable. The hard service of Napoleon had become a slavery. His severity towards the Pope also assisted in alienating the Italians, and throughout the Roman States he was hated by the population.

His pacific protestations, however, deceived nobody. The Czar had no wish for war; he dreaded it, and his people had also long dreaded it; but now he felt it to be inevitable, and the patriotic passion of defending their soil took possession of the Russian nation. Lauriston was besieged with attentions, but he lived alone, having no intercourse with the Russian upper classes, who were now urging the emperor forward. "Everything will be against us in this war," said Napoleon boldly to some of those about him who knew Russia well, especially Caulaincourt and Ségur. "On their side, love of country and independence; all private and public interests, even to the secret wishes of our allies! On our side, against so many obstacles, glory alone, even without the hope of plunder, since the frightful poverty of those regions renders it impossible."

The events proved, in a startling manner, the justice of what the military diplomatists anticipated. From the history of the secret negotiations we learn that advices and promises were largely bestowed by Austria and Prussia upon the Emperor Alexander. The leaders of our armies, which had for several months occupied Germany and Poland, could not pretend not to see the increasing hatred which was silently brooding under the disguises of popular submission and princely attentions. General Rapp, who commanded at Dantzig, felt it his duty to inform Marshal Davout of the precarious state in which our rule in Europe then stood. "If the French army has a single check," wrote the general, "there will quickly be from the Rhine to the Niemen only one single insurrection." Davout, in transmitting this information to Napoleon, made only one remark: "I recollect, sire, true enough, that in 1809, without the miracles wrought by you at Ratisbon our situation in Germany would have been very difficult."

It was upon those miracles of his genius, and upon a destiny which he justly considered superhuman, that the Emperor Napoleon always reckoned. The information brought vexed him without persuading him, and made him somewhat distrust those who ventured to give it him. The brilliant renown of Marshal Davout, the justice and consistency of his administration in Poland, and the admirable order which reigned in his army, had made Napoleon somewhat displeased and gloomy. The rivals and enemies of Davout skilfully utilized the occasion. "One would think that the Prince of Eckmühl commanded the army," they said constantly in the emperor's

presence.   Some even accused him of aiming at the throne of
Poland.   Napoleon had dispensed with Masséna's services ;
and now he showed a coolness towards Davout, as if he were
jealous of his glory and power, and at the moment of engaging in the supreme struggle wished to be surrounded with
servants only !

Marshal Davout, nevertheless, went on his way, executing
the emperor's instructions with consummate skill and prudence.   There were now 450,000 men marching against Russia ;
an army of reserve of 150,000 men was about to be formed in
Germany from the recruits sent from all parts of France ;
120,000 men of the national guard were to protect the French
soil, in combination with 150,000 soldiers sick or new, who
were still in the military depots.   According to the " cadres,"
which were often deceptive, there were 300,000 men engaged
in Spain.   On leaving Italy to march to Germany, Prince
Eugène had left about 50,000 soldiers in the strongholds.   Thus
for one man's quarrel, and in his name, there were under arms
more than 1,200,000 soldiers.   The Russian army did not exceed 300,000 men : on their side they had the weather, extent
of country, and climate.   " Don't come into collision with the
Emperor Napoleon," said Knesebek, the Prussian envoy to the
Czar; " draw the French into the interior of Russia.   Let
fatigue and hunger do the rest."   The Emperor Alexander had
just learnt that Davout had appeared at Elbing : having crossed
the Vistula, he was on his way to the Niemen.   The feeling of
the people as well as the ardor of the court called the Czar to
head-quarters, but he still hesitated, having a repugnance to
give the sign of general conflagration ; and at last, on the 21st,
set out for Wilna after telling Lauriston that there was still
time for negotiations.   The population of St. Petersburg were
all present at his departure, earnest and full of interest ; and
the churches were crowded with people praying at the altars.
" I go with you.   God will be against the aggressor."   Such
was the Czar's proclamation on reaching his head-quarters.

Europe was no more deceived than Russia and France herself ; in spite of Napoleon's precautions, nobody was ignorant
as to the real aggressor. The emperor remained at St. Cloud till
9th May, 1812, waiting till an act of the Czar's should give him
the liberty of his movements.   Before leaving France, and as
a last indication of his pacific intentions, he despatched Narbonne to Wilna, with instructions to propose to the Czar an
interview and armed negotiation, on the Niemen.   " My aide

de-camp, Count Narbonne, who is the bearer of this letter to
your Majesty, has at the same time important communications
for Count Romanzoff," wrote Napoleon on the 25th April;
"they will prove to your Majesty my desire to avoid war, and
my constancy to the sentiments of Tilsit and Erfurt. In any
case your Majesty will allow me to assure you, that if fate
renders this war inevitable between us, it will make no change
in the sentiments with which your Majesty has inspired me,
and which are safe from all vicissitude or alteration."

It was at Dresden, whither he had gone on leaving France,
that Napoleon received the refusal to negotiate, brought by
Narbonne from the Czar. England had replied by a similar
refusal to the pacific manifesto which the emperor, as usual,
had addressed to her before recommencing new hostilities in
Europe. The orders for the positions of the troops were already given. Davout was to concentrate between Marien-
werder, Marienburg, and Elbing: the Prussians had been appointed to the advance-guard, and still remained on their right,
advancing to the banks of the Niemen. Marshal Oudinot occupied the suburbs of Dantzig, forming Davout's right; while
Ney's body, at Thorn, supported his left. Prince Eugène, with
the Bavarians, advanced to Plock, on the Vistula; the Poles,
Saxons, and Westphalians were united at Warsaw, under
the orders of King Jerome; and the guard, who held Posen,
were commanded by Mortier and Lefebvre. General St. Cyr
was appointed to lead the Bavarians in the field, and General
Regnier was responsible for the Saxons. The Austrians were
to invade Volhynia. Already wherever the troops passed there
was raised a chorus of complaints from the pillaged and ill-
treated populations, and from the King of Prussia, who had
seen Spandau and Pillau occupied by the French troops, on
pretext of depositing the war-material there. King Frederick
William had set out for Dresden, to present his claims personally to the conqueror.

In the sight of the crowned crowd which at Dresden thronged
around Napoleon, there was something at once brilliant and
sad. Amongst the sovereigns who claimed the honor of presenting their homages, there were very few who did not cherish
against him some secret grievance or bitter rancor. All
dreaded some new misfortunes, and were endeavoring to
charm them away by servile flatteries. The Empress Marie
Louise accompanied her husband, showing her delight and
want of tact in displaying her splendor so near her native

country, before the eyes of her father and mother-in-law, who had just met her in Dresden. All purely military display had been forbidden at the magnificent court around Napoleon. Murat and King Jerome themselves had been ordered to their head-quarters, yet the couriers followed each other night and day, frequently disturbing the brilliant *fêtes* by the fear of the first cannon-shot ready to go off. At Paris, Prince Kourakin, discontented and uneasy, had asked for his passports, thus anticipating the official rupture. At St. Petersburg, Lauriston received the order to join the Emperor Alexander at Wilna, and again lay before him the proposals of peace. It was necessary to let the grass grow—to let the sun dry the roads—to give Napoleon's emissaries the opportunity of acting on the minds of the Poles, and stirring up amongst them a national movement in favor of France, a mission to which Abbé Pradt, afterwards Bishop of Malines, had been appointed. Talleyrand, of whom the emperor at first thought, did not then enjoy his good graces. "Set out, my lord," said Napoleon to the bishop, "set out at once; spare no expense; rouse their enthusiasm; set Poland a-going without embroiling me with Austria, and you will have well understood and fulfilled your mission." The prelate's vanity was fired, surrounded as he was by the apparatus of his new grandeur. He set out to stir up Poland in the name of France!

The work was more difficult then than it had been in 1807, when Napoleon had personally remarked the distrust of the great lords and the apathetic indifference of the peasantry. The formation of the grand-duchy of Warsaw did not please the Poles, who had already seen their hopes vanish. They were poor, and a large number of their best soldiers were serving under Napoleon. The continental blockade had ruined the trade of the Jews, who had always been numerous and influential in Poland. The Abbé Pradt had to use his efforts in the midst of an excited people, who wished for the future something different from promises. His mission was to produce but trifling results, because the penetration of the Poles guessed Napoleon's thoughts, and his resolution to wage no decisive battle in their favor. He set no great value on the political spirit of the race, their patriotic passions meeting with scarcely any response in him. He wished to drag the living force of Poland in his train, in order to support him in his struggle; but it was in vain that he gave to the new aggression which he was about to attempt the name of a second

Polish war—the public voice was no more deceived than history.   The campaign of Russia was about to begin.

On leaving Dresden, Napoleon at last urged forward the advance of his armies.   In spite of the precautions he had taken,
the transports moved slowly and with difficulty, the staff officers dragging after them much useless baggage, and on reaching Thorn he ordered some important reductions.   When pushing on towards Marienburg and Dantzig he was attended by
Davout and Murat.   Cold in his manner to Davout, who was
perpetually quarrelling with Marshal Berthier, he was uncivil
to Murat, who was tired and ill.   "Are you not satisfied with
being king?" he asked, dryly.   "I scarcely am king, sire," retorted Murat.   "I did not make you kings, you and your
brothers, to reign as you liked, but as I liked," returned the
emperor; "to follow my policy, and remain French on foreign
thrones."   Napoleon had given orders for the last supply of
provisions for the strongholds, and completed the organization
of inland navigation by streams and rivers.   On the 17th June
he arrived at Intersburg, having resolved to cross the Niemen
at Kowno, in order to direct his march upon the Dwina and
Dnieper by the road leading to Moscow, passing first by Wilna,
the capital of Lithuania.   It was, in fact, upon those two
rivers, the real frontiers of the Russian empire, that the Emperor Alexander had concentrated his forces.   The army of the
Dwina was commanded by General Barclay de Tolly; the army
of the Dnieper marched under the orders of Prince Bagration.
The emperor went straight towards the enemy, hoping to open
the campaign by one of those brilliant strokes by which he had
been accustomed to terrify Europe.   He reckoned upon passing the Niemen on the 22nd or 23rd, and on the 16th wrote
from Kœnigsberg, authorizing Lauriston to ask his passports.
The despatch was dated the 12th, from Thorn, the ambassador
having been told of the artifice.   Napoleon soon learned that
Lauriston had not been allowed to leave Wilna.   It mattered
little now; having reached the banks of the Niemen, his proclamation was everywhere read to the troops:—

"Soldiers!   The second Polish war is begun.   The first finished at Friedland and Tilsit!   At Tilsit Russia swore an
eternal alliance with France, and war with England.   To-day
she is violating her oaths.   She will give no explanation of her
strange conduct unless the French eagles recross the Rhine,
thus leaving our allies to her discretion.   Russia is drawn on
by fate; her destiny must be accomplished.   Why does she

think we are degenerated? Are we no longer the soldiers of Austerlitz? She places us between dishonor and war. Our choice cannot be doubtful! Let us march forward; let us pass the Niemen; let us carry war into her territory. The second Polish war will be glorious to French arms; but the peace which we shall conclude will bring with it its guarantee; it will bring to a close the fatal influence which for fifty years Russia has exercised upon the affairs of Europe."

The river was there, rolling at Napoleon's feet, like a natural and majestic barrier, fulfilling its function of holding him back from ruin; the enormous mass of his army surrounded him; on the opposite bank reigned silence and solitude. Several sappers who had crossed in a small boat, having landed, a Cossack came up to them, in charge of a patrol, who followed him at a short distance. "Who are you? and what do you want here?" he asked. "We are Frenchmen, and we are come to make war upon you," replied one of the sappers. The Cossack turned his horse round, and disappeared in the forest, unhurt by the bullets which they fired after him. They were there to throw a bridge across.

On the morning of the 25th, Napoleon himself crossed the river on horseback, galloping as if he wished to find the enemy, still absent and invisible. The light cavalry had already taken possession of Kowno. The emperor wishing bridges to be thrown over the Vilia, ordered a squadron of Polish lancers to cross the river, in order to sound the depth, and a large number of the unfortunate men perished in the attempt. When they felt themselves carried away by the current, they turned round to shout "Long live the emperor!" Meanwhile the army was still defiling across the Niemen, and it was only on the 30th June that it had entirely reached the left bank.

After a violent discussion among the Czar's advisers, Alexander decided to evacuate Wilna, the minister of police being appointed for the last time to carry a conciliatory message to Napoleon. A detachment of cavalry disputed for a moment with the French the gates of the capital of Lithuania, the passage being forced by Murat. On the 28th June, about mid-day, Napoleon made his entry into Wilna, annoyed at not meeting the enemy, whom he would have liked to fight, overcome, and crush on the first day. The Lithuanians received him eagerly, as in expectation of freedom. The same day the Diet assembled at Warsaw proclaimed the re-establishment of the kingdom of Poland, and several members of the Senate hastened to Wilna, to announce officially to Napoleon the resurrection of their country. "The Poles have never been subjected by either peace or war," said they, "but by treason! They are therefore free *de jure* before God as well as before men, and to-day they can be so *de facto;* and their right becomes a duty. We demand the independence of our Lithuanian brothers, and their union to the centre of all the Polish family. It is from Napoleon the Great that we ask this word, 'The Kingdom of Poland exists!' It will then exist if all the Poles devote themselves ardently to the orders of the chief of the fourth French race, before whom the ages are but a moment, and space an infinitesimal point."

Napoleon did not believe in the restoration of Poland, and was resolved not to create beforehand an insurmountable obstacle to peace by forming engagements with the Poles. He received the deputies of the Diet coldly, and did not yield to their desire of seeing Lithuania at once joined to Poland. A special government had just been organized, which seemed to be entrusted to the great Lithuanian lords, but was practically administered by young "auditors" of the Council of State. Distrust had already secretly begun, and mutual recriminations; the Lithuanians dreaded the vengeance of Russia, not being certain of having permanently got rid of her government; robbery was scandalously common; the weather was bad, and many soldiers were ill. Everywhere throughout the province, corn, cattle, and forage were requisitioned for the army, and a dearth threatened Lithuania as soon as the French entered upon their soil. Half of the carriages, a third of the horse, and a fourth of those in charge of the transports, had already perished on the roads from the Elbe to Wilna. Napoleon had ordered a levy of four regiments of infantry in Lithuania, and five regiments of cavalry; but the money and military outfits were both wanting. It was necessary to organize some columns of militia, to pursue those who pillaged, and protect the peaceful inhabitants. Our soldiers were ordered to look after the burial of the dead. From the reports of chiefs of divisions the emperor was fully informed of some of the wretched consequences. The Duke of Trevisa wrote:— "From the Niemen to the Vilia I saw nothing but houses in ruins, wagons and carriages abandoned; we found them scattered on the roads and in the fields; some upset, others open, with their contents strewed here and there, and pillaged, as if they had been taken by the enemy. I thought I was following a routed army. Ten thousand horses were killed by the cold stormy rains and the green rye, which is their only food, and new to them. They lie on the roads and encumber them; their bodies exhale a poisonous smell—a new plague, which some compare to famine, though the latter is much more terrible. Several soldiers of the young guard have already died of hunger."

The necessity for a speedy victory was being already felt. The Russian army had been cut in two by the rapid march of the French, Prince Bagration being isolated on the Dnieper, where Marshal Davout was already hemming him in, and soon after gained an important victory, at Mohilew, 23rd July, 1812. The Czar, with General Barclay de Tolly, had fixed himself in the intrenched camp at Drissa before the Dwina; and it was upon this principal division that Napoleon directed his march when he left Wilna, on the evening of the 16th July. Murat commanded the advanced guard, followed first by Ney, and then by Oudinot; Prince Eugène, who advanced towards the right, was to join Marshal Davout.   The forces of King Jerome and Prince Poniatowski remained in the rear. Desertion and fatigue were already decimating the soldiers.   The King of Westphalia, placed under Marshal Davout's orders, had with difficulty accepted that secondary position. Difficulties having arisen, the prince returned towards Germany, and thus lessened the marshal's success at Mohilew.

Before leaving Wilna the emperor had dismissed, without satisfying him, Balachoff, the bearer of the Czar's last offers. Napoleon repeated his former complaints, going back bitterly to the happy future which was unrolled before Russia when her emperor walked in harmony with France. "What an admirable reign he might have had, if he had liked!" repeated Napoleon; "all that was necessary was to keep on good terms with me. I gave him Finland, and promised him Moldavia and Wallachia, which he was about to obtain, when all at once he allowed himself to be surrounded by my enemies, and turned against me the arms he ought to have reserved for the Turks; and now his gain will be having neither Wallachia nor Moldavia. And now, what is your object in coming here? What are the Emperor Alexander's intentions? He is only general on parade: whom will he put against me? Kutusof, whom he does not like, because he is too Russian? Benningsen, who is old and only recalls to him frightful memories? Barclay, who can manœuvre, who is brave, who knows war;

but who is a superannuated general? Bagration is the best soldier; he has no imagination; but he has experience, quickness of vision, and decision; he cannot prevent my throwing you beyond the Dnieper and Dwina. These are the results of your rupture with me. When I think of the reign which your master might have had!" Napoleon summed up by a demand to occupy Lithuania, Russia to undertake to resume permanently her alliance against England. Balachoff set out again, assuring Napoleon that if the sentiment of religious patriotism had disappeared throughout Europe, it still remained in Spain and Russia. The bitterness of the discussion envenomed several wounds already deep enough. When Balachoff rejoined the Czar in order to give account of his mission, Alexander was no longer at Drissa. Waiting in an entrenched camp tired and humiliated the Russians. The plan of campaign was the work of Pfuhl, a German general, high in the emperor's favor; but the feeling of the whole army was expressed so emphatically against the tactics at first adopted, that the Czar agreed to quit head-quarters, and fall back with his staff upon Moscow. There, they assured him, the mere fact of his presence was enough to animate the national enthusiasm of the old Russians, and stir up the whole country against the invader. General Barclay, henceforward free in his movements, began on the 10th July to march up the Dwina as far as Vitebsk, hoping to be joined by Bagration opposite Smolensk. Our road to Moscow was thus intercepted; and Count Wittgenstein, with 25,000 or 30,000 men, was to cover St. Petersburg between Polotsk and Riga. Marshal Macdonald, at the head of the left wing of the French army, threatened the coasts of the Baltic.

Napoleon guessed this movement of the Russian general, and determined to push forward, prevent the junction of the two armies of the enemy, attack them by suddenly crossing the Dwina, and thus render impossible the continuous retreat of the Russians, who were now drawing him in their pursuit into the interior of the empire, without giving him an opportunity of striking the blow which was to be their destruction. He therefore left Glouboko̧é on the 23rd July, advancing upon Vitebsk; and two brilliant engagements of the advance-guard, by Murat and Ney, on the 25th and 26th, redoubled the ardor of our troops. On reaching Vitebsk after another engagement, the Russian army was seen, drawn up in order of battle, beyond a small tributary of the Dwina. Napoleon urged for ward the march of all his forces. The Russian forces seemed to count about 90,000 or 100,000 men. The French army was reduced by illness, by the desertion of some Poles and Germans, and by the death of young recruits who could not endure the heat, fatigue, and bad food. The body accompanying the emperor, however, still amounted to 125,000 men, excellent troops. Napoleon felt certain of success.

Barclay de Tolly was of the same opinion. At first he had resolved to give battle, in order to keep the roads open for Prince Bagration, with whom he had made an appointment to meet at Babinowiczi; but the news of the check received by the Russian army at Mohilew convinced him that their junction must now be delayed, and that his colleague felt himself compelled to look forward to a long movement before succeeding in passing the Dnieper. A battle was no longer necessary, and, on the night of the 27th, Barclay raised his camp, to advance upon Poreczie, behind the Kasplia. Thus the St. Petersburg and Moscow roads were covered by the Russian army, and the two main divisions might look forward to a junction in the neighborhood of Smolensk.

Napoleon was excessively annoyed on learning of the enemy's retreat, and in spite of the overpowering heat ordered immediate pursuit. Count Pahlen, however, at the head of the Russian cavalry, protected their main body, while at the same time retiring before us. After a day's work as fatiguing for the troops as a long engagement, Napoleon returned to Vitebsk, where he encamped several days, in order to rest his soldiers, and rebuild the store-houses, everywhere overthrown by the Russians, who also destroyed the crops and every kind of forage. Up to this point, in spite of his able combinations, the plan of campaign decided upon by Napoleon at Wilna was a complete failure; and by the persistent retreat of the Russians, the circle of his operations had to be constantly increased. The immense space spread out before us, solitary and vacant; and for the future it was impossible to prevent the junction of the enemy's forces. On our side Marshal Davout had just joined the great army; and the emperor took advantage of this combination of the greater part of our forces to inspect his troops. In every regiment, except the old guard, the leaders were struck with consternation at the results ascertained by the roll-call.

It is a good thing to know the cost of enterprises begun in folly and pursued through excessive difficulties, whatever may have been the superior genius, the consummate foresight and experience, of the general. Ney counted 36,000 men as they crossed the Niemen, but only 22,000 were in line at Vitebsk. The King of Naples had lost 7000 men out of 28,000. The young guard had seen 10,000 men disappear out of 28,000. Prince Eugène reckoned 45,000 on the banks of the Dwina, and entered Kowno with 40,000. Even Davout, the most skilful in drilling and managing his soldiers, saw his 72,000 men diminished by 20,000. In King Jerome's division, 22,000 were wanting, the number formerly being nearly 100,000 men. The emperor still had at his disposition 255,000 soldiers; but Macdonald on the Baltic, and Oudinot at Polotsk, ought still to have 60,000, and General Reynier remained on the Dnieper with a body of 20,000 soldiers. Napoleon already spoke of calling Marshal Victor, with his 30,000 men of reserve, cantoned between the Niemen and the Rhine. Thirty thousand Austrians advanced towards Minsk under the orders of Prince Schwartzenberg. The emperor sent orders to Paris to despatch all his guard still left in the depots. He rejected the idea of an establishment on the Dnieper and Dwina being a sufficient result of the campaign. Better than all his lieutenants he at last foresaw the dangers and difficulties of the work which he had undertaken, which he still wished, but which he was anxious to finish in a brilliant manner. Europe was waiting for the news of a victory. Napoleon had reached the centre of the Russian empire, but without a battle. The pretige of his glory and his power demanded a decisive blow; and the emperor prepared for it at Vitebsk.

Marshal Macdonald, however, had taken possession of Courland, after one battle before Mittau. The Russians everywhere retreated before him, evacuating even the stronghold of Dunaburg. The marshal laid siege to Riga, but his forces were insufficient to guard this vast territory, and he in vain asked for reinforcements. Everywhere the men succumbed under the extent of the task imposed upon them. Marshal Oudinot, who formerly supported Macdonald at Polotsk, had crossed the Dwina, and was advancing, by the emperor's orders, against Count Wittgenstein. After a brilliant engagement at Jakoubowo on the 20th July, he found it prudent to retreat upon the Drissa. On the 1st August there was another successful battle, but the troops were tired, and had lost many men; the enemy were threatening. Oudinot returned to Polotsk, requiring rest and more soldiers, like Macdonald. The marshal did not succeed in demolishing the entrenched camp at Drissa, as he had been instructed to do.

On the south-east, in the upper part of the course of the Bug, General Reynier found himself at last obliged to retreat, in order to protect the grand duchy of Warsaw, and invade Volhynia. This expedition was at first intended for the Austrians, but the will of the Emperor Francis, as well as that of Napoleon, called them to head-quarters; and Reynier's forces were to replace them in the posts which they held.

Nevertheless, the Russian General Tormazoff threatened the grand duchy, after taking possession of Kobrin, which was badly defended by the Saxons. The Diet of Warsaw took alarm. A large number of wealthy Poles collected their most valuable property, and crossed to the left bank of the Vistula. They asked assistance from the Abbé Pradt, who was as disturbed as the Poles. He wrote to Wilna, where Bassano was installed as the emperor's representative, and at the same time addressed himself to General Reynier. The latter having called Prince Swartzenberg to his assistance, they both advanced upon the Bug, thus protecting the grand duchy, without being able to rejoin the grand army or support the general movement. Admiral Tchitchakoff had just signed the peace with the Turks, and was expected to come to Tormazoff's assistance.

Following Marshal Davout's advice, after mature consideration the emperor resolved at Vitebsk to advance with his main body from the banks of the Dwina upon those of the Dnieper, cross the latter at Rassasna, and ascend quickly to Smolensk. He reckoned upon finding the town without defence, and then by a sudden movement taking the Russian in flank, and so at last inflicting upon his enemies a great military disaster. The movements of the French army were to be concealed from the enemy behind the forests abounding everywhere. It was important to conceal our march from the Russians, who were about to form their junction at Smolensk.

The Emperor Napoleon was not alone in his enthusiastic ardor for battle. Prince Bagration was, like him, fervently wishing for the moment of conflict. The soldiers of high rank who were of Russian birth and manners, were greatly vexed and prejudiced against Barclay de Tolly, and his prudent tactics, every day accusing him of cowardice, and suspecting his patriotism. Born of a Scottish family which had long been settled in Russia, Barclay was ardently devoted to his adopted country, and could scarcely endure their unjust reproaches. The passion of the Russian generals at last gained the day, and the council of war resolved to take the offensive against the French cantonments. The projected march of our armies was unknown to the enemy when, on the 9th August, their vanguard made an attack upon General Sebastiani, who was badly defended. He at once called General Montbrun, and they both charged the Russian squadrons forty times in the course of the day, and then fell back upon Marshal Ney's forces. The Russians observed the solidity of our lines, saw the large force under Prince Eugène, and believed there were indications of a march towards St. Petersburg. Barclay took advantage of the uneasiness which he saw around him, and fell back upon Smolensk. The Emperor Napoleon now commenced the march.

On the morning of the 14th August, the whole army had crossed the Dnieper. With 175,000 men under the flags, an immense artillery, wagons and innumerable troops, the vast solitude of the ancient Borysthenes was suddenly transformed into a camp. The march continued towards Smolensk: before Krasnoe, after a rather keen fight, General Névéroffskoi was driven back to the town of Korytnia. Nearly all the corps had rejoined the emperor when, on the 16th August, the advance guard debouched before Smolensk. At a single glance of the eye, the generals were convinced that the town was in a state of defence. A useless attempt was made to take the citadel by storm; Ney, who had imprudently advanced, fell into an ambush, and was only with difficulty rescued by his light cavalry. The Russians were already seen occupying the heights on the right bank of the Dnieper, in the suburbs, and above the new town. Barclay had taken up his position there, and a large force occupied the old town on the left bank, both parts of the town being connected by a bridge. Prince Bagration had advanced beyond Smolensk, to protect the banks of the Dnieper, and prevent Napoleon, on crossing the river, from attacking the town and its defenders from behind.

Though the taking of Smolensk formed no part of his original plan, Napoleon was obliged to make the attack. The possession of that ancient and venerable town had great importance in the eyes of Russians. Nevertheless the emperor had the river sounded some distance off, hoping to find a ford which would allow of a surprise. It was impossible to throw over bridges, on account of the nearness of Prince Bagration, whose troops lay on the banks of the Kolodnia, a tributary of the Dnieper; and, so far as these observations were taken, the river was not fordable. Napoleon waited for a day, hoping that Barclay would leave the heights of the new town to offer him battle; and, on the Russian making no movement, the assault was ordered.

The fighting was continued a whole day on the 17th. The suburbs of the old town were in our hands, but the old enclosure, with its irregular brick towers, still resisted our attack. The Russians no longer made sallies, but defended themselves heroically behind the walls. Most of the emperor's lieutenants had been opposed to the siege, and Murat, it is said, wished to be killed. He went to a part which was incessantly battered by the guns from the ramparts, and said to his aides-de-camp, "Leave me alone here." Napoleon gave orders to cease the assault. Marshal Davout sent a party to reconnoitre, General Haxo braving a storm of fire to discover the weak point of the enclosure: and the attack was to begin again next morning at daybreak. "I must have Smolensk," said the emperor.

The Russians had already seen Napoleon's obstinacy, and felt that they could no longer repulse the efforts of our arms. The bombshells had already set fire to several parts, and during the night the whole of the town was in flames, kindled by the Russians. Their battalions were withdrawn, and the old town gradually evacuated. Barclay de Tolly prepared to follow their example. At sunrise Davout entered without difficulty into Smolensk in flames. The women and children, collected in the ancient Byzantine cathedral, seemed the mere remnant of a wretched population. Many men had fled; and the bridge, which joined both banks, being cut, the Russian army had started before us on the road to Moscow, without any possibility of our at once pursuing them. Napoleon passed on horseback through the smoking and blood-stained streets. Surgeon Larrey, faithful to the sentiments of humanity which always distinguished him, had the Russian wounded collected as well as the French.

The emperor looked gloomy and discontented. Though victorious, the army was depressed: the first town taken by assault, burnt before them by the determined hatred of its defenders, seemed to the soldiers a sinister omen. They were all tired of a war which imposed upon them unheard-of efforts without any glory coming to console them with its accustomed

intoxication. "The war is not a national one," said Count
Daru recently at Vitebsk; "the importation of a few English
goods into Russia, or even the rising of the Polish nation, is
not a sufficient reason for so remote an enterprise. Neither
your troops nor your generals understand the necessity of it.
Let us stop while at least there is still time."

The same advice was repeated at Smolensk, on that bank of
the river gained by such bravery, and difficult to leave without danger, in order to plunge into an unknown and hostile
country, far from the reinforcements which were still being
prepared in Germany. Before attacking Smolensk, Napoleon
said to Prince Eugène, "We are going to give battle, and then
we shall see Moscow." "Always Moscow! Moscow will be
our ruin," muttered the Viceroy of Italy as he left the emperor. Nearly all the military leaders felt the same fears.

Marshal Ney rushed with his troops in pursuit of Barclay,
and overtook two Russian columns on the plain of Valoutina
behind a small muddy stream, over which they had to throw a
bridge. Here a keenly contested fight cost us the life of General Gudin, when obstinately carrying the passage at the point
of the bayonet. Our columns were embarrassed in their attack
by the marshy ground. The Russians kept their positions till
night; and when at last obliged to quit the plateau more than
13,000 to 14,000 of both sides lay dead on the field of battle.
The enemy's columns resumed their retreat, and continued to
intercept our route to Moscow.

Thus, without a single check to diminish the prestige of our
arms—after constantly defeating the Russians in the partial
engagements which had taken place—after occupying, without
fighting or taking by assault, every place in our way, we
found ourselves, after two months' campaigning, with an army
less by a half, in the very heart of Russia, unable to reach the
enemy, who were retreating without running away—further
than when at Wilna from that peace, desired by all, which Napoleon wished to impose under glorious circumstances immediately after a victory. The pacific messages of the Emperor Alexander had long accompanied our invasion of his
states. Now they ceased, and the sudden summer of the north
was soon about to disappear. "That would make a fine
station for a cantonment," said Count Lobau, the heroic General Mouton, as he looked at the position and old walls of
Smolensk. The emperor made no reply.

He was hesitating or reflecting, because he waited. On our

right, General Reynier and Prince Schwartzenberg, with the Saxons and Austrians, had dislodged the Russians from the important position of Gorodeczna at several leagues from Kobrin; thus opening, with considerable difficulty, the intercepted road to the grand duchy. On the left, Marshal Oudinot, hurt at the emperor severely blaming him because when victorious he took the position of the conquered, had advanced against Count Wittgenstein, although the Russians would not accept battle. The marshal again fell back on the Drissa and Polota; a strong detachment, however, covered the latter river, and on the Russians presenting themselves for the attack they were repulsed. Oudinot was wounded, and the command devolved upon General Gouvion St. Cyr, who was also slightly wounded. On the 18th August, having resolved to give battle, he directed his troops from a small Polish carriage, which was overturned in the thick of the conflict, and the general was trodden under foot. In spite of the exhaustion of the soldiers, and their leader's pain and ill-health, the feigned retreat which had deceived the Russians, as well as the battle itself, were crowned with brilliant success. After the battle of Polotsk, Wittgenstein was compelled to withdraw, and Gouvion St. Cyr received at last his marshal's baton. His instructions were to guard the Dwina, while Macdonald was kept before Riga, unable to take it or raise the siege. The two corps were now deprived of communication, as soon as the main body was still further removed from its wings, now isolated on the right and left. The emperor was resolved to leave Smolensk, and at every cost pursue the battle which was running from him. Davout and Murat, always at the head of the army, and perpetually at strife in their military operations, agreed, however, in affirming that the Russians certainly showed a real intention of fighting. Napoleon went himself towards Dorogobouje.

A last effort was attempted by those about him to make him stop at Smolensk. General Rapp, just arrived from Germany, could not conceal his emotion and astonishment. "The army has only marched a hundred leagues since the Niemen," said he. "I saw it before crossing, and already everything is changed. The officers, arriving by posting from the interior of France, are frightened at the sight which meets their eyes. They had no conception that a victorious march without battles could leave behind it more ruins than a defeat." "You have left Europe, as it were, have you not?" said Murat and

Berthier. "Should Europe rise against your Majesty, you will only have your soldiers for subjects, and your camp for empire; nay, the third of that even being foreign, will become hostile." Napoleon granted the truth of the facts. "I am well aware that the state of the army is frightful. From Wilna half of them could not keep up, or were left behind; and to-day there are two thirds. There is therefore no more time to lose. Peace must be had at any cost, and it is in Moscow. Besides, this army cannot now halt; its composition and disorganization are now such that it is kept up by movement alone. One can advance at its head, but cannot stop or retreat. It is an army of attack, not of defence; an army of operation, not of position. I shall strike a great blow, and all will rally."

When leaving Smolensk, on the 24th August, with his guard, the emperor had not yet come to a final decision as to his advance, but all his measures were taken with that result in view, and his skilful lieutenants were not deceived. Marshal Victor was already on his way to Wilna, and Napoleon sent him orders to march at once towards Smolensk. Two divisions of the army of reserve, left in Germany under the orders of Marshal Augereau, were summoned to Lithuania. When the emperor learned, on arriving at Dorogobouje, that the enemy was again escaping from him, he concluded that General Barclay was ready to fight him, and was seeking for a favorable position. "We are told that he awaits us at Wiazma," wrote Napoleon to the Duke of Bassano on 26th August; "we shall be there in a few days. We shall then be half-way between Smolensk and Moscow, and forty leagues, I believe, from Moscow. If the enemy is beaten there, nothing can protect that great capital, and I shall be there on the 5th September."

The day was in fact come, and the battle which Napoleon had so long desired was at last to be offered, given, and gained —with no other result except more deeply involving us in a desperate enterprise and consummating our ruin. The Russians having evacuated Wiazma, it was only at Ghjat that the emperor at last felt certain of encountering the enemy. The command of the Muscovite armies had changed hands: the cry raised since the beginning of the campaign against Barclay's prudent tactics, at last overbore the Czar's confidence in that able general, and old Kutusof had been placed at the head of the troops. Keenly patriotic, and long engaged in the struggle against the man who had conquered him at Austerlitz, the new general-in-chief appealed to all the national and religious passions by which his soldiers were animated. "It is in the faith," said he, "that I wish to fight and conquer; it is in the faith that I wish to conquer or die, and that my eyes shall see victory. Soldiers, think of your wives and children who claim your protection; think of your emperor who is looking upon you; and before to-morrow's sun has disappeared, you shall have written your piety and fidelity upon the fields of your country with the blood of the aggressor and his legions." The priests, clothed in their most sumptuous robes, were already carrying the holy images at the head of the regiments, while the soldiers knelt down to receive absolution. The French army was near.

The emperor having been ill for several days, his assistants found him depressed and undecided at the very moment when he was at last attaining the object of his desires. There was still a constant quarrel between Murat and Davout. The marshal blamed the King of Naples for imposing too much work upon the cavalry, and forbade the infantry of the advanced guard to manœuvre without his express orders. The complaints of his lieutenants reached Napoleon, but he made no more efforts to reconcile them. Having a fixed ill-will against Davout, he compelled him to place under Murat's orders one of his divisions which had been refused to the King of Naples. The emperor had shown more ill-temper than usual; and on one occasion he said to Berthier himself, the most devoted of his old friends "And you, too, are you one of those who wish to stop? As you are only an old woman, you may go back to Paris. I can do very well without you." For several days the Prince of Neuchâtel refused to appear at the emperor's table.

The imperial staff had now left Wiazma. When occupying that small town, Napoleon had himself run after and horse-whipped some soldiers who were pillaging and destroying a shop. He pursued his journey under the blue sky and an exhausting heat, listening to the simple talk of a young Cossack, who had been taken prisoner that very morning amongst the Russian soldiers who had lagged behind. Lelorgne d'Ideville, the excellent interpreter who attended the emperor, put questions to the soldier. "Nobody wishes to keep Barclay," said the young Cossack; "they say that there is another general. They would all have been beaten long ago but for the Cossacks. No matter, there is going to be a great battle. If it takes place within three days, the French will gain it; but, if it is delayed longer, God only knows what will happen. It seems the French have a general called Bonaparte, who has always con-quered all his enemies. Perhaps he will not be so fortunate this time; they are waiting for large reinforcements in order to make a stand." The emperor having made a sign, Lelorgne leant over towards the young Cossack's saddle and said, "That is General Bonaparte beside you—the Emperor Napoleon." The soldier opened his eyes and looked at the face of the great conqueror whose name had, like some tale of wonder, reached even his savage tribe: he said nothing, when Napoleon gave orders that he should be restored to liberty.

The weather becoming bad, the rain fell in torrents, and rendering the march of the army difficult, many soldiers left the ranks to pillage, their provisions being short; and the em-peror bitterly reproached his lieutenants with a state of things which they could not prevent. "The army is in that way threatened with destruction," wrote Napoleon, "even from Ghjat. The number of prisoners made by the enemy amounts every day to several hundred. Let the Duke of Elchingen know that he is daily losing more men than if we were fight-ing, and that it is therefore necessary that the foraging expe-ditions should be better managed, and the men should not go so far away."

Order was not restored in the army when, on the 5th Sep-tember, it debouched upon the plain of Borodino. Following the table-lands extending between the Baltic and Black Sea, we descended the slopes by which the Moskwa on the left, and the Protwa on the right, flow towards the Oka, a tributary of the Volga. The rain ceasing, Napoleon was encouraged by the appearance of the sky to hope for fine weather. At one time he thought of returning towards Smolensk; but when the sun reappeared he cried, "The lot is cast; let us set out." He at last found himself face to face with the Russians.

General Kutusof had taken advantage of the natural posi-tion. Entrenched on the left behind the river Kolocza, he had raised a series of earthen redoubts, furnished with a formid-able artillery, to defend the small heights at the foot of which were extended the Russian battalions. The course of the river changing its direction at the point where the village of Borodino was placed, the heights were there protected only by hollows. It was this position which Napoleon first gave orders to attack, in order to carry a detached redoubt placed on a mamelon. Our troops had scarcely arrived, and night was approaching, but after a very severe engagement the advanced work of Schwardino remained in our power. The whole of the 6th of September was spent in reconnoitring. Several of the corps had not yet joined the main body. Marshal Davout proposed to cross the thick curtain of forest extending on the left of the Russian army, and by taking the old Moscow road, turn the enemy's positions and seize their troops between two fires. Napoleon refused, thinking this movement too dangerous. He himself seemed disturbed and ill at ease; with his head in hand, and deeply plunged in thought, he all at once tore himself from his meditations to make sure of the execution of some orders. "Are you confident of victory?" he asked General Rapp, abruptly. "Certainly," replied he, "but with much bloodshed." "Ah! that is true," said the emperor. "But I have 80,000 men; if I lose 20,000, I shall enter Moscow with 60,000; the soldiers who have fallen behind will join us, and then the marching battalion. We shall be stronger than before the battle." In enumerating his forces, Napoleon did not reckon his cavalry or the guard. He was still ill, being under an attack of fever, but it was with a voice of the greatest firmness that he again harangued his troops. "Soldiers!" said he, "this is the battle which you have so much wished for. The victory now depends upon yourselves. It is necessary for you; it will give us abundance, good quarters in winter, and a ready return to our own country. Behave as you did at Austerlitz, Friedland, Vitebsk, and Smolensk, and so that the most remote posterity may quote your conduct this day. Let them say of you, 'He was at that great battle under the walls of Moscow!' "

On the 7th, before daybreak, Napoleon was already on the battlefield, near the redoubt which had been gained on the evening of the 5th. The troops had received orders to look their very best. Stretching his hand towards the sky the emperor exclaimed, "See! it is an Austerlitz scene!" The bright rays, however, were in the soldiers' faces, and the Russians had more advantage from their brilliancy than we. At seven o'clock the combat broke out on the left: Prince Eugène carried the village of Borodino, but his troops, being too eager, crossed the bridge instead of breaking it down, and were crushed under the fire of the enemy's artillery, placed on the heights of Gorki. The attack became general—so passionate and violent, that on both sides they scarcely took time to manœuvre. For the first time in his long career as head of an army, the emperor remained in the rear, looking on the strug‑gle without taking part in it, yet opposing the eager demands of his generals for reinforcements. "If there is a second bat‑tle to-morrow, what troops shall I give it with?" he replied to Berthier, who entreated him to send assistance to Murat and Ney, on their carrying the enemy's redoubts. Generals fell on every side, dead or severely wounded. They hurriedly bound up the wounds of Marshal Davout, who was seriously hurt; and Rapp, wounded for the twenty-second time in his life, was carried before the emperor. "Always Rapp!" said Napoleon; "and what is going on over there?" "Sire, they want the guard, in order to put an end to it," replied the gen‑eral's aide-de-camp. "No," retorted the emperor, "I won't have them destroyed. It is not when 800 leagues from home that one risks his last resource."

During this long day this was Napoleon's constant reply to all the leaders of divisions who believed they held in their hands the foretaste of victory, or who saw officers and soldiers slaughtered around them. Napoleon was waiting for a pro‑pitious moment, to decide himself the success of the day. "It is too soon," he repeated several times; "the hour for me to join in the fight personally is not yet come; I must see the whole chess-board more clearly." The reserve artillery, how‑ever, had been authorized to advance, and crowned the heights which had just been taken from the Russians. The enemy's cavalry came to dash against that unsurmountable obstacle; their infantry fell in dense files, without withdrawing or breaking. For two hours the Russian regiments remained ex‑posed to this terrible fire. Marshal Ney at last turned what were left of this heroic corps, commanded by Prince Bagra‑tion. The struggle gradually ceased in the plain; the heights remained partially in the hands of the Russians; Prince Eugène used his utmost endeavors to take the great redoubt; and Prince Poniatowski was unable to force the old Moscow road. In vain did Murat and Ney demand loudly for the ad‑vance of the guard, still remaining motionless. For a mo‑ment the arguments of General Belliard seemed to take effect, and the order to march was given to the young guard. Count Lobau was already putting them in motion under the pretext of rectifying their lines, but Kutuzoff, till then motionless and inactive, had anticipated Napoleon in his final determination, and throwing forward his cavalry of reserve, the forces again formed in the plain, and a charge of the enemy, came pouring upon the divisions which held it. The emperor stopped the guard, forbidding an operation which, though recently likely to be successful, was now dangerous from the delay. The gap made in the centre of the Russian army by the untiring efforts of Murat and Ney was now closed up; the Russians again occupied their outer works; their ardor and courage never slackened under the fire of our artillery. The great redoubt, however, having been carried, and the Moscow road being abandoned, the generals who still miraculously survived after having a hundred times exposed their lives, asked to try a supreme effort to throw back the enemy and drive him into the Moskwa. Napoleon left his post, and came to inspect himself the point of attack. Marshal Bessières was not disposed to risk the guard; and Napoleon once more resisted all urgent demands. He instructed Marshal Mortier to occupy the field of battle with the young guard; and night being come, the battle at last ceased. "I do not ask you to advance, or commence any engagement," repeated Napoleon twice; and calling back the Marshal as he was going off, "You thoroughly understand? Keep the battle-field, without advancing or retreating, whatever may happen." The Russians had not yet evacuated all their positions, and the conquered and conquerors, both equally heroic, were extended in confusion on the plain. Several Russian detachments threw up a rampart of dead bodies. When on the morrow General Kutuzoff effected his brave retreat, he left no soldiers lagging behind, and the wounded who died on the march were religiously buried. The Emperor Alexander's army left 60,000 dead or dying on the plain of Borodino—or the battle-field of the Moskwa, as Napoleon himself named that terrible day. Prince Bagration was killed.

The battle of the Moskwa caused in our ranks 30,000 dead and wounded. Ten generals had succumbed, including Montbrun and Caulaincourt, brother of the Duke of Vicenza. Thirty-nine general officers were wounded: and ten colonels killed, and twenty-seven wounded. Three days were scarcely sufficient to attend to the dead and wounded. The abbey of Kolotskoi and the neighboring villages were converted into provisional hospitals, under the direction of General Junot, commandant of the Westphalians. The emperor had advanced towards Mojaisk, and Murat followed with his decimated regiments. Napoleon refused Davout the command of the advanced guard. The town was attacked on the 9th: some attempts had been made to set it on fire, but the walls and houses were still standing when the emperor fixed his abode there for several days. It was there that he reviewed the state of his losses on the 7th. He had gone over the battle-field, showing more emotion and compunction than usual at the sight of the frightful carnage which had signalized the battle. Only 800 prisoners remained in our hands. The soldiers well knew that the number of captives was an indisputable sign of the importance of a victory. They beheld with terror the heaps of their enemies' corpses. "They all prefer death to being taken!" said they. "Eight days of Moscow," exclaimed the emperor, "and the enemy will not be seen again." He still remained ill and moody, however; and on the previous evening wrote to Marshal Victor, "The enemy when attacked in the heart no longer attends to his extremities; tell the Duke of Belluna to direct everything, battalions, squadrons, artillery, and isolated men, upon Smolensk, so that he may come from there to Moscow."

It was indeed upon Holy Moscow, the traditional capital of old Russia, that the hopes of Napoleon were now concentrated, hoping there to conclude a peace, and finish a war which he himself felt to be above human strength. Several weeks previously the Czar had left Moscow and returned to St. Petersburg, whence he watched at a distance, and without military skill, the defence of his empire. He upheld the courage of his subjects, however, and had personally obtained from them great sacrifices. The lords assembled round him, in the cradle and tomb of nobility, as they called Moscow, had voted the levy of every tenth serf, armed, equipped, and supplied with three months' provisions. The merchants offered the emperor half their wealth. On the approach of the French, and while waiting for the defence of the old capital, the orders of Rostop-chin, the governor, forbade the evacuation of the town. Women, children, old men, on carts and carriages, loaded with goods, money, and furniture, slowly removed from the town, where their husbands, sons and brothers still remained. "The less fear the less danger," said the governor. Kutuzoff's proclamations at first represented the battle of Borodino as a disputed combat, which left the Russian army standing, and capable of defending Moscow; but when their battalions appeared before the gates of the capital the sad truth struck the eyes of all. Whatever it might cost the invader, the national army was beaten, and Moscow could not repulse an attack. There was an immediate and constantly-increasing rush to leave the place. Popular rumor described the French as fierce monsters, worthy of that emperor whom Alexander himself had portrayed as a "Moloch, with treason in his heart and loyalty on his lips, come to efface Russia from the surface of the world."

In his real heart Kutuzoff had decided what to do. Skilful and cunning, without presence of mind or great courage on the field of battle, he could direct the operations of a campaign, and choose the proper mode of leading his country's enemies to their downfall. Nevertheless, he held a council of war, being determined to make the other generals share the weight of a terrible responsibility. Must they defend Moscow by a second battle in open field, wait for the enemy behind the walls, and dispute with him, foot by foot, the possession of the town? Must they abandon the capital, and, as it was recommended by Barclay de Tolly, always bravely true to his original purpose, retreat to Vladimir, and thus cover the road to St. Petersburg? All these proposals were proposed, and keenly discussed. Several spoke in favor of immediate and unflinching resistance, who would have bitterly regretted the adoption of their advice. At last the old general rose: he had listened to all their speeches without speaking, and only shook his head, to signify, as it were, his strong conviction that whether his head were good or bad, it had to make the final decision of the question.

He gave his orders, which showed great skill and prudence. The army was to pass through Moscow without halting, without assisting in any preparation for resistance, or joining in any skirmish even when on the rearguard; then falling back upon Riazan, it was, after several days, to occupy the road to Kalouga, and thus intercept the way to the French, while preserving communication with the provinces in the south of the empire, which are the richest and most fertile. The troops at once began to defile. Behind them long convoys hurried to escape the French. Five sixths of the population had quitted the town when the columns of those wounded in the battle of Borodino appeared at their doors, and they were obliged to crowd their hospitals and churches with 15,000. By abandoning their capital the Russians entrusted these wretches to the pity of their enemies.

The governor of Moscow, Count Rostopchin, had not yet

left the town. On the previous evening he trusted to the assurances of Kutuzoff, that the capital would be keenly defended. "There will be fighting in the streets," said he, in his proclamations. "The courts are already closed, but that does not matter; there is no need of courts to do justice to ruffians. I shall soon give you the signal; take care to provide yourselves with hatchets, and especially three-pronged forks, for a Frenchman does not weigh more than a sheaf of corn. I shall have mass said for the wounded, and holy water to hasten their cure. I shall then join General Kutuzoff, and we shall soon set about sending those guests to the devil, forcing them to give up the ghost, and reducing them to powder."

Kutuzoff, nevertheless, withdrew, not less resolute, but more skilful than Count Rostopchin. It was then that the latter conceived an idea, the responsibility of which, as well as the honor, rests entirely upon him. Nobody was consulted; and it is not known whether the Emperor Alexander, with some anticipation of gloomy fate crossing his mind, may not have beforehand granted the dread authority to the governor of his capital. For several days inflammable substances had been collected in the garden of his palace. At the moment of leaving the town, Rostopchin ordered the prisons to be opened, and the hideous crowd of condemned prisoners jostled and mixed with the half-frantic citizens who were fleeing before the French. The governor retained two prisoners—one a Frenchman, lately come to Moscow to earn a living; the other, a Russian, and both accused of having acted as agents of the enemy. "Go," said Rostopchin to the Frenchman, "you have been ungrateful but you have the right to prefer your country; you are now again free, go back to your own people. As for you," he added, turning to the Russian, "let even your own father be your judge." An old merchant came near, tottering under the weight of his grief. "You may speak to him and bless him," said the governor. "Me bless a traitor!" exclaimed the old man; and, raising his hands to heaven, he cursed his son, who was immediately beheaded. The mob showed their keen vindictiveness in their treatment of his body.

Count Rostopchin at last left Moscow, letting all precede him, like the captain who hesitates to abandon the sinking ship. He had given all his instructions. All the baggage all the wealth, he took with him, were the fire engines of that great city, which was nearly entirely built of wood. "Of what use are those in the country?" asked Colonel Wolzogen, with astonishment. "I have my reasons," replied the governor; then, leaving the last friends who still accompanied him, he turned round, and pointing with his finger to Moscow, and then touching the sleeve of his coat, he said, "I take away nothing except what is on my back." He went towards his country house at Voronovo.

Meantime, however, the French advanced guard were approaching Moscow. Several slight skirmishes had taken place during the march, and Kutuzoff succeeded in protecting his retreat. When Murat appeared at the head of the first columns, General Miloradovitch, who commanded the Russian rearguard, made a verbal agreement with the King of Naples to suspend hostilities for several hours, for the protection of the troops, and the safety of the citizens. Murat agreed to it, limiting himself to the pursuit of the Russians when they should have completed their evacuation of Moscow.

The soldiers, as well as the generals and Napoleon himself, were delighted at the distant sight of that town, illuminated by the rays of the setting sun, which brought into full relief the Oriental brilliance of its palaces and churches. "Moscow!" Moscow!" they repeated from one end of the ranks to the other. The emperor added to the enthusiastic expression of his troops another thought: "Not a moment too soon!" he muttered.

The great conqueror was deceived, and divine justice punished more completely than he anticipated his guilty ambition and insatiable pride. The dense ranks of the French soldiers presented themselves before the gates of the capital, without any one coming to open them. Several ragged wretches, with gloomy looks appeared on the turrets of the Kremlin and fired a few shots; but while passing along the streets of Moscow, among palaces mixed with cottages—before golden-domed churches, adorned with paintings of a thousand colors—our soldiers wondered, and felt uneasy at the solitude which reigned around them. "What is become of them?" they asked. It was not thus that the French army had entered Berlin or Vienna. "Let the head men of the town be brought to me!" ordered the emperor. The population of Moscow had no longer any head men. Those who hid themselves in terror in the houses, or wept in the churches, felt themselves at the mercy of the ruffians whom the governor, by quitting Moscow, had let loose upon them. The door of the Kremlin had to be burst open with cannon-balls before the old palace of the Czars could be rid of the wretches who had shut themselves up in it. Napoleon took possession of it, without at first fixing his abode there, curious to admire its barbarous magnificence, not yet subjected to the influence of French elegance like the houses of the rich merchants already occupied by his generals.   The whole army gazed with delight upon this strange and long-anticipated sight.   On the 15th September, 1812, the Emperor Napoleon and his soldiers passed through the streets of Moscow, deserted, but still standing.   They examined the concentric quarters, like a series of ramparts round the Kremlin; the old or Chinese town, the centre of Oriental commerce; the white town, with its broad streets and gilt palaces, the quarter of the great nobles and rich merchants; and all round the privileged districts: the "land town," composed of villages and gardens, interspersed with magnificent houses.

All the military posts were chosen, On the north-west, south-west, and south-east, between the roads to Riazan and Vladimir, the forces of Prince Eugène, Davout, Poniatowski, and Ney had taken their quarters.   The guard occupied the Kremlin.   Soldiers and generals enjoyed the luxury which had been preceded by the cruel privation of the months immediately preceding.   "We have provisions for six months," said the soldiers.

On the morning of the 16th fire broke out in a spirit-warehouse, and some hours afterwards in a magnificent bazaar which was filled with valuable goods.   The officers blamed for it the stupidity of a drunken soldier.   They at once battled with the fire, but the wind was contrary, and the wealth heaped up in the warehouses became a prey to the flames and pillage, which it was impossible to prevent.   The fire soon spread even to the neighborhood of the Kremlin, and the sparks, carried by the equinoctial breeze, fell from all parts on the gilded roofs. The courts of the palace being crowded with artillery wagons, and the cellars heaped up with ammunition which the Russians had neglected to take with them, a horrible catastrophe seemed imminent.   The generals had great difficulty in persuading Napoleon to leave the Kremlin.   The imperial guard, acting as firemen, inundated incessantly the roofs and walls.   The fire-engines of the city were searched for in vain.   Soon there was a rumor spread that incendiaries had been arrested in several quarters.

The emperor ordered these wretches to be brought before

him.   They were proud of the terrible mission with which they
had been entrusted, taking a delight in the fatal disorder produced under their hands, pillaging and murdering in the
houses which they delivered up to the flames.   They all made
a bold declaration of the orders they had received, and underwent unflinchingly the extremest punishment.   The poor population, who had remained concealed in the lowest haunts of the
capital, now fled in terror, the women carrying with them their
children, the men dragging behind them the most valuable of
their household goods, or the shameful results of pillaging the
shops.   The flames extended from street to street, house to
house, church to church: thrice the wind seemed to fall, and
thrice it changed its direction, driving the fire into quarters
previously untouched.   The Kremlin remained always surrounded by fire.   The imperial guard had not quitted the
palace.   The army carried their cantonments outside the town.
When scarcely fallen into the hands of the conquerors, Moscow succumbed before a more powerful enemy, enrolled for
the defence of the country.   Palaces and huts were both become uninhabitable, and the hospitals, filled with wounded
Russians, had perished in the flames.   The emperor quitted
Moscow, and took up his quarters at Petrowskoi.   For three
days the conflagration remained alone in possession of the
capital.

The wind falling, was succeeded by rain.   The fire everywhere brooded under the dead ashes, ready to burst out afresh
at the contact of air; but the spectacle had lost its avenging
beauty.   The roofs left standing were relieved against the columns of smoke.   The Kremlin still rose majestic, and almost
untouched, as if protecting the city against its various enemies.
The soldiers soon began to steal from their cantonments into
the streets; and in the cellars of the houses, under heaps of
rubbish, protected by walls blackened with the flames, they
found provisions collected by households for the winter; valuable clothes; plate which had been carefully concealed in
hiding-places which no longer existed; objects of art, of which
the finders did not know the value; strong drink, which they
madly used to intoxicate themselves.   After the fire, in spite
of the efforts of the officers, Moscow was delivered up to
pillage.

So much disorder and mad prodigality shocked all the Emperor Napoleon's instincts of order and government.   Returning hastily to Moscow, he repressed by his mere presence the

outrages of the soldiers. Regular search was everywhere organized for the collection of provisions buried under the ruins, and bringing them into stores. The resources collected in a few days were sufficient to supply the troops for a long time. Forage alone was wanting, and companies were formed for the purpose of scouring the country round Moscow. The prices offered to the peasantry for their stock was expected to encourage them to supply the markets of the capital. Napoleon even considered the interests of the wretches who wandered, defenceless and houseless, in the streets of Moscow, or timidly glided into the town at the opening of the gates to look for those they had been compelled to abandon, and the remainder of their property concealed under ruined walls. Huts were erected to shelter them.

The desire for peace daily took stronger possession of Napoleon's mind, and he had already authorized several indirect overtures. On the 20th September he thus wrote the Czar:

"My brother, having learned that the brother of your Imperial Majesty's minister was at Moscow, I sent for him, and had some conversation with him. I requested him to wait upon your Majesty, and acquaint you with my sentiments. The handsome and superb city of Moscow no longer exists. Rostopchin has had it burnt. Four hundred incendiaries were taken in the act; and having all declared that they had lighted the fire by order of that governor and the director of police, they were shot. The fire at last seems to have ceased. Three fourths of the houses are burnt, and one fourth remain. Such conduct is atrocious, and serves no purpose. Was the intention to deprive us of some resources? But those resources were in the cellars, which the fire could not reach. Besides, why destroy one of the finest towns of the world, and the work of ages, to accomplish so paltry an object? It is the procedure followed since Smolensk, and it has reduced 600,000 families to beggary. The fire-engines of Moscow were broken or carried off, and some arms from the arsenal given to ruffians, who could not be driven from the Kremlin without using cannon. Humanity, the interests of your Majesty and this great city, demanded that it should have been entrusted to my keeping, since it was deserted by the Russian army. They ought to have left administrations, magistrates, and civil guards. That is what was done at Vienna twice, at Berlin, and Madrid; and what we have ourselves done at Milan, when Souwarof entered. Incendiarism causes pillage, the soldier abandoning himself to it to rescue what is left from the flames. If I thought such things were done by your Majesty's orders, I should not write you this letter; but I consider it impossible that, with your principles, heart, and sense of justice, you have authorized such excesses, unworthy of a great sovereign and a great nation. While carrying away the fire-engines from Moscow, they left 150 field cannon, 60,000 new muskets, 1,600,000 infantry cartridges, more than 200 tons of powder, 150 tons of saltpetre, and also of sulphur, etc.

"I made war upon your Majesty without animosity. A letter from you before or after the last battle would have stopped my march, and I should have been ready to forego the advantage of entering Moscow. If your Majesty still retains aught of your former sentiments, you will take this letter in good part. In any case, you must feel indebted to me for giving an account of what is taking place in Moscow."

When thus writing to the Emperor Alexander, Napoleon well knew that the material disasters of the burning of Moscow were exceeded by the moral results, and that the ruins of the capital were a proclamation to the French army, to Russia, and to the whole of Europe, of the implacable resolution of the old Muscovites. Rostopchin himself had written on the iron door of his splendid country-house at Voronovo: "For eight years I have been improving this estate, and have lived here happy in the bosom of my family. The inhabitants of this estate, to the number of 1720, leave it at your approach, and I set fire to my house that it may not be polluted by your presence. Frenchmen, I have left you my two houses in Moscow, with contents worth half a million of roubles. Here you will find nothing but ashes."

The hatred which he had excited against the invader was afterwards to fall back upon himself. Count Rostopchin, driven from Russia by the execration of all those whom he had ruined, was compelled to take refuge in France, where he died in peace, honored by his former enemies. He had nevertheless rendered to Russia one of those terrible services excused by a state still half barbarous, and that violent patriotism by which the soul is possessed in presence of foreign invasion. He revived in the Russian people the unconquerable ardor of resistance. Moscow on fire was an appeal to the eyes and hearts of all.

Napoleon understood this well. Besides, other difficulties were becoming extreme. Time was passing; no reply arrived from St. Petersburg, and the emperor's overtures made to Kutuzoff by Lauriston remained without result. The attempt to continue hostilities was unsuccessful, General Sebastiani having been deceived as to the direction taken by Kutuzoff, and, after following him in vain for two or three days, compelled to return to Moscow. Murat being again put in command of the advanced guard, met the enemy on the Pakra, after being joined by Marshal Bessières. In spite of the cries of his army, who were furious at the burning of Moscow, and wished to march to battle, Kutuzoff slowly retreated before the French generals, and finally pitched his camp at Taroutino on the road to Kaluga. Two cavalry engagements terminated successfully for our arms. Napoleon's lieutenants waited for his orders. A sort of armistice reigned between the two armies. Murat had several times seen Kutuzoff; and the Russian officers overwhelmed him with attentions. He showed himself in favor of peace, concluded by him and through his exertions. The Cossack chiefs celebrated his exploits, one of them surnaming him the "hetmann." Kutuzoff had sent Prince Wolkonsky to St. Petersburg, with instructions to communicate to the Czar the pacific advances which had been made. Alexander replied on the 21st October: "All the opinions which you have received from me, all the determinations expressed in the orders addressed to you by me—everything ought to convince you that my resolution is immovable, and that at the present moment no proposal of the enemy can make me think of terminating the war, and so failing in the sacred duty of avenging our outraged country."

Before the Emperor Alexander thus expressed his resolution of listening to no offers of peace, his enemy had already evacuated Moscow—beginning, whatever pain it cost him and whatever care he took to conceal it, a retrograde movement, which was soon to be the consummation of his ruin. Napoleon long hesitated as to what route he should take. By advancing upon Kaluga in pursuit of Kutuzoff he should plunge further into Russia, towards regions where he should be without winter-quarters and communication with the rear. By resuming the road to Poland, as all his lieutenants wished, he should tacitly admit his defeat. He conceived the idea of making the Duke of Belluna march upon St. Petersburg, reckoning that, on his arrival and while threatening the capital and court, he could effect an oblique movement northwards by Woskresensk, Wolokolamsk, and Bieloi, and then concentrate all his forces at Smolensk.   Winter being past, Napoleon would then be in a position to attack St. Petersburg in earnest.   To satisfy his own mind, the emperor wrote out this plan before speaking of it to the generals, who were waiting, full of serious thought, to know his determination.

They all opposed Napoleon's new plans; all repeating that he did not take into account the hardships of the army, that he over-reckoned the strength of the corps, that the soldiers were incapable of any fresh effort.   He went over, with Count Lobau, the statistics of the different regiments and the detachments in charge of generals at a distance.   "There, six thousand."   "Four thousand, sire," said the general.   "Ten thousand here."   "Five at the most."   "You are perhaps right," the emperor admitted.   But on coming to sum up the total of his resources, he always went back to his first inaccurate reckoning, the truthful and blunt obstinacy of Lobau being unable to overcome his master's voluntary illusions. Nevertheless, Napoleon understood that he could now no longer, by the mere superiority of his genius, take his lieutenants along with him without discussion or hesitation.   He did not insist upon marching northwards.   Count Daru's proposal was to spend the winter in Moscow.   From his administrative experience, he concluded that their supplies were sufficient for the army, while the troops should thus be spared all the hardships and difficulties of travelling.   In spring, all the army corps would be again brought together, there would be a rising in Lithuania, and the emperor could complete his conquest. Napoleon turned toward his faithful servant, and looked upon his energetic features, his robust figure, and the resolution which shone in his looks.   "My dear Daru," said he, "that advice is lion-like, but I should require lions to put it in execution.   You are right, Moscow is not a military position, it is a political position.   Yet what would be said in Paris? what would become of France during that long absence, without possible communication?   No, it is impossible.   Austria and Prussia would take advantage of it to betray me."

The emperor came back to the idea of marching upon Kaluga, and driving Kutuzoff from the camp of Taroutino, summoning the Duke of Belluna to join him in order to keep up communications with Smolensk, at the same time leaving Marshal Mortier in the Kremlin with 10,000 men to occupy and preserve Moscow.   Preparations were being made for this purpose, when, on the 18th of October, cannon were heard on

the road which Napoleon was making ready to follow, and
speedily one of Murat's aides-de-camp appeared.   The King of
Naples, who had long complained of the isolation in which he
was left, was careless in his guard, and had been attacked by
Kutuzoff at Winkowo.   The Russian army taking advantage
of all the delays which gradually diminished our forces, had
increased theirs; and their general had 100,000 men at his disposal, when he yielded to the urgent request of his lieutenants,
and all at once made an attack with two corps upon our positions.   Murat's personal courage and skill in the field partly
compensated for the faults of his imprudence.   He repulsed
the enemy's attack, and fell back upon Voronovo, continuing
to cover the road to Moscow.   Kutuzoff, however, held our
positions, and the King of Naples lost the greater part of his
cavalry.   Napoleon immediately resolved to march to the
enemy.   According to the plan already decided upon, Mortier
fixed his quarters at the Kremlin, over the mines laid ready to
blow up the citadel and palace of the Czars.   All the rest of the
army defiled through the open gates of the city, recently so
eagerly longed for, and now only occupied for thirty-seven
days, which had been full of agitation and terror.   The long
trains of carriages, the soldiers' booty heaped upon the wagons
or their shoulders, the furs fastened to their haversacks or
arms, were all proof enough that the troops were no more
deceived than the generals as to the possibility of a return to
Moscow.   The Duke of Trevisa's friends and comrades looked
upon him as a man condemned beforehand to death, and
sorrowfully bade him adieu without shaking his courage.
The French families formerly settled in Moscow fled from the
anger of the Russians, and joined the march of their fellow-
countrymen.   The long train on its march seemed more like a
convoy defiling, than the progress of an army advancing
against the enemy.   Napoleon, however, had not yet said anything to imply that the evacuation was final; he was marching against Kutuzoff, whom he wished to chastise, and, if
possible, crush.   Before leaving Moscow, his last instructions
were devoted to the defence of the Kremlin.

It was on the morning of the 20th October that the emperor
left the city, in fine autumnal weather which prevented any
one from yet anticipating the rigors of winter.   On reaching
the castle of Troitskoi, he was struck with a new idea; Kutuzoff held the old Kaluga road, and a battle was necessary to
dislodge him; and the French, even if victorious, would lose

men and be encumbered with a crowd of wounded. The new road to Kaluga was protected by Broussier's division, and had not been cut up by the passage of troops; if it were possible to deceive Kutuzoff by a sudden détour to the right, and to gain the new road, Kaluga would be reached without a battle, and the positions for winter secured. The occupation of Moscow must now no longer be insisted upon, and Mortier immediately instructed to leave Moscow and join them. Having made up his mind, the emperor in the evening sent his orders to the Duke of Trevisa: "My cousin," said Napoleon to the Marshal Berthier, "give orders to the Duke of Trevisa to put on march, to-morrow, at daybreak, all the tired and lame soldiers of the corps of Prince Eckmühl and the viceroy, of the foot-cavalry, and the young guard, and to direct the whole upon Mojaisk. On the 22nd or 23rd, at two o'clock in the morning, he will set fire to the brandy storehouse, the barracks, and the public buildings, except the Foundling Hospital.* He will have the palace of the Kremlin set on fire. He will take care that all the guns are broken into pieces, that powder is placed under the towers of the Kremlin, that all the gun-carriages are broken, as well as the wagon wheels.

"When these orders are attended to, and the Kremlin is on fire in several places, the duke will leave the Kremlin, and advance on the Mojaisk road. At four o'clock, the officer of artillery appointed to that duty will blow up the Kremlin, according to instructions.

"On the march he will burn all carriages left behind, use every endeavor to bury all the dead, and burn all the muskets he can find. On reaching the Gallitzin palace, he will take the Spanish and Bavarians stationed there, and put fire to the ammunition wagons, and everything which cannot be removed. He will collect all the commanders of posts, and order the garrisons to fall back.

"He will reach Mojaisk on the 25th or 26th, and there receive further orders to put himself in communication with the army. He will naturally leave a strong advanced guard of cavalry on the Mojaisk road.

"He will be particular in remaining in Moscow till he has himself seen the Kremlin blown up; and also in setting fire to the governor's two houses and that of Rasomowsky."

---

* This establishment, founded by the dowager empress, had been patronized by Napoleon. The governor, General Toutelmine, had been one of the agents of his communications with St. Petersburg.

Thus Napoleon himself put hands to that burning of Moscow with which he had recently blamed the Russians, and the originator of which he did not forget to punish even then! The march upon Kaluga was already begun, and one of Prince Eugène's divisions, being in advance, had already occupied Malo-Jaroslawetz, on the Lougea. General Delzons, who was in command, was engaged in repairing the bridges, when Kutuzoff was informed of the direction which the French seemed to take. General Doctoroff at once advanced with a large body, and Kutuzoff raised his cantonments to follow him.

The small town of Malo-Jaroslawetz was built on a chain of heights, of which the Russians at once took possession, cannonading the French, who in their turn dislodged them. Six times was the town taken and retaken, the fire of the burning houses combining with the cannon-balls to repulse the combatants on both sides. Seven French generals fell on the field towards evening; yet, in spite of the keen determination of the Russian recruits, who had scarcely arms or clothes, the ruins of the town remained in our hands. When the emperor arrived on the banks of the Lougea with the main army, he beheld a sight as painful in proportion to its extent as had been the plain of Borodino. Many of the corpses were scorched by the fire. Ten thousand men fell on both sides. The emperor saw that all future movements implied new and terrible battles. The generals appointed to reconnoitre, considered the enemy's positions impregnable; and on Napoleon himself going to take observations he narrowly escaped being taken by a body of Cossacks, who surprised him when crossing the Lougea. General Rapp had only time to get him out of the way of those troublesome enemies, bands of whom incessantly harassed the army. A council was held in a ruined hut on the banks of the small river.

The emperor was still inclined to attempt a march towards Kaluga, for the sake of the battle, victory, and consequent rest in a rich district not yet exhausted. The generals were as confident as their chief in the success of our arms, but they thought that the loss of 20,000 men and a charge of 10,000 wounded would themselves constitute a check in presence of the Russian army, constantly recruited by new forces. A retreat to Mojaisk, and thence to Smolensk, was decided upon. The attempt on Kaluga had cost ten days, and exhausted the greater part of the provisions brought from Moscow, and it was now necessary to submit to a retreat pure and simple. Marshal Davout proposed to effect this by a new road, which should still supply some resources for the troops; but his advice was not listened to. A passionate desire for return, and terror of the frightful evils which threatened the army, had seized all those men who were recently so daring, and ready to try any danger. Napoleon still hesitated. "What do you think about it, Mouton?" he asked Count Lobau, standing beside him. "That as quickly as possible, and by the shortest road, we must get out of a country where we have stayed too long," was the immediate reply of the hero of so many battles. The emperor hung down his head. In his inmost soul he felt himself beaten.

The whole army also felt itself beaten, and every heart was filled with dejection. Already, during the march from Moscow to Malo-Jaroslawetz, many carriages and badly harnessed wagons were left behind; but the train was still enormous, accompanied by defenceless women and children. The wounded of the last battle had been distributed amongst the different wagons and carts. The dying were abandoned to their wretched fate on the battle-field, under the cold rain which began to fall, or in the huts to which they had been carried. The army left Malo-Jaroslawetz on the 27th October, marching to Vereja, where Marshal Mortier rejoined them after accomplishing his terrible mission. The ground was still quaking under his feet when he left Moscow, bringing with him all the wounded. Such was the emperor's express order, though the army convoys were already insufficient for that necessary duty.

Mortier brought to Napoleon a prisoner, Count Wintzingerod, who had fallen into his hands during the second burning of Moscow. That general was in command of a body of partisans, and believed the French had evacuated the capital. The emperor's anger burst forth against this German on finding him in the Russian ranks. "You belong to no country!" he exclaimed excitedly. "I have always found you among my enemies—with the Austrians when I fought with Austria, with the Russians when Austria became my ally. Yet by birth you belong to the Rhenish Confederation; you are a traitor—I have the right to judge you. You will be tried by court-martial." Then pointing to Count Narischkin, Wintzingerod's aide-de-camp, "This young man does you too much honor by serving with you."

The general made no reply, even by the slightest movement or gesture. The emperor's staff looked on in silence, and the French officers tried by their attentions to make the prisoner forget the treatment. Every one knew the cause of so much bitterness rising from Napoleon's heart to his lips. For the first time in his life the conqueror was retreating.

He was retreating, and every day of their march made them feel more and more the terrible difficulty, while proving its necessity. Napoleon marched at the head of his army with his staff, without joining the main body of the troops, or troubling himself about the fatigue and difficulty experienced at every step by Marshal Davout, who had been appointed to command the rear-guard and protect the retreat. General Grouchy's cavalry were already exhausted, and could not assist him in this painful duty. The marshal's old foot-soldiers alone remained—those who had so long fought under his orders, having been formed under his strict and severe discipline, and loving him while they feared him. At every stage Davout found some carriage or cart had disappeared, left behind by the exhausted horses and drivers, and he heard the cries of the wretched wounded men, henceforward delivered up to the lances of the Cossacks or the severities of the approaching winter. He saw unrolling and lengthening out before him that train behind the army, despised by the soldiers remaining under arms, and reinforced every day by laggards from all the corps. He was the last to arrive at the hindmost posts after the troops defiling past had eaten up all the resources of the villages and farms, burnt the shelters, and sacked what they were unable to carry off. The complaints and demands of the distinguished chief of his rear-guard made no impression on Napoleon. "March quicker!" he kept repeating, without admitting the marshal to see him, without ever going himself towards the rear of his army—apparently indifferent to the sufferings he had produced, absorbed in gloomy silence, surrounded by his lieutenants equally dejected. When passing Borodino, where the battle-field was still covered with the corpses, of which savage beasts were in undisputed possession, the rear-guard were still further encumbered by the transport of the wounded, who had formerly been left at Kolotskoi. Those whose wounds did not allow them to be removed were entrusted by Dr. Larrey to the cares of the Russians, whom he had cured. The army left Ghjat on the 1st November.

In spite of what was constantly being left behind from the

baggage train, the difficulty of the march daily increased on account of fatigue, the want of horses, and the rigor of the climate. Marshal Davout often found himself compelled to blow up artillery wagons which he could not take further with him; and the cannon which were still dragged on became for the most part useless. Immediately before him marched Prince Eugène's forces. The viceroy, young and courageous, had not yet gained consummate experience of war: the marshal urged him to make haste first in crossing the Czarewo-Zaimitché and afterwards in the suburbs of Wiazma. Kutuzoff, at first deceived as to our movements, had advanced southwards after the battle of Malo-Jaroslawetz, but soon changed his direction and marched upon Wiazma. A preliminary engagement near the bridge of Czarewo had opened a passage for us. Then the march was again interrupted before Wiazma. The Russian army occupied the ground on the left of the road. Prince Eugène's forces, embarrassed by the convoy, had an engagement with the enemy on the morning of the 2nd November, and the cannon were making havoc in his ranks when Davout came to his assistance, and General Gerard making a dash at the enemy's artillery, quickly cleared the road again. At the noise of the cannon Marshal Ney halted in his march, and advanced behind a small tributary of the Wiazma. The battle began so vigorously on the part of our old soldiers that General Miloradowitch, who commanded the Russians, did not dare longer to intercept their retreat. The regiments defiled into Wiazma, but still continued firing. General Morand, who was in command of the last battalions, was not rid of the pursuing enemy till he reached the very camp, his soldiers presenting their bayonets. The troops, who had thus gained another victory, encamped in the woods, with no resource except the dying horses, which they slaughtered as they required them, roasting the joints at the bivouac fires. The exhausted soldiers slept.

Marshal Ney, in his turn, had charge of the rear-guard. The emperor felt himself condemned by the stern and impassible judgment of Davout, whom he had left alone to bear the heaviest burden; and he blamed the slowness of his movements for the unfortunate battle of Wiazma, and the responsibility of all the hardships undergone by the rear-guard. Like Masséna in Portugal, Davout found himself in disgrace because he was blamed with faults which he had not committed, and which he was unable to rectify.

Meantime they had approached Smolensk. Alarming news awaited Napoleon at Dorogobouje. He had long reckoned on the assistance of the 9th corps, which Marshal Victor was bringing him from Germany. Scarcely had the new troops arrived at Smolensk, according to the emperor's order, than they found themselves obliged to go to the assistance of our left wing, which was threatened by Count Wittgenstein. A large reinforcement had joined the Russian army at this point. After a conference at Abo, in Finland (28th August, 1812), between the Prince Royal of Sweden and the Emperor Alexander, the Russian forces promised to Bernadotte for the conquest of Norway had advanced from Finland into Livonia. Marshal Macdonald was compelled to abandon the siege of Riga in order to support the Prussians on the lower Dwina. Marshal St. Cyr, in his turn, found himself threatened on the 18th October by forces superior to his own, and had fought a second battle before Polotsk, and successfully defended the town; but when attacked by Wittgenstein and the forces arrived from Finland, on both banks of the Dwina, he was compelled to withdraw behind the Oula (connected with the Berezina by the Lepel canal). Being severely wounded in the last engagement, he had given up the command to Marshal Oudinot, who was anxiously waiting for Marshal Victor's arrival. The approach of Admiral Tchitchakoff was already announced; returned from Turkey with a large army, the negotiator of the treaty of Bucharest had, with Tormazoff's assistance, driven General Reynier and Prince Schwartzenberg behind the marshes of Pinsk; and, after leaving General Sacken with 25,000 men to keep the allies in check, was now advancing towards the upper Berezina, to support Count Wittgenstein. Thus, on reaching Smolensk, Napoleon was about to find the place almost destitute of troops, while the left wing was in very great danger, attacked at the same time by Wittgenstein, the Finland troops, and Tchitchakoff. The supplies even were smaller than was expected, on account of the difficulty of conveyance. The soldiers were delighted as they came near Smolensk. The emperor knew that the halt must be short; nevertheless, he ordered Victor to join Oudinot immediately in order to make a joint attack upon Wittgenstein; and wrote General Reynier and the Austrians to pursue Admiral Tchitchakoff. He also asked for one of the divisions of Marshal Augereau to be sent from Germany; and separating the troops which still remained, in order to facilitate the food-supply during their journey, he continued his march upon Smolensk, whilst Prince Eugène took the road for Doukhowtchina, with instructions to protect Vitebsk if necessary.

The main army resumed its march on the 6th November. On the 7th and 8th the cold became so keen, and the ice on the roads so dangerous, that the horses could not advance, and it was necessary to leave behind some cannon. On the 9th the viceroy reached the banks of the Vop, a small stream which in winter becomes a rapid torrent, its channel being already choked with ice. Before the engineers had completed a bridge, the crowd of the soldiers and runaways rushed headlong upon it and broke it down. The cavalry forded the stream, the troops following them with the water up to their shoulders. The field-pieces, the baggage, and ammunition-wagons, one after another crushed down the banks and ploughed through the channel, frequently plunging into the mire, and being left there. It became impossible to cross; and the wretches who were following the army found themselves left behind, and delivered up to the vengeance of the Russians or the cruelties of the Cossacks, who ran up in eager hordes. In despair and terror, they struggled to cross the river, leaving behind them the wagons which still afforded them some supplies, and many perished. Even the soldiers who had fallen behind the army pillaged the baggage which had been abandoned on the bank. Blood flowed also in the midst of this horrible confusion, for the Cossacks, eager for booty, joined with the disbanded soldiers. Some brave men several times braved the dangers of crossing the stream to save the lives of the defenceless women and children.

On reaching Doukhowtchina, Prince Eugène learned that Vitebsk had fallen into the hands of Wittgenstein. Thus the cruel day's march just made by the army of Italy proved useless. The viceroy set fire to the small town where he found temporary shelter and a few supplies, and then advanced towards Smolensk, where Napoleon had arrived on the evening of the 9th.

There also there was nothing but discontent, dejection, and, for a short time, disorder. The emperor had only allowed the guard to enter the town, and both lodgings and provisions were reserved for this favorite corps, the only remnant saved from shipwreck, who had only undergone the hardships of the campaign without any share in the battles. The mob of camp-followers, deaf to discipline, forced open the gates, and general

pillage had commenced when the emperor's order was modified. The troops lay down in the streets and squares, overpowered by fatigue, and fell down exhausted beside the fires
which had been lighted. Then arrived Prince Eugène's troops,
more decimated than all the others by the frightful disaster on
the banks of the Vop. Marshal Ney had been fighting since
they left Dorogobouje, sustaining all his soldiers by his indomitable courage and the steadiness of his physical and mental
energy, playing in turns the part of general, captain, and soldier, seizing the musket as it fell from the hands of a dying
grenadier to fire, himself, upon the enemy, and purposely
slackening the march of the rear-guard in order to give time
to all to reach Smolensk.

The news brought there from all quarters, like bulletins of
some deadly agony, no longer allowed even the soldiers the
vain hope of several days of rest. General Hilliers, who had
advanced according to orders on the Jelnia road, was surprised
by the Russians, and having lost 2000 men, returned to Smolensk, to find himself degraded in the eyes of all the army, and
was sent back to France, to be tried there by court-martial.
Prince Schwartzenberg was doubtful, he said, about leaving
Warsaw unprotected; and Admiral Tchitchakoff advanced
unchecked, and was already threatening Minsk, where the
great bulk of our supplies was collected together. Victor and
Oudinot had not dared to risk a decisive engagement; and the
two Russian armies were about to combine in order to bar our
passage over the Berezina, the only way of safety to return to
Poland. There was not a moment more to be lost in effecting
that fatal junction. The emperor resolved to march immediately towards Vilna, still intending to make an attack upon
Admiral Tchitchakoff, and entrusting the leaders of his left
wing with the duty of at last defeating Wittgenstein. But
by one of those blunders which seemed to indicate some failure in his genius and foresight, he ordered the marshals to
follow him one after another; and taking no account of
Kutuzoff's army, he left Smolensk on the 14th November.
Prince Eugène, Davout, and Ney were to evacuate their cantonments on the 15th, 16th, and 17th respectively, and the gallant leader of the rear-guard was to bury the cannon, destroy
the ammunition, and blow up the walls surrounding the town.
The great army by this time scarcely amounted to 36,000 fighting men; and the cavalry, entirely under the orders of General Latour-Maubourg, only counted 1800 horse. Napoleor

followed on the left bank the road from Smolensk to Orscha, without taking the precaution to place between him and General Kutuzoff the rapid current of the Dnieper. He was soon to pay dearly for this fault. Scarcely had he reached Krasnoe than he found General Sebastiani, who had preceded him, blockaded in a church by a body of the enemy. Kutuzoff was approaching with 50,000 soldiers, and making ready, with the assistance of several bands of Cossacks, to cut our long columns. On his march Napoleon found at every step ambulance-wagons, and those of runaways, half buried in the snow, and still containing frozen corpses. The emperor halted to wait for those corps which were to rejoin him, and were seriously exposed by their isolation. Prince Eugène had already forced a passage before Krasnoe upon the Lossmina, being therefore compelled to sacrifice Broussier's division, which remained in battle order, threatening the Russian army with a renewal of the attack upon the heights which had been vainly attempted on the evening before. All the rest of the main army succeeded in escaping, with the assistance of the darkness, and the snow, which deadened the noise of the footsteps. The troops left in the rear could only be saved by the approach of Davout and Ney.

On this occasion, once more, Napoleon recovered that unconquerable resolution which had carried him to the summit of power. Determined not to leave his army and lieutenants, he marched before them on the Smolensk road with his guards, who were henceforward subjected to all the hazards of battle. The village Koutkowo, occupied by the Russians, was retaken, the emperor himself being on foot, because the icy ground made riding impossible. The Russian batteries ploughed up the ground held by the French, and the noise of the battle was heard. Davout was at hand, after rallying the poor remainder of the Broussier division, and the artillery with Generals Lariboisière and Eblé; and dashing in dense columns with his four divisions upon General Miloradowitch, who defended the valley of the Lossmina, he soon opened a bloody passage, and rejoined the guard grouped round Napoleon. Krasnoe was thus surrounded by a semicircle of our troops, disputing the enemy's positions step by step; but Admiral Tormazoff was now on our rear, in order to hold the Orscha road. The emperor saw that he should be speedily hemmed in, and resolved to resume his march, without waiting for Ney's regiments. He thus devoted him to certain loss; but in the stern neces-

sity which compelled him, Napoleon had not the courage to
accept the responsibility of the act which he was about to
accomplish.   Ordering Mortier to start with the guards, he imposed on Davout the double duty of waiting for Ney and not
separating himself from Mortier.   In presence of these contradictory instructions, and with an overwhelming sense of
their responsibility, Davout made an effort to hold his ground,
his divisions having replaced on the plateau of Krasnoe the
regiments of the young guard, which had now begun defiling
towards Orscha.   Napoleon marched in front with the old
guard, undergoing as they went a deadly fire from the Russians.   Tormazoff's columns seemed to wait for the final orders
to cut the passage of what were left of the great army.   Kutuzoff resisted the urgent advice of Tormazoff as well as the arguments and excitement of General Wilson, who had been sent
to him by the English Government.   "You think the old man
is a fool," he said repeatedly, "that he is timid, and without
energy: you are young, and don't understand.   If Napoleon
turned back, none of us dare meet him; he is still terrible.   If
I bring him back to the Berezina, ruined and without an army,
I shall have accomplished my task."   Thus protected by the
terrible renown of his name, the emperor advanced to Liady.

Davout resisted to the last moment; but Marshal Mortier,
who was hurrying to leave Krasnoe, urged him to start.   The
roads were about to be barred; the bullets were falling in
showers on the little town; the marshal's three divisions only
amounted to 5000 men, and all the rest of the army were being
withdrawn.   As he left the plateau of Krasnoe, Mortier ordered
the guard to keep step.   "You hear, soldiers?" cried General
Laborde; "the general orders the ordinary step.   Slow time,
soldiers.   March!"   It was in the same way that Davout's
troops defiled, constantly turning round to fire at the squadrons of the enemy's cavalry, closely pursuing them.   When
the exhausted corps were again brought together at Liady, the
faces of all were still more gloomy than on the previous evening.   Besides their physical sufferings, there was now added
the burden of a bitter regret.   Their desertion of Marshal Ney
weighed on the consciences of all.

Ney had been warned neither of the danger which threatened him nor of the isolation in which he was to be left, because a courier sent by Davout was taken by the enemy.
When he came face to face with Kutuzoff's army, before
Krasnoe, he still felt sure of passing there, where his comrades

had gone before him. A determined attack under a rain of shot having been unsuccessful, the marshal saw the uselessness of the attempt, and without for an instant losing his presence of mind or his courage, he resolved to effect a movement during the night towards the Dnieper, cross the river, and escape by the right bank, in order to regain the main army. "But if the Dnieper is not frozen, what shall we do?" said some of the officers. "It will be frozen!" retorted the general, curtly; "besides, frozen or not, we shall do as we can—but we shall cross."

They did cross, to the profound astonishment of the Russians, who believed the general and his soldiers were at last caught, and to the unspeakable delight of the forces collected at Orscha. Prince Eugène and Marshal Mortier took up their positions in front of their companions-in-arms, saved by a de termination and courage really marvellous. Only 1200 men rejoined the army, out of 7000 forming the third corps when they left Smolensk. On the plateau of Krasnoe, in the skirmishes against the Cossacks of Platow, and by the sides of the ice-covered roads, Ney had everywhere left dead bodies, wounded and dying men, besides men overpowered by the hardships and incapable of any effort.

Even at Orscha the disorder was so great that it threatened to infect the regiments of the old guard. The emperor harangued them energetically. "Grenadiers," said he, "we are retiring without being conquered by the enemy; let us not be so by ourselves; let us give the example to the army! Several from amongst you have already deserted their eagles, and even their arms. It is to you alone that I address myself to have this disorder stopped. Act justly towards each other. It is to yourselves that I entrust your discipline!" An appearance of order was restored; but the regular distributions were impossible. Famishing wretches, soldiers, and those of the camp-followers who still remained, all rushed upon the provision-stores. Panics also continually increased the tumult. "The Cossacks! There are the Cossacks!" was frequently shouted.

At Orscha, moreover, as well as at Smolensk and Dorogoubouge, ominous news reached the emperor. Tchitchakoff, who had not been pursued by Schwartzenberg, had carried Minsk, one of the most important rallying-points on the Vilna road, and the centre of our principal supplies. The Polish general Bronikowski being unable with 3000 men to defend the place, had joined Dombrowski, who was covering the Dnieper, and both guarded the bridge of Borisow on the Berezina with insufficient forces. Should the bridge fall into the hands of Admiral Tchitchakoff, the army would be blockaded behind the Berezina, or compelled to ascend to its source at the risk of being attacked by Count Wittgenstein. Marshals Victor and Oudinot, with their weak and decimated regiments, could not succeed in dislodging the enemies from their position near Smoliantzy on the Oula. Thus marching a second time over the roads which he had recently trod full of hope, Napoleon found himself threatened on his left by Tchitchakoff holding Minsk, on his right by Wittgenstein and Steinghel; behind him Kutuzoff was advancing; before him it was now doubtful if the Berezina could be crossed. The conception of a last and powerful combination arose in that inexhaustibly fertile mind. He sent to Oudinot the order to march towards the Berezina to support the Poles at Borisow. Victor was to check Wittgenstein, so as to give the great army time to cross the river. Napoleon could then rally the two marshals, whose forces still amounted to 25,000 men; he should attack and recover Minsk, send for Schwartzenberg, and when thus master of all the scattered remnants of his army, make a crushing attack upon the Russian troops, and gain a victory before returning to Poland. With this hope, Orscha was evacuated on the 20th November, under a cold rain, which penetrated the soldiers' clothes, and then froze on their bodies. The emperor ordered the greater part of the convoys to be sacrificed. The leaders of divisions alone kept carriages. The wounded and several fugitive families still followed with great difficulty on carts and wagons.

On the 22nd, at Tolocsin, the emperor learned that, after a keenly-fought battle, the Russians had taken Borisow and the bridge over the Berezina. He dismounted, and showing more uneasiness than he had yet done, called to his side General Dode de la Brunerie, an officer of the engineers, whom he had already distinguished. "They are there!" said he, without further explanation. The general easily divined the emperor's meaning. They both entered a hut, and Napoleon, spreading out his maps on a rickety table, discussed with Dode the resources still at his command. The general's plan was to ascend the course of the Berezina, declaring that he knew several fords, and that they could then advance quickly upon Wilna by Gloubokoi. They might indeed be met by Wittgenstein, but Tchitchakoff covered Borisow, and would be certain to burn the bridge over the Berezina if he saw it threatened.

The emperor listened as he kept looking at his maps. At last something arrested his attention, the sight of a name of ill-omen: "Poltava! Poltava!" he repeated. Then, as if more conscious than ever of the superiority of his glory and destiny over the heroic adventures of King Charles XII., he went up to General Jomini, who had just entered, and said, "When one has never met with defeats, he ought to have them great in proportion to his success." At the same time, while considering vaster plans, now chimerical by reason of the exhaustion and dejection of his troops, he resolved to push on to the Bere-zina, retake the bridge of Borisow, and throw another over the river in spite of the Russians, and thus, at any cost, recover Wilna by the shortest road. Scarcely was his mind made up, when the means of effecting it were presented. General Cor-bineau, formerly despatched by General St. Cyr to assist the Bavarians, found himself at liberty on account of their inac-tivity; and conceiving the idea of rejoining the great army, he crossed the Berezina by a ford which he had long known, and brought Napoleon 700 horse, a valuable reinforcement at such a moment of extreme distress. He learned at the same time, that Marshal Oudinot had driven the Russians from Borisow without being able to prevent them from burning the bridge. He could there check Tchitchakoff, and leave Napoleon time to throw over the ford at Studianka a simple bridge of tressels, which was the only apparatus General Eblé had been able to preserve during their rout. The engineers were secretly and expeditiously ordered to go to this place.

The attempt was one of difficulty and danger, but it was still possible, and offered several chances of success. General Eblé, still indomitable in spite of his age and the fatigues of the cam-paign, collected his workmen, and made them understand that the fate of the army depended upon their exertions. Exhausted by marching and want of food, the soldiers bravely went into the icy water, and worked incessantly during the 25th and night of the 26th, in the midst of frozen blocks perpetually dashing against them, without time to eat, without rest, with-out even a dram of spirits. The houses of Studianka having been demolished, their beams were utilized as buttresses and tressels for the bridge; and on the 26th, at daybreak, prepara-tions were made for crossing. The Russians, deceived by a pretended attempt near Borisow, had not moved far from that quarter ; General Corbineau had already crossed the ford with his cavalry, to protect the right bank. The hopes and looks of all were concentrated upon the exertions of the bridge-makers, who worked incessantly, and seemed to be uncon-scious of fatigue. On the right, one of the bridges was at last opened for infantry and cavalry, and they began to defile across ; the passage was to occupy two days. When the second bridge was completed, Eblé said to the engineers, " Let half of you lie down on the heaps of straw; the others will watch the passage, and sleep in their turn "—he himself not having had a moment's rest by day or night. The imperfect construction of the bridges caused serious danger ; the tressels shaking under the weight of the wagons and cannon ; and during the night the bridge intended for the artillery suddenly gave way. The soldiers again went into the water, several times assisted by the general himself, who bravely exposed himself to every hard-ship and danger. The cold had now become extreme, and the bridge-engineers worked in the midst of large masses of ice ; yet the work went on, and the passage was again begun. The emperor was one of the last to reach the right bank ; a disor-derly crowd of camp-followers and fugitives were huddled to-gether on the left bank, encamped on the frozen marshes, and no authority was sufficient to hasten their movements. Every day the number of soldiers faithful to their colors became smaller and smaller, on account of the general discouragement and re-laxation of discipline. Davout himself had not more than 4000 men in his divisions. On Marshal Victor rejoining the remains of the great army between Studianka and Borisow, his troops, though themselves weak and fatigued, were amazed at the piti-ful state of their comrades, whom they had not seen for so many months. " Your turn will come," said those who were coming back from Moscow, marching in any order, officers and soldiers mixed together all equally dejected, even though suf-fering did not bring all minds to one level. Human nature, often a miserable sight under disaster, then also displays its greatness. Along with a selfishness sometimes brutal, the more noble characteristics of courage and devotion raised their dejected minds. Some of the women saved their children through a thousand hardships ; others remained close beside their husbands ; soldiers continued loyal to their chiefs ; and one officer for a long time carried on his shoulders his *half-frozen* servant, who in his turn did him the same friendly turn.

The battle which was preparing promised to be a terrible one, as Napoleon knew; yet he insisted on leaving at Borisow the Partouneaux division, which belonged to Marshal Victor, hoping at this expense to continue the mistake of Tchitchakoff. The enemy's circle was now closing round that handful of brave men, condemned beforehand. Wittgenstein and Milora-dowitch had intercepted the Studianka road. On the evening of the 27th, the Partouneaux division was attacked on both sides, and defended its positions heroically, but without being able to break through. On the morning of the 28th, after being twice summoned by the Russians, the general, in despair, gave himself up a prisoner. Almost at the same moment the second corps, under Oudinot, was attacked by part of Tchitchakoff's army, which had collected at Pahlen, on the left bank of the Berezina. Being soon wounded, as usual, the marshal was re-placed in command by Ney, who made a vigorous charge upon the enemy, and drove them back to half-way between Brill and Borisow, and placed over a pass a battery of artillery, which kept the Russians at a distance. Marshal Victor had since morning kept up on the left bank a vigorous fight against Wittgenstein, to cover the passage over the bridges; on the other bank the guards used their cannon against the enemy, who were perpetually driven back by the charges of our cav-alry, and perpetually returning to the charge. At nightfall they were still fighting. The Russians, however, withdrew, beaten, but carrying off their wounded, and certain of return-ing next day, as numerous and daring, against an expiring army, which was sustained only by despair and the tradition of an heroic past.

The soldiers fought and died with courage. The confused mob crowding on the bank of the river also died, but in all the agonies of terror and helplessness. After having for a long time refused to take advantage of the bridges, which lay open, the multitude, terrified by the noise of the cannon and the ap-proach of the enemy, rushed in a body towards the river, heedless of discipline, or the necessity for reserving one road for those on foot and the other for carriages. The throng was so dense that they could not advance; cries were succeeded by cries, and exertions by exertions. Occasionally the hissing of a bullet was heard, as it came to open a horrible gap in the compact mass, who shrank in terror. The weak, drawn into the confused crowd, succumbed, and were trodden under foot, without those that crushed them even observing their fall. Night and darkness brought back a moment of calm. Many of the wretches perished in the river when endeavoring to escape. The reaction of unreasonable panic kept from the bridges those who, shortly before, entreated General Eblé with tears to let them pass; nobody would venture in the darkness —the engineers, assisted by their officers, urging those who stayed behind; but they had again lighted their fires on the bank. During that long night of winter the bridges remained deserted and useless, and General Eblé, who had orders to blow them up at daybreak, delayed till eight o'clock, grieved to his very soul by the despair of the crowd, which had again begun to throng the entrances. When at last the fire appeared, with its omnious gleam, both bridges were crowded with carriages, horses, men, women, and children. The wretches plunged into the waters, and struggled vainly against the current. Their cries were mingled with those of the crowd who remained on the bank, now without defence. The Cossacks soon arriving, galloped round this human herd, and pushed them forward with their lances. When they withdrew, loaded with booty, the remains of the army took the road for Smorgoni. At every step Ney and General Maison protected the retreat, and again met the Russians at Molodeczno, after burning the bridges of Zembin. From league to league the march of the army was indicated by a long series of corpses—soldiers who had fallen in the snow without rising again, runaways who had at last succumbed under the weight of their hardships. The emperor was still surrounded by officers, some without soldiers, and generals without officers. The forces who recently rejoined him had in their turn undergone the terrible disorganization by which the whole army was infected. Napoleon saw that every chance was lost, and felt in danger of being hemmed in by the enemy, and falling alive into their hands. He was now in haste to escape finally from the overwhelming realities which urged him on every side. For several days he secretly matured a plan to set out for France alone with several faithful companions, resolving to leave to his lieutenants the glory and pain of bringing back to Germany, on a hostile though allied land, the shapeless remnant of the great army. In spite of the objections of Daru and the Duke of Bassano, to whom he had spoken and written about it, he held a council at Smorgoni of his marshals—who arrived one after another, wounded, ill, exhausted by fighting, sleepless nights, and constant vigilance, followed only by a few thousands of men. He announced his departure, saying that he handed over the command to the

King of Naples, and whom he trusted they would obey the same as himself. Then, shaking hands with some, embracing others, and talking kindly to all, even those whom he had often badly used, he stepped into a sledge during the night of the 5th December, with Caulaincourt, Duroc, Mouton, and Lefebvre-Desnouettes. His lieutenants still looked, as if to see the last trace of him in the darkness: he had disappeared, taking with him the last remnants of hope, and leaving in each of those brave hearts a deep and bitter sense of being cruelly deserted.

The Emperor Napoleon had fled—selfishly fled. He had escaped from the frightful sight of, and contact with, unlimited pain, incessantly renewed, without respite or issue, the responsibility of which rested entirely upon himself. Secondary faults had been committed by his generals, but he was really blamable for them all; for he had asked from men more than they could accomplish, without any earnest intention or proper pretext. For the first time in his life he took care, as he left Smorgoni, to address Europe in explanation of his retreat and rout. The twenty-ninth bulletin of the great army no longer resounded with the report of brilliant victory. One could read in it the secret humiliation of a pride which admitted of no conqueror but winter, and did not yet confess its lamentable errors. It appeared that the Russians had in no way assisted towards this defeat, which had to be recognized, and that the French army were everywhere victorious. "The army was in good condition on the 6th November," wrote Napoleon, "and till then the weather had been perfect. The cold began on the 7th, and from tha time we lost every night several hundred horses, which died during bivouac. Soon 30,000 had succumbed, and our cavalry were all on foot. On the 14th we were almost without cavalry, artillery, and transports. Without cavalry we could gain no information beyond a quarter of a league. Without artillery we could not fight battle, or keep positions steadily. It was necessary to march, to avoid a battle, which the want of supplies made undesirable. It was necessary to occupy a certain space, to avoid being taken in flank, and that without cavalry to gain information and unite the columns. This difficulty, together with the excessive and sudden cold, rendered our position difficult. Some men, whom nature had tempered strongly enough to be above all vicissitudes of fate and fortune, seemed staggered, lost their cheerfulness and good humor, and thought of nothing but disaster and

destruction; those whom she has created superior to everything, preserved their cheerfulness and usual disposition, and
saw a now glory in the various difficulties to be surmounted.

"The enemy, seeing on the roads traces of the frightful calamity which struck the French army, tried to take advantage
of it. Our columns were all surrounded by Cossacks, who, like
Arabs in the desert, carried off the trains and carriages which
had separated from the army. That despicable cavalry, which
comes silently, and could not repulse a company of light-horse
soldiers, became formidable under those circumstances. The
enemy, however, had reason to repent of every attempt of importance which he made, and after the French army crossed
the Borysthenes, at Orscha, the Russian army, being fatigued,
and having lost many men, ceased from their attempts.
Nevertheless, the enemy held all the passages over the
Beresina, a river eighty yards wide, and carrying much ice,
with its banks covered with marshes 600 yards long, all
rendering it very difficult to cross. The enemy's general
placed his four divisions at different points, where he concluded the French army would pass. On the 26th, at daybreak,
the emperor, after deceiving the enemy by several feint movements made on the 25th, advanced to the village of Studianka,
and, in spite of the presence of one of the enemy's divisions,
had two bridges, thrown over the river. The Duke of Reggio
crossing, attacked the enemy in a battle lasting for two hours;
the Russians withdrew to the head of the Borisow bridge.
During the whole of the 26th and 27th the army crossed. To
say that the army has need of being redisciplined and re-
formed, and of being re-equipped in cavalry, artillery, and
supplies, is to be inferred from the statement just made. Rest
is its principal want. Supplies and horses are arriving. General Bourcier has already more than 20,000 new horses in the
different depots. The artillery has already repaired its losses.
The generals, officers, and soldiers have greatly suffered from
fatigue and sca city. Many have lost their baggage on account of their horses being lost, and several by the Cossacks in
ambush. The Cossacks took a number of isolated men—engineers who wer) surveying, and wounded officers who marched
imprudently, preferring to run risks rather than march regularly in the convoys.

"Throughout all those operations, the emperor has always
marched in the midst of his guard; the cavalry under the
Duke of Istria, and the infantry under the Duke of Dantzig.

Our cavalry was deprived of horses to such an extent that the officers who were still mounted had to be collected, to form four companies of 150 men each. Their generals acted as captains; the colonels as under-officers. This sacred squadron, commanded by General Grouchy, and under the orders of the King of Naples, did not lose sight of the emperor in all his movements. The health of his Majesty has never been better."

It was always a part of Napoleon's cunning to mix truth with falsehood, and conceal his lies with an appearance of honor. The "twenty-ninth bulletin of the great army" contained facts which were partly true. He admitted the hardships, and palliated the faults; but he neither gave, nor wished to give, a true idea of the disasters, or a candid statement of the frightful miseries which had ravaged the French battalions, and reduced our army as snow is melted under the sun of summer. There were still too many who had seen those catastrophes, and undertaken to establish the truth of the facts. In Napoleon's mind the evils he had seen, and that he himself had caused, were to leave less permanent impressions. He regretted the destruction of his armies, without wishing to state all their losses. "We left 300,000 men in Russia," said Marshal St. Cyr, in Germany. "No, no!" replied Napoleon; "not so many as that." Then, after a moment's reflection, "Ah! 30,000 at the Moskwa; 7000 here, 10,000 there; and all those who strayed on the marches and have not returned. Possibly you are not far wrong. But then there were so many Germans!" The Germans did not forget it!

The solitary consolation left to the army was that which the emperor had himself presented to Europe—the presence of Napoleon; his physical and mental energy and vigor. His flight from Smorgoni deprived the soldiers of this last resource of their confidence; from that day, as soon as the report spread, despair seized upon the strongest hearts. Nothing is more enduring than the instinctive courage which resists pain and death, because it becomes a man to strive to the last. All the ties of discipline, military fraternity, and ordinary humanity were broken together. I borrow from the recollections of the Duke Fezensac, then colonel of the 4th of the line, the following picture of the horrors which he saw, and of which he has given the story with a touching and manly simplicity:—
"It is useless at the present day to tell the details of every day's march; it would merely be a repetition of the same misfortunes. The cold, which seemed to have become milder only

to make the passage of the Dnieper and the Berezina more difficult, again set in more keenly than ever. The thermometer sank, first, to from 15 to 18 degrees, then from 20 to 25 degrees (Réaumur), and the severity of the season completed the exhaustion of men who were already half dead with hunger and fatigue. I shall not undertake to depict the spectacle which we looked upon. You must imagine plains as far as the horizon covered with snow, long forests of pines, villages half-burnt and deserted; and through those pitiful districts an endless column of wretches, nearly all without arms, marching in disorder, and falling at every step on the ice, near the carcasses of horses and the bodies of their companions. Their faces bore the impress of utter exhaustion or despair, their eyes were lifeless, their features convulsed, and quite black with dirt and smoke. Sheepskins and pieces of cloth served them for shoes; their heads were wrapped with rags; their shoulders covered with horse-cloths, women's petticoats, and half-burnt skins. Also, when one fell from fatigue, his comrades stripped him before he was dead, in order to clothe themselves with his rags. Each bivouac seemed next day like a battle-field, and men found dead at their side those beside whom they had gone to sleep the night before. An officer of the Russian advance-guard, who was a witness of those scenes of horror—which the rapidity of our flight prevented us from carefully observing—has given a description of them to which nothing need be added: 'The road which we followed,' says he, 'was covered with prisoners who required no watching, and who underwent hardships till then unheard of. Several still dragged themselves mechanically along the road, with their feet naked and half frozen; some had lost the power of speech, others had fallen into a kind of savage stupidity, and wished, in spite of us, to roast dead bodies in order to eat them. Those who were too weak to go to fetch wood stopped near the first fire which they found, and sitting upon one another they crowded closely round the fire, the feeble heat of which still sustained them, the little life left in them going out at the same time as it did. The houses and farms which the wretches had set on fire were surrounded with dead bodies, for those who went near had not the power to escape the flames which reached them; and soon others were seen, with a convulsive laugh rushing voluntarily into the midst of the burning, so that they were consumed also.'"

I hasten to avoid the spectacle of so many sufferings. Yet

it is right and proper that children should know what was en-
dured by their fathers. In proportion as the last survivors of
the generations who saw and suffered so many evils disappear,
we who have in our turn undergone other disasters owe it to
them to recount both their glory and their misery. The time
will soon come when our descendants in their turn will include
in the annals of history the great epochs through which we
have lived, struggled, and suffered.

Napoleon crossed Germany like an unknown fugitive, and
his generals also made haste to escape. They had at last
reached Wilna, alarming Lithuania by their rout, and themselves terror-struck during the halt on ascertaining the actual numbers of their losses, and the state of the disorderly
battalions which were being again formed in the streets of the
hospitable town. For a long time the crowd of disbanded
soldiers, deserters, and those who had fallen behind, were collected together at the gates of Wilna in so dense a throng that
they could not enter. Scarcely had the hungry wretches
begun to take some food and taste a moment's rest, when the
Russian cannon was heard, and Platow's Cossacks appeared at
the gates. The King of Naples, heroic on the battle-field, but
incapable of efficient command in a rout, took refuge in a
suburb, in order to set out from it at break of day. Marshal
Ney, the old Marshal Lefebvre, and General Loyson, with the
remains of the division which he recently brought back from
Poland, kept back the Cossacks for some time, and left the
army time to resume its deplorable flight. A large number of
exhausted men fell into the hands of the enemy; the fragments of our ruined regiments disappeared piecemeal. At
Ponare, where the road between Wilna and Kowno rises, the
baggage which they had with great difficulty dragged so far,
the flags taken from the enemy, the army-chest, the trophies
carried off from Moscow, all remained scattered at the foot of
the icy hill, neither horses nor men being able to take them
further. The pillagers quarrelled over the gold and silver in
the broken coffers, on the snow, in the ditches. Then the
Cossacks coming upon them, some of the French fired in defence of treasures which they were no longer able to carry.

When the ruins of the main army at last reached Kowno,
where they found supplies of food and ammunition, they were
no longer able to make use of it, or to resist the pursuit of the
Russians, still keenly determined to drive us from their territory. The generals held a council. In their weariness and

despair some gave vent to complaints against Napoleon, and Murat's words were susceptible of a more sinister meaning. Marshal Davout, honorable and unconquerable though still strongly prejudiced against the King of Naples, boldly expressed his indignation against the falling off of the lieutenants whom the emperor had made kings. All with one accord handed over to Ney the command of the rear-guard, and that defence of Kowno which was for a few minutes longer to protect the retreat. General Gerard alone remained faithful to this last despairing effort. When at last he crossed the Niemen with General Ney, on the 14th December, 1812, they were abandoned by all: their soldiers had fled, either scattering before the enemy or stealing away during the night from a useless resistance. When, in Kœnigsberg, he overtook the remnant of the staff, Marshal Ney, with haggard looks and clad in rags, entered alone into their room. "Here comes the rear-guard of the great army!" said he bitterly.

The Prussian General York had abandoned Marshal Macdonald, making a capitulation with his forces in presence of the Russians, whose friendly intentions he had been long conscious of. Being disarmed by this neutrality of York's, Macdonald in his turn fell back upon Kœnigsberg, pursued by the Russians. The hospitals were ravaged by disease: men who had resisted all fatigues and hardships, such as Generals Lariboisière and Eblé, at last succumbing. Murat withdrew to Elbing, to start soon after for Naples, leaving Prince Eugène in command of the remains of the army. From Paris, where he was already preparing for other battles, the Emperor Napoleon sought for his army in vain. The old guard itself only amounted at Kœnigsberg to 1500 men, of whom not more than 500 could carry a musket. When the scattered fragments of the regiments left this last place of refuge, 10,000 sick men were still left in the hospitals.

END OF THE SEVENTH VOLUME.